REBELS

NEW AMERICANISTS

A series edited by Donald E. Pease

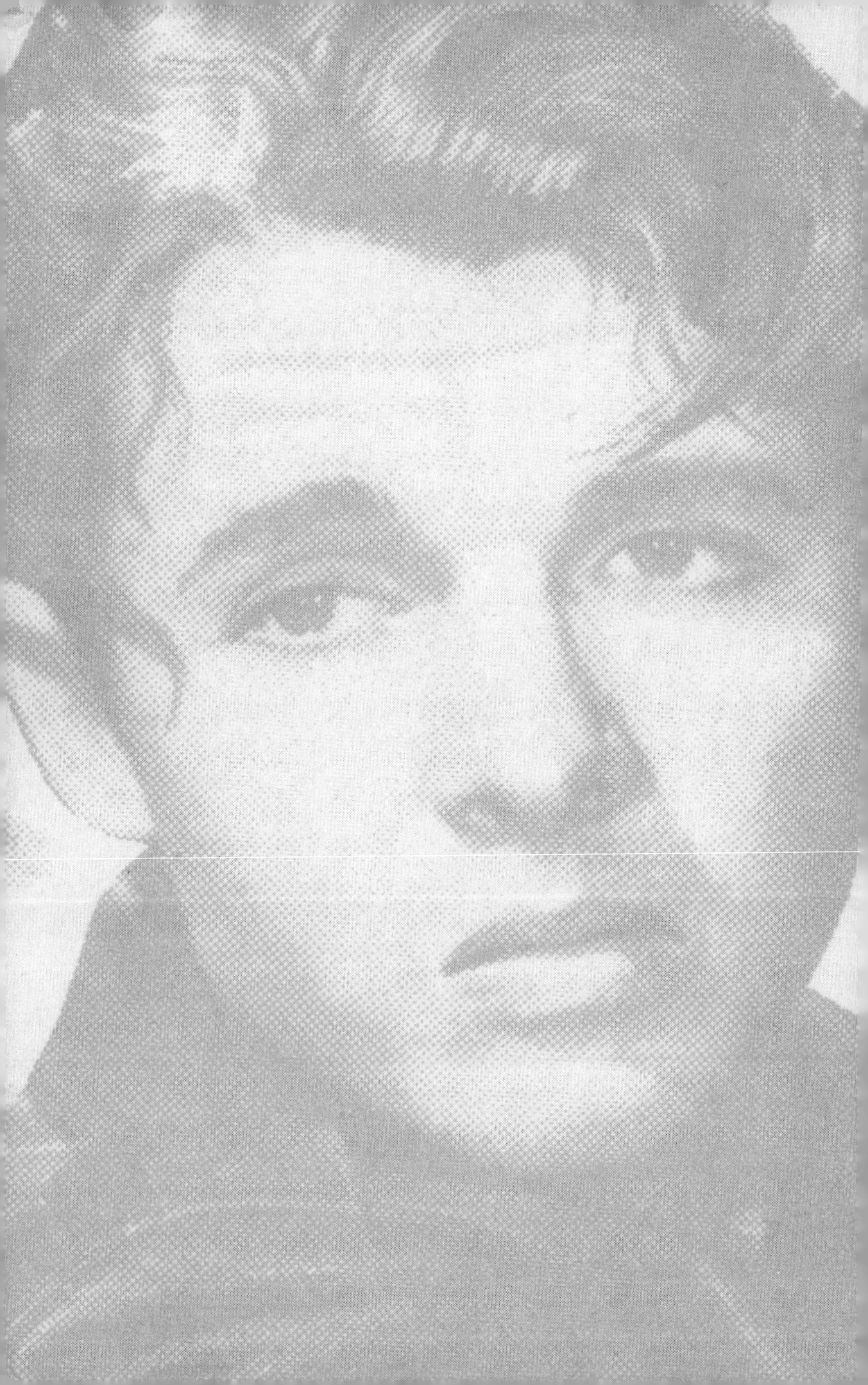

REBELS

YOUTH AND THE COLD WAR ORIGINS OF IDENTITY

LEEROM MEDOVOI

Duke University Press   Durham and London   2005

© 2005 DUKE UNIVERSITY PRESS
All rights reserved
Printed in the United States
of America on acid-free paper
Designed by Amy Ruth Buchanan
Typeset in Scala with Shortcut display
by Tseng Information Systems, Inc.
Library of Congress Cataloging-
in-Publication Data appear on the
last printed page of this book.

CONTENTS

	Acknowledgments	vii
1.	Identitarian Thought and the Cold War World	1
2.	Cold War Literature and the National Allegory: The Identity Canon of Holden Caulfield	53
3.	Transcommodification: Rock 'n' Roll and the Suburban Counterimaginary	91
4.	Identity Hits the Screen: Teenpics and the Boying of Rebellion	135
5.	Oedipus in Suburbia: Bad Boys and the Fordist Family Drama	167
6.	Beat Fraternity and the Generation of Identity	215
7.	Where the Girls Were: Figuring the Female Rebel	265
	Conclusion: The Rise and Fall of Identity	317
	Notes	331
	Works Cited	359
	Index	377

ACKNOWLEDGMENTS

I am daunted by the numerous thanks that I owe. So many people contributed to the writing of this book in so many different ways that I hardly know where to begin. For lack of a more elegant idea, I will simply begin at the beginning. I launched a very different version of this project while still in graduate school, at a time when I was blessed with a cohort of some of the most wonderful intellectual comrades I could have hoped for. I thank Shay Brawn, Elaine Chang, Alex Chasin, Lisa Hogeland, Diane Nelson, Kristin Nussbaum, Shankar Raman, David Schmid, and Eric Schocket for their generous help in shaping the questions and issues with which I began this project. I especially want to thank Robert Arch Latham, for his unstinting loyalty and for the way in which he always pushed me to think harder and with greater care. I likewise feel special gratitude to Kim Gillespie, whose indefatigable commitment to my Marxist education changed the way I saw the world. Finally, Benjamin Robinson remains my comrade in mind and heart. I thank him for always being there, as a profound interlocutor but most of all as a dear friend.

My dissertation advisor, Regenia Gagnier, offered me moral and professional support in difficult times, not to mention her thoughtful criticism of this project's early drafts. David Lloyd and Russell Berman were also important faculty mentors whose keen insights I deeply appreciate. I thank Sandra Drake for her warmth and historical acumen. Harry Stecopolous and Joel Foreman, who both helped me to publish early pieces of this book, gave me the courage to continue the work.

Robert Corber and Donald Pease played vital roles in bringing this book to fruition. It is they who helped me to imagine the book it might become. I also thank Ranjana Khanna, Tomo Hattori, Ranita Chatterjee, and Karen Engle, who were important intellectual comrades and friends during some difficult years. I especially want to thank Srinivas Aravamudan, whose keen mind and generous encouragement kept me thinking and writing. It was in dialogue with him that I began to explore the vital relationship between postwar U.S. culture and the moment of decolonization.

I thank Jane Newman and John Smith for their caring friendship and for their deep intellectual integrity. They are scholars in the finest sense of the word. My gratitude also goes to Julian Carter, who helped me to think through several key problems in the latter half of the manuscript. Rey Chow, Mark Poster, and Robyn Wiegman, all in different ways, kept me professionally engaged and energized when I needed it. Thank you all. Thanks also to two wonderful people, Fred Pfeil and Henry Schwarz, for showing me what it means to be an engaged scholar. Clara Maclean, a dear friend, was kind enough to read, correct, and engage my work at a crucial moment. I can't thank her enough. I appreciate the rich comments and encouragement that Judith Halberstam offered me for my final chapter. The UCI Humanities Center offered me deeply appreciated support.

Several people offered me guidance with this project's final transformations. Rayna Kalas, Nic Sammond, and Andy Hoberek offered me invaluable suggestions as I rewrote the introduction to this book. So too did Miranda Joseph, whose friendship and support have meant so much to me over the years. Amy Greenstadt is the finest colleague and the most generous friend I could hope to have. She is also a profound interlocutor, who rescued me when I was hopelessly lost in revisions of my second chapter. I cannot be too grateful to the two anonymous readers who submitted reports to Duke Press. Their criticisms and suggestions improved the manuscript in incalculable ways. Reynolds Smith and Sharon Torian have been wonderful people to work with at the press. I thank them for all their support and advice.

Sections of this book have been published previously and I appreciate the permission from these venues to reprint them here. One section of chapter one previously appeared in *Minnesota Review* for their special issue on the 1950s, edited by Andrew Hoberek (55:57 [2002]: 167–186). Several short sections in chapter two also appeared in an earlier version of my argument that may be found in the anthology *The Other Fifties: Interrogating Midcentury American Icons*, edited by Joel Foreman (University of Illinois Press 1997). Lastly, chapter four draws substantially from an essay that appeared in the anthology *Race and the Subject of Masculinities*, edited by Michael Uebel and Harry Stecopoulos (Duke University Press 1997).

My parents, Jorge and Cepora Medovoi, supported me in many different ways as I labored with this book. My brother, Amir, and sister, Ornah, were also great comforts and joys to me. Bob and Martha Klotz were endlessly supportive of me and my family. They are kind and generous people. My closest friend, Jim Fina, kept me feeling loved even when I was most down on myself. The spirit of his care and wise encouragement inhabit this book. Lena Roth and Rosa Celestine both cared for my very young children as I struggled to complete the manuscript. In the most material of ways, my book would not have been possible without them.

My deepest thanks goes to my life partner, Marcia Klotz. What can I say? She saw me through it all. She gave me the most precious of company, she loved me, thought every thought with me, she read every page. I can't count the number of times when she put me back on the right path as I was veering away. She inspires me again and again with her intelligence, her articulateness, her strength of character, and her generosity of spirit. This book is as much hers as it is mine, and I dedicate it to her, as well as to those dear ones that we care for together.

IDENTITARIAN THOUGHT AND THE COLD WAR WORLD

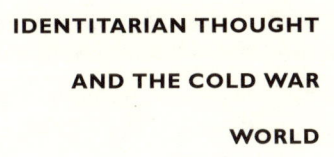

> The study of identity, then, becomes as strategic in our time as the study of sexuality was in Freud's time.
> —Erik Erikson, *Childhood and Society*

This book examines the figure of the young rebel in postwar American culture, including such avatars as Holden Caulfield, the beat writers, Elvis Presley, Chuck Berry, and James Dean. These figures emerged at the dawn of the Cold War era because the ideological production of the United States as leader of the "free world" required figures who could represent America's emancipatory character, whether in relation to the Soviet Union, the new nations of the third world, or even its own suburbs. The personality of the postwar rebel heralded new historical conditions that would soon inaugurate what we now call the "politics of identity." By the 1960s, new social movements and countercultures would begin to articulate themselves as emergent identities, pitted against a status quo cast as parental, repressive, and authoritarian. The motivating argument of this book is that the very concept of "identity" as it is commonly understood today was a new one in the 1950s. The meteoric rise of "identity politics" and the breakneck speed with which it had eclipsed class-based left politics by the 1960s and 1970s demand a historical explanation that both acknowledges how recently this concept came into use and investigates the ideological grounds from which sprang its rapid appeal.

For some time now, leftist thinkers and activists have grown skeptical of identity, whether as a proper basis for political action or, more radically, as an ontologically meaningful paradigm. Identity is frequently judged an essentializing category that articulates a political subject by denying difference and enforcing exclusions.[1] Even worse, identity sometimes stands accused of necessarily reiterating the very terms of the social relations of oppression that gave rise to it.[2] Yet, for all these critiques of identity, the discourse itself has yet to be systematically historicized.

Even so trenchant a philosophical critic of identity as Judith Butler, who persuasively argues that identity is the result of our practices and not their ground or origin, has not attempted a genealogy of identity of the sort that, for instance, Foucault once offered for sexuality. *Gender Trouble*, her groundbreaking first book, presents itself as a genealogical study that means to force the question, what kind of politics might be possible after the critique of identity? Nonetheless, in offering only a theory of identity rather than a history, it foregoes a philosophically hard-won opportunity to redescribe identity, not as the universal product of human practices, but instead as a bounded one tied to the contingencies of a historical moment. Butler instead limits herself to providing an antirealist and antifoundationalist ontology of identity. She declines to ask, as a genealogist should, when and how did "identity" become the product of our performative practices? What is the history of its emergence? And what, for that matter, might be provoking its discursive subversion at present?

This book, taking the antirealist account of identity at full face value, brackets what might be called the "identity hypothesis" of most contemporary leftist criticism: the notion that there has always been something we call "identity" in human history whose relevance to any given political situation should be theorized, critiqued, or deconstructed. Instead, I attempt to answer the question of when and why "identity" was first produced. Terms such as "nationalism" or "race" are routinely granted generative histories by their critics—explained as the discursive result of print capitalism or the colonial contest, for instance. Yet with a few exceptions, "identity" has remained without such a history.[3] Why, for example, does it not appear in a book such as Raymond Williams's *Keywords*? The answer surely has something to do with the fact that, unlike the bulk of Williams's entries, "identity" is not a word bearing the mark of social struggles dating back to the sixteenth century, nor even to the nineteenth century. It is in fact so recently coined that Williams did not have the historical perspective to trace its development.

As I will show, our contemporary politicized conception of identity first emerged a mere fifty years ago, as a lynchpin to the ideological contradictions in the Cold War order. Even as anticommunist ideology authorized the suppression of an Old Left rooted in radical class politics, the rise of a New Left, animated by identity politics, was actually abetted by a different face of the Cold War imaginary that envisioned the young American rebel as guarantor of the nation's antiauthoritarian democratic character.

After the 1960s, the narrative of youth, which subtends "identity politics," receded from view as identity became principally attached to race, gender, and sexuality. Nevertheless, its continued presence can be perceived in the youthful face through which the new social movements' insurrectional spirits were figured. The liberation movements of the late sixties (black, Chicano, women's, or gay) articulated as their political subject an *emergent* identity, a young self establishing its sovereignty against the forces of a racist, patriarchal, or homophobic "parent culture." While race, gender, and sexuality have come to represent the manifest content of modern identity activism, age has remained latently present, a structuring element in the post–New Left political unconscious. If we wish to understand why the identity paradigm seems less potent today than it did in previous decades, the answers therefore will likely be found in a historicotheoretical consideration of the end of the Cold War and its attendant identitarian ideology of age. This hidden history of identity is important not only for what it tells us about the recent past but also for how it might frame the political upheavals of the present. How are the political configurations of globalization reworking or engaging the identitarian rhetoric that saturated political culture in the Cold War years? What place might identity continue to have within an emerging *new* New Left associated with antiglobalization struggles? These are questions to which I will return in the conclusion.

The Postwar Emergence of Identity

Prior to the 1950s, the word "identity" did not apply to a collective sense of self, let alone to a notion of self understood as embattled or emergent. It was not modified by the terms of peoplehood as it now is in such locutions as "national identity," "racial identity," or "cultural identity." Nor, with a single exception, did it function adjectivally, as it would in such later locutions as "identity issues," "identity crisis," or "identity politics." In philosophy and mathematics, the word "identity" named a quality or condition of sameness or equivalence between several objects. One might, for instance, argue that the Phoenicians were originally Canaanites by observing the "identity" of their languages, or one might suggest that there is no identity of interest between capital and labor.⁴ Near the end of the nineteenth century, "identity" became an adjective, used only to designate objects manufactured so as to "identify the holder or wearer," such as identity cards, bracelets, or certificates. In this usage, "identity" indicated a person's entry in an informational system of reference. One could assume, for instance, a "false identity"—a counterfeit name or social position. Nevertheless, identity did not yet capture a psychological sense of personhood.

Until 1957, the *Reader's Guide to Periodic Literature* listed only one form of the word "identity": a subject heading entitled the "Identification of Criminals." In that year, however, a new entry appears in the periodical: "Identity, Personal. See Personality." Under "Personality," one finds a variety of articles listed, including such revealing titles as "What It Means to Find Yourself," "Traps of Identity," "Person in a Machine Age," and "Teenagers in Search of Themselves." Both the New Left and the counterculture of the 1960s seem to have made a decisive impact on the establishing of identity as a periodical topic. By 1971, the *Guide* no longer refers its readers to "Personality." Instead, it begins to log an independent subject heading entitled "Identity (psychology)" that lists such articles as "Identity Crisis in Black Americans Visiting West Africa" and "Masculinity and Racism: Breaking out of the Illusion: The White Middle-Class American Identity Role." By 1973, the first subcategory appears: "Negroes—Race Identity." Over the next few decades, other ethnic identities are gradually added to the *Guide*, while the politicization grows more explicit in such article titles as "American Identity Movements: A Cross-Cultural Confrontation" and "Liberated Woman: Identity Crisis."

These articles, of course, were merely publicizing a lexicon of identity already in use by post–New Left movements to describe the motives and goals of their activism. Although "identity politics" are today typically traced back no further than the mid-1970s, often to the rise of black feminism, its origins are in fact explicitly earlier and more disparate.⁵ Already by 1966, for example, "Black Identity" would appear as the subtitle to a key section of a SNCC (Student Non-Violent Coordinating Committee) manifesto meant to justify the organization's famous decision to reconstitute itself as an all-black youth organization: "Any re-evaluation that we must make will, for the most part, deal with identification. Who are black people, what are black people, what is their relationship to America and the world?" (SNCC, 158)

This political usage of identity was an early one, but by no means unusual. Nor was it restricted to activists of color. In 1969, for instance, Tom Hayden explained the irreconcilable differences between Judge Hoffman's generation and his own during the Chicago 7 trial with the simple assertion, "Our crime was our identity" (Hayden, 440), arguing that the court had indicted them for living in a "liberated zone" that threatened adult America, not merely with its political opinions, but "even more around 'cultural' and 'psychological' issues" (442). In that same year, the Gay Liberation Front Women stated in their manifesto: "We denounce the fact that society's rewards and privileges are only given to us when we hide and split our identity. We encourage self-determination and will work for changes in the lesbian self-image, as well as in society, to permit the 'coming out' of each gay woman into society as a lesbian" (Gay Liberation Front Women, 606).

In all these cases, it is notable that "identity" is conceived as the product of self-defining and self-affirming acts that confront a punitive, authoritarian Other: "America and the world," Judge Hoffman's generation, or a heteronormative society. The rhetoric of politicized identity hinges on proclaiming the subject's triumphant self-transformation as it detaches itself agonistically from the coerced expectations of "society," "America," or one's "elders."[6] Black politics takes its identitarian turn, for instance, through explicitly asserting the arrival of black power and black pride. To this day, gay identity politics draws on the rhetoric of pride, and not only at annual marches. In the metaphorics deployed above by the Gay Liberation Front, we see an early example of how the collective identity's "coming out" functions as a political debut, a coming into one's own "self-determination" that may be replayed by the gay individual. What I will call the psychopolitics of identity begins then, not with a wounded attachment to one's victimization, but rather with a proud declaration of emergence into power, a rhetorical move that has carried strategic value for many decades. The history taken up by this book begins by asking the question, what conditions spawned this new sense of identity as realized psychopolitical sovereignty? How and from whence did this identitarian discourse become available to help launch the new social movements?

Inventing Identity: Erik Erikson and the Cold War Psychopolitics of Youth

"Identity" as we know it was coined in 1950 with the publication of Erik Erikson's *Childhood and Society*, a text that would exert a powerful influence on postwar American culture.[7] Erikson's book was the first to define the word "identity" as the normative psychic achievement of selfhood. It was also the first, as Jonathan Arac notes, to attach identity to such elements as individuality, nationality, racial grouping, and even sexual orientation (20).[8] In just a few years time, Erikson's concept of "identity" would become hegemonic across the social sciences, come into use as an exciting new term in the humanities, and win a wide popular following. Many other writers and thinkers would take up the mantra of "identity," but they would refer back endlessly to Erikson's work, and to his first book especially, which became a college textbook bestseller. Robert Bellah is said to have remarked, "If there's one book you can be sure undergraduates have read, it is Erikson's first one. You can't always be sure they've read Shakespeare, but you know they've read Erikson" (Friedman, 335).

Identity discourse rapidly permeated postwar U.S. culture in no small part through its now largely forgotten relation to two key terms: "youth" and the "Cold War." It is rarely remembered that Erikson erected the concept of identity as part of his influential model of the stages of human development, with adolescence playing the pivotal role. Moreover, Erikson relied heavily on the ideological terrain of Second World War and Cold War geopolitics to promote his understanding of the identity concept as part of what would soon become an emergent postwar common sense.

The identity concept began as a key feature in Erik Erikson's account of the human life cycle—the so-called eight ages of man. Erikson schematized individual human development through an ascending series of psychosocial stages, each characterized by a new polarity in the self's possible relationship to the outer world. Despite the title's emphasis on childhood, Erikson's book is actually most concerned with the fifth stage, "puberty and adolescence." Adolescence, according to Erikson, replays all the earlier conflicts of childhood, but now at a level that requires the self to negotiate its way between the poles of identity and role confusion (273). For Erikson, adolescence constitutes the crucial staging ground of identity formation. It names the moment at which a person establishes, not so much a cognitive distinction between self and other (which clearly begins far earlier) but rather what might be considered a *psychopolitical* one.

In Erikson's account, childhood ends and "youth begins" when young people start to wrestle with the basic issue of "what they appear to be in the eyes of others as compared with what they feel they are" (261). In one respect, the "search for identity" that comprises the stage of adolescence for Erikson reenacts a classical political metanarrative of the enlightened individual entering into full possession of his/her right to self-determination.[9] Much like the ideals of liberty and independence that it incorporates, therefore, "identity" is a normative term and not just a descriptive one. It names an accomplishment and a positive good. What Erikson adds, however, is a post-Hegelian psychological requirement to the liberal political narrative: the self must be capable of formulating a satisfactory self-image that is determined by neither blind acceptance nor unthinking rejection of the image offered by the other. Identity pivots on what has sometimes been called a "politics of recognition" derived from the Hegelian model of lordship and bondage.[10] However, what specifically distinguishes the politics of identity is that the project of an uncoerced "self-recognition" becomes a prelude and a precondition to achieving recognition by the other. Because youth occupies the transitional stage between childhood and adulthood, it represents, in the context of the liberal theory that Erikson appropriates, a normative passage into self-determination.

Identity's political potency, however, derives from the fact that it has applied—from its inception—to collectivities as well as to the individuals that comprised them: for Erikson, it was not just persons that sought identity, but also tribes, nations, races, and even sexes. From the perspective of such collectivities, the political ideal upon which the concept of identity drew most directly was that of sovereignty. Like personal liberty, sovereignty too is a political norm, but the rights that it historically designates belong not to individuals but to states, which are entitled first to domestic autonomy (self-determination within their borders) and second to international recognition (acknowledgment and respect for that right by other states).[11] As scholars of international law have shown, however, the doctrine of sovereignty is itself based upon what is sometimes called the "domestic analogy," in which the liberal individual's natural rights are writ large, so that each state is itself conceived as an individual among other individuals, equally entitled by natural law to self-determination.[12] State sovereignty therefore acts as the projection of individual liberty onto the level of the body politic. Insofar as identity likewise moves from the individual's achievement of psychopolitical autonomy to an analogous one sought by the figure of the collectivity, it mirrors the political ideal of sovereignty.

Identity expands upon sovereignty in one very important way, however, for sovereignty, as a normative attribute of states, constitutes in Alexander Murphy's words a "political-territorial ideal" that takes primacy over peoplehood, or that at the very least makes state governmentality and territory into the obligatory complements of peoplehood. It assumes, in short,

IDENTITARIAN THOUGHT AND THE COLD WAR WORLD 7

that "the land surface of the earth should be divided up into discrete territorial units, each with a government that exercises substantial authority within its territory" (81). At the level of collectivity, identity may therefore be thought of as *a psychologized conception of sovereignty detached from territory and the state.* It treats both the person and the people as bearing a right to psychopolitical self-determination that precedes any questions of statehood or territory, and that indeed constitutes them as fully endowed persons or a people. Identitarian governmentality (insofar as it conceives one) begins with the self-rule of the personality.[13]

It is no accident that this decisively new locus for sovereignty's application coincided with the beginning of the Cold War, at a moment when U.S. political culture was being permeated and redefined in complex ways by the critiques of totalitarianism and colonialism. As we shall see, the new discourse of identity aimed to resolve a paradox for the traditional ideal of political sovereignty, namely that a state (like Nazi Germany or like a former European colony) might be nominally independent while its people remain psychologically subjugated. This was a problem that concerned thinkers and writers from many backgrounds, but it received special attention from psychoanalytically trained thinkers, including Wilhelm Reich and Eric Fromm (on fascism) and Franz Fanon (on colonialism). Erikson's work, and the discourse of identity that it spawned, belong to this tradition.

The politics of identity began in the metanarrative of youth's psychopolitical struggles, which Erikson brought directly to bear on the broad geopolitical dilemmas posed by the Cold War world. The study of identity, he famously asserted, "becomes as strategic in our time as the study of sexuality was in Freud's time," but the reason Erikson considered identity so indispensable a concept was because it enabled analytic judgment of the psychopolitical stakes involved in different paths to industrialization. Though titled "Youth and the Evolution of Identity," the important concluding section of Erikson's book does not examine individual identity formation but rather compares the respective national identity crises that the industrial revolution provoked in fascist Germany, communist Russia, and liberal capitalist America. This section of his book thus carves up the world according to the Cold War logic of the Vital Center, with the United States neatly balanced between the right-wing and left-wing extremes of fascist and communist totalitarianism.[14]

Adolescence remained just as central to Erikson's discussion of national identity as it was to individual identity, underscoring his conviction that all nations and collectivities possess group psychologies that must pass through a youthful stage of identity formation. Indeed, Erikson's book seems to take as axiomatic (setting the table, as it were, for development theory) that the moment of industrialization represents a collective "coming of age" for nations, in which the achievement of identity appears even more vital than economic growth.[15] Mediating between individual and social psychology, Erikson uses representative youth figures to analyze both German and Russian national identities. In the study of Germany, for instance, Erikson brings Freudian group psychology to bear on Hitler's youth-based charisma. If, for Erikson, excessive rebellion and sycophantic obedience represent the dueling risks of the adolescent struggle for identity, then Nazism emphatically embodied the former pathology. Erikson characterizes Hitler as an ersatz adolescent gang leader whose bid for political power began with an appeal to estranged adolescents, whom he induced to defy their parents. Eventually, Erikson argues, Hitler swayed the entire nation to the antiadult position that Germany had been betrayed by the parental afflictions of adjustment and conscience. In their place, Hitler offered them an aggressive, amoral "imagery of ideological adolescence" (344).[16]

In his discussion of Russia, Erikson directs his study of national identity through the "legend of the young Maxim Gorky," whom he presents as an apostle of an emergent industrial society. Working with a Soviet biopic about the famous novelist and playwright, Erikson interprets the events of the young Alyosha's boyhood in a backward, tribal world on the fringes of the Russian empire. Over the course of his childhood and adolescence, the young Alyosha develops a revolutionary identity that prepares him for a future in the Soviet intelligentsia. Though Erikson endorses Gorky's developing struggle against tsarist feudalism, he also hints at the eventual failure of his Bolshevik solution to Russia's identity crisis, which yielded only a totalitarian "machine logic" captured in such nicknames as "Stalin."

Toward its conclusion, the Gorky section turns decisively to a new topic, as the young Alyosha suddenly becomes representative of something other than merely Russian identity: "We must be able to demonstrate to grim Alyoshas everywhere that our new and shiny goods (so enticingly wrapped in promises of freedom) do not come to them . . . as so many more opiates to lull them into the new serfdom of hypnotized consumership. They do not want progress where it undermines their sense of initiative. They demand autonomy together with unity; and identity together with the fruits of industry" (402). This passage bears a complex relationship to the analysis of

Russian identity for which it serves as an epilogue. Erikson's "we" transparently designates an affluent postwar America. The "grim Alyoshas" of the passage, however, represent not the Soviet Union but instead, as we shall see, the nations of the third world. Moreover, what "we" need to demonstrate to "them" is emphatically not what one might expect in a time of Cold War, namely the perils of Bolshevik revolution, but rather the *lack* of perils posed by "our new and shiny goods." Put another way, the danger that occurs to Erikson following his analysis of Russian identity is not the Soviet threat to America, but instead the third world's erroneous suspicion that American affluence leads to unfreedom. Erikson's seemingly peculiar fear points toward yet another secret of identity's potency as a Cold War political concept.

The Age of Three Worlds

Erikson's "grim Alyoshas" come into focus only if we approach the Cold War era less as a simple squaring off between two postwar superpowers than as what I have elsewhere called a triangulated "age of three worlds."[17] As James Cronin has observed, the Cold War was first and foremost a postwar settlement that, following the defeat of the Axis powers, established highly stable geopolitical spheres of influence for both the United States and Soviet Union, even while it incited vigorous ideological conflict between them. Militarily speaking, the United States and the Soviet Union typically waged their territorial battles through proxy forces, but they confronted one another directly on the ideological playing field as self-appointed harbingers of rival universalisms: the world-historical claims of liberal capitalism and state socialism respectively (5–6).

The special urgency of these ideological conflicts derived from the main historical event of the era: the rapid decolonization of much of the earth. Even as the Soviet Union and the United States competed with one another to widen their respective social systems and spheres of influence, the old European world empires were breaking up. Between 1945 and 1960, Penny von Eschen points out, "forty countries with a total of eight hundred million people—more than a quarter of the world's population at that time—revolted against colonialism and won their independence" (125). U.S.-Soviet rivalry thus did not play out on a dichotomous globe in a simple scenario of "us against them," as a "containment" approach to Cold War culture implicitly presumes. Rather, it took the form of a triangulated rivalry over another universe that only now became known as the "third world."

The emergent nation-states in South and East Asia, the Middle East, Africa, and the Caribbean collectively became, as Eric Hobsbawm notes, "the zone in which the two superpowers continued, throughout the Cold War, to compete for support and influence, and hence the major zone of friction between them" (227). By the mid-1950s, the "three worlds concept" had become the globe's dominant topological imaginary.[18]

Hobsbawm's choice of the oddly gentle words "support" and "influence" inadvertently offers a vital observation to be made about the altered geopolitics of the postwar moment: although the United States and the Soviet Union, without question, aimed to win new territories for their social systems, it was no longer permissible to do so in the old modality of empire. The ideological as well as the material waning of formal imperialism, already well under way by the First World War, only accelerated during the Great Depression and the Second World War. By the moment of the post–World War II division of the globe, an anticolonial "global common sense" had firmly found its place as a necessary element in the formation of any hegemonic Cold War discourse. The very term "third world" was thus meant to name a region of the earth for which the experience of colonization was putatively now in the past, and whose present would therefore encounter only problems of "modernization," not foreign domination.

Put another way, the third world designated a region in which newly sovereign "national characters" were emerging from their former "dependence" upon colonial masters. After the First World War, the Versailles Treaty had fashioned for the tottering colonial order a new political rationale and juridical code whose "ideological origins [lay] in Western legal instruments for the protection of minors and the tutelage of children" (Grovogui, 121). This Kantian rhetoric of colonial nonage, according to which some people were "not yet able to stand by themselves under the strenuous conditions of the modern world" imaginatively positioned colonized populations as up-and-coming peoples, approaching though not yet arrived at a state of self-determination (Grovogui, 121). Already by 1918 then, the ruling ideology of colonialism hinged upon the human life cycle as its master metaphor.

The three worlds imaginary of the postwar years constituted a key turning point in this rhetoric, for it envisioned the colonized as having finally begun the passage out of nonage, a transition that Erikson would emphatically associate with adolescence and the quest for identity. Within this network of meanings, the first and second worlds benightedly represented, in turn, rival paths to modernization between which the nations of the third world would have to choose as they passed through national adolescence toward maturity.[19] It is within the terms of this global imaginary of emergent sovereignty that the United States competed with the USSR to win client states among the emergent nations. As the newly elected Harry Truman proclaimed in a 1949 speech promoting a new program of assistance to the third world, "Our aim should be to help the free peoples of the world, through their own efforts, to produce more food, more clothing.... The old imperialism—exploitation for foreign profit—has no place in our plans. What we envisage is a program of development based on the concepts of democratic fair-dealing" (916–917).

Truman here advances a by now familiar Cold War rhetoric, positioning America as "inherently anti-imperialist, in opposition to the empire-building of either the Old World or of communism and fascism, which collapse together into totalitarianism" (Amy Kaplan, 12). The United States, stressing whatever anticolonial credentials it could muster, presented itself as the only reliable model for achieving national self-determination. It promoted its first world as the genuinely "free world," a truncated but hopefully expanding version of the free and equal "one world" that Senator Wendel Wilkie had famously espoused following his travels through colonial Asia and Africa in the midst of the Second World War.

One principal way the United States validated itself as the proper model for developing third world nations was by mobilizing its claim to a history of colonial revolt. As even the hawkish secretary of state John Foster Dulles proclaimed in 1954, "We ourselves are the first colony in modern times to have won independence.... We have a natural sympathy with those everywhere who would follow our example" (Paterson et al., 504). With these words, Dulles enjoined an influential postwar national fantasy through which the United States transfigured itself from an informal imperial superpower into the first of the world's postcolonial states. It depicted itself, in other words, not as the imperial parent but as an elder sibling to the world's new nation-states, which had at last begun to follow in the footsteps of America.

This geopolitical fantasy served several ideological purposes. Not only did it explain why third world nations should gravitate toward the American over the Soviet alliance, but it also bolstered a proprietary relation to the discourse of freedom. As nation after nation cast off the colonial rule of European states, these newly independent countries possessed, on the geopolitical playing field, immediate legacies of national liberation movements that could make a rhetorically stronger claim to the title of the free world than the United States. The third world's claim on freedom was in many ways furthered by efforts made by many new nations to escape domination by either the United States or the USSR, particularly after the concept of a "third path" gathered force following the 1957 Bandung Conference of so-called nonaligned countries.

In contrast to the culture of containment nourished by the "red scare," Cold War America's phantasmagoric affiliation with the third world led in notably different political directions. Specifically, the newly independent nations of the third world prompted assertions of America's status as their historical precursor, and thus as a postrevolutionary society. Among the most influential of such assertions was Erikson's identity concept, which explicitly shared this Cold War fantasy of a postcolonial revolutionary American character. Decolonization had unleashed, in Erikson's view, a wave of new national self-images whose "common denominator is the freeborn child who becomes an emancipated adolescent" (299). Yet in this respect, they followed a path already blazed by American identity since "the American farmer's boy is the descendant of Founding Fathers who themselves were rebel sons" (399). Implicit in Erikson's reasoning, then, is the geopolitically vital question, would the new freeborn children of the world recognize their likeness to America?

These, then, are the "grim Alyoshas" of Erikson's Russia chapter. The historical Alyosha, it would seem, stands in metonymically for the young Russian nation as it moves beyond feudalism and into a revolutionary moment of "identity crisis." Against the Cold War backdrop for Erikson's book, "Alyosha" names not the Stalinist totalitarian enemy (who will be known by the name "Maxim Gorky") but rather a Russia in the pivotal moment *before* it had become the metropole of the second world, when it was still a third world nation, seeking a path to "autonomy together with unity; and identity together with the fruits of industry." The many other Alyoshas, following suit, would appear to be the new cast of young nations mounting the postwar stage, now poised (like prerevolutionary Russia) to make a choice between state socialism or liberal capitalism as their path to sovereignty.

Erikson, as a famously patriotic emigré to the United States and a partisan of Franklin Delano Roosevelt's New Deal, does not even bother to denounce the communist model. It is taken for granted that the young Alyosha's commendable struggle for identity ends tragically in Stalinist tyranny. Communism, the false road to industrialization, promises collective sovereignty and an industrial future, only to send one hurtling back, in the damning words of Cold Warrior Robert Hayek, on the road to a second serfdom. It may provide unity (a communist empire), but not autonomy. It may deliver the fruits of industry, but only at the bitter price of identity. Gorky's new regime thus proves as unfree as the old one that his earlier self, the young Alyosha, had sought to overthrow.

It remains less clear, however, why Erikson would expect the young Alyoshas of the third world to view America's "shiny goods" as embodying, not its "freeborn" passion for identity but instead yet another "new serfdom," here based upon industrial consumerism rather than communist tyranny. Erikson's poetic language, which describes "shiny goods" as "enticingly wrapped" to seduce their buyers into a "hypnotized consumership," paradoxically draws his reader toward a threat that he ostensibly believes does not exist. In other words, he insists that consumerism does not represent a "new serfdom" for emerging nations even as the rich detail of his description suggests that it must. The passage marks Erikson's profound ambivalence toward American mass consumption as a threat to identity, an attitude that was not untypical of the generalized social anxieties wrought by the new relations of postwar U.S. capitalism.

Cold War Suburbs as a Mode of Regulation

The emergence of identity discourse in the United States was conditioned, not only by the postwar decolonization of the globe but also by the rapid transformations of everyday life within the nation's borders. While decolonization led to an intensified rhetoric of American freedom, the emerging postwar culture of consumption called forth a more complicated response in the United States, one that was often self-congratulatory, but at times also included palpable fears that Americans were becoming more passive and unfree. The identity concept spoke directly to these fears that plagued the social arrangements of postwar life.

Because my reading of the culture of postwar U.S. capitalism relies heavily on the technical and theoretical insights of the French regulation school, it will be necessary at this point to make a slight theoretical detour.[20] Like its post-Marxist cousin, British cultural studies, the French regulation school theorists have developed a complex account of the relationship between economics and culture. While both schools reject the traditional base-superstructure model, however, the regulation school has focused, not on the degree of autonomy between spheres (as has been the tactic of cultural studies) but instead on the extent of their mutual interdependence; special stress is placed on the political, juridical, and cultural as sites for preconditions of capitalist economies.[21] In lieu of "base" and "superstructure," the regulation school theorists distinguish instead between what they call a "regime of accumulation" and a "mode of regulation." The "regime of accumulation" describes the particular processes utilized in production for profit at any given moment in the history of capitalism. The "mode of regulation" describes the ensemble of regulating institutions, formations, and subjects that make for the stability of a particular "regime of accumulation." In this respect, the regulation school treats cultural and political institutions not as superstructural, but in fact as potentially *infrastructural*, as genuine conditions of possibility for the reproduction of any particular historical form of capitalism.[22]

The 1950s, as it happens, launched an episode in economic history that regulation school theorists have studied carefully under the rubric of the Fordist regime of accumulation. The term "Fordist," borrowed from Antonio Gramsci, is taken from Henry Ford, who combined a Taylorist production model (fragmenting the work process so as to intensify labor productivity) with compensatory higher wages that, along with a system of credit, would enable his workers to purchase the cars they manufactured. In the crudest sense, Fordism represents an economic system in which an assembly-line model of mass production was articulated with a culture of mass consumption, all under the regulatory guidance of an expanded professional managerial class and a Keynesian welfare state. Roughly speaking, the regulation school traces the roots of Fordism to the Great Depression, which it describes as a crisis precipitated by the incompatibility between an old "competitive mode of [economic] regulation," the laissez-faire political arrangements of nineteenth-century capitalism, and the new Taylorist production model, which they describe as an "intensive regime of accumulation."[23]

The difficulty posed by this intensive regime's vast improvements in economic productivity was that it required social demand to keep pace with the potential increase in supply. Left to the vagaries of market forces in a laissez-faire "competitive mode of regulation," late-nineteenth- and early-twentieth-century capital experienced repeated crises of overaccumulation, culminating in the Great Depression. The solution to these recurring crises came through the development of what the regulation school calls a "monopolistic mode of regulation," spearheaded by the Keynesian state's use of fiscal policy (i.e., government spending and taxation) and monetary policy (manipulation of the money supply) to stabilize aggregate demand. Though governmental regulation of the U.S. economy had roots in early-twentieth-century progressivism, it expanded rapidly with the New Deal, and took hold in earnest when the state took command of industrial output during the Second World War. The proto-Fordist wartime model demonstrated that, by providing big business with a secure market that would allow it to safely increase its output, a Keynesian state could provide much of the institutional structure necessary for capital accumulation.

Seen against this historical preface, the Fordist regime that motored the "peacetime" economic boom appears to have been achieved by finding suitable replacements for the peculiar conditions of the wartime economy, thereby forming, in combination, what I will call the Cold War mode of regulation. Wartime state coordination of industry, in other words, evolved into the standard set of "peacetime" Keynesian legal, fiscal, and financial state institutions. But in another sense, as many have argued, the state of war never ended, as Cold War hostilities led to a perpetually militarizing security state, and consequently, a means of upholding aggregate demand. Postwar Fordism became regulated, to borrow Herbert Marcuse's term, by a "welfare/warfare state."[24]

Fordism also entailed a new mode of regulation for labor, similarly modeled on a wartime precedent: an ideology of compelling national interest. During the Second World War, the state had managed its labor problems through a propaganda apparatus that mobilized workers as self-sacrificing Americans willing to labor heroically to defeat their fascist adversaries. Soon after 1945, as it declared a "cold" war with Soviet Russia, the state mandated, once again in the name of national security, that American labor desist from challenging capital. As America's right-wing fascist nemesis was supplanted by a left-wing communist one, the Cold War succeeded in justifying far greater hostility to the radical politics of labor than had the comparatively benign atmosphere of the war's antifascist agenda. Left-wingers who challenged the terms offered to labor in the Fordist social contract could be vilified, not merely as unpatriotic saboteurs of a war effort, but as apologists for the totalitarian ideology of the communist enemy.

The Cold War undermined class politics in other ways as well, some more indirect but no less effective. Fordism, for instance, greatly expanded in size a more politically acquiescent white-collar managerial class, both in the public sector, where this class administered the regulatory state, and in the private sector, where it managed the Taylorized workforce on behalf of corporate elites. Though they labored for wages just as surely as their blue-collar counterparts, white-collar workers, as critics have often noted, imagined themselves as a middle class situated between capital and labor, at least in part because the labor they performed was deemed mental rather than physical. They thus possessed a sort of "knowledge capital," which set them apart from the working class.[25]

Fordism found its most powerful means of social regulation, however, in the great postwar suburbs, which brought the blue-collar working classes together with the expanding white-collar managerial class into a single system of everyday life. Politically, the suburbs deradicalized labor; culturally, they interpellated Americans as consumers; economically, they propped up social demand. As it matched the new scale of production offered by the Taylorized assembly line with a new mode of mass consumption, Fordism completely transformed the way of life for the wage-earning classes (Lee, 73). During the late forties and fifties, the state helped to finance, build, and administer an entirely new form of the everyday: suburban living. As developers assembled concentric rings of suburban housing tracts around urban centers, government subsidized them by providing the infrastructure necessary to sustain them, including water, power, and crucially, a highway system of beltways and interstates linking the new suburbs to urban workplaces. As workers purchased the new homes, using their hefty wage increases and state-supported Federal Housing Administration financing, they launched what London Jones describes as the single largest internal migration in the history of the United States:

> In the twenty years from 1950 to 1970, the population of the suburbs doubled from 36 million to 72 million. No less than 83 percent of the total population growth in the United States during the 1950s was in the suburbs, which were growing fifteen times faster than any other segment of the country. As people packed and moved, the national mobility rate leaped by 50 percent. The only other comparable influx was the wave of European immigrants to the United States around the turn of the century. But, as *Fortune* pointed out, more people moved to the suburbs every year than had ever arrived on Ellis Island. (38)

Suburbanization on such a mass scale allowed automobile companies in turn to market cars that the millions of relocated workers now needed to commute on the new highway system. It also eventually led to the rise of the shopping mall, a suburban alternative to urban commercial districts that added further convenience to new rounds of purchases for the home. In short, suburbanization established the mode of mass consumption necessary for Fordism to stave off another accumulation crisis, absorbing as it did the excess production capacity unleashed by postwar demobilization.

For a working class with few material assets, which had survived the depression in miserable urban tenements or even in tent cities, suburban home ownership was a deeply attractive postwar opportunity. Yet this process of suburbanization quickly came to regulate postwar labor insofar as it led them to reimagine themselves, no longer as proletarians, but at last as fully enfranchised nationals, as Americans whose socioeconomic system could now "deliver the goods" and thus no longer deserved to be criticized. The suburbs facilitated this imaginative work on numerous fronts. To begin with, the suburban home relocated the worker both physically and imaginatively at a distance from the site of production, where worker consciousness might be nourished; in its stead, it offered an environment that reorganized life around the pleasures of private consumption.

The suburbs also radically reordered race and ethnicity to the detriment of class consciousness. During the Second World War the city became a rich space for proletarian affinities, as workers across ethnic and racial groups labored and lived together, building solidarities amidst the war effort.[26] Suburbanization rent asunder this emergent wartime working class. European immigrants, whose class-stratified enclaves in the cities had encouraged a strong sense of themselves as ethnic groups akin to "other" nonwhites, were now enticed to the suburbs by appeals to their understandable post–depression era desire to escape urban tenements for the security of home ownership. Once dispersed among the suburbs, however, their prior friendship and kinship networks were increasingly supplanted by patterns of sociable consumption to be shared with their new neighbors. Blacks, Latinos, and Asians, meanwhile, were pointedly excluded from the new suburbs through an ensemble of policies that included "redlining" by banks and the FHA, as well as "restrictive covenants" enforced by developers and homeowner associations.

The Cold War suburbs transformed not only the basic terms of race, but also those of family, gender, and sexuality through its prevailing ethos of domesticity. As it removed people from the city, Fordism eroded the institution of the extended family, erecting in its place a streamlined nuclear family, the new atomic unit of postwar consumer society characterized by ownership of a home, at least one automobile, a television set, refrigerator, washer and dryer, and much more. Like suburbia itself, this new domesticity served a political as well as an economic purpose. As Elaine Tyler May points out, "Purchasing for the home helped alleviate traditional American uneasiness with consumption: the fear that spending would lead to decadence. Family-centered spending reassured Americans

18 CHAPTER ONE

that affluence would strengthen the American way of life. The goods purchased by middle-class consumers, like a modern refrigerator or a house in the suburbs, were intended to foster traditional values" (166). The Cold War American family was thus a radically new institution that paradoxically took on a status as a traditionalist bulwark against communist (and analogized forms of) amorality, thereby easing the transition into a mass-consumption society.

For all these reasons, the postwar suburb must be understood, not simply as a geographical phenomenon, nor even as a new mode of mass consumption, but as a primary Cold War ideological apparatus. A "machine for living," the suburban home (in contrast to the city apartment) hailed its subjects not as a multiracial working class with common laboring interests to defend, nor even as citizen members of a heterogeneous public, but instead as white Americans participating in a national ideal (the much ballyhooed "American dream") that itself needed defending against its communist enemies.[27] Moving to the suburbs was tantamount to doing one's national duty by building the affluence and strength of America's Fordist order.

*From Containment to Identity Culture:
A New Cast of Cold War Characters*

Insofar as the new regime of accumulation depended upon a Cold War ideological system of social regulation, it can be said that Fordism and the Cold War worked neatly together as the respective economic and the political faces of a powerful postwar hegemony. Cold war discourse proclaimed the new suburbs as the apotheosis of American freedom, a utopian space of national abundance in which people could at last fully realize their individuality by making consumer choices that expressed and satisfied their inner wants. From this perspective, Americans who questioned or opposed the promise of suburbia could be constituted as the internal enemies of American freedom who, like the external Soviet enemy, needed to be prevented from acting out their subversive intentions.

This dimension of Cold War culture in the fifties has been widely investigated by numerous scholars under the rubric of "containment," and Cold War culture is indeed often conceived in the scholarship as above all an ideologically driven system of sociopolitical repression. Originally, "containment" named a foreign policy, first devised by diplomat George Kennan in his famous Long (or X) Telegram, in which the United States to "contain" or restrict the expansionary intentions of the Soviet regime. As a number of critics have argued, the policy of containing communism abroad provided flexible terms for a repressive cultural logic on the home front that identified various "un-American" characters and forces as domestic equivalents of the Soviet menace.

The most obvious (and also least figurative) example of such Cold War "domestic containment" is surely McCarthyism, the right-wing political campaign that rolled back New Deal progressive politics by accusing its partisans in Washington, Hollywood, and elsewhere of serving Soviet interests.[28] But, as Elaine Tyler May first suggested in her groundbreaking book *Homeward Bound*, a version of containment policy was also brought to bear on postwar gender relations, as fear of the bomb—and the Soviet threat generally—drove women and men into the sense of security offered by suburbia's powerful new norms of nuclear family living. May's arguments find revealing parallels in the work of John D'Emilio, Robert Corber, Gerald Horn, Alan Nadel, and others, who have each shown in quite different ways how the "red scare" dimension of postwar culture set in motion far-reaching forms of social regulation, with detrimental effects for unmarried or working women, gays and lesbians, sexual bohemians of all stripes, political radicals, labor unions, racial minorities who challenged white privilege, and numerous other deviants from the norms of the Cold War suburban imaginary.[29]

It would be a mistake, however, to assume a seamless relationship between the material relations of Fordism and the ideological imperatives of the Cold War. Indeed, one of the era's most distinctive cultural features was an abiding fear that Fordist consumer culture and the Cold War were not aligned, that the new suburbs did not at all constitute the sort of "free world" that the three worlds imaginary of the Cold War required America to be. One highly condensed expression of this fear is found in Erikson's concern that America appeared more as a system of "hypnotized consumership" than as the preeminent democratic society of the "freeborn son." But while objections to the "soft tyranny" of postwar culture— its suburbs, its white-collar world, its system of mass consumption—were legion, the image demanded of Cold War America as land of the "freeborn sons" made Fordist masculinity into an especially sensitive site of social critique. William Whyte's renowned sociological study *The Organization Man* and Sloan Wilson's best-selling novel *The Man in the Gray Flannel Suit* provided two well-known monikers for a widening critical discussion of the "new" white-collar, suburban masculinity, as did a high-profile *Life* magazine article entitled "The New American Domesticated Male."

Too often, scholars have viewed these figures as instituting a new normative model of American manhood, when what they in fact connoted was at best a distressed form of masculinity, and at worst a degenerate one.[30] As Barbara Ehrenreich reminds us, Sloan Wilson's protagonist represented what she calls an "early rebel," or a "gray flannel dissident" who was "adjusted; he was mature; he was, by any reasonable standard, a success as an adult male breadwinner. But . . . he knew that something was wrong" (29). William Whyte's classic treatise likewise polemicizes *against* the Organization Man, denouncing him for his conformist "social ethic" and entreating him instead to "fight the Organization" in defense of his own individuality (13).[31] Indeed, as Whyte suggests in his introduction, for all his Fordist affluence, the Organization Man's dilemma seemed very similar to that of a people ruled by communist tyranny: "The word 'collective' most of them can't bring themselves to use—except to describe foreign countries or organizations they don't work for—but they are keenly aware of how much more deeply beholden they are to organization than were their elders" (4). Such criticisms were widely extended, not merely to the Organization Man, but to the suburban world in which he lived. As Helen Puner noted with exasperation in her 1958 magazine article "Is It True What They Say about the Suburbs?" these naysayers included the entire range of "sociologists, psychologists, playwrights, novelists and assorted peerers at the American scene" (42).[32] In the popular forays against the Fordist world, a consistent theme appears: the new system of mass consumption was depriving Americans—and most vitally its men—of their hitherto distinctive autonomy, and thus diminishing the very value of freedom held to distinguish the first world from the second. Suburbia, in one of the jokes that Whyte quotes, was "a Russia, only with money" (310). Timothy Melley has referred to this ubiquitous, often paranoid anxiety of the era as "agency panic," precisely because it imagined that powerful yet invisible new structures were coming to determine the self's every action.

Exemplary of this postwar "agency panic" was the most influential sociological treatise of the decade, David Riesman et al.'s *The Lonely Crowd*, a text which argued that the new consumer society (associated with suburbs, white-collar workplaces, and other scenes of the Fordist order) was fundamentally redirecting the American character toward compulsory social conformity: "from invisible hand to glad hand," as he succinctly puts it. Where once they were "inner-directed," by which Riesman and his co-authors mean that they behaved in accordance with an internalized set of moral codes, Americans were increasingly becoming "other-directed," conditioning their behavior in response to social pressures and communicated directives (13–25).[33]

At the conclusion of their enormously influential text, the authors close with a grim question: might "other-directed" Americans find themselves increasingly reduced to a miserable choice between "adjustment," in which larger social needs will simply recalibrate their personalities for a proper "fit," or "anomie," a state of disfunctionality or failed dissent? Against these equally dismal alternatives, Riesman and company pinned their hopes on a third possibility, that Americans might develop an "autonomous" form of other-directed personality capable of "conforming to the behavioral norms of their society—a capacity the anomics usually lack—but are free to choose whether to conform or not" (242). This figure of the "autonomous other-directed personality" fulfilled a widespread cultural wish of the times. Like the writings of Whyte, Wilson, and many others, *The Lonely Crowd* struggles to imagine how the sovereign American personality might be rejuvenated in the face of a widespread conviction that it had been compromised by Fordism's cryptototalitarian system of mass consumption.

These common attacks upon the suburban ideal, organizational manhood, and the like, suggest that the much-touted "Cold War consensus" never actually existed. Instead, they indicate that postwar American culture was deeply troubled by ideological tensions between the norms of Fordist suburbia and the America idealized by the three worlds imaginary. While "agency-panicked" critics like Riesman never doubted that the Fordist first world remained more conducive to sovereign selfhood than the communist second world, they nevertheless condemned the former as far from ideal. Soviet Russia's "modern totalitarianism . . . must wage total war on autonomy," Riesman noted, but the "diffuse and anonymous authority of the modern democracies is less favorable to autonomy than one might assume" (251).

Like most liberal social critics of the day, David Riesman sought to imagine an autonomous but still Fordist American character, capable of freely choosing its "other-directed" suburban consumption and white-collar employment. One major difficulty with this hope, however, concerned how such an "autonomous" conformity might ever be demonstrated. Fordism, because it articulated mass production with mass consumption, brought into existence an undeniable standardization in the object world of everyday life for Americans. The advertising system, to be sure, insisted that mass consumption gave Americans the means to achieve individual self-expression. Nevertheless, the standardization of Fordist assembly line products was often seen instead as eroding the sovereign selfhood of Americans. Moreover, if someone has already chosen to live, like "everyone else," as an Organization Man or to don the ubiquitous gray flannel suit, how might one show that a choice had been made at all? What might visibly distinguish a chosen conformity premised on one's autonomy from a coerced one stemming from adjustment? Only in refusing to conform to the Fordist standard, it seems, could the individual's sovereign independence from the directives of others be ascertained. This dilemma was particularly troubling given its appearance at the precise moment when the Cold War required that the sovereign American character be celebrated.

Understood both as the antithesis of second world totalitarian mass societies and as the model for third world developing societies, Erikson's concept of identity, when understood as a project of self-development for the young, offered a resolution to the ambivalence expressed by critics like Riesman or Whyte. It is here that the immediate and tremendous appeal of the identity concept becomes intelligible, as does its general political utility. The adolescent self-generates his or her identity through a process that must be at least partially agonistic, refusing "roles" and "self-images" offered up by others, and challenging what later critical theorists of identity would term "subject positionings." In Erikson's model, successful identity formation depends upon the legitimate exercise of rebellion. The Eriksonian drama of adolescence, therefore, describes the development of an individual or social character that successfully reconciles "autonomy" and "other-directedness" in Riesman's sense.[34] The patent appeal of the Eriksonian adolescent's "character" is that she enacts the requisite dramas of rebellion *prior* to adulthood. Thus, if an adolescent exhibits a properly rebellious spirit before growing into a conforming suburbanite or an Organization Man, then she has effectively displayed the American self's sovereignty without necessarily sacrificing the eventual conformity of the adult.

Given that the containment culture of Cold War suburbia was repeatedly plagued by agency panic, the adolescent, as a figure who represented the autonomous character of American identity, on both the national and individual levels, offered an imaginative remedy. The youthful figure of American identity likewise offered a pleasing mirror image with which to reflect back the gaze of the "young Alyoshas" of the third world. For emergent nations seeking to define themselves as independent of their former colonizers, what could be a better antidote to the geopolitically deleterious image of a "hypnotized consumership" or an "other-directed" mass than a young America, endlessly restaging its own revolutionary moment in a struggle to assert its emergent identity? Within this field of ideological forces, the ideal of the young rebel thus became the nodal point around which a secondary Cold War formation was assembled: an identity culture whose dialectical relationship to containment culture conveyed a celebratory rather than a panicked relationship to agency.

Cold War Youth and the Invention of the Teenager

The quickly embraced concept of identity was only one in a cluster of lexical terms that articulated the ideologically motivated desire for a youth that could represent Cold War America's self-determination in a "conformist" Fordist era. Another key term was the "teenager"; yet another was the "rebel." By the mid-fifties, as these terms came to orbit around an emerging Fordist youth market, they gave rise to a rebel metanarrative. The typical protagonist of this narrative (but not the only possible one) was a figure I shall call the "bad boy" of Cold War American culture. It is through this figure that a definitive political culture of identity first came into existence. Before discussing the bad boy, however, I want to trace his sources in the "teenager" and the "rebel," each of which offers a slightly different genealogy.

Like "identity," "teenager" is a word whose recent coinage has been largely forgotten. Not only did both terms enter the lexicon at the same moment, but they did so under similar ideological pressures and determinations. According to historian William Manchester, the word "teenager" made its very first appearance at the close of the Second World War, in an article published by Elliot Cohen in a 1945 issue of the *New York Times Magazine*. From this very beginning, the word claimed a powerful political connotation, as the article's title, "A Teen-Age Bill of Rights," readily suggests.[35] In a noteworthy echo of Woodrow Wilson's fourteen-point program for national sovereignty, Cohen's article proposes another postwar bestowal of autonomy: a "ten-point charter" drafting the rights of the teenager. In this case, however, psychopolitical rights define the endorsed arena of sovereignty. This politicized vocabulary of rights and charters for teenagers might read today as overblown, pseudopolitical rhetoric, yet for Americans in 1945 it intelligibly responded to an apparent crisis in the historic relations of age inherited by the wartime years.

Only in the late nineteenth century had a space of representation opened up between childhood and adulthood, to be occupied by the "adolescent." The figure of the adolescent condensed together various socioideological developments in the pre-Fordist era of industrial capitalism that lie beyond this study's scope, but several important determinants deserve at least to be mentioned. In part, the adolescent represented a difficult compromise between labor and capital over where to draw the line between child and adult labor within the industrial wage system. Meanwhile, in the emerging system of education, the adolescent also became central to norms of reproduction for the professional middle class. Fears of urbanization and overcivilization were also spoken to by the adolescent, whose stage in life allowed for intervention in such nature and recreation organizations as the Boy Scouts. Finally, the adolescent also functioned as part of the legitimation narrative for Western imperialism, which, as earlier noted, was steeped in the symbolics of age dependency and development.

Taken together, these determinants tended to produce the adolescent as a dependent whose physical maturity belied a need for adult supervision and instruction. As Joseph Kett has shown, adolescence became a stressful preparatory stage in life, initiated by puberty, when the instinctual energies of young people presumably climaxed even while they lacked the cultural or psychological maturity needed to master their physical powers. Schooling, broadly understood as subjection to adult pedagogical training, became the central drama of adolescence. This new category of transitional age placed its subjects (who formerly had exited childhood directly into the position of young adulthood), in a formalized state of legal, economic, and intellectual subordination to their elders (Gillis, 98). The very meaning of adolescence, associated as it was with sexual, moral, and intellectual immaturity, precluded youth from the rights of personal autonomy that liberal enlightenment doctrine granted to the mature individual. Youth, in the emergent professional middle classes, became increasingly administered by "new educational and recreational systems of social control" (Gillis, 98). Meanwhile, as a normative ideal, "adolescence" served to pathologize the lives of working-class and immigrant youth, since their participation in "street-corner societies" only confirmed the neglect shown by lower-class families and communities toward these vital years of their children's development.[36] Far from symbolizing the achievement of sovereignty, then, adolescence represented a condition of—and case for—a lengthening state of dependency.

The Second World War brought the category of adolescence into crisis.

With so many fathers abroad and mothers at work, the proper supervision of adolescents seemed increasingly unworkable, precipitating tremendous anxiety. A campaign of hysteria ensued in the wartime press, supported by social experts who predicted a coming epidemic of juvenile delinquency. As James Gilbert argues, this "rehearsal for a crime wave" derived from widespread social scientific and psychoanalytic beliefs that "delinquency was a problem rooted in the family structure. When this [normal structure] was disrupted, then crime was one inevitable result. Thus as the war split families apart, first by conscription and then because women entered the labor force, children were more and more subjected to pressures that in theory, at least, would lead them to misbehave" (28). The social dislocations caused by the Second World War seemed to place middle-class adolescents, for the first time, on the streets alongside their less privileged peers, whose street culture had long been pathologized by social workers and social scientists as delinquent.

The war did not, in fact, throw an entire population of middle-class youth onto the streets. Rather, the war actually led many young people of all social classes to enter the workforce, much as it had for adult women (Gilbert, 19–20). Youth, in short, became part of the wartime proto-Fordist economy. Many adults, however, perceived youth employment as yet another road to delinquency, since it seemed to provide adolescents with an unacceptable level of independence. "We've all heard about teen-age girls who pick up servicemen, and about the easy-come-easy-go way of teen-age boys with newly acquired pay checks," observed a typical article pleading for recreation facilities for "Teen Ages" (Mackenzie, 27). The war was seen as rushing youth prematurely into adulthood, which was perhaps an anxious way of acknowledging that the young were regaining some measure of adult economic and social privilege lost to them since the invention of adolescence.

It is this politicized context that made possible the "teenager" and such attendant articles as the "Teen-Age Bill of Rights." In important respects, the new category of the teenager embodied a compromise that became foundational to the postwar regime of age. The young waived any claims on adulthood per se, but they retained certain privileges acquired during the war. These rights, moreover, would be explicitly justified in relation to the wars waged against the Nazis and the Soviets. At a remarkably early date, the "Teen-Age Bill of Rights" framed the liberties it endorsed in terms of the Cold War. The text of the charter begins with the "right to let childhood be forgotten," drawing an emphatic distinction between the dependency of nonage and the growing capacity for autonomy in the teen years (Cohen, 16). Unlike the "adolescent," the teenager of the "Bill of Rights" does not require continuous supervision by adults. Indeed, such supervision is presented as both a violation of the teenager's rights and a political pitfall. The article introduces us to "Don," "a boy on the debating team who only last week took the affirmative of the question, 'Should the United States pledge its armed forces if necessary to preserve the peace?' His teacher said he was very convincing. He knows a lot about the Cardinals, Congress, Crosby and communism, and he's learning fast. But when he gets home, he's still a kid. . . . [H]e feels his parents are living in his past, and don't understand him. There's nothing quite as infuriating as the tolerant smile—'After all, you're still just a child' " (Cohen, 16). The article's language converges strikingly with an Eriksonian concept of identity. Don's political intelligence promises an important future as an effective defender of American geopolitical interests. Yet the satisfyingly autonomous image Don has of himself threatens to lead into an unneeded confrontation with his parents, who mistakenly continue to regard him as a mere child (or perhaps as a prewar "adolescent"). Without recognizing that, as a teenager, their son has already begun his quest for identity, Don's parents also risk failing to honor his corollary rights as a teenager, including "a 'say' about his own life," "the right to make mistakes, to find out for himself," "to have rules explained not imposed," and "to question ideas." The "Teen-Age Bill of Rights," in short, petitions its readers to honor and respect youth as *the embodiment of emergent identity*.

The ideologically saturated meaning of the "teenager" is also revealed in two child-rearing advice books written by Dorothy Baruch. In her first book of 1942, *You, Your Children, and War*, Baruch expresses concern that, as personal freedoms are suspended in wartime, "our children see in the world about them no very true picture of democratic living. They see, instead, a kind of autocracy in action" (89). Amidst the war on fascism, and on the very eve of decolonization, Baruch calls for a renewal of democratic attitudes toward youth, including respect for their efforts at independence, so as to avoid "either [their] open and extreme revolt, or continuing dependence. The ones who revolted had to prove their independence blindly and with violence. The ones who continued their dependence were trying to prove to themselves by 'dutifulness' that they were not wicked after all. They could still be nice and good and obedient children" (101–102). These dual negative options noticeably echo the two pathological extremes of adolescence asserted in the psychological writings of Erik Erikson. Also like

Erikson, Baruch normalizes a middle route between "extreme revolt" or "continuing dependence," one that leads to the "democratic" formation of an independent identity. By 1953, Baruch had become an active promoter of the new youth lexicon, publishing a follow-up book, *How to Live with Your Teen-Ager*, whose basic philosophy is suitably captured in the title to her final section, "Toward Growing Independence" (167).

The Cold War rationale for teenage autonomy was spelled out in even greater detail by Dorothy Gordon, moderator of the *New York Times* Youth Forums, as she recalls the "indoctrination of the young" she had witnessed in mid-thirties fascist Germany and communist Russia:

> Indoctrinated with ideologies utterly opposed to the ideals of democracy, how much did those youngsters threaten the future of America? . . . Suddenly I knew I had to do something about it! A man does not come by his democratic conscience overnight in his manhood. He is not born into it. Instead it must be instilled into his thinking from his alphabet days on in order to make him fit for liberty. I realized then that the greatest hope for a lasting democracy lay in an awareness of the principles of freedom on the part of our youth in America, and that awareness could best come through participation in one of the strongholds of democracy which is freedom of speech. . . . The danger and threat of the totalitarian ideology could best be met by a reaffirmation of faith in our democracy. With that firm conviction in mind, I brought the idea of youth forum discussion to *The New York Times*. (173)

Gordon illustrates here a complicated slippage in postwar youth discourse between the "is" and the "ought" of the autonomous American teenager. Though America's democratic character could sometimes be dramatized by comparing its independent-minded teenagers with the slavish obedience of a Hitler youth or a communist youth group member, at other times it seemed equally evident that autonomy was a fragile value requiring active cultivation and encouragement. In *The American Teenager*, a "general report" on America's youth from 1957, culled from detailed social opinion surveys, Herman Remmers and D. H. Radler concluded that, while America's teenagers exhibited distinctly democratic ideals, their commitments were too often driven by "other-directed" motivations in exactly Riesman's sense. Teenagers, in other words wanted so much to "fit in" that they exhibited a susceptibility to fascist and communist political precepts. Remmers and Radler considered this situation fundamentally unacceptable in a Cold War world: "The internal stability of any democratic society, as well as its effectiveness in meeting the challenge of rival ideologies, is dependent on the constant and active exercise of those freedoms and those responsibilities that epitomize the democratic orientation. Passive acceptance of choices made by others is actively destructive to the American ideal" (230). In the end, therefore, Remmers and Radler prescribed something very much like the "Teen-Age Bill of Rights," as a means of shoring up the agential, sovereign status of American youth: "The capacity of the American teenager is vast. Helping him achieve self-realization is more than mere duty; it can become sublime satisfaction. And the debt will be more than repaid. Aided to 'come into his own,' the American teenager will contribute to our society much more than that society could possibly give him. He will be, indeed, an inspiration to his family, his community, and the world" (259).

Such endorsements of the teenager as the bearer of youth's autonomy did not come without struggle. On the contrary, parents and the media would repeatedly bemoan the "scandalous behavior and rebellious nature of the nation's young people" (Oakley, 268). For conservatives in particular, youth's increased claims to autonomy signaled a calamitous deterioration in age relations.[37] The political concession ultimately made to a sovereign teenhood was deeply fraught and circumscribed by powerful fears and rhetorical turns that were themselves clearly associated with the conservative Cold War culture of containment. The bogey of the juvenile delinquent therefore did not disappear with the end of the Second World War. Public anxiety persisted through the fifties that freedom for middle-class youth might devolve into criminality. In the nineteenth century, the middle-class adolescent and the juvenile delinquent from the "other half" had once functioned as a normative binary, with clear class and ethnic lines separating them. The teenager, however, could not be so easily distinguished from the juvenile delinquent, for s/he had incorporated a degree of freedom from adult supervision previously associated only with lower-class youth. Middle-class teenagers might, for example, form gangs of their own that — unlike the Boy Scouts of the prewar eras — mirrored those more frightening gangs associated with delinquent culture.

The suburbanization process did not help matters. The suburbs were widely seen as a space of assimilation into a white, middle-class consumer ethos that would alleviate social conflict. When it came to the new teenage subculture, however, it was not always clear whether ethnic and working-class youth would become middle-class teenagers, or whether middle-class teenagers would absorb the taint of delinquency that for nearly a century had been associated with non-middle-class youth cultures. Criminality, in any event, became the widely perceived risk of the teenager's relative independence. Within the Cold War discourse on youth, then, the easily ruled, always obedient young person susceptible to totalitarianism represented only one pole of political danger, balanced by the image of the young criminal. If teenage autonomy led to something other than gradual acceptance of adult standards and values, if it merely seemed to enable amoral behavior that led to criminality, then the teenager became, not a democrat-in-training, but a juvenile delinquent. Popular discourse on teenagers often bitterly attacked consumerist teen culture, precisely because it perceived that culture as taking advantage of the autonomy that adults had tentatively granted teenagers (stepping into the vacuum, so to speak) and filling young people's heads with sex and violence which they would never have come up with themselves. In part, postwar fears of juvenile delinquency expressed a broader anxiety that parents and children had been divided by a "new peer culture spread by comic books, radio, movies, and television" (Gilbert, 3). Part of this adult frustration, however, stemmed from the feeling that just when parents had initiated a great experiment in democracy by enabling the "teenager" to think for him- or herself, the mass media were exploiting that situation for a petty profit, sending the teen on an ill-deserved fast road to juvenile delinquency. Lurking as a continual risk for the teenager, therefore, was the lure of juvenile delinquency, the Scylla which adults needed to weigh against the Charybdis of incipient authoritarianism resulting from excessive adult control.[38]

Authorizing the Rebel

In all of its complexity, the teenager of postwar U.S. culture represented nothing less than a figure of psychopolitical sovereignty, a Cold War instantiation of Erikson's "freeborn American son" as defined against his antithesis, the compliant youth of totalitarian society. Moreover, whenever a young person exercised his or her autonomy in a way that visibly defied adult wishes, s/he crossed over an important threshold of Cold War cultural meaning. In defiance, autonomy passed into the even more charged state of rebellion, transfiguring the teenager into the young rebel. If the teenager provided the metanarrative of identity with its character, the rebel provided it with a plot: dissent, defiance, or even insurrection mounted against a social order of conformity.

At times, as noted, the rebel represented the threat of juvenile delinquency, yet another Cold War menace to the nation that needed containing. At others, however, the rebel served to animate a vital national allegory, not simply for American identity, but for an America in which "identity" itself *became* the central feature of the nation's identity. Broadly recapitulating the Eriksonian drama, the rebel conveyed the spirit of a young America in revolutionary action, forging identity through a politically necessary struggle against the forces of undemocratic coercion.

Like the concept of identity itself, the rebel figure was popularized by an eminent psychoanalyst, Robert Lindner, whose writings are less well remembered today in their own right than are his inestimable cultural influences. In 1944 Lindner published his first book, a case study entitled *Rebel without a Cause: The Hypnoanalysis of a Criminal Psychopath*, which describes his sessions with a boy named Harold who had suffered early deprivation and considerable abuse at the hands of his tyrannical father. Unable and unwilling to internalize the paternal imago, Harold had entered his youth a "pyschopath," whose "sickly superego" lacked the capacity to inhibit his criminal drives (9).

What Lindner found most important about Harold's case, however, was its relevance to the interpretation of contemporary social systems. Like Erikson and many other Freudian theorists, Lindner believed that psychoanalysis offered the most persuasive account of fascism and its mass appeal. Harold's psychopathology, he argued, closely resembled the shared personality disorder of German Nazis, whose tyrannical socialization had driven them to the Nazi Party as a venue where they might express their violent urges. In Lindner's view, therefore, the psychopath represented the personality type best suited to unreservedly serving a charismatic fascist leader: "the psychopath is not only a criminal; he is the embryonic Storm-Trooper" (16).

Despite his chilling description of Harold, however, Lindner actually endorsed rebellion as a basic human instinct at the heart of our capacity to overcome social obstacles and limitations. In his second book, *Prescription for Rebellion*, Lindner began to foreground the importance of the rebel for opposing what, with increasing virulence, he condemned as the "lie of adjustment." For Lindner, "adjustment" was the pseudotherapeutic goal of a modern mass society, its technique for producing a psychologically subservient line of conformist "mass men" with the same dearth of political agency as David Riesman's "other-directed" personality: "The propagation of adjustment as a way of life is leading inexorably to the breeding of a weak race of men who will live and die in slavery, the meek and unprotesting tools of their self-appointed masters" (Lindner, 23). Psychopathic, negative rebels like Harold offered resistance to the tyrannical demands of conformity. They did so, however, in fundamentally antisocial and politically exploitable ways. Against these, Lindner proposed the counterfigure of the "positive rebel," a type of person who controls the rebellious instinct and who, in the name of universal self-assertion and autonomy, demands "revolution" against the forces of adjustment.

Like Erikson's concept of identity, Lindner's allied principle of rebellion cannot be separated from a Cold War imagination. Neither can it be separated from youth as the human figure through which that Cold War imagination was embodied. Stepping back from the individual to discuss larger sociohistorical issues, Lindner compared the youthful moments of the Russian and American revolutions. "Negative rebellion is clearly illustrated in the case of the U.S.S.R.," claimed Lindner, for the reasons that it embodied "a Mass Man ideal" and was therefore "antibiological and unprogressive in the widest sense" (222). By contrast, the revolution "made by the [American] colonies against Great Britain" offered a "positive symbol" because its democratic principles protected the human instinct to rebel against social constraints and thereby create social progress (222–223). Hailing the American revolution as one of colonies against empire, Lindner (like Erikson before him) implicitly affiliated America's history to that of third world revolutionaries seeking similar national self-governance. Such democratic struggles always constituted positive forms of rebellion because, as Lindner explained, "In the permissive atmosphere of true democracy, the horizons are never limited, the boundaries never set. . . . Moreover, inherent in the democratic formula is the acceptance of the principle that a certain amount of positive rebellion and a spirit of vigorous protest are essential to its realization" ("Political Creed" 112–113).

Lindner's writings reiterate endlessly America's dismaying decline from these sound democratic values into a mass society. When too crushing a level of social conformity was demanded of Americans, Lindner contended, they reconciled it with their rebellious instinct by what he called "rebelling within the confines of conformity": becoming obedient members of such socially destructive oppositional groups as delinquent gangs, or fascist and communist parties. It was among youth, of course, that these negative rebellions were most evident, for it was in adolescence that the human instinct to rebel most naturally expressed itself. "It is a commonplace of folk-wisdom that the state of youth is always and everywhere one of rebellion," asserts Lindner in the opening line of "The Mutiny of the

Young," the opening essay in his influential collection *Must You Conform?* "Recalling his own adolescence, each parent resigns himself to a period of distressful concern, ordinarily of predictable length, when his child will pass through a state of active insurrection, when his offspring will fault convention, dispute authority, and vigorously, if at times rather recklessly, oppose the institutions that traditionally regulate society" (3).

Today, however, under the overriding pressures of conformity and adjustment in America's mass society, the rebellious instinct has been tragically transformed into a psychopathic "mutiny of the young" that endangers America's social stability. The solution, however, lies not in a moralistic crackdown on delinquency, for this would merely strengthen the lie of adjustment that had generated the problem in the first place. A genuine and successful rebellion against mass conformity, launched at the level of parenting, was the only possible solution.

Borrowing Erikson's key concept, or perhaps coining it independently, Lindner is quoted as having argued that "from loss of identity has come insecurity" (*Time* 64), and he therefore urged adults, in the title words of his 1956 essay in *McCall's*, to "Raise Your Child to Be a Rebel." Of six virtues that Lindner attributes to the positive rebel, the most important two both name versions of psychopolitical self-recognition: "awareness" and, once again, "identity." A child needs "awareness," which Lindner defines as a "freedom from unconscious, hidden compulsions" if s/he is to avoid becoming "a slave to the irrational pressures of any authoritarian system" (104). Guiding Lindner's argument here is the assumption that "hidden compulsions" serve a disavowed master, an "other" who aims to colonize one's consciousness. Without awareness of the border between the self's desires and those of the (authoritative) other, one cannot even discriminate between acts of rebellion and conformity. Unlike conformists, who generically confuse their own desires and interests with those imposed upon them by mass society and who hence become indistinguishable from other "mass men," the positive rebel is also an "identified" person who thereby possesses "a sense of his own individuality, his uniqueness as a human being, his assets and potentialities as a person. Because of this he is able to care for his welfare, assert his interests and participate . . . as an important, distinct and necessary instrument in the great human orchestra" (104). In thus positing the rebel as the guarantor of such future democratic community, Lindner weaves together the various threads of the Cold War imaginary into an incipient master narrative of identity politics: a young person—or in its collective variation, a young *people*—rebels against the authoritarian aspect of the social order in a way that simultaneously secures identity and restores the democratic promise of that order.

Though Lindner himself never achieved the fame of Erikson, Fromm, or Marcuse, his writings diffused widely and influentially through Cold War American culture. When today the fifties are schizphrenically presented both as a "decade of conformity" and as the "age of the rebel," we are mobilizing constructs indebted to Lindner. It was he who binarized the verbs "rebel" and "conform," valorized the former term, and thereby bestowed a mythic sanction on images of defiant youth for expressing a needed resistance to the "organized society" and its compliant "organization man." Like the language of "identity" (and for much the same reasons) the rebel figure quickly multiplied and spread about in a highly receptive postwar culture. His book *Rebel without a Cause*, inspiring the eponymous film, provided underpinnings for James Dean's emergence as a young star in American culture. That film's tremendous success in turn spawned a host of subsidiary "rebels" within youth culture. From a literary point of view, Lindner's "psychopathic" account of the rebel also became the primary source for Norman Mailer's famed description of the hipster in his influential essay "White Negro." Lindner's rebel thereby became a presupposed reference point for the confrontation of the hip with the square, as well as the rationale for understanding the former's personality type as a living indictment and negation of its adversary. By the close of the 1950s, so deeply ensconced and influential was Lindner's concept of the young rebel that a radical critic like Paul Goodman could actually title his polemic against the "organized society" *Growing Up Absurd*: youth's alleged revolt ("the mutiny of the young") and the moral vacuity of the organized society would appear as one and the same problem.

Rebelling against Fordism from the Inside:
the Paradox of the Youth Market

Working through the nodal points of these new terms—"identity," "teenager," and "rebel"—a politically potent discursive formation began to emerge out of the gap between a Cold War political imaginary that envisioned the United States as democratic, self-determining, and agential, and a Fordist economic order whose system of mass consumer standardization posed a threatening contrary national appearance. In effect, this discourse imaginatively split America in two: the America of identity or rebellion, as represented by the subject of youth, and the America of conformity, as embodied in the object world of Fordist mass culture.

The irony, of course, is that the emergent culture of youth was itself a *vital part* of Fordist mass culture, even when it was paradoxically pitted against it at a symbolic level. It is common knowledge that, following the Second World War, the United States experienced not only an economic boom but also a procreative one. The baby boom reversed nearly two continuous centuries of declining birthrates in the United States, including especially steep drops during the Great Depression, to bring into existence an astonishing 76,441,000 babies in the years between 1946 and 1964.[39] The remarkable duration and intensity of the baby boom derived, in fact, from the central importance of children to the suburban mode of consumption. The new suburban home was celebrated, not only for the economic benefit it brought to young couples, but also for the ease it offered in the raising of children. Parenthood triggered a vast cycle of consumer needs and purchases in its own right. Landon Jones observes,

> As early as 1948, *Time* noted that the U.S. population had just increased by "2,800,000 more consumers" (*not* babies) the year before. Economists happily predicted that the new babies would set off a demand explosion for commodities such as homes, foodstuffs, clothing, furniture, appliances, and schools, to name only a few examples. *Fortune* pronounced the baby boom "exhilarating" and with an almost-audible sigh of relief concluded that the low birthrates of the 1930s were a "freakish interlude, rather than a trend." "We need not stew too much about a post-armament depression," the magazine wrote. "A civilian market growing by the size of Iowa every year ought to be able to absorb whatever production the military will eventually turn loose." (36)

Rather than increasing gross sales for suburbia's domestic market, however, much of this added consumption instead came to form the core of an entirely new market, organized around the commercialization of the teenager. From the start, the ideal of teenage autonomy had included an independent relation to leisure time. The fifth entry in the 1945 "Teen-Age Bill of Rights," for example, had declared youth's "right to have fun and companions" on its own terms, free of family supervision. Historians have universally observed that in the postwar years, well before the baby boomers reached adolescence, teenagers already appeared to have gained control of their own spaces (in cars, at hangouts), to spend more time in unmonitored peer group situations, and most remarkably, to have these forms of autonomy treated tolerantly by adults as a "right." Over the course of the 1950s, moreover, this particular "right" was rapidly translated into the forms of consumer culture, giving rise to a secondary suburban market that stood definitively apart from the primary family market, and which was characterized by its own array of products, codes of advertising, and cultural imagination.

Fordism has been typically analyzed as an economic order premised on a single homogenizing system of mass consumption, which was fragmented only much later when a flexible production process enabled its replacement by a post-Fordist system of market segmentation. In actuality, Fordist consumption was segmented by age almost from the very beginning. The teenager, who began as a political citizen-subject bearing his/her own rights, rapidly became an economic consumer-subject as well, bearing a peculiar set of goods. Indeed, if Fordist capital growth depended upon persuading wage earners to imagine themselves not as laborers but instead as consumers, then the teenager became a kind of exemplary Fordist subject, a type of person hardly acknowledged to be a producer at all, but identified almost exclusively with consumption.[40]

As suburbia grew, so did the teen market such that, by 1964, teenagers would account for overall sales of "something like $12 billion a year and, counting the money their parents were spending on them, the total market was heading for a spectacular $25 billion, . . . 55 percent of all soft drink sales, 53 percent of all movie tickets, and 43 percent of all records sold. They owned 10 million phonographs and were spending $100 million a year on records before the industries had their biggest years" (Jones, 73). The striking feature of teen consumption revealed here is how weighted it was toward the products of the entertainment industry. Youth obviously did not buy many appliances or homes, but they had a disproportionate impact on paperback books, films, records, and radio broadcasts. As an increasing sector of books, film, and records began explicitly to hail its audiences as teenagers with distinct priorities, desires, and attitudes, many products that would be considered exemplary of American culture (works of literature, cinema, and music) also became artifacts of youth culture. This broad turn by the Fordist culture industry toward a youth market was partly facilitated by the relative disposability of teenage income. Equally important, however, were an ensemble of new conditions, both social and technical, faced by each branch of the culture industry in the Fordist era.

Subsequent chapters will lay out the distinct conditions that shaped the representations of young rebel identity in each industry. In the next chapter, for example, I analyze the conversion of "identity" into a measure of American literary value by examining the massive critical endorsement of J. D. Salinger's *The Catcher in the Rye*. Literary critics quickly assimilated *Catcher* into a Cold War national allegory according to which its young protagonist became emblematic of American identity determining itself against the forces of social conformity. This literary valorization of identity, however, was both shaped and abetted by the so-called paperback revolution, which delivered Salinger's novel (among other texts) to young American readers on a mass scale. During the 1940s and 1950s, a product revolution in the book industry launched the twenty-five-cent disposable paperback, which allowed the distribution system for books to be extended well beyond the traditional hardcover network of libraries and carriage-trade bookstores, into the traditional magazine market located in newstands and dimestores. In the process, a host of new book companies moved to the head of the industry, including Pocket Books, Bantam, and New American Library.[41] Although the paperback revolution created vast new sales opportunities for the book industry, it also pushed publishers into increasingly fierce competition for market share.

The resulting struggle for the allegiance of new readers led in turn to the formation of a youth book market. In 1945, the very year the word "teen-ager" was coined, the leading publisher of paperbacks, Pocket Books, toured a "Teen-Age Book Show" that introduced American youth to the concept of disposable books. The following year, on the heels of the show's success, Pocket Books formed a "Teen-Age Book Club," while Bantam Books, one of Pocket's main competitors in the emerging market, formed a new "Scholastic" imprint (Davis, 125). The apparent emergence of a young mass readership was a key determinant for the critical attention that Salinger's novel began to receive in 1957 on its rapid path to canonization. *Catcher* thus concretely demonstrates the intimate connection between the identity concept's growing cultural authority and the emerging power and influence of the youth market.

No industry mobilized the motif of young rebel identity more dramatically than the music industry, which became entirely reoriented toward a teen market. The rise of rock 'n' roll, as chapter 3 discusses, constituted a new youth imaginary defined against the very suburban world that had led to the music industry's changes. As radio was dethroned from its national network status by the new, suburbanized medium of television, it began to recreate itself as locally based entertainment. Radio therefore became unique among the postwar media for its special ability to transact cultural relations between urban centers and the suburban belts growing up around them. It is in this general context that radio propelled the rise of rock 'n' roll as a youth genre. The light and affordable 45 rpm disc was also invented at around this time, which allowed radio hits to serve as advertisements for a growing market in vinyl records. This potent combination not only created a new means to make radio profitable; by the mid-1950s it had also prepared the way for the youth market to overwhelm the pop charts. As the chapter shows, rock 'n' roll is best understood as a product of the "transcommodification" of both rhythm and blues and country music, a process that assigned each an imaginatively new relationship of identitarian opposition to the world of the Fordist suburbs.

Hollywood cinema's incorporation of the identity concept came, unlike the book or music industries, during a period of decline. With the collapse of the prewar studio system, Hollywood came under increasing pressure to cultivate product lines that would find a reliable audience and therefore predictable box office draw. By the mid-fifties, the film industry had tapped into the lucrative rock 'n' roll market, developing as one of its product lines the so-called teenpic, a specialty picture for teenagers whose subgenres included delinquency crimes movies, horror, and romantic "clean teen" films.[42] Although the teenpic arose somewhat later than the teen novel in the book industry, when it finally arrived, the niche market orientation of an ascending "new Hollywood" would allow the movies to take a leading role in the new youth culture.

Chapter 4 explores the special role played by rebel identity in the development of the teenpic by reconstructing the reception of the 1955 Hollywood feature film *Blackboard Jungle*. A transitional text, *Blackboard* held together, in complex tension, adult concern and youthful pleasure in the figure of the juvenile delinquent. Though it functioned for adults as a social problem film of the sort developed during the thirties and forties, it simultaneously operated as a prototype for young adult audiences of the first rock 'n' roll film. This second capacity is enabled in the film by its depiction of an imaginary multiracial alliance of city youth, grounded in a masculine vision of defiance against a suburban ideal of parental authority. The split reception of this film, I argue, suggests that the film industry effectively learned how to segment its market into adult and youth sectors by deploying the young rebel as representative of the youth audience itself, conceived as an emergent identity.

Together, the first four chapters of this book show that figures of young rebel identity quickly became staple features of American literature, film, and popular music. They remained conspicuously rare, however, on television. The growth of national network television closely paralleled the general expansion of the suburban family market. As the television set became a standard feature of the new suburban home, its programming came to reflect what the technology itself symbolized: the new leisure forms of family togetherness (Belton, 259). As the music and film industries sought alternative customer bases—local, specialty, and niche markets—they therefore also began to promote desires and pleasures that television had bypassed or excluded from its vision of the close-knit, consuming American family. Even the book industry, though not as directly threatened by the rise of TV, soon learned to profit from the new market opportunities of the countersuburban imaginary. Youthful defiance of a suburban mass society, already widely criticized for its "hypnotized consumership," its other-directedness, or simply its squareness, thus became a powerful advertising tool for the nontelevisual media. In paperback books, at the movies, and on the radio airwaves, the figure of the young rebel promoted "identity" in its narrative of struggle against Fordist conformity.

Engendering the Rebel: Bad Boys and the Hegemonic Face of Identity

The first four chapters of this book emphasize the broad conjunctions of identity, Cold War culture, and the youth market for rebellion. In the final three chapters, I train my attention on a more focused problematic, namely the significance of the persistently masculine forms taken by these early figures of rebel identity. If one quickly lists the chief icons of the fifties youth rebel—the beats, Elvis, Little Richard, James Dean, Holden Caulfield—one common feature rapidly becomes clear: all were imaged as male. With few exceptions, the rebel of the fifties conventionally took the form of a "bad boy" who agonistically defined his identity along axes of both age and gender.

The term "bad boy" is meant to emphasize how postwar identity discourse presided over the reinvention of a certain tradition in representing young American men. During the latter half of the nineteenth century, as Steve Mailloux observes, a so-called bad boy boom took place in American letters, which included among its texts Thomas Aldrich's *Bad Boy* and Mark Twain's *Huck Finn*. Circulating alongside early "juvenile delinquency" pan-ics in the United States, these novels tended to challenge the predominance of morally didactic fictions about "good boys." Instead, bad-boy fictions offered "realistic" depictions of mischievous boys whose antics in no way doomed their moral futures as adults. While these stories promoted a more tolerant perspective on adolescent indiscretions, they also prepared the way, according to Mailloux, for a disciplinary society that is historically related to the age category of adolescence, with its attendant institutions of adult supervision over youth, including public schools, scouting organizations, and the like.[43]

The postwar years propelled what might be called the second major "bad-boy boom" in American culture, but by the time this figure resurfaced in the age of identity and the Cold War, he had changed considerably. These changes are already evident in a film release of 1949 that is actually entitled *Bad Boy*. Like its nineteenth-century counterparts, the film presents its protagonist as a juvenile delinquent to be redeemed. Where the earlier bad boy needed only to be domesticated and bourgeoisified, however, the latter also needed to satisfy concerns about America's geopolitical challenges. *Bad Boy* starred Audie Murphy, the single most decorated soldier of World War II, whose appearance in a film about juvenile delinquency foregrounded the bad boy's readiness for combat (McGee and Robertson, 14–15). By casting Murphy, the film sets to rest any doubt as to whether the bad boy is strong, brave, or independent enough to fight for his country, qualities that the cooperatively minded figure of the Organization Man was feared to lack. The question raised by the bad boy concerns, rather, his commitment to the public good, and whether the rage, defiance, or alienation that has prompted him to be "bad" can be rechanneled into patriotic feeling. In the film, the answer is emphatically yes. At a home for delinquent boys, the rebellious Murphy is guided back to national service by the understanding headmistress (played by Jane Wyatt). The film ends with Murphy triumphantly graduating from Texas A&M's ROTC program.

The movie *Bad Boy* anticipated a parade of nationally celebrated bad-boy characters who would soon begin to populate the imaginative landscape of Cold War American culture. In 1951, J. D. Salinger's *The Catcher in the Rye* introduced an adulatory American readership to the disaffected teenage character of Holden Caulfield. In 1953 *The Wild One*, starring Marlon Brando as leader of a gang of bad-boy bikers loose in a small midwestern town, became an instant Hollywood classic. The floodgates opened wider in 1955 as Hollywood simultaneously released *Rebel without a Cause*, star-

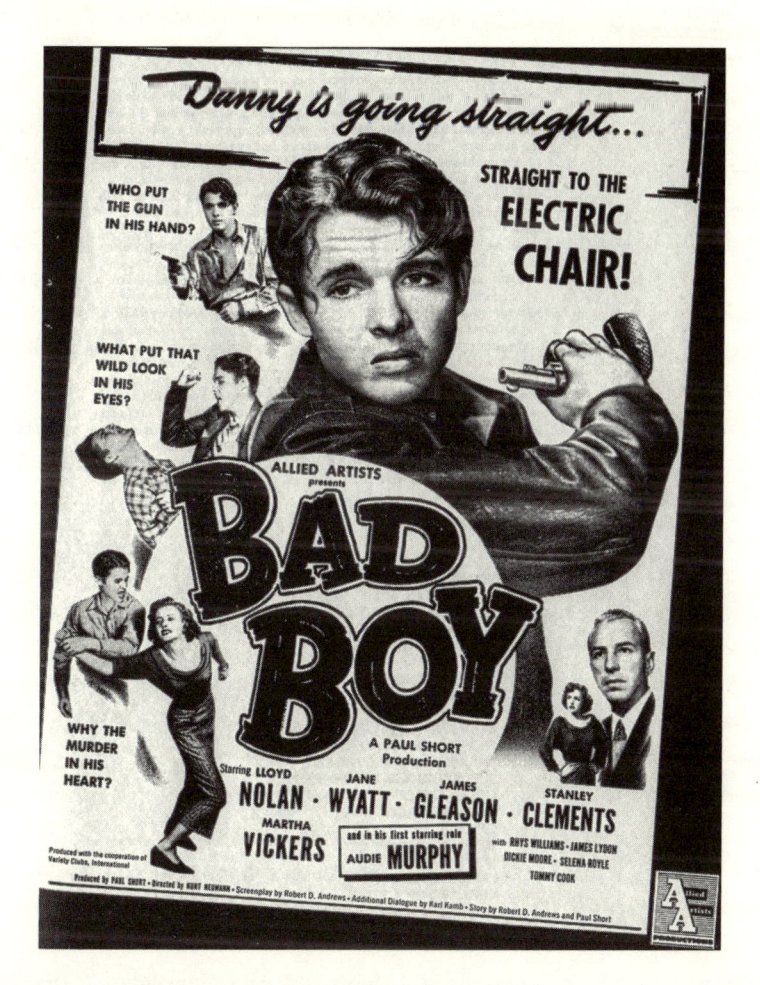

1. Movie poster for *Bad Boy* (Allied Artists, 1949).

ring James Dean in his famous role as a troubled middle-class boy from the suburbs of Los Angeles, and *Blackboard Jungle*, an urban drama featuring a gang of delinquent boys who dance to the film's title rock 'n' roll tune of "Rock around the Clock." That song in turn became the opening gambit to a rapid takeover of the popular music hit charts by rock 'n' roll, an entirely new "youth sound" featuring numerous performers who adopted bad-boy personae. In 1957, a literary wing of the bad-boy phenomenon was launched as the obscenity trial for Allen Ginsberg's poem "Howl" catapulted the beat generation writers into sudden, iconoclastic fame. "Bad Boy" also became the title for two rock 'n' roll songs, one by the Jive Bombers in 1957, and another in 1960 by Marty Wilde, a performer who coined his stage name by combining the title character of *Marty*, a film about leaving city life for the suburbs, with a playful conception of wildness, borrowed perhaps from Marlon Brando's 1953 portrayal of *The Wild One*. Unlike his nineteenth-century progenitor, then, the 1950s bad boy represented a youth spawned in the new suburbs, but refusing its domestication (hence the wildness) and thereby ensuring the continuity of American freedom in an age of three worlds.

By 1957, these representative figures for the identity of the nation had become so ubiquitous that literary critic Leslie Fiedler would explicitly anoint the bad boy as "America's vision of itself, crude and unruly in his beginnings, but endowed by this creator with an instinctive sense of what is right" (*No!* 263).[44] Though Fiedler sometimes simply called this figure the "Bad Boy," he also sometimes called him the "Good Bad Boy" to spell out his compound moral character. In some respects, this split description echoes the dual moralities traced by Nietzsche in his *Genealogy of Morals*. Following Nietzsche, who had observed that the word "good" signifies differently depending on whether it is opposed to "bad" or to "evil," Fiedler distinguishes between two moral ledgers. Like the "blond beast," the bad boy defies the flaccid moral conventions of his age, thereby displaying his strength of character. The bad boy's badness demonstrates that he is no slave, no conformist to an external coerced moral code. At the same time, however, he is also "good" in that he only rebels for the higher purpose of serving the public interest (a self-loathing morality of altruism in the Nietzschean perspective). Unlike the "bad bad boy," he is no self-serving psychopath but instead what Lindner called a "positive rebel." The bad bad boy is strong but evil, an unambiguous juvenile delinquent. The good good boy, conversely, is conventionally virtuous but materially weak (like Nietzsche's slave moralist).[45] It is only the good bad boy who, in combining virtue and strength, can seize historic opportunities to transform social morality, particularly at moments when moral conventions have become overly coercive, massified, and thus destructive of personal and national identity. The bad boy becomes a figure for the insurrectional citizen, one who challenges the polity precisely in the name of that polity's higher good.

Fiedler's description of the bad boy's rebellion uses terms that are complexly gendered. The "Good Bad Boy," Fiedler explains, though "sexually as pure as any milky maiden . . . is a roughneck all the same, at once potent and submissive, made to be reformed by the right woman" (*No!* 270). This combination of "potency" and "submissiveness" reiterates in different terms Lindner's political imperative that young Americans should be "rebels" but "positive" ones, so that their defiance can ultimately enter into the orbit of good citizenship. Here, however, the binary explicitly masculinizes the bad boy's potency while feminizing his submissiveness. The former represents the purely masculine "bad" attribute of the "roughneck" American self, while the latter aspect, which makes him ultimately good, anticipates the bad boy's eventual romantic compromise with women, and thus with femininity, as the other to his American self. Indeed, Fiedler defines his bad boy—technically a "good bad boy"—by his relationship to his mother. Unlike the good good boy, whom Fiedler says, "does what his mother must pretend that she wants him to do: obey, conform; the Good Bad Boy does what she really wants him to do: deceive, break her heart a little, be forgiven" (*No!* 270).

Fiedler's drama of the bad boy and his mother, and indeed the entire problem of the rebel's masculinization, gain ideological clarity when placed alongside an article that appeared in a 1948 issue of *Parents* magazine. Written from a mother's perspective, this article, in a clear allusion to the 1945 *New York Times Magazine*'s article, was titled "A Bill of Rights for Teenagers" and captioned "Parents must have the faith and courage to let their adolescent children pursue happiness in their own way, with a minimum of questioning and objection." Unlike its predecessor, however, the *Parents* magazine article recounts the story of a girl rather than a boy in its opening parable. The author, Kathleen Doyle, begins by recalling an argument with her daughter over whether she might wear a black satin formal to a dance party (20). Doyle's quarrel, which her husband later persuades her was ill-advised, clearly involves her daughter's consumer autonomy, and looks ahead to the future expansion of teenage discretionary spending. It also overtly concerns sexual autonomy, the right of a teenage girl to eroticize her presence among other teenagers. In this respect, the dispute seems to recall the wartime controversy regarding sexually delinquent "Victory Girls." The content of the conflict between parent and teenager, in other words, appears decisively different here from Don's, the boy in the *New York Times Magazine* who had debated whether to pledge American armed forces against communism. Its focus is on the terrain of culture rather than politics, and on acts of consumption rather than those of diplomacy or war.

To be sure, Doyle quickly moves to politicize the quarrel's significance, alluding to the U.S. Constitution and the Declaration of Independence as she derives a lesson on the necessity for a teenage "bill of rights" guaranteeing youth's "pursuit of happiness." As she does so, however, her prose shifts increasingly into a masculine register. The ideal approach to the teenager, she decides, is "to let a child proclaim his independence, to encourage him to stand alone" (83) so that he can find his own way to "bridge the gap between childhood and maturity" (86). Doyle, moreover, emphatically attributes her insights to men, who intuitively grasp the virtues of youth autonomy. It is her husband who persuades her that she has made a mistake in picking the fight, and it is an anonymous "gentleman" at a dinner party who reminds her that "it's respect for another's rights that's the very stuff of which democracy is made" (83).

As early as Philip Whylie's 1942 polemic *Generation of Vipers*, the discourses of anticommunism had begun to feature a rhetoric known as "momism," a misogynistic attack on American women who smothered their children and henpecked their husbands.[46] In the postwar period, with explicit misogyny buried underneath the celebration of domesticity, momism was mainstreamed and assimilated into the Cold War discourse on youth. Embracing the assumption that mothers posed a danger to the agential (and often the heterosexual) masculinity of their boys, postwar parenting ideology often stressed, as Elaine May notes, that "fatherhood was important . . . to counteract the overabundance of maternal care. Although mothers were, of course, expected to devote themselves full-time to their children, excessive mothering posed dangers that children would become too accustomed to and dependent on female attention. The unhappy result would be 'sissies,' who were allegedly likely to become homosexuals, 'perverts,' and dupes of the communists. Fathers had to make sure this would not happen to their sons" (146). Spelled out here are a complex set of sexual and gender norms that guided the points of attachment between Cold War political culture and family arrangements. When fathers encouraged their sons' rebellious impulses, what they effectively safeguarded was a masculinized public sphere, the same one that Youth Forum moderator Dorothy Gordon had, as quoted earlier, characterized as the realm of "man's democratic conscience," and that Erik Erikson associated with the American legacy of "freeborn sons," the "backbone of the nation" (321). On the one hand, homosexuality often connoted a menacing weakness and vulnerability for the "freeborn sons" who constituted the national public. But on the other, heterosexuality also constituted a potential threat in the form of excessive "female attention" that might domesticate and distract the boy from his pursuit of masculine sovereign selfhood. The Cold War realm of "man's democratic conscience" projected a long-standing public/private opposition between a homosocial domain of male citizenship and a domestic space of heterofamilial companionship. It was through the former that national agency was posited, like an army or a bourgeois public, in the collective form of a young male fraternity. Yet such fraternity could itself evoke a specter of impending homosexualization, thus signifying the vulnerability of masculine agency in the very image that should have expressed its triumph.

Three consequences resulted from this network of gendered meanings. First, it was boys who became the focus of attention. Identity usually took a male form because it was a masculine conception of the people's sovereignty and self-determination that Fordist conformity allegedly jeopardized. Second, given that it was the suburban man who typically symbolized this conformity, fatherhood became (like "organizational manhood") more a subject of criticism than praise. Cold war culture, one might say, became characterized not only by "momism," in which the bad boy asserted his badness by defying his mother's expectations, but also by a related form of "dadism" in which fathers were repeatedly damned for failing to uphold their sons' struggle for identity. Third, the representation of collective identity often took the form of the fraternal boy gang, though this representation was plagued by sexual doubts.

Chapters 5 and 6 each examine the political complexities of the bad boy's sexual and gender dynamics, on the levels of the family unit and the collective fraternal public respectively. Chapter 5 considers oedipal dramas of the suburban family, tracking a narrative pattern in which identity emerges through a rebellious son's struggle against an impotent father who lacks the capacity for autonomous self-assertion. In two films that serve as the occasions for this chapter, *Rebel without a Cause* and *King Creole*, the sons assert a masculinized rebel identity that challenges the father's suburban domesticated manhood. Bad-boy masculinity, as this chapter suggests, drew on codes of blackness and working-classness to establish its difference from a father lacking in political agency; it expressed both homo- and heteroeroticism to establish its difference from the father's lack of sexual agency. In these texts, the father's erotic deficiency amplifies his distressing inability to defend himself against characters who would dominate and humiliate him. In the midst of a Cold War, these films declared the son, and not his father, as ready for action.

Chapter 6 explores the collectivization of young rebel identity by looking at the constitutive bonds of the bad-boy gang as celebrated in key texts by the beat generation writers. The very trope of the "beat generation" was productive in its ambiguity, vacillating in meaning between a small group of writers and an entire cohort of postwar Americans. Literary texts such as *On the Road*, "Howl," and John Clellon Holmes's beat manifestos openly claimed to represent in their particular stories a universal young American identity. The cultural authority of the beats, I argue, derives from this proprietary relation to America's "tradition" of sovereign identity. By writing generational identity in the form of a boy gang, however, the beat texts reenacted and had to variously resolve the paradoxical demands posed by the ideological equation of the democratic public and agential masculinity. Women, predictably, are placed on the outside of the beat fraternity of bad boys, and heterosexual relations with them must be devalued relative to the homosocial bonds that constitute beat identity. Male homosexuality, meanwhile, openly appears in certain beat texts as a face of rebel identity, and as a challenge to sexual conformity, but it is almost always restricted to the boy gang's external relations with other men, where it cannot threaten the "horizontal comradeship" subtending the beat claim that, as a fraternity of bad boys, they constituted the champions of democratic American identity.

Identity: A Modality in Which Racial, Sexual, and Gender Justice Is Demanded

The hegemonic status of the bad boy in early identity discourse raises pressing questions regarding his ideological relationship to subsequent identity politics, for not only was he a male figure, he was also usually white and straight (at least nominally, if not latently). Yet "identity politics" as we know it is usually the name we give to the social movements of women, people of color, and gays and lesbians. In what meaningful way, then, can the young rebel of the 1950s be said to have prepared the way for them?

This important question must be approached with care. Feminism, anti-racism, and even gay activisms have long histories that quite obviously predate the politicocultural formation I am tracing in this book. What the rebel figure facilitated, therefore, was not gender, race, or sexual politics per se, but a model for their *identitarianization*. By casting "woman," "black," "Chicano," "gay" or "queer" as their protagonist in the Cold War metanarrative of identity narrative, postwar social movements embraced and deployed the rebel figure as a new subject of history: an emergent self establishing its psychopolitical autonomy in a struggle against an authoritarian world of "role expectations." Black liberation, women's liberation, or gay liberation, drawing from the three worlds imaginary of national liberation, asserted psychopolitical emancipation from the compliant subjectivity associated with the coercive expectations of patriarchal, white supremacist, or heteronormative self-definition. Identity, to loosely paraphrase Stuart Hall, became the modality through which antiracist, antisexist, or antihomophobic struggles could be fought with considerable potency.

The fifties rebel, as I have argued, upheld the principle of insurrectional citizenship against a threat of "conformity" and corresponding loss of agency posed by a Fordist suburban world. Precisely because whiteness and heterosexuality were foundational features of this suburban imaginary, their norms were often exactly what the rebel narrative of identity formation symbolically challenged or resisted, even when the rebel remained manifestly white or straight, as was the case with such figures as Elvis or Norman Mailer's "White Negro" hipster. Consider, for instance, that Leslie Fiedler himself fashioned the bad boy as both a racialized and homoeroticized character. Drawing on *Huck Finn* as the urtext for his version of the American literary tradition, Fiedler insisted not only on the bad boy's affinity with blackness but also on the same-sex eroticism of this affinity, which for Fiedler expressed the bad boy's (and thus America's) utopian longing to escape a domesticated manhood.[47]

Given that racial and sexual difference both represented ways of declaring an identity in righteous rebellion against the conformities of Fordist heteronormativity and whiteness, it hardly seems surprising that black and queer representations of the bad boy did in fact circulate in postwar culture: rock 'n' roll's black stars such as Chuck Berry and the flamboyantly queer Little Richard, Sidney Poitier as a borderline delinquent in *Blackboard Jungle*, the zoot suit hipsters who fascinate the protagonist of Ralph Ellison's *Invisible Man*, Johnny Nash, the black teenage star of the film *Take a Giant Step*, and the homoerotic rebel biker featured in underground gay filmmaker Kenneth Anger's *Scorpio Rising* are among the most obvious examples. One cannot divorce the Cold War bad boy from the incipient racial and sexual politics of identity that his rebel narrative promoted.

The Girl as Rebel

This genealogical link is more complicated when we come to the issue of gender politics. Initially at least, the liberatory promise of identity was often complicit with an insistent masculinization of the insurrectional sovereign citizen. As the maligning of the Organization Man and the Man in the Gray Flannel Suit demonstrates, it was the white, middle-class man of the suburbs whose inadequate self-determination constituted a national crisis. Nevertheless, the postwar rebel was not as rigidly masculine as one might assume. In many of the central bad boy texts—*Rebel without a Cause* and *On the Road* for example—girls play important supporting roles in the rebel drama of identity. Identitarian narratives about rebellious girls, moreover, carried on an important subterranean life in the postwar years.

These rebel girl narratives form the subject of this book's final chapter. Treating examples from both literature and film, I explore the two principal forms in which the female rebel appeared: the sexual bad girl and the tomboy. Both types received considerable cultural attention as romantic counterparts to the bad boy who shared his desire for something other than a domesticated or organizational future. As attested by the delinquent heroine of the film *Girls Town* and the black daughter in Douglas Sirk's maternal melodrama *Imitation of Life*, girls too could embody emergent identity by "breaking their mother's heart," to use Fiedler's words, declining a future like their mothers' in favor of a different life imaginatively shared with the bad boy. In parallel with the bad boy, the bad girl often enacted her rejection of Fordist womanhood by way of racialized and classed self-assertions.

The tomboy evinced an even more powerful refusal of maternal domesticity, embodying a female masculinity potentially suited for participation in the bad-boy gang. As texts such as Hal Elson's juvenile crime novel *Tomboy* and the blockbuster teenpic *Gidget* demonstrate, the tomboy's character is typically established through her initial denial of sexual desire. Eventually, however, her erotic awakening to the bad boy creates an uneasy but important opportunity for imagining a heterosexual romance compatible with (rather than antithetical to) the fraternal collective identity of the gang. The tomboy, in short, produces the utopian fantasy of having it both ways, getting to be one of the bad boys while also getting to have one of them.

Though she bore lesboerotic meanings only covertly in the fifties, the tomboy (like the sexual bad girl) nevertheless signified antisuburban female sexuality as a version of rebellious identity.

Because the sexual bad girl and the tomboy were both associated with a longing to be coupled romantically with someone other than a domesticated male, both afforded the bad boy a partner who might allow him to win over an ambivalent Cold War mainstream. The bad boy's coupling with a girl suggested that his struggle for identity would yet be redeemed in a future that reconciled sovereign citizenship and Fordist heteromaturity. If, for such mainstream meanings, girls were licensed to rebel primarily because they thereby drew bad boys back into heterosexual romance, and thus back into the wider orbit of potential marital adulthood, their stories nonetheless opened up important spaces of representation. Once female figures also came to represent the youthful quest for identity, they could be (and eventually were) decoupled from heteroromance to embody alternative narratives of emergent identity. It is through the trope of the rebel girl, for instance, that Beneatha in Lorraine Hansberry's *A Raisin in the Sun* could come to represent the assertion of black female identity, or that the heroine of Ann Bannon's first lesbian pulp novel, *Odd Girl Out*, came to dramatize the coming out of lesbian identity. These texts offer an early precedent for the identitarianization of the young woman as a political subject, and hence for a politicized discourse of identity that would become available to women's liberation and lesbian activists by the end of the 1960s.

Identity and the Other Fifties

According to the containment model of Cold War culture, the fifties were, above all, years of reaction in which political possibilities were closed down. The politics of labor (often class-based, but not exclusively) certainly suffered a precipitous decline under the aegis of the Cold War regime. Once we reread the decade as the inaugural moment of identity, however, it is not difficult to see that these were also times in which new political potentialities were born. The dramatic rise of rock 'n' roll, with its distinct challenge to the authority of the color line, was a youthful declaration of identity in its symbolic opposition to the suburbs. Similarly, the beat generation writers achieved literary celebrity through their self-presentation as rebels against suburban, domestic America. Further, as Wini Breines has pointed out, young white women developed a distinct sensibility of disaffection along similar lines. And outside the arena of youth culture, it was in the 1950s that the civil rights movement actually achieved its first high-profile victories, beginning with the Supreme Court's decision in *Brown v. Board of Education*, and then the dramatic populist victory of the Montgomery bus boycott. These victories involved an insistence on the place of blackness in American identity in contradistinction to the suburban presumption of universal whiteness. Finally, although gays endured a distinctly anticommunist mode of postwar homophobia, it was in the 1950s, as Robert Corber points out, that gay writers such as Tennessee Williams, Gore Vidal, and James Baldwin became highly visible cultural figures who could assert their alternative sexuality publicly as a form of "oppositional consciousness" meant to challenge Fordist manhood (*Homosexuality* 4).

Taken collectively, these various phenomena suggest that an "other fifties," to use Joel Foreman's useful term, existed alongside the culture of containment, one that made themes of revolt and liberation available to the youth, black, feminist, and gay movements of the 1960s and the 1970s.[48] The challenge, today, is to avoid reifying the identitarian terms that the discourses of the "other fifties" initiated. By and large, critics of the 1950s have celebrated the figures in question (civil rights activists, beats, young women, rock 'n' rollers, gay writers, and so forth) by taking their insurrectional identities and status as self-professed rebels at face value. Agents of the "other fifties" have been touted as lonely voices in the night who spoke out against the Cold War order, but whose capacity to do so was not in any way itself a product of that order.[49]

Rather than historicizing the psychopolitical narrative of identity first devised by Erikson and Lindner, this typically hagiographic literature on the "other fifties" has tended to reproduce it. The "rebels" of the 1950s are installed as the urprotagonists in the metanarrative of identity politics, the first postwar characters to defend their identity against an industrial/consumer society's errant expectations (Erikson), or the first to defy the "conformity" proscribed by a repressive mass society (Lindner). Tacitly, this approach presupposes that postwar radicalism was extrinsic to Cold War culture because it expressed a psychopolitical refusal to be "contained." If we approach the Cold War as producing something other than just a "containment culture," however, we can begin to understand the emergence of identity discourse, not as an extrinsic response to Cold War culture based upon the ontological truth of identity, but rather as the production of identity itself as the dialectical antithesis of containment within the cultural matrix of the Cold War world. If "containment" offered a rhetoric of repression, identity countered with a rhetoric of "liberation" that was no less imperative in its reference to the three worlds imagination of its time.

This argument implies that the various social movements and critiques of race, gender, and sexuality that have come to be associated with the broad term "identity politics," all appealed, more or less explicitly, to a rhetoric of the Cold War era that represented political agency itself as a struggle with the regulatory norms of postwar suburbia. Racial identity was thus pitted against the mass standards, privileges, and exclusions of suburban whiteness. Feminist identity politics challenged woman's subjection to the breadwinner/homemaker hierarchy of suburban gender relations. And sexual identity politics, perhaps the most explicitly antisuburban of them all, defied the Fordist heteronorm of the monogamous, procreative couple. By no means are these movements defined or wholly captured by this historic linkage; this was not their raison d'être. All the same, this genealogy illuminates what they have shared in drawing on the discourse of identity, as well as what made their appeal to identity so politically effective for so many decades.

In the conclusion, I trace forward the genealogy of identity, exploring the ways in which appeals to identity evolved after the fifties, alongside their grounding condition of possibility in the articulations of Fordism and the Cold War. The changes were perhaps most vivid in the mid-seventies, when Fordism itself entered crisis. But at least until the end of the Cold War, the politics of identity were steadfast. The discourses of identity moved through a series of changes—they became more openly tied to struggles against "stigma," they were gradually demasculinized, they were pluralized and then multiculturalized. But throughout, they maintained a set of psychopolitical claims that could not be denied their effectivity. Today, however, the widely registered dissatisfaction with identity politics can in fact be traced to the severe erosion of the geopolitical conditions that once propped up their ideological potency. Race, gender, and sexuality obviously remain indispensable sites in crafting the politics that might combat economic "globalization" or the neoimperial "war on terror." And yet, "identity" does not provide the articulatory traction that it offered us in the sovereignty-centered "age of three worlds." I offer this genealogy in the hopes that it can clarify for us our discomfiting political present.

COLD WAR LITERATURE AND THE NATIONAL ALLEGORY: THE IDENTITY CANON OF HOLDEN CAULFIELD

> The wheel has come full circle, and now America has become the protector of Western civilization, at least in a military and economic sense. Obviously, this overwhelming change involves a new image of America. Politically, there is a recognition that the kind of democracy which exists in America has an intrinsic and positive value.... If [however] a reaffirmation and rediscovery of America is under way, can the tradition of critical non-conformism ... be maintained as strongly as ever?
> —*Partisan Review*, "Our Country and Our Culture"

In 1952 the prominent liberal intellectual and literary journal *Partisan Review* published an influential symposium on postwar intellectual life. Entitled "Our Country and Our Culture," the symposium opened with an editorial statement (quoted above) announcing the rise of a "new image" of America suited to its stature as the "protector of Western civilization."[1] This statement, which served to define the parameters of acceptable debate regarding the role of America's writers and thinkers, was followed by a series of responses to it by a virtual "who's who" of postwar intellectual life. While many respondents disagreed with particular claims made in the editorial, few contested its essential, liberal, anticommunist premises.[2] The statement began with the happy observation that U.S. intellectuals were increasingly integrated into national life. No longer a figure of left-wing political alienation, the typical intellectual had grown into a staunch advocate of the American system who grasped the totalitarian nature of its Soviet rival. At the same time, however, the editors expressed their concern that this affirmative stance might itself paradoxically jeopardize what they called America's "tradition of critical non-conformism." In their estimation, it was incumbent on postwar intellectuals to negotiate between two conflicting priorities. On the one hand, they were called upon to ideologically defend America's democratic ideals against the communist threat, and yet the political practice of democracy obliged them just as surely to speak out as the nation's conscientious critics and dissenters.

This latter task the editors closely associated with the arena of culture. Although American *political* democracy stood unambiguously as a global beacon of hope, the "cultural democracy" of America's mass arts and letters troubled them. "Cultural democracy," explained the editors, was a natural "outgrowth of political democracy under conditions of modern industrial development," and yet in practice the conformity that it imposed could undermine the basic democratic capacity of American citizens to think as free individuals (285). As *Partisan Review* explained, "We cannot evade the fact that at present America is a nation where at the same time cultural freedom is promised and mass culture produced" (285). "Critical non-conformity" thus served for *Partisan Review* as a placeholding term for the kind of cultural iconoclasm that might uphold the apparently fragile ideal of cultural freedom.

Implicitly for the *Partisan Review* editors, this dilemma had special consequences for the state of American literature. Among the symposium contributors, critics and writers of literature outnumbered those of any other intellectual endeavor, and repeatedly America's "new image" became a question of the nation's *literary* self-representation. *Partisan Review*'s two concerns may be expressed concisely. On the one hand, was American literature sufficiently patriotic and affirming of the nation's political principles in a time of Cold War? On the other, did not a firmly celebratory vision better suit the straitjacketed literary and intellectual culture of the nation's perennial adversary, a totalitarian society that brooked no dissent? Could American literature, in other words, reconcile wartime national loyalty with the public spirit of critique and questioning called for by a functioning democracy? Did it, to use *Partisan Review*'s words, carry on the democratic tradition of "critical non-conformity"?

Beginning in the 1950s, and increasingly in the 1960s and 1970s, critics and other readers would begin to interpret works of literature in terms of the "identities" they depicted or explored. This development, I propose, marked not simply one more swing in literary interest, but a far more profound change: the adaptation of "identity," itself a newly invented concept, into a primary standard for judgments of literary meaning and value whenever the literature of a "people" was in question. As the preceding chapter argues, "identity" first became a word freighted with political meaning during the early years of the Cold War when, beginning with its initial popularization by Erik Erikson, it came to signify the achievement of a self-made and self-governing personality equally vital to individual persons as they approached adulthood and to collectivities as they developed into sovereign nations or peoples. Indeed, one of the most distinctive aspects of "identitarianism" is that, from the start, the ideal it espoused sought to reconcile the traditional liberal tension between the individual and the collectivity by mediating between their respective claims to sovereign self-determination. The identity of a collectivity, after all, typically appears as its individual member writ large, just as the political sovereignty of a state is modeled upon the liberal doctrine of the self-determining individuals who are its citizens.

From a literary perspective, we might say, identity operates through the modality of national or popular allegory in its requirement of two reciprocal conditions of representation. First, the individual's trials and tribulation must serve to dramatize and instantiate the larger identity struggles of his or her people. At the same time, the politics of identity demand that the sovereignty of the people remain commensurate with the self-determination of its individual members. The collectivity otherwise becomes a totalitarian mass, formed through a coerced equivalence of its members that denies them identity precisely by robbing them of their right to psychopolitical sovereignty. Rather than pit the individual against society, in short, identity as a pychopolitical ideal works to harmonize them as necessarily reciprocal images of one another in the struggle for sovereign selfhood.

This chapter analyzes the celebration of rebellion as an American ideal by the public arbiters of Cold War culture, a formation usually associated with repressive demands for national loyalty. As suggested by the intellectual's dilemma as staged by *Partisan Review* (to affirm or to criticize?), rebellion was a necessary price exacted by the ideologically potent discourse of identity. For in expressing their dilemma as a problem of the individual writer/intellectual's ability to represent national culture, *Partisan Review* had already begun the work of adapting identity discourse to the domain of literature. On the one hand, the editors desired an identity—that is, an allegorical equivalence—between the work of individual writers and their country's culture (the former no longer "alienated," as writers presumably had been in the 1930s). Yet paradoxically, they also did not want the work of these individuals to espouse unmitigated affirmation, for such a culture of blanket obedience threatened to cast America as an irredeemable mass society whose people's fading grasp on political agency was spotlighted by the dearth of dissenting voices. The political dilemma posed by rebellious writing resolved itself, however, if writers and intellectuals instantiated in their work, not simply the revolt of an individual or a movement, but rather a great American tradition of "critical non-conformity" that exemplified the innate resistance of American identity to regimented mass mentalities.

I shall explicate the identitarianization of American literature by tracing the extraordinary process of national canonization that J. D. Salinger's *The Catcher in the Rye* underwent during the 1950s. Like few other literary works, *Catcher* epitomized the triumph of the young rebel as a requisite figure for representing the national identity of America. The fifties was the "Decade of Salinger," asserted Warren French confidently in his introduction to one of the very first critical anthologies about the era, a claim that was often repeated, even though this brief novel was the only one that Salinger wrote in that decade—or any other. Salinger's overwhelming association with fifties America—and the other way round—constitutes a clear example of what Jonathan Arac has called "hypercanonization," the excessive investment by criticism in a very small number of texts from a literary period or tradition that leaves a multitude of their contemporaries to languish. *Catcher*'s overwhelming critical acclaim, I argue, grew from the demand for a "new image" of America as *Partisan Review* had expressed it. It hinged on an ideological reciprocity between literature and politics that could be called the protagonization of the American character; this was a process by which the literary value of American texts, old and new alike, became measured for their hermeneutic capacity to be read as allegories of national identity.[3]

Allegory has traditionally been defined as the extension of metaphor, and in particular of a "figure" across narrative time, one thing standing for something else through the duration and transmutations of a story.[4] Allegorical figuration often takes the form of a personification, and this is especially so in the case of national allegory, in which the nation's situation is commonly expressed through the story of an individual character. Even when personified, however, a figure is not merely a character, but also, as Erich Auerbach's etymology of "figura" reminds us, an idea rendered plastic in form. A figure materializes an abstraction into a shape whose "definition" becomes a bordered interior in an inside/outside relationship. In this respect, figuration closely resembles the process of imagination itself,

56 CHAPTER TWO

whose etymology suggests a similar tracing of its object within a field of vision. One cannot create an allegorical figure, in short, without also having produced a "ground," an exterior topos against which the otherwise "illegible" image or figure may be distinguished.

The visualization of a figure/ground relationship additionally presupposes a discerning eye that brings one shape to the fore, while consigning other possible ones to the back. Although some critics have understood allegory as a sort of genre, determined by the structural properties of the text, this focus on the figure/ground relation favors an alternative understanding of allegory as the outcome of a reading process or critical intervention, a second-order decoding of the text by the reading subject that was well understood by classical rhetoricians in their use of the term "allegoresis": the allegorization of a text.

In the case of national allegory, this production of an inside/outside relation between figure and ground by no means requires that the latter become the "outside" of the nation. On the contrary, both figure and ground often come to represent the nation in what becomes a dialectical imaginary. Pictorially speaking, one might say that national allegory may function simultaneously as both portrait and landscape, a figure against a background, each differently representative of the nation, and indeed mutually so. It is precisely in their contradictory signification that national allegories often owe their rich semiotic and ideological effectivity.

Catcher was subject to allegoresis in just this doubled sense, at both an immanent and a contextual level. In textual criticism, Holden Caulfield *became* America, yet so too did the notoriously phony world against which he railed. As a paperback book, meanwhile, *Catcher* also came to figure America, but once again only against the distressing backdrop of a mass market for commercialized literature. In each case, it is the figure/ground relationship that established America's political character as a young and rebellious identity, discernable as such through its adversarial relationship to a no less American landscape of Fordist conformity.

The Protagonization of the American Character

The canonization of *Catcher in the Rye* did not take place in isolation but rather alongside the institution of the "classic" canon of American literature during the early postwar years. As several literary scholars have demonstrated, until the 1950s a quite different Americanist canon had reigned, one responsive to the issues of early-twentieth-century progressivism and grounded in the ideals of realism and social commentary. A series of literary histories ranging from Vernon Parrington's *Main Currents in American Thought* to Alfred Kazin's *On Native Ground* assembled an American literary tradition valued for its efforts to represent and address the various ills and blessings, crises and opportunities, that modernity had delivered to American life. Loosely speaking, this canon centered upon the works of the self-described realists and naturalists (Howells, Wharton, and Dreiser, among others), moved from there to the "lost generation" of modernist writers, then onward to the proletarian and populist fictions of the 1930s. Yet in the 1950s, just when American literature was consolidating its legitimacy as a topic worthy of academic study, this progressive canon was pushed aside by a different ensemble of works championed by a new generation of Americanist critics.

This new edition of the American literary tradition expressed a decisively different set of literary values that reflected the general political perspective of its principal advocates: the anticommunist liberal New York intellectuals, whose principal organ was none other than *Partisan Review*. Realism became tainted as a politically naive aesthetic through its association with the left-wing genre of socialist realism. In its place, the newly invented tradition erected a vision of American literature as inherently antitotalitarian, aesthetically and politically hostile from its very inception to the closed-minded simplifications of both left-wing and right-wing world visions. In this regard, both the new canon and its critical apparatus functioned, in Geraldine Murphy's apt words, as an "aesthetic counterpart to the vital-center liberalism of the first Cold War" (738), locating the visionary character of American freedom somewhere between the opposite extremes of fascism and communism.

Where the old canon had emphasized the development of American literary realism, the new canon placed at its apex the works of the so-called American Renaissance. As Donald Pease has shown, Melville, Hawthorne, and Twain, whose texts had in fact been responding to quite different conditions in antebellum America, were now redeployed as a coherent tradition that dramatized the emergence of American freedom as a literary ideal, somehow already waging its heroic struggle against a prefigured totalitarianism. In the process, Pease argues, *Moby-Dick*, *The Scarlet Letter*, *The Adventures of Huckleberry Finn*, and a handful of other texts were assembled as a hypercanon that would transform American literature itself into an "arena of cultural discussion" completely dominated by the Cold War (*Moby-Dick*, 112). Pronouncing these novels to be literary monuments to American freedom, postwar criticism transfigured their protagonists into allegorical representatives of an extraliterary "American character." *Moby-Dick*, for example, was declared the greatest of American novels through readings in which Ishmael came to stand for a larger America that "proves its freedom by opposing Ahab's totalitarian will" (113).[5] Similarly, Mark Twain's *Adventures of Huckleberry Finn* secured its reputation as the quintessentially American novel alongside its eponymous character's transformation into the archetype of the freedom-loving American, a youth who instinctively refused to conform to the proslavery morality of his day.[6]

A doubled process of representation operated in these politicizations of American literature. To draw on a distinction employed by Marx in "The Eighteenth Brumaire," and usefully elaborated by Gayatri Spivak and David Lloyd, fictional characters became representatives of the American national character in the discrete senses of both the German words *darstellen* and *vertreten*.[7] They served to "represent" America in the sense of an aestheticized "portrayal" or "image" (Darstellung), but in the process they also came to "represent" America by becoming its political "proxies" or "substitutes" (Vertretung), figures that could stand in and speak for the values and interests of the democratically "represented" nation. In this way, the domain of literature was politicized: novels now came to profess the nation's geopolitical struggle for a free world.

It was not simply that literature was politicized, however, but that politics were rendered literary through these processes of national representation. The literary criticism of the day, through its uses of allegory, worked to *protagonize* the "American character." As in the "mirror-relation" of ideology so famously described by Althusser, the "little" American characters depicted in the new canon, when hailed as figures for a current struggle, rendered the U.S. nation-state imaginable as the general American character, and the Cold War itself as the Great American Novel, the paradigmatic story about the free spirit of the American people battling heroically against History's most recent incarnation of political tyranny.

This deep politicization of the new canon as "antitotalitarian" did not however bear a unitary meaning. It tended rather toward two different meanings related to the conflicting imperatives advanced in the *Partisan Review* symposium: at times the new canon projected an affirmative image of America as antithetically defined against the likes of Soviet communism. At others, it envisioned the American tradition as one of critical nonconformity, whose only antithesis was its own "conformist" (and therefore incipiently totalitarian) American double, namely the nation's uncritically affirmative "new image." Though dialectically linked, these imperatives pulled in opposite ideological directions. The affirmation of America demanded that the canon serve as an unambiguous endorsement of the freedom actually embodied in the U.S. social order, thus equating "what is" with "what ought to be." Critical nonconformity, meanwhile, employed the canon to stage America's democratic credentials at one level of abstraction, as an immanent critique of an actually existing America, a challenge to the inadequacy of "what is" that paradoxically demonstrated America's higher-order commitment to "what ought to be" in a genuinely antitotalitarian democracy.[8] The canon, in short, was alternately patriotic and dissenting in its nationalism, finding its validation in two joined yet distinctive metanarratives that may respectively be termed the national allegory of development and that of rebellion.

The Allegory of Development: Protagonizing Liberal Maturity

The development allegory interpreted American literature first and foremost as the dramatization of a maturing political character. This story, which Thomas Schaub has simply described as the "liberal narrative," often took an autobiographical form, allowing numerous intellectuals—Reinhold Niebuhr, Lionel Trilling, and Leslie Fiedler among them—to explain the rightward shift in their own postwar politics. It also functioned as a national allegory, however, for in this story *liberalism itself* became the name for America's political personality as it evolved from the thirties to the fifties. The story begins with an old liberalism, rooted in the early-twentieth-century progressive movement, that was heady, hopeful, and therefore naively sympathetic to communism. From here, Schaub describes the trajectory of this "liberal narrative" as "a Blakean journey from innocence to experience, from the myopia of the utopian to the twenty-twenty vision of the realist. . . . Their [liberals'] decisions were invariably accompanied by narratives of maturation and realism, of awakening to a more sober and skeptical perception of political reality and human nature" (5–6). Chastened in particular by the disillusioning betrayal of Stalinism, a new liberalism emerges painfully by the end of the story—realistic, responsible, and vigilantly wary of manipulation by those to its left.

Although Schaub only mentions the word in passing, "maturity" played a crucial part in constituting this liberal narrative as a figural allegory. Repeatedly, intellectuals represented the transition from the "old" to the "new liberalism" (terms Schaub borrows directly from the fifties critic Richard Chase) through an age-coded personification. In this Bildung narrative, the young or adolescent liberalism becomes a protagonist, wide-eyed, naive, and uncompromising. By the story's end, however, after a series of bitter experiences with political manipulation, an older, more reflective (and thus less infantile) liberalism with a deeper appreciation for human fallibilities has learned how to strike the proper balance between ideals and practical considerations. Seen in hindsight from the "mature" liberal perspective, the "young" liberalism appears above all as infantile. As Newton Arvin put it in his contribution to the *Partisan Review* symposium, the "negative relation to one's culture," though valid in certain periods, becomes at moments like the present "simply sterile, even psychopathic, and ought to give way, as it has done here, in the last decade, to the positive relation. Anything else suggests too strongly the continuance into adult life of the negative Oedipal relations of adolescence—and in much of the alienation of the twenties and thirties there was just that quality of immaturity" (*Partisan Review*, 287).

The Rebel Allegory and the Rise of Identity Criticism

The allegory of development, however, was not the only "liberal narrative" through which the value of the new canon was established. No less important was an allegory of rebellion that may be understood as a variation of the development allegory, though with a substantively different ideological thrust. In this second allegory too, America had arrived at a new level of maturity, but here its terminus point was the rebelliousness of a youthful nation rather than the generic wisdom of adulthood. The rebel allegory dramatized the revolutionary moment of national self-declaration, reflective of the moment (stressed by Erikson) when a self came to establish itself as a free and sovereign character by repudiating all coerced "role expectations" placed upon the conduct of its personality. Like the concept of "critical nonconformity," the rebel allegory safeguarded "cultural freedom" as a core feature of the American character by facing down the same blanket loyalty that was celebrated in the development allegory.

It was precisely at the moment when the allegory of development turned into its opposite—a tale of rebellion—that the concept of identity emerged as that story's protagonist. When *literary* characters from the "American Renaissance"—Huck Finn, Ishmael, and the like—were transfigured by critics into a young *American* character declaring cultural independence from old world tradition, they also became figures for the identity concept itself in its newly politicized sense as a prescriptive discourse of autonomous selfhood. Although the term "identity" did not become a common word in the American lexicon until approximately 1952, it began to saturate the discourses of literary criticism—and in particular the criticism of American literature—very rapidly thereafter. By 1954 Richard Chase would already seize upon the word to establish the central importance of Walt Whitman's "Song of Myself" to American literature. Whitman's great poem, he argued, thematizes what he called the "paradox of 'identity'" in American literature, the tension that the poem explores between the value of an American individual's self-expression, and, granting the democratic values of American art, that individual's status as synecdoche for the nation (181). Chase's reading of Whitman's poetry as a self-reflective allegory of national identity also tacitly informs his most famous work of criticism, *The American Novel and Its Tradition*, in which Chase reconceived the romance as a uniquely American narrative tradition that unlike the realist European novel, veered "toward mythic, allegorical, and symbolistic forms" (13). Though somewhat coy about the American romance's literary merits, Chase, in associating it with the nation's "'democratic' quality of mind" (8), ultimately presented it as a "freer, more daring, more brilliant fiction" (viii) than the comparatively staid realism of the British novel.[9] While confessing that some might find the social texture of the British novel more mature, Chase challenged those who might dismiss the romance as a product of the "unenlightened youth of our culture," arguing that—whatever its limitations—its originary status had enabled subsequent American literature to fuse "realism and romance" in ways that encouraged the "repeated rediscovery" of a young America's sense of its literary freedom and possibility (xii).

"Identity" is also briefly referenced in R. W. B. Lewis's *The American Adam*, yet another influential account of the American renaissance as the foundation of the nation's literary tradition. In the process of asserting that one can deduce a general account of American culture from the nineteenth-century debates making up his book's archive, Lewis argues that "a culture achieves identity not so much through the ascendancy of one particular set of convictions as through the emergence of its peculiar and distinctive dialogue" (2). Even while introducing the word "identity" here to specify the possibility of something "peculiar and distinctive" about American culture, Lewis's study soon concludes not only that America's identity is distinct but that what characterizes this distinctiveness is its very passion to *be distinct*. In essence, *American Adam* argues that the identity of American culture consists precisely in insisting on its identity, in distinguishing itself as free and independent of the European culture from which it descends. The American character, claimed Lewis, reveals its inner nature through allegories of the "American Adam" in which the nation appears personified as a new man with a novel personality, somehow simultaneously innocent of and antagonistic toward the constraining codes of the ancestral "old world," and therefore ever "hopeful" about the prospects of remaking the world outside the traditional norms earlier generations had prescribed (7). For Lewis too, then, the word "identity" served to express, above all, American literature's essential movement toward the sovereign expression of a free national character, suited for leadership of the "free world."

Like its developmental counterpart, the rebel allegory defined the national figure through the binary of young and old. The latter allegory, however, reversed its hierarchy of values. Development condemned youth for its idealistic naïveté and foolish "moral crusading," while praising adulthood for its cautionary wisdom. The allegory of rebellion retained youth's association with idealism, but celebrated it instead as a positive challenge to the stultifying expectations of maturity. Thus for Chase, romance was the vibrant counterliterature of a young America, whose fresh imagination flouted the more sober and mature outlook of European fiction. Lewis, meanwhile, in his figure of the American Adam, conjured up the nation as a man who (like liberalism at the *start* of the development allegory) was young, and eager to liberate himself from the chains of human tradition. Rebellious acts deserved praise, for they had won the nation an important identity marker: an autonomous literature of its own.

The tropes of development and rebellion also implicitly imagined different relationships between America and the third world. Development erected a conservative Bildung in which political moderation and transcended youthful naïveté became signs of a positive maturity. As in the eponymous social science literature, therefore, the literary allegory of development framed the United States as an appropriate guide for aspiring third world countries seeking their own industrial maturity. Like these emerging nations, the United States had once been young, socioeconomically ambitious, and morally uncompromising in its quest for social justice. It too had been inclined toward dangerous revolutionary ideologies like communism. Through a process of political and economic maturation, however, it had discarded the false promises of utopian politics and come to recognize the complex truth that capitalist democracy provided a sufficient if imperfect state of freedom, prosperity, and social equality. The allegory about the movement of American intellectuals from the thirties into the fifties thus also served, paradoxically enough, as an allegory for third world nations as they made their transition from preindustrial to Fordist national economies.

It was equally vital to American interests, however, that the first and third worlds not always be hierarchically differentiated by development, but that they also be ideologically aligned against the communist second world in a common creed of each nation's right to freedom from tyranny. To this end, the rebel allegory offered something that the development allegory could not: it enacted a revolutionary ethos in which the American character always already endorsed the efforts of the young (nations) to free themselves from the tyrannies of the old (world). Only in the rebel allegory, then, was identity affirmed as a psychopolitical ideal.

The Rise of the Identity Novel

Postwar literary critics obviously took an interest in the literary present as well as the past. In addition to cultivating the "American Renaissance" as an origin story for the nation's literary tradition, they also hypercanonized a handful of contemporary novels using the same pair of allegorical reading strategies. But while an era of understood national emergence such as the American Renaissance lent itself to the discourse of identity, the older, "developed" America of the present did not, particularly given its widely professed evolution into a mass society. As previously observed, the Fordist conditions of suburban and organizational life were widely alleged to promote the mass—and incipiently totalitarian—values of adjustment and conformity, presumably at the direct expense of the American individual's sovereignty. Critics partial to the rebel allegory's promise of identity, therefore, found the culture of postwar America especially troubling. As for instance R. W. B. Lewis complained in his epilogue to the *American Adam*, too many Americans in this "age of containment" took the classic Adamic hopefulness of their nation as an embarrassing symptom of "the culture's youthful indiscretions and extravagances. We have had to get beyond such simple-minded adolescence confidence, we suppose; . . . and we sometimes congratulate ourselves austerely for having settled, like adults or Europeans, upon a course of prolonged but tolerable hopelessness" (195). Yet, as Lewis admonished his readers, the current remnants of the nation's classic adolescent headiness should be deemed vitally important to postwar America because "recalling the moral and artistic adventurousness of a century ago may help release us a little from our current rigidity" in this "conformist" era when we pathetically "huddle together and shore up defenses," both in "our literature and our public conduct" (196).

Lewis was hardly alone in his fears and hopes concerning the present literary age; he echoes *Partisan Review*'s anxiety concerning the mass conformity dictated by "cultural democracy." Numerous critics feared that American culture had traveled, per the subtitle of *American Moderns*, Maxwell Geismar's 1958 study of contemporary American literature, "From Rebellion to Conformity." The American writer's traditional "rebelliousness," his commitment to social commentary and criticism, Geismar morosely explained, had succumbed to "the historical setting . . . of the uneasy 'peace,' the tensions of the Cold War, the return to 'normalcy,' and the epoch of conformity" (ix). John Aldridge likewise began his book *In Search of Heresy: American Literature in an Age of Conformity?* with a plea for literary challenges to the "conformism" of modern American mass society that might reanimate the "ideal of creative independence and free critical dissent which has come down to us in the central tradition of American thought and letters and which has energized the work, even as it has debilitated more than a few of the lives, of most of the writers whom we now consider to be important" (8). This "search for heresy" led many critics directly to a cluster of rebellious characters who might be deployed as literary avatars of the identity concept.

In the closing pages of *The American Adam*, R. W. B. Lewis singled out three contemporary novels for their praiseworthy fidelity to the idealistic spirit of the Adamic American character: Ralph Ellison's *Invisible Man*, Saul Bellow's *The Adventures of Augie March*, and J. D. Salinger's *The Catcher in the Rye*. Written by the three most celebrated authors of the immediate postwar years, these novels shared certain noteworthy characteristics. Each is voiced in the first person. In each the narrator takes us along on his picaresque journey through a social environment bent on controlling or manipulating his sense of self. In each, the protagonist's resistance to these forces of manipulation may be read as a defense of personal identity. And lastly, the struggle for personal identity may be allegorized in each as a national narrative.

All three novels, it must be noted, were also susceptible to conservative "development" readings, in which a young protagonist outgrows his ill-considered social naïveté, moving into a more mature comprehension of social and moral complexity. These texts, in other words, accrued literary merit in part because they could be enlisted to the cause of liberal anticommunist ontology. Nevertheless, as Lewis's selection of them as "Adamic" texts attests, they were also (if in different degrees) valued for the rebelliousness of their protagonists, who thereby expressed the unflagging struggle for identity that characterized America. Not only did this latter reading strategy create a distinct axiological basis for their literary canonization, but it grounded its concept of literary merit in the aesthetic vindication of what might be called the "antiauthoritarian personality" of their American protagonists, whose defense of their psychopolitical rights point broadly in the direction of identity politics.

The anticommunist development allegory is particularly evident in *Invisible Man*. As Thomas Schaub observes, Ellison's novel touted a "new liberal" vision of ontological complexity and paradox that was explicitly offered as an anticommunist fable: the Invisible Man must learn to reject the dogmatic "laws of history" propagated by the "Brotherhood," a blatant fictional counterpart to the American Communist Party in the 1930s. *Invisible Man*'s charm for postwar literary critics derived in no small part from its Trillingesque invocation of an anticommunist "liberal imagination" that rejected all simplifications of sociopolitical reality (91–93).

This assessment of the novel's appeal does not reckon, however, with its pioneering use of the identity concept. Ellison's nameless protagonist relates to his reader a personal history of naive efforts to please a train of authority figures who successfully dominate his sense of self. It is in the scene that makes the Invisible Man's psychopolitical domination most explicit, at the factory hospital when he is strapped to an electroshock device bent on "entirely changing the personality," that the word "identity" makes its first major appearance. "What was my identity," he asks himself, realizing that he no longer has any idea. It is at this point that the Invisible Man actively begins his efforts to rebel against the Bledsoes, Nortons, and others whom he has heretofore faithfully obeyed, speaking out against those who would dispossess people like himself of their humanity.[10] Identity reappears as the novel's central theme in a scene that, at first glance, would seem to assert the illusory nature of what we take for granted as social reality. Repeatedly mistaken for the street hipster Rinehart, and recognizing the power of such misrecognition, the Invisible Man asks himself: "If dark glasses and a white hat could blot out my identity so quickly, who actually was who?" (111). In the end, however, though attracted to Rinehart's technique of manipulating what Erik Erikson would have called the "role expectations" of others, the Invisible Man embraces a more robust concept of identity, one that stems from both self-discovery and a self-assertive refusal to submit blindly to the equally blind demands of those who embody social authority.

Andrew Hoberek has astutely noted that the Invisible Man's others represent a world of mass institutions—the black college, the paint company, and the Brotherhood—that mirror almost exactly the mass organizations imperiling the agency of the so-called white-collar Organization Man." And if the Invisible Man in fact begins his story as something of a victim of the organization, a "yes-man" served up to mass society, then in Ellison's novel, as in the culture at large, the cure will be found in a prescriptive category of identity. This is not the nominalistic sense of "identity" manipulated by Rinehart, but rather a psychopolitical brand: the emerging, but still unnamed protagonist must achieve self-recognition in order to then declare independence from his tyrants.[12] As Jonathan Arac points out, the Invisible Man ends his story by declaring it to have been just such an identitarian voyage of self-discovery and self-assertion, both as a personal narrative and as a national allegory ("Toward," 195–96). The Invisible Man at least understands "who I was and where I was and knowing too that I had no longer to run for or from the Jacks and the Emersons and Bledsoes and Nortons, but only from their confusion, impatience, and refusal to recognize the beautiful absurdity of their American identity and mine" (550). In the novel's closing sentence, "Who knows, but that at lower frequencies I speak for you?," the Invisible Man incorporates even the reader into this agonistic search for identity. It is hardly surprising that R. W. B. Lewis and other critics fixated on Ellison's *Invisible Man*, for above and beyond its participation in the developmental narrative, few other postwar novels were so ripe for inclusion in a canon of allegorical identity novels.

Though lacking a similarly direct use of the term "identity," Saul Bellow's *The Adventures of Augie March* was similarly read and valorized through the emerging discourse of identity. Generally speaking, Bellow's conservative cultural and political temper, his impatience with utopian or romantic simplifications of the world, closely allied his fiction to the paradigm of development. As Schaub notes, however, *Augie March* was an exceptional work in Bellow's oeuvre, widely acclaimed as a break with the careful formalism and modernist despair of his earlier writings. In contrast to them, it was taken as a literary "declaration of individual freedom," driven by the "cocky American self-reliance" of its narratorial personality, a work that would influence later countercultural fiction writers such as Thomas Pynchon (80–81).

As Andrew Hoberek has convincingly argued, we can witness through *Augie* the inauguration of identity as a key feature of what he calls the "so-called Jewish novel." Stressing the novel's organization around a "series of submissions to and rebellions from various figures who want to eliminate his personhood by turning him into an instrument in their own plans" (*Twilight*, 121), Hoberek argues that the Jew became the postwar exemplar of American identity for the reason that, in a mass age, s/he could paradoxically be understood both as an outsider (to the traditional WASP conception of American nativism) and the consummate insider (the most quickly and thoroughly assimilated of people to the Fordist white-collar world). The Jew therefore, like the black in Ellison, becomes an ideal character to be pressed into service for a national allegory whose protagonist serves simultaneously as patriot and critic, conformist and rebel. While, in each episode of his life, the chameleonlike Augie March continuously benefits himself by meeting the expectations of his various authority figures (thus appearing other-directed in Riesman's sense, "Rinehartish" in the Ellisonian sense), he also insists upon the inner-directed character of his insurgent national selfhood, most famously expressed in the novel's opening sentence, "I am an American, Chicago-born . . . and go at things . . . free-style, and will make the record my own way" (5).

One striking feature of the postwar canon, namely the rise of the "outsider" writer to a paradigmatic position in American letters can thus be traced to the ascendance of the identity concept in criticism. This was particularly true for Jewish authors, whose writings had been previously perceived as a minor immigrant or ethnic literature, but black and gay writers were likewise elevated to a position of national prominence as definitively *American* writers (including Ellison, but also James Baldwin, Lorraine Hansberry, Tennessee Williams, Allen Ginsberg, and others). The canonization of both Ellison and Bellow's fiction, in short, directs our attention to typifications of the young American self as a "critical nonconformist," someone who struggles to live and think in his own way, particularly in a present age of "other-directed" conformity.

If this list of postwar authors demonstrates a growing deployment of the racial or sexual outsider as the representative rebel against social conformity, it reveals even more consistently that the rise of the "identity" concept in criticism was reflected in dramatic narratives of youthful emergence from one's marginality or, more precisely, from one's minority (a coming into majority both as canonical literature, as allegorical representative of the nation, and more literally as a claiming of the right to sovereign self-determination, something denied to "minorities"). Beyond the characters of the Invisible Man and Augie March, we can add here the oedipal struggles of John Grimes in Baldwin's *Go Tell It on the Mountain*, the insubordinate daughter Beneatha in Hansberry's *Raisin in the Sun*, and the various sexy young men whose eroticism disrupt their drab surroundings in the plays of Tennessee Williams and William Inge. To the young protagonists of these racial and/or queer literary works, we can further add a cluster of young women: Mick Kelly and Frankie Jasmine from Carson McCuller's *The Heart Is a Lonely Hunter* and *The Member of the Wedding* respectively, Allison MacKenzie and Selena Cross from Grace Metallious's *Peyton Place*, the beat heroes of Jack Kerouac and Allen Ginsberg, and, finally, the character certified by R. W. B. Lewis as the last of the American Adams, arguably the single best-known "American character" of fifties fiction, Holden Caulfield of J. D. Salinger's *Catcher in the Rye*.

Holden Caulfield and the Birth of Identity Criticism

Holden Caulfield, the protagonist-narrator of J. D. Salinger's *Catcher in the Rye*, is male, white, and a member of the professionally elite upper middle class of New York City. He fails, in other words, to look anything like a representative subject of what we now call identity politics. Nevertheless, Holden occasioned one of the earliest applications of the identity concept to a contemporary novel. David L. Stevenson, arguing in 1958 that Salinger's novel had brilliantly captured the "crisis" of the individual in America's "Lonely Crowd," praised *Catcher* as a "boy's comment, half-humorous, half-agonizing, concerning his attempts to recapture his identity." "Through him," Stevenson contended, "Salinger has evoked the reader's consciousness of indefinable rejections and rebellions that are part of the malaise of our times" (43). While Stevenson's explicit citation of "identity" came exceptionally early, it merely made visible the guiding influence that the new concept had already begun to exert on critical understandings of *Catcher in the Rye*, and ultimately on postwar literary culture at large. Indeed, the very fact that *Catcher*'s protagonist lacks the overt racial, ethnic, or sexual casting that we have come to expect of an "identity novel," yet was read as one all the same, lays bare the ideological work that identity performed in the early years of the Cold War.

The Catcher in the Rye, J. D. Salinger's one and only novel, was published in 1951. The story begins with Holden, in convalescence at a sanitarium in California, offering to recount to the reader the events that led to his recent breakdown. Holden's recollections begin at the moment when he has flunked out of an East Coast prep school, and extend through a three-day odyssey of feverish wanderings in New York City. *Catcher* is most famous, of course, for Holden's critical perspective on most of the people around him, his denunciation of what he calls their "phoniness," and his repeated efforts to find solace, advice, and ultimately a possible future with others who might escape this phoniness. While it is difficult to pin down the precise meaning of "phoniness" for Holden, the word assuredly involves an indictment of American mass culture and all those who submit to its logic. Holden directs his first denunciation at his own elder brother D.B., who once wrote sincere short stories but now composes instead commercial screenplays in Los Angeles. Holden includes on his "phony list" a range of typical culture industry products: Hollywood movies, magazine fiction, Broadway theater, slick lounge music, and so forth.

As a strong-selling Book-of-the-Month-Club selection, *Catcher* received solid but unremarkable attention from magazine reviewers following its release. Its literary fortunes shifted drastically in 1956 and 1957, however, as critics began casting an increasingly obsessive gaze upon the novel. Short and simply written though it was, *Catcher* became the subject of dozens of articles and several scholarly books between 1956 and 1963.[13] So rapidly did this interest in *Catcher* overtake the critical establishment that several other novelists, feeling slighted, decried the unjustified burst of articles, essays, and speculations as pandering to Salinger's work.[14] Only a small minority of critics disputed *Catcher*'s merit, however, while the vast majority celebrated the authenticity of its teenage narrator's colloquial voice, the steadfastness of its utopian commitments, and—in what proves a combination of these two—its efficacy as contemporary national allegory. Ihab Hassan's advocacy of Salinger's work as "seriously engaged by a current and a traditional aspect of American reality" (260) stemmed from his more general views concerning the adolescent's role in American literature: "The life of the adolescent or youth still in his teens mirrors clearly the ambiguities of rejection and affirmation, revolt and conformity, hope and disenchantment observed in the culture at large. In his life as in our history, the fallacies of innocence and the new slate are exemplified. His predicament reflects the predicament of the self in America" (41). It is noteworthy that all of the binaries offered by Hassan derive from the cultural dilemmas specifically associated with the Fordist moment.[15] The predicament of "rejection and affirmation" echoes the problem raised in *Partisan Review* of reconciling the positive anticommunist patriotism of the postwar intelligentsia with their duty as nonconformist critics of American mass society. The binary of "revolt and conformity" explicitly taps into the figure of the American rebel who spoke to the agency panic that was triggered by Fordist mass regimentation. "Hope and disenchantment," finally, alludes to the Adamic figure of a young America (Lewis's "party of hope"), but also to the inordinately naive hopefulness of Popular Front "old liberalism," from which American intellectuals had supposedly now sobered up. Hassan, in short, condenses into the character of the adolescent all of the deeply contradictory judgments associated with both national allegories, development and rebellion, the tension between which implicitly constitutes for Hassan the nation's so-called predicament. Subjecting it to this powerful hermeneutic, Hassan, like many other critics, came to interpret *Catcher in the Rye* not simply as a psychological tale tracing the pitfalls of growing up but rather as a fable in which the adolescent Holden expresses the paradoxical meaning of the nation's development.

Although his vague language remained open to either developmental or identitarian readings of *Catcher*, like the vast majority of other critics Hassan tended to prioritize the latter, endorsing Salinger's novel about "adolescence in revolt" for what Robert Lindner's, the famed psychotherapist of youth, would have called Holden's "positive rebellion." In Salinger's work, claimed Hassan, "the retreat to childhood is not simply an escape; it is also criticism, an affirmation of values which, for better or worse, we still cherish; and the need for adolescent disaffiliation, the refusal of initiation, expresses the need to reconceive American reality" (260–261).

In lauding Holden as an allegorical figure for America's aspirations, Hassan alludes to another study of Salinger that had already become the single most influential assertion of *Catcher*'s literary importance: Arthur Heiserman and James Miller's essay "J. D. Salinger: Some Crazy Cliff." Heiserman and Miller were among the first critics to praise *Catcher* for its quintessentially American heroization of "the outcast, the person who defies traditions in order to arrive at some pristine knowledge, some personal integrity." They also designated Holden a Fiedlerian "bad boy" whose personal sense of virtue led him into conflict with various "institutions" (24–25). In adulthood, one must capitulate to a barrage of institutional demands, but childhood in Salinger's work offers a prelapsarian innocent freedom from those impending demands. Adolescence, in turn, represents the transitional moment when one recognizes the loss of personal integrity that adulthood entails. Thus adolescence provides a heroic opportunity for defiance: "In childhood he [Holden Caulfield] had what he is now seeking—nonphoniness, truth, innocence. . . . Still, unlike all of us, Holden refuses to compromise with adulthood and its necessary adulteries: and his heroism drives him berserk" (75–76). Following the spirit of the development allegory, Heiserman and Miller assume a consensus (their "all of us") that accepts the inevitable "compromise with adulthood" and recognizes the price of refusal: psychosocial breakdown or what Riesman called "anomie." Yet Holden's defiance remains an act of "heroism," presumably because his uncompromising search for personal integrity also "speaks for us," just as the Invisible Man claims to do at some lower frequency. In that sense, Holden as the figure of a national allegory represents America's better side, its submerged commitment to a sovereign selfhood, which survives intact beneath pragmatic compromises made with mass society.

Early influences of the identity concept are apparent in the critics' ubiquitous references to *Catcher*'s special relationship to teenagers and in their heroization of Holden as the quintessentially American rebel. Critics writing in the late fifties and early sixties almost invariably noted *Catcher*'s apparent popularity among youth, explaining it in terms of an "identity" between Holden and his young readers. Dan Wakefield, in his celebratory essay "The Search for Love," claimed that teenagers find "in Holden Caulfield, and to a lesser extent in James Dean, an expression of their own most fundamental attitudes." In "Everybody's Favorite," Alfred Kazin claimed that Salinger writes to young people "in a language that is particularly honest and their own, with a vision of things that captures their most secret judgments of the world" (48). By the early sixties, the language of identity would become entirely explicit. "What was it about the novel that struck Americans so squarely ten years ago and continues to hit the mark still?" asked Robert Gutwillig. "Primarily it was, I think, the shock of recognition. Many of my friends and this writer himself identified completely with Holden" (5). Henry Grunwald's anthology even included a short essay by an adolescent (and a self-professed "crazy kid"), who explained:

> I knew at least ten Holden Caulfields at ITT. . . . every boy who reads *The Catcher* thinks he's just like Holden and I think that's one of the reasons for its great success; we can all identify ourselves with his plight. . . . It's also sort of a fad among us to be very critical of everything and everyone, and those who are most critical are the strongest and most independent. . . . You could say he was trying to find himself, his identity, and all that, but that's a lot of categorical nonsense—who isn't? (Parker, 254, 257)

Being "critical" provided the substance for critics asserting Holden's "identity" with America's youth. Young people, as the critics saw it, "recognized" themselves in Holden precisely because they too desired to establish a sovereign identity that resisted the "age of conformity" they inhabited.

The beginnings of the "rebel" reading of *Catcher* trace back to Salinger himself, who in 1945 and 1946, on the heels of both Robert Lindner's *Rebel without a Cause* and the *New York Times*'s "Teen-Age Bill of Rights," published two early Holden sketches titled "I'm Crazy" and "Slight Rebellion off Madison." Like the rebel in Robert Lindner's later works of psychopolitical commentary, such as *Prescription for Rebellion* and *Must You Conform?*, Holden was a youth mistaken for a madman merely because he had refused to become a mass man. It is not surprising, then, that one of *Catcher*'s first reviewers was Ernest Jones, the famous Freudian analyst of childhood and adolescence, who in "Case History of Us All" contended that the novel reflects in Holden's sense of alienation "what every sensitive sixteen-year-old since Rousseau has felt, and of course, what each one of us is certain he has felt" (8). Maxwell Geismar, in a 1957 essay, made an even more direct connection to Lindner and James Dean, asserting that "if this hero [Holden] really represents the nonconformist rebellion of the Fifties, he is a rebel without a past, apparently, and without a cause" (96). In "J. D. Salinger: Search for Wisdom," Granville Hicks would explicitly assert the equivalence of rebellion and identity for young readers. "There are, I am convinced, millions of young Americans who feel closer to Salinger than to any other writer," wrote Hicks, for the two reasons that "he speaks their language . . . a voice we instantly recognize," but also because "he expresses their rebellion." Students, Hicks writes, "admired his [Holden's] intransigence, too, which he so often refers to as his craziness, and rejoiced in his gestures of defiance," yet this identification with Holden's rebelliousness was commendable precisely because of its utopian affirmations (88–89). In a conciliatory gesture toward the priorities of the development allegory, Hicks wrote: "Holden is not rejecting maturity but is looking for a better model than his elders by and large present" (91).

The Age of Simple Truth:
Huck, Holden, and the Boyhood of America

As Alan Nadel has shown, the doubled readings of *Catcher* corresponded closely to the complex pressures of anticommunism. Holden's obsession with veracious speech simultaneously satisfied two different demands of the era: on the one hand, for testimony that demonstrates one's "loyalty," but at the same time for a critique of the "phoniness" or untruthfulness of any such testimony (71–78). In short, Holden paradoxically satisfied both the need for McCarthyite conformity and a rebellion against it. This raises the question, however, as to why it was that critics so tenaciously associated *Catcher* with the second of these imperatives.

Identity after all did not always trump maturity as a value in literary criticism. Ralph Ellison's *Invisible Man* and Saul Bellow's *Adventures of Augie March*, as noted, drew praise as novels of the rebelling self in its search for autonomy and internal direction; that is, as novels of identity. Such praise, however, was always more than balanced out by stronger developmental readings, which valorized them as novels of education whose characters (with the readers in tow) advanced from blindness to insight, from innocence to experience, and from infantilism to maturity. *Catcher in the Rye* by contrast provoked very few such readings. Although a small handful of critics, most notably John Aldridge and Maxwell Geismar, condemned Salinger's novel as an adolescent protest that seemed overly "cynical, defiant, and blind" (Aldridge, 26), even they persisted in interpreting the novel as a (poor) instantiation of the rebel allegory. The only essay to interpret *Catcher* actively as an allegory of development, Peter Seng's "The Fallen Idol," which first appeared in *College English*, found no allies and was indeed rebuked by a run of letters in the journal challenging his interpretation.[16]

This absolute primacy of rebelliousness in Salinger criticism derives from the allegorical meaning of age itself with which critics approached both Holden Caulfield and the America that he represented for them. Consider, for instance, the widely praised kinship of Holden Caulfield and Huckleberry Finn, a lineage that many critics proffered as evidence of *Catcher*'s literary merit. No critic was firmer about this link than Charles Kaplan, who in "Holden and Huck: The Odysseys of Youth" asserted that "Huck Finn and Holden Caulfield are true blood-brothers. . . . [T]hese two novels thus deal obliquely and poetically with a major theme in American life, past and present—the right of the nonconformist to assert his nonconformity" (80). Kaplan's nationalist argument for *Catcher*'s canonization can be crudely expressed by a simple deductive chain of equivalences: *The Catcher in the Rye* = *Huckleberry Finn*, *Huckleberry Finn* = great American literature. But, as we can also see, identity itself becomes the criterion that sets this equation in motion. America's "national character" here actually becomes its "nonconformity." In literature, this takes the form of the people's willingness to honor the right of youth to reject the mandates of the adult world. Great American literature is that which endorses the nonconformity of the young. The language of "right" is crucial here in discerning the implied linkage to the discourse of identity. Like the "Teen-Age Bill of Rights" that the *New York Times* published in 1945, Kaplan imagines the emergence of the young into selfhood as a matter of justice, representable as a *right* to psychopolitical autonomy.

In noting this theme's relevance to both "past and present," however, Kaplan points to a temporal complication of identity that deeply concerned the critics of American literature. This complication appears somewhat more explicitly in Heiserman and Miller's essay, which along with Kaplan's was among the very first to stress *Catcher*'s affinity with *Huckleberry Finn*. Twain and Salinger's common genius, Heiserman and Miller suggest, lay in their masterful use of a colloquial American adolescent's voice to convey their respective "childism," by which they mean the nostalgic wish to recover our inner Adamic child. "Each of us does indeed carry an Adam inside us," they argue, a new and innocent self whom we wish we could rescue from "childism's" opposite: "adultism," the ideology of compromise with adult corruption (220). Because Huck flees from the adults who would "sivilize," Twain's novel became the quintessential *anti*developmental narrative, rebuking the pedagogical principle of maturity, while Holden, the prep school dropout, became Huck's twentieth-century counterpart. Both characters, asserted Heiserman and Miller, are "fugitives from education," adolescents who defiantly seek their own path in life in lieu of the one to which adults would direct them (223).

By alluding to R. W. B. Lewis's "American Adam," Heiserman and Miller make a subtle but highly consequential move. While they understand childhood as a timeless phase in the human life cycle, the "American Adam" signifies for them a literary character type specific to an earlier era of American literature. Huck Finn, in this sense, is an Adamic American character in a novel that properly belongs to the nation's Adamic moment of cultural emergence during the American Renaissance. Holden Caulfield, by contrast, is a latecomer, equally Adamic, yet out of step with his era. It is for this reason, they speculate, that Holden is driven to insanity; there is little room for characters like Huck or Holden in the mid-twentieth century. In this respect, Heiserman and Miller echo Lewis himself, Geismar, Aldridge, and many others, who saw the present age of conformism as deeply inhospitable to the idealistic individualism of the Adamic American.

Nowhere are the political stakes of this assertion clearer than in Lionel Trilling's essay on *Huckleberry Finn*, which lurked in the background of these numerous comparisons of Twain and Salinger. Trilling's essay, originally published in 1948, one year after the House Un-American Activities Committee began its hearings on Hollywood communists, was reprinted as part of *The Liberal Imagination*. In the essay Trilling affirms the greatness of *Huckleberry Finn* as "one of the central documents of American culture," which he locates in its boyish power of telling the truth: "No one, as he [Twain] well knew, sets a higher value on truth than a boy. Truth is the whole of a boy's conscious demand upon the world of adults. He is likely to believe that the adult world is in a conspiracy to lie to him, and it is this belief, by no means unfounded, that arouses Tom and Huck and all boys to their moral sensitivity, their everlasting concern with justice, what they call fairness" (101).

Catcher criticism unmistakably echoed Trilling's reading of *Huckleberry Finn* whenever it praised Holden Caulfield for allegorizing a moral and truthful America whose idealism always demands far more of the world than it has inherited from the last generation. Trilling, however, describes such boyishness with considerable ambivalence. On the one hand, he admits to a sort of lying conspiracy in the adult world and praises Twain's novel for offering the "very voice of unpretentious truth" (113). The character Huck Finn possesses a "liberal imagination," a utopian desire for fairness, justice, and democracy that leads him to reject compromise with an institution so ethically adulterated as slavery. At the same time, Trilling also suggests that the novel "is a hymn to an older America forever gone," an age of innocence that was ushered to its close by what Trilling calls "money-capitalism" (110).

Indulging here in a sentimental and nostalgic discussion of Huck Finn's world, Trilling only hints softly that today such "unpretentious truth" may no longer be affordable. By contrast, in the essays that precede it in *The Liberal Imagination*, such sentimentality is not simply avoided; it is derided as dangerous. America's liberal character must be tempered, for pure idealism is easily manipulated by political cynics. In his famous attack on the famous progressive critic Vernon Parrington, Trilling complains that "ideals are different from ideas; in the liberal criticism which descends from Parrington ideals consort happily with reality and they urge us to deal impatiently with ideas—a 'cherished goal' forbids that we stop to consider how we reach it, or if we may not destroy it in trying to reach it the wrong way" (19). Trilling decodes this cryptic comment by way of illustration: the errors of Theodore Dreiser, who late in life became affiliated with the Communist Party. Since communism is, for Trilling, the self-evidently "wrong way" to actualize one's liberal ideals, Dreiser's lack of *political* judgment confirms the lack of *literary* judgment by progressive critics like Parrington, who foolishly embraced him as "one of the great, significant expressions of [liberalism's] spirit" (18–19).

Trilling's literary criteria here flatly contradict those he espouses in his essay on *Huckleberry Finn*. The very qualities that he praises in Twain's work—its simple expression of America's democratic desire for human equality and justice, and most of all its idealism—are those he here denounces in Parrington. In celebrating Theodore Dreiser's novels, Parrington reveals the profound naïveté of his liberalism, which can be readily exploited and turned against itself by communism, its worst enemy. Trilling papers over the contradiction between his positive reading of political idealism in Twain and his negative evaluation thereof in Dreiser precisely by manipulating an allegory of age that fixes an appropriate relationship between national development and fictional character. Twain's novel is a boy's novel, written from the point of view of a boy, but also written at a time when America was young, when an era prior to "money-capitalism" could still be remembered. For Trilling, therefore, Huck Finn locates idealism in the nation's youth (in both senses), where it belongs. Dreiser's fiction, by contrast, neither places idealism in the mouth of a boy, nor does it reserve its democratic impulse for America's precapitalist past. Where Twain's democratic spirit can be safely dealt with in nostalgic, bygone terms, Dreiser's raises the spectre that American democratic idealism, placed in conflict with market values, might yield sympathy for twentieth-century communism.

Like *Huckleberry Finn*, *Catcher* embodied liberal idealism in the figure of a boy. Like Dreiser's fiction, however, *Catcher* had been written in the age of America's maturity, not its wide-eyed youth, and the sorts of principles motivating its protagonist's rebelliousness, in the view of liberal intellectuals like Trilling, therefore needed to be tempered with a measure of skeptical conservatism. Nevertheless, *Catcher*'s boyish voice rendered it an appropriately aged work with which to *recall* the radical origins of American liberalism, even if those origins were taken to belong to a youthful stage of national character development, a crucially valuable, if now completed, phase in America's identity formation. *Catcher*, in other words, was not typically held to espouse a viable alternative to the "mature" liberalism of America's present. Its canonical value lay in its recapitulation of a more principled American past, a resurrection of the spirit of Huck Finn, with which the present could be confronted, criticized, and literally rejuvenated. *Catcher*, as Heiserman and Miller implied, allowed America to recover its inner Adamic youth, to rediscover its sense of hope and assertive self-creation by confronting the conformist pressures of present-day adult America with accusations voiced by the adolescent character of its own past.[17]

For all that *Catcher* is set entirely in the present moment, therefore, its promotion to the canon of American literature proceeded through a temporally displaced national allegory that reconciled the identitarian and the development liberal narratives through a manipulation of national time. At the level of *Darstellung* or likeness, Holden appeared as an earlier America, the blood brother of Huck Finn, but at the level of *Vertretung*, as a proxy for the nation, Holden spoke for "all of us" in present-day America, the deeper level at which Americans presumably wished to recover that young, Adamic America, and thus implicitly hoped, in Stevenson's words, to "recapture" identity as the American ideal at a moment of "crisis" brought on by the forces of "conformity." As Hassan put it in his closing sentence, Salinger's heroes "play upon our nostalgia for a mythic American past. They also manage to raise nostalgia to the condition of hope" (289). The mainstream of liberal critics thus at least tacitly sided with Mr. Antolini on the point that Holden needed to "mature," to find a way to live in the present day. In this sense *Catcher*'s reception remained shaped by the developmental liberal paradigm championed by Trilling. Nevertheless, the critics found Holden no less admirable in his "immaturity," since his conviction for national ideals was sorely needed in the Fordist present.

Earlier I suggested that national allegories signify precisely through the contradiction they delineate between the representative figure and the ground of the nation. In the case of Salinger's novel, this contradiction was projected across a temporal axis. *Catcher*'s allegorical value was grounded in precisely this "age of conformism," a present-day America that Holden rightly deemed "phony." In the ground of this allegory—acknowledged often enough but far more briefly than was its figure—America appears as a "lonely crowd" of "other-directed" people, a landscape of characters who have fully internalized a mass cultural logic of mutual equivalence, commerce, and sign exchange. It is they who allow Holden to stand out as an identity figure, against a nation that has become phony because it caters or prostitutes itself to a system of commerce. Holden did so, however, as a figure for a *younger* America, like Huck Finn himself, and therefore not yet compliant with its commercial logic. On the allegorical level, Holden's resistance issued from a time before the "adulthood" of the nation, a youthful era prior to—yet standing in judgment of—the "age of conformity." Holden figures the justified recalcitrance of a former (young) America to melt into the topos of its contemporary ground, the "lonely crowd" of characters arrayed in its background.

This temporal strategy played a key part in what might be called the "first worlding" of American literature. While the development allegory confirmed the nation's mature reconciliation to industrial capitalism and its market values, the rebel allegory foregrounded by *Catcher* demonstrated the survival of a national passion for freedom and sovereignty that America shared with the new nations liberating themselves from colonialism. In readings of *Catcher*, Holden's demand for identity took priority over the theme of maturity, and Salinger's novel thereby became a far more emphatic icon of American critical nonconformity than most other canonical works.

Catcher *among the Paperbacks:*
Figuring America in the Mass Marketplace

In its standing as national allegory, *Catcher* operated both at the level of the national individual (the allegory's "vehicle"), an American teenager battling for self-definition in a mass society, but also at the level of the people (its "tenor"). His story became, to paraphrase Ernest Jones, a "case history of us all," a metonym for America's "lonely crowd" fighting to retain its collective sovereignty against the disempowering force of its own mass culture. Paradoxically, however, *Catcher* was also often read as a product of the very mass culture that it appeared to criticize. Phenomenally successful in paperback form, *Catcher* became a paradigmatic case study of the great shifts in postwar book culture. Here again, *Catcher* was taken to be representative of American literature, which faced either a fate of degradation (as it was massified by the marketplace) or else a realization of its deepest promise if the paperback were taken instead as a means to literary democratization.

Among the various sectors of the culture industry, the book industry was unique in that its production process underwent a Fordist revolution in lockstep with the industrial core of the postwar American economy.[18] The mass-market paperback, whose centrality to print culture we now take for granted, was actually a product innovation of the 1940s and 1950s that drastically transformed the book industry. Until World War II, the book market had been dominated by a handful of small but prestigious hardcover publishing houses. In less than ten years, new companies that had begun modestly enough as softcover reprint houses for the majors—Pocket Books, New American Library, Bantam, and several others—would overwhelm the traditional book companies with tremendous sales figures made possible by their innovations in mass production and distribution. As Kenneth Davis writes in his *histoire de livre*, "Before these inexpensive, widely distributed books came along, only the rarest of books sold more than a hundred thousand copies; a million-seller was a real phenomenon.... Overnight, the paperback changed that. Suddenly, a book could reach not hundreds or thousands of readers, but millions, many of whom had never owned a book before" (xii). Soft binding and the replacement of hand stitching with machine-applied glue allowed the price of a book to be reduced to as low as twenty-five cents. Now comparable in price to magazines, books began selling for the first time outside of bookstores, at magazine stands, in dime stores, and even in airports. Books in effect became yet another sort of disposable text affordable even to the casual reader.

Because paperbacks circulated outside the traditional network of book distribution, their sales figures appeared relatively immune to the opinions of critics, librarians, or booksellers, the very people who had traditionally guided readership. Instead, paperback companies began to rely heavily on advertising copy to woo their customers, beginning first and foremost with the book's graphic covers. The vast expansion of book readership enabled by paperback print capitalism thus led to a perceptible decline in cultural authority by the traditional arbiters of literary merit. Literary intellectuals already concerned about their "age of conformity" therefore found themselves particularly anxious over what they perceived as a tendency toward *literary* conformity, driven by the paperback's massification of literature.

If the majority of Salinger's critics read his novel as a narrative of national identity, running close behind came their interest in how it evidenced the paperback market's growing influence on American literary culture. Although Little, Brown's hardcover version had sold respectably well, in 1953 New American Library, the most prestigious of the paperback companies, won the rights to a softcover edition, which they quickly converted into a commercial success. New American Library's mass-market edition sold a steady quarter million copies in every year of its publication, often it seems to young readers. It was only after the established success of this paperback edition that literary critics began to take a serious inter-

2. Original cover design for paperback edition of *The Catcher in the Rye* (1951).

est, and they repeatedly made note of its appeal as a paperback. Typical was Robert Gutwillig's pronouncement:

> Many an observer of the manners and mores of American youth contends that a first novel published ten years ago occupies much the same place in the affection of today's college generation as F. Scott Fitzgerald's *This Side of Paradise* did for their parents in the Nineteen Twenties. The novel is *The Catcher in the Rye*, by J.D. Salinger, which since its publication on July 16, 1951, has sold a total of 1,500,000 copies in the United States alone—1,250,000 of them, significantly enough, in paperbound form. (1)

In such comments as this, youth again played a crucial role, but for the somewhat different purpose of designating who exactly had enabled readership to be transformed into another site of mass consumption. Not only were adolescents assumed to be the principal purchasers of America's new mass literary product, but they were also understood to be transforming its very substance in the process. In a discussion of the new directions taken by postpaperback American fiction, Leslie Fiedler argued that

> we have been ... living through a revolution in taste, a radical transformation of the widest American literary audience from one in which women predominate to one in which adolescents make up the majority.... And the mode demands, in lieu of the teen-age novelists who somehow refuse to appear, Teen-age Impersonators, among whom one might list, say, Norman Mailer, Jack Kerouac, even William Burroughs — certainly the Salinger who wrote *The Catcher in the Rye* and invented Holden Caulfield, a figure emulated by the young themselves. (236)

Such an argument in fact makes little empirical sense. Teenagers have never made up an overwhelming majority of book readership. Paperbacks, which from the start came in an enormous variety of genres and styles, have likewise always been marketed to a highly heterogeneous audience. It was thus the literary critics themselves who, in fixating on a highly selective handful of literary works (by Mailer, Kerouac, Salinger, and so forth), had elevated youthfulness to the status of a paradigm for judging the nature of paperback literature and its mass readership.

Fiedler's conflation of mass culture and youth culture, a commonplace in liberal culture debates of the fifties, grew out of several related ideological issues. On the one hand, a new teenage consumer market was indeed coalescing in the postwar years. Often it was feared that this new market might compromise the ability of adults to raise their own children according to their own values.[19] In some ways, this was an assumed risk associated with the new concept of the "teenager," defined as a young person bearing a certain right to independent social relations with others his or her own age. Neither were these fears that teen culture might lead to an uncontrollable rebellion entirely fanciful, for by promoting among youth a peer culture assertive of its identitarian sovereignty, the new youth market did in fact encourage, over the long run, new forms of cultural and political dissent in American life.

The association of paperback culture *in general* with a young readership, however, was also related to a postwar indictment of kitsch, which liberal critics construed as a degenerate culture of predigested meaning. In this account, kitsch was akin to children's culture, designed for people unable or unwilling to perform the cognitive labor of decoding the texts. Like baby food, mass culture infantilized *anyone* who consumed it, as Dwight Macdonald argued in his influential essay "A Theory of Mass Culture," making the United States into a nation of "Adultized Children" and "Infantile Adults," so that "Peter Pan might be a better symbol of America than Uncle Sam" (66).

Here again, America is analogized to a young character, but here that figure takes on a sinister appearance. In the culture industries at least, Macdonald's comment suggests that industrial development was leading, not to national advancement or maturation, but to characterological regression instead. Critics dismayed by *Catcher*'s mass popularity typically condemned the novel as just such a Peter Pan narrative, a story about a boy who refuses to grow up, and a novel whose mass appeal could be equated with its shameless juvenilization of American literature. As George Steiner made clear in the title of his bitterly polemical essay "The Salinger Industry," both *Catcher* and its intellectual cheerleaders were complicit with the assembly-line Fordization of both American literature and American literary criticism. Strenuously insisting on a difference between genuine and commercial literature, Steiner castigated literary critics for pandering to the latter, and argued, of course, that the work of Salinger himself leaned heavily in the direction of commercialization: "Salinger flatters the very ignorance and moral shallowness of his young readers. He suggests to them that formal ignorance, political apathy and a vague *tristesse* are positive virtues" (116). He also "writes briefly," noted Steiner, "no need to lug home a big book or something, Lord help us, not available in paperback" (116). A faithful lackey of mass-market product guidelines, Salinger was, in Steiner's estimation, a prostitute to his audiences, giving them what they want to read rather than what is good for them. Critics who lauded Salinger only encouraged this dismal literary conformity driven by the paperback industry's interest in maximizing book sales.[20]

The irony of these claims that *Catcher* promoted the commercialization of American literature was, of course, that Holden Caulfield shared Steiner's distaste for commercialization. Holden consistently condemns anyone at all who produces himself or herself for exchange: the schoolmaster who sells himself to the parents of the wealthy students, Ernie the black pianist who panders to his college crowd, the Lunts with their self-inflated acting, and the audience members at their performance who have only come to be seen by one another in the lobby. Holden views these and many other people as phonies, whose self-promotion for the consumption of others is an index of their inauthenticity. What should ideally be a social world built upon acts of communication, hence communion, has instead become one in which people are instrumentalized as objects of one another's exchange. Holden thus condemns precisely the sorts of literary phenomena that Steiner would have represented by someone like J. D. Salinger: a successful, commercial writer of what Holden calls those "dumb stories in a magazine" (52). Holden even attacks the very institution that propelled *Catcher* to its initial successes, the Book-of-the Month Club. Holden's brother D.B., whose writing now makes "lots of dough" in Hollywood, is thus condemned by Holden as a literary "prostitute" in terms virtually identical to Steiner's attacks on Salinger himself (1–2).

Catcher's paradoxical relationship to mass culture was not lost on the novel's many proponents. Fully aware of *Catcher*'s impressive sales figures, they suggested that *Catcher* actually illustrated the good that could come of paperback readership. *Catcher*, precisely *through* its status as a mass-market hit, had successfully popularized Holden's compelling denunciation of massified literature and of the tendency of all too many Americans to ape its other-directed logic. When combined with a classically American willingness to defend the ideal of identity, mass culture could thus generate its own internal challenge to the conformity that it otherwise seemed to encourage. A book like *Catcher* therefore appeared as the solution to *Partisan Review*'s problem, offering both cultural democracy and critical nonconformity. The well-known cultural critic David Manning White had championed paperbacks against their critics, arguing that they, like the other mass media, "hold out the greatest promise to the 'average' man that a cultural richness no previous age could give him is at hand" (19). For Salinger's advocates, *Catcher* realized just this richness, uniting literary quality and quantity, artistic merit and cultural democracy.

Celebratory interpretations of *Catcher* typically pressed ahead with this defense, stressing the novel's appeal to young paperback readers as a prelude to their allegorical reading of Holden as an exemplar of America's youthful idealism. This position found its greatest symbolic force in Dan Wakefield's contribution to the inaugural issue of New American Library's mass-market literary journal, *New World Writing*. The journal, which was candidly created in order to prove that paperbacks could actually usher in a "new world" of literary possibilities, alluded with its title to Lewisonian Adamic American literary tradition that it "hoped" to renew. It offered an ideal forum, therefore, for defending Salinger's work as both quintessentially American and as an exemplary paperback novel. Wakefield warned that, "it seems to follow in the eyes of some older observers that if Salinger is indeed a myth and mentor of many young people, interest in his work is restricted to young people and that this is symptomatic of the fact that it is really childish, sentimental, adolescent, and irrelevant" (195). In fact, argued Wakefield, Salinger's youthful appeal was not at all restricted to physically young people but spoke readily to anyone who remained young in spirit, and who thereby resisted what Wakefield slyly called "moral senility" (197). The "adolescent" character that Salinger promulgated so widely and successfully therefore signaled not literary degradation but rather the persistence of what Wakefield called the "search for love," a hunt for connection with others based upon mutuality rather than on the lonely pressures exerted by social conformity. And if the American literary character had always been youthful, Adamic, and opposed to moral senility, then the youthful appeal of J. D. Salinger's paperback fiction, far from threatening the American literary tradition, promised to rejuvenate it. For critics like Wakefield, it was not only Holden who represented the best of America but *Catcher* itself as a popular paperback book, standing conscientiously against the mass book market that surrounded it, pressing forward its demands for a better world, a better morality, and evidently a better contemporary literature.

Identity Canons, Rebel Allegories, and the First World Imaginary

> In order to answer the question of what "representation in the canon" means within the larger context of American political culture, we must acknowledge at the outset that our concept of "social identity" is a product of that culture, and that only within that culture can the category of an author's racial, ethnic, or gender identity found a politics of curricular revision. Any reconsideration, then, of canon critique in its political context must begin with the notion of "social identity."—John Guillory, *Cultural Capital*

> Judging from recent conversations among third-world intellectuals, there is now an obsessive return of the national situation itself, the name of the country that returns again and again like a gong, the collective attention to "us" and what we have to do and how we do it, to what we can't do and what we do better than this or that nationality, our unique characteristics, in short to the level of the "people." This is not the way American intellectuals have been discussing "America."—Fredric Jameson, "Third World Literature in the Age of Multinational Capitalism"

> It is not only the Asian or the African but also the American writer whose private imaginations must necessarily connect with experiences of the collectivity. One has only to look at black and feminist writing to find countless allegories even within these postmodern United States.—Aijaz Ahmad, "Jameson's Rhetoric of Otherness and the 'National Allegory'"

Normally, when we discuss "identity" as a value constitutive of American literature, we think not of the 1950s but rather of the multicultural American canon that a new generation of critics began to establish in the 1970s and 1980s. "Identity," in this context, names the previously excluded or marginalized cultural voices that deserve to be recognized within a more diverse and representative gathering of American literature. The drama of literary representation, as John Guillory notes, was thus construed by direct analogy to political representation, with the canon itself serving as a literary proxy for the social totality whose political culture needs to be opened up to all those it has historically disenfranchised. Guillory, who favors a materially grounded institutional approach that would locate the political significance of literature in "cultural capital" rather than in "representation," attacks the premise that literary and political representation are in any way analogous. The persuasive force of this analogy, he argues, issues from "our concept of social identity," a historically bound and problematic product of American culture that we need to contextualize and reconsider.

In this chapter, I have offered just such a reconsideration of identity, tracing its origins as a literary value that measures the representation of a collective self. In so doing, however, I have demonstrated that the identity concept entered the literary domain considerably earlier than the moment that Guillory presumes: the point at which postsixties critics began mobilizing "identity" on behalf of writings by people of color, women, gays, and lesbians. By the 1950s, critics had *already* begun to demand a "new image" of America suitably representative to the nation's "democratic" character. Authors, their works, and finally even their protagonists were obliged to affirm and represent "our country and our culture" in terms of its sovereign identity, by expressing its perennial spirit of "critical nonconformity." In the fifties, this rebel allegory was dramatized by a young American character who refused the depersonalizing expectations of a mass society. During the seventies, in the wake of the black, yellow, and brown power and gay and women's liberation movements, new versions of the American literary character would continue to represent rebellious identity, but their "critical nonconformity" would now directly express acts of racial, gender, or sexual insubordination as offered up by allegorical figures of black, Chicano, Asian American, female, or gay identity. In both moments, then, the critical search for identity would become an act of literary judgment and canon formation.

Given this history, it would be inappropriate to blame the positing of identity as literary value on "faulty thinking" by postsixties activist critics, as Guillory sometimes implies, for this was a criterion they merely inherited and indeed put to important use. If we are to assess the literary politics of identity, we must contend with the fact that it issued from conditions that, at least twenty years earlier, had *already* begun to work upon the political imaginary of American critics. It is the "age of three worlds" itself that offers the widest possible political context for considering the "identitarianization" of U.S. literary politics, with its allegories of representative selves. And this process of identitarianization, I submit, was largely synonymous with what might be called the "first worlding" of the American literary canon.

This first worlding of American literature, as I have shown, proceeded through the critical application of two national allegories: that of development and that of rebellion. The allegory of development, as I noted earlier, attested to the "maturity" of the American character in a way that implicitly celebrated American *industrial* development. America was no longer susceptible to left-wing naïveté precisely because its tremendous postwar influence rendered self-evident the notion that the first world's liberal version of capitalism (with all its imperfections) was preferable to the "return to serfdom" entailed by the communist alternative. The rebel allegory, while also first-worlding American literature, proceeded quite differently. Unlike the allegory of development, it conceded that industrial mass culture threatened the autonomy of the people, yet it simultaneously insisted on the capacity of a truly democratic people to defy this threat, thereby demonstrating their autonomy anew. The rebel allegory thus showed the American character to be not mature (i.e., industrial, like the second world) but young (i.e., seeking independence, like the third world). It is for this reason that Holden Caulfield was cast as the expression of an earlier America, one associated with the identitarian spirit of the nation's precapitalist past, hearkening back to the anticolonial spirit of revolutionary, democratic America, much like Huck Finn.

It is striking that this role of national allegory in the first worlding of American literature mirrors in a curious way the argument once made by Fredric Jameson that it is *third world* literature that is characterized by the national allegory. Jameson, of course, was taken to task for what many postcolonial critics saw as a grotesque homogenization of the literatures and cultural conditions of Asia, Africa, and Latin America.[21] Yet Jameson's argument makes considerable sense if reformulated so as to conceive the third world, not as an empirically homogenous space, but instead as a loosely knit geopolitical project shared by formerly colonized, nominally independent states who sought national self-sufficiency at multiple levels (economic, political, cultural, psychological). Taken thus, the "national allegory" of third world literature no longer appears as a universalizing account of the literature produced on three continents but rather as a literary insight into a narrative structure that often animated and guided the disparate strategies of decolonization.

As the hypercanonization of *The Catcher in the Rye* attests, however, national allegory was no less crucial to first world literary projects. Contrary to Jameson's claims, postwar American intellectuals and writers did indeed sound the gong of the "nation" and its "situation" with an obsessiveness rivaling that of any third world country.[22] The very basis of the era's revised canon rested upon national allegory, and many of the new literary works to gain stature alongside *Catcher in the Rye*—Ellison's *Invisible Man*, Allen Ginsberg's *Howl*, Ken Kesey's *One Flew over the Cuckoo's Nest*, Thomas Pynchon's *The Crying of Lot 49*, among others—did so by making the story of the first world individual stand in for that of the first world people. This first world individual, when imagined as a rebel identity, typically stood as a psychopolitical outsider, and already in the fifties racial, gender, or sexual difference was affiliated easily enough with this outsider status; writings by and about blacks, Jews, women, and gays began to assume a representative role for American literature. One can see, therefore, the ease with which the rebel allegory would later serve to create a multicultural identity canon.

This allegorical turn in postwar American literature and criticism is disavowed by Jameson's essay, largely because it posits the first and third world relation as that of a Hegelian contradiction. For Jameson, while "third world" names the address of the politicized but embattled national community, the "first world" always embodies its lack, as the place where resident intellectuals fail to voice the national situation precisely because its systemic privilege within world capitalism manifests itself imaginatively in depoliticized personal-libidinal narratives. The first world, as the "other" of the third world politicized community, maps (as Jameson's contemporaneous work on postmodernism makes explicit) a degraded commodity culture in which the very possibility of historical and collective narration has been foreclosed. Paradoxically, however, this means that Jameson's essay writes its own unacknowledged national allegory for the "industrialized" countries: the libidinally self-oriented first world national, disconnected from the world of political meaning through his or her absorption into privatized consumption, becomes emblematic of his or her people's forfeiture of collective agency to the culture industry.

88 CHAPTER TWO

What I would like to stress here is how both of Jameson's national allegories can be respectively traced back to the figure and ground that together constituted the national allegory derived from *Catcher in the Rye*. The social world through which Holden Caulfield moved, composed of phony people subjected to the instrumental rationality of a mass culture, elevated *Catcher* to the status of a "mirror of crisis" that would be used imaginatively to corroborate the grim analyses of David Riesman, William Whyte, C. Wright Mills, Paul Goodman, and Herbert Marcuse concerning mass conformity in the new age of American Fordism. This loose tradition of first world self-critical pessimism, more or less tacitly promoted in much of the commentaries about an age of conformity in Salinger criticism, sketched the first world as an ironic reflection of the completely administered second world, a space of personal and collective subjection to the totality. Jameson drew from this tradition for his theories of first world postmodernism and the loss of political agency it entailed.

Holden himself, meanwhile, represented for postwar critics precisely what the third world protagonists meant for Jameson, the contrary image of a national character as political agent who offers hope against the degraded landscape of a mass consumer society. It is important to see this relation as a motivated one, for Holden as an allegorical figure for America (and an earlier one at that) served to mirror the nations of the third world. He too was young and like them struggling to establish his psychopolitical sovereignty in a hostile setting. Where Holden himself figured American identity defending itself in a time of crisis, the "phony" American ground that he inhabits provided the needed *tableau* of crisis (an organizational society, a lonely crowd, a mass culture, a paperback literature) through and against which his heroic struggle might be discerned.

Contrary to what Jameson would have expected, then, there was no separation for American intellectuals between Holden's personal-libidinal narrative and the nation's public affairs. Rather, as a pivotal text in first world U.S. thought and literature, *Catcher* embodied not a separation of the political and the psychological but an emphatic fusing of the two that was expressed nowhere so clearly as in the psychopolitical concept of identity itself. The mobilization of this concept as a right of the young or the emergent self would have reverberations, both inside and outside of literature, for decades to come. When the multicultural American canon arrived on the scene, it too would feature protagonists mirroring the third world in their assertion of identity: the rightful emergence of an embattled people into the space of representation.

TRANSCOMMODIFICATION:

ROCK 'N' ROLL AND THE SUBURBAN

COUNTERIMAGINARY

At least part of the motivation for the middle-class white youth adoption of Afro-American and working-class music as their own in the 1950s stemmed from a collective judgment about the demise of the urban industrial city and the rise of the suburb.... Visible markers of class and ethnic identity disappeared as the single-family, detached suburban home replaced the multi-family dwellings of ethnic neighborhoods, as network television eclipsed the neighborhood movie theater, and as a culture of consumption and conformity encouraged standardization of dress and behavior as the entrance requirements into the burgeoning, corporate white-collar world. Facing a choice between the sterile and homogenous suburban cultures of their parents or the dynamic street cultures alive among groups excluded from the middle-class consensus, a large body of youths found themselves captivated and persuaded by the voices of difference. Mass consumer culture had become so hegemonic that middle-class young people flocked to the cultures of the dying industrial city for connection to the past, for emotional expression, and for a set of values that explained and justified rebellion.
—George Lipsitz, *Time Passages*

I want to emphasize the way in which this context [of liberal consensus] constrained the political possibilities of the rock formation, rather than romanticizing rock as a radical statement of political resistance or an expression of alienation.... This goes hand in hand with the assumed image of the 1950s rocker as the isolated and agonized rebel and delinquent, antisocial, antidomestic, and anticonsumerist. Apart from the fact that this image is simply an inaccurate portrait of the vast majority of rock fans, there is also little evidence (even in the songs themselves) that rock rejected the dominant liberal consensus or the major ideological assumptions (sexism, racism and classism) of that consensus. It is not merely that most rock fans lived somewhere inside the vast center of U.S. society; it is also that they imagined themselves remaining within it.

—Lawrence Grossberg, *We Gotta Get Out of This Place*

An interpretation is not authentic unless it culminates in some form of appropriation (*Aneignung*), if by that term we understand the process by which one makes one's own (*eigen*) what was initially other or alien (*fremd*).

—Paul Ricoeur, *Hermeneutics and the Human Sciences*

In this chapter and the one that follows, I shift my attention from the arbiters of American culture (literary critics, journalists, intellectuals) to the young people actually being positioned by the ascendance of identity discourse. Specifically, I will be tracing the imaginary processes through which youth audiences began to identify with "identity," viewing themselves as emergent personalities entitled to rebel against suburban conformity in the name of their own sovereign self-definition against adults. This is a historic event that did not happen automatically. It depended, rather, on a series of material and ideological contingencies that brought the various entertainment industries to embrace the new discourses of identity as the marker of a new and sorely needed market. Youth rebellion became a thematic device with which the so-called mass audience could be segmented along the axis of age. Nowhere was this process more dramatically evidenced than in the birth of rock 'n' roll, understood as a sector of popular music marketed exclusively to and for the young, and in particular to an enormous and highly lucrative suburban teenage market.

While it is quite evident that the themes of youth autonomy and even rebellion were integral to fifties rock 'n' roll, scholars have passionately argued as to whether or not the music expressed a genuine shift in the protopolitical sentiments of young Americans. In so doing, they have also implicitly made judgments about the ubiquitous class, racial, and geographic claims that so many postwar countercultures since early rock 'n' roll have made. For celebratory scholars such as George Lipsitz, rock 'n' roll's fan base among suburban teenagers demonstrates that white, middle-class youth from the fifties onward willfully chose to reject suburbia and ally themselves with minority and working-class culture. For critics such as Lawrence Grossberg, rock 'n' roll's roots in working-class and minority culture lose importance in the face of suburban youth culture's participation in the broader scene of postwar consumption. Whatever rock 'n' roll's origins, suburban youth's adoption of the music effectively drew it into the liberal consensus.

As the coauthors of *Rock over the Edge* accurately observe, a tenacious "authenticity myth," a certain binary of "real" versus "fake" music, has stymied the study of rock, making it exceedingly difficult to "discuss rock music apart from rock's rhetoric" about itself (Beebe et al., 3). It is no coincidence, however, that this obsession with the authentic is something that the discourses of identity share with those of rock. The birth of rock 'n' roll bears an affiliation with the emergence of identity that, here, I will be tracking in terms of new imaginary relationships that arose in the fifties among suburb, city, and country. For reasons that include changes in social geography, mass media, and youth culture itself, it became possible by the mid-fifties to remarket urban and rural musical forms—themselves already commercial products with distinct ideological and historical trajectories—to suburban teenagers who thereby invested them with identitarian meanings that were new, yet also related to their earlier ones. I call this process "transcommodification" in order to suggest that the advent of rock 'n' roll can be reduced neither to a transition from authenticity to commerce nor to a solidarity of middle-class youth with the oppressed and exploited. Both positions *assume* a logic of identitarian authenticity rather than treating it as a historically new value that rock 'n' roll's theme of youthful rebellion actually helped to create. Lipsitz, for instance, presumes the postwar authentic-identity/inauthentic-conformity binary by arguing that because the suburbs aimed to crush identity (implicitly conceived as the self-defining ethnic or working-class personality), youth reclaimed identity by finding it elsewhere (in the cities). To refute this argument, Grossberg is compelled to reverse it by flatly denying that the rebel figure for identity carried any "authentic" cultural force. Rock fans, by and large "conforming" to postwar culture, never did truly embrace the avatar of identity (i.e., the "isolated and agonized rebel"). Paradoxically, Lipsitz and Grossberg end up sharing an ontology of identity that aligns it with authenticity against commercialism. For both critics, identity implicitly requires (as Erikson first insisted) a political fidelity to the self. For Lipsitz, rock 'n' roll expresses youth identity because it expresses a genuine (self-authentic) revolt against the standardized system of suburban commerce, even if it is borrowed from elsewhere. For Grossberg, youth is part of the American commercial consensus, so that the only identity it can have is social conformity, which signifies precisely the *absence* of an authentic identity since mass incorporation precludes the possession of psychopolitical autonomy.

I will approach rock 'n' roll, not as the site of opposition between authenticity and commerce but instead as the marker of a complex ideological and economic shift from one commodity system to another. It is therefore just as misleading for Lipsitz to celebrate rock 'n' roll as an authentic embrace of black and working-class culture as it is for Grossberg to condemn it as the encroachment of postwar consumerism. In quoting Paul Ricoeur alongside Grossberg and Lipsitz, I want to anticipate a quite different analysis of rock 'n' roll. Using metaphoricity as a hermeneutic model for thinking about transcommodification, I will argue that authenticity and appropriation should be seen as collaborative terms rather than antithetical ones. Although derived from black and working-class culture, the music that became rock 'n' roll was suburbanized in ways that changed its meanings substantively. Rock 'n' roll therefore did not align suburban teenagers in any straightforward way with black/working-class culture. But this does not mean that teenagers neutralized black/working-class music in appropriating it. Rather, I will suggest, rock 'n' roll allowed youth culture to constitute a Fordist counterimaginary, a way of seeing oneself as simultaneously within, yet implicitly critical of, postwar suburbia.

The Dual Imaginaries of Suburbia

Perhaps the quickest way to index the intimate relationship between rock 'n' roll and suburbia is to point to their shared codes of spatial hybridity. Rock 'n' roll, as its critics always note, fused the respective urban and rural traditions of rhythm and blues and country-and-western music.[1] As such, rock 'n' roll's origin narrative mirrors exactly the suburban ideal itself. As many historians have noted, suburbia maps out a long-standing modernist project, at least as old as industrialization, that has aimed to fuse the respective benefits of inhabiting the city and country.[2] If rural life is wistfully celebrated for its proximity to nature and traditional life rhythms, it has also been commonly disparaged as parochial, boring, and too distant from the socioeconomic activity of the city. And while the vast possibilities, kineticism, and cosmopolitanism of the city offer a vibrant alternative, urban life is widely faulted for its noise and dirt, its cramped spaces, disruption of tradition, and its intensified occasions for social conflict. Suburbia, then, as a bourgeois ideal for sublating these lifestyles, has always promised continued access to the city's modern opportunities while recreating the peacefulness and pastoral values of the country.[3]

Particularly in the form it took throughout the building boom of the Fordist era, suburbia was constituted through a series of binary oppositions derived from the public/private distinction: consumption versus production, leisure versus work, the familial versus the social. By and large, suburbia associated the city with the public terms and itself with the private ones.[4] Within the suburban vision, the city remained a place for the collective enterprises and zones of industry, production, work, public space, and nonfamilial social encounters; by contrast, the suburbs offered, at affordable prices, a protected private space for the exercise of household consumption and leisure situated within one's nuclear family. Urban and rural cultures had traditionally seen themselves as constituted by *both* sets of terms in these binaries (the city and country for their inhabitants were places for both production *and* consumption, work *and* leisure, family *and* sociality). One of suburbia's innovations is thus the way that it imaginatively split the terms of these binaries, expelling the public ones from itself and locating them (both imaginatively and materially) at distances transversible, in the postwar period, only by automobile.[5] Suburbia became conceived, therefore, as a locale where people could freely enjoy leisure time, albeit in specifically private and domestic forms.[6]

Suburbia was also organized according to a vision in which class and race were rendered invisible. To the extent that work defines one's class position, suburbia aimed to conceal its class differences by literally placing distance between its residents' jobs and their private lives, as well as by privileging consumption over production as the locus of social activity. Whatever the differences in their work lives, people in a suburban neighborhood presumably shared a home life that involved the ongoing improvement of domestic space through the purchase of commodities. Racial difference was "vanished" in a very different way, through the infamous practice of redlining, in which mortgages for racially mixed urban neighborhoods were regularly refused as a financial risk by banks and the Federal Housing Administration even while they rubber-stamped mortgages for mostly white buyers in the new neighborhoods of the expanding suburbs. Developers and homeowner associations meanwhile routinely enforced "restrictive covenants" that adopted property value protection as grounds for keeping nonwhites from buying into the new suburban neighborhoods (Jackson, 208–210). Such financial rationalizations of these exclusionary policies nominally disavowed that these new neighborhoods represented a racialist project. Suburbia was presented as a politically neutral place for the building of equity and family, a place whose creation was motivated not by prejudice but by the personal dreams of its residents. Implicitly, however, these covenants and redlining practices functioned as codes, in both the legalistic and semiotic senses of the word, that established suburbia—at once imaginatively and demographically—as a zone of protected whiteness over and against the racially marked zones of both the country and the city.

These various codes initially constituted suburbia for its residents as a utopic form of modern living—an enclave adjacent to the energy and opportunity of the city, yet pastoral like the country, close to nature and free from the risk of class or racial conflict. Yet these same codes have been easily reversible, even for those living there, into a powerfully dystopic image. Roger Silverstone has astutely observed a historically split vision of suburbia in which it has served simultaneously as a "dream for those wishing to escape the density of the city or the emptiness of the country," and as a "nightmare for those who regard . . . [it] as a sterile hybrid, the bastard child of unculture" (56). The reason for such a split vision, I propose, rests on the very ambivalences that draw people to suburbia in the first place. Suburbia, after all, proposes a compromise between people's hopes and doubts about both the city and the country. An appreciation and antipathy for both animates the suburban ideal. Suburbia's founding anxiety, therefore is that it might inadvertently wed, not the best elements of each world, but the worst. To put this uneasiness in the form of a nagging question for the bourgeois imagination: what if suburbia should prove itself to be a sterile hybrid, a third place between city and country which ultimately provides access to neither culture nor nature, which lacks heterogeneity and excitement, yet is also too densely populated, too new, too contrived an environment to be genuinely rustic or traditionalist? If, as Silverstone concisely puts it, suburbia represents "a form of life that modernism has created almost to escape from itself" (171), one might add that, especially in the Fordist era, as it grew increasingly hegemonic, suburbia became a place where the bourgeois experience of modernity repeatedly found itself torn by its own self-ambivalence. It became, in short, a place from which one might also wish to escape.

Mass-Mediating Suburbia:
TV, Rock 'n' Roll, and the Dual Imaginaries

Two major events in the history of American mass media occurred in the 1950s. First, television grew into the nation's dominant medium of entertainment. Second, rock 'n' roll became a dominant new force in popular music.[7] In ways that need to be better understood, these two developments were mutually linked through the process of suburbanization. Their interconnection, I will suggest, emerged through the alternative ways in which each medium accommodated mass entertainment in suburbia. Broadly speaking, television and rock 'n' roll came to center themselves on opposite sides of the split imaginary of suburbia: utopic for the visual medium, a wasteland for the audial. This antonymic mirroring of television and rock 'n' roll derives, I argue, from their shared prehistory in the prewar institution of radio.

Rock 'n' roll critics tend to recall the prewar era of network radio—dominated by four national broadcast systems—as reflecting the bland homogeneity of the Tin Pan Alley sound. Reebee Garofalo, for example, claims that the radio networks perceived the nation "as one monolithic audience" desirous only of "middle-class, family-oriented fare" (86). From the viewpoint of TV critics, however, network radio seems anything but an era of monolithic broadcasting. While it is true that network radio usually presumed a family audience, national domesticity openly cut across various lines of social difference. Presuburban in both the fictional spaces it created and the listeners it interpellated, network radio aired shows set in various ethnic and working-class urban neighborhoods, and presented social interactions (serious and comic) that cut across class, race, and ethnic lines. Musical radio shows were admittedly dominated by live performances of the generic middle-class sound of Tin Pan Alley, but they also often included performances of regional, folk, and ethnic music. Moreover, radio broadcast a wide range of genres, including not only dramas, comedies, and news, but also vaudevillian and variety shows drawn from working-class traditions of entertainment. In short, while network radio interpellated a national audience united across the lines of social difference, it acknowledged—and played with—the existence of these lines. Domesticity, for prewar radio, was imagined as a condition in which private and public situations interpenetrated one another, where family life intersected with forms of urban or rural sociability that might involve class, ethnic, and racial relations of difference.

In 1948, television began to supplant radio's status as the preeminent national broadcast medium. CBS and NBC, both previously radio networks, rapidly transferred their programming onto television. As Lynn Spigel has shown, TV took only seven years to become the chief medium for domestic entertainment. Television did not simply replace radio as the preeminent domestic medium, however. It also suburbanized the very meaning of domestic entertainment. The very apparatus of television seemed to require, in a way radio had not, the spaciousness of a suburban home. Whereas people could be arranged in many ways while listening to a radio, television demanded that they occupy a space organized into a field of vision.[8] This often required not only more room, but more sitting furniture than before. TV sets were also tied, for the most part, to a logic of "bigger is better," in which televisual images stood to improve by increasing their size. As a result, consoles tended to become bulky, space-demanding items of furniture consonant with the impetus of suburbanization.

In practice, television's commercial availability in the forties and fifties grew alongside the postwar suburban building boom, at times even serving as a built-in feature of new tract homes.[9] It took only four years, as Spigel notes, for the TV set to replace the radio as the "central figure in images of the American home," appearing in magazines, advertisements, and of course on TV itself as the "cultural symbol par excellence of family life" (39). Television became viewed as a means toward suburban forms of domestic togetherness, an entertainment medium that unified husbands and wives, parents and children within a single household space.

The suburbanization of domestic entertainment was also effected through TV programming's new combinations of generic form and personal address. From its earliest years, TV interpellated its viewers as family members of a "new suburban unit, which had left most of its extended families and friends behind in the city" (Spigel, 39). This interpellation was manifested, not only in the direct address of commercial messages, but often implicitly in TV's genres of entertainment. While at first TV simply adapted radio shows to the screen, it soon began to recode genres in marked ways. Several genres, such as the live drama and the variety show, largely disappeared from TV by the late fifties, with the noticeable exception of *The Ed Sullivan Show*, which survived well into the 1960s. Other genres increasingly drawn from Hollywood, particularly the western and the crime show, gained air time (Oakley, 98–103). But the shows most explicitly marked by suburbanization were the situation comedies. The earliest of TV sitcoms, such as *The Goldbergs, Amos and Andy, The Honeymooners,* and *I Remember Mama*, like the radio shows from which they were adapted, typically featured working-class ethnic families living in city apartments. Yet even in these adaptations, as George Lipsitz notes, TV quickly began to replace extended family casts with nuclear families.[10] After 1955, these programs were increasingly supplanted by shows unique to television that featured class and ethnically unmarked suburban families: *Ozzie and Harriet*, *Leave It to Beaver*, and *Father Knows Best* among them. Rarely featuring nonwhite or even ethnically marked characters, and keeping the world of work offscreen, these shows recast the sit-com in the very image that TV broadly ascribed to its viewers: the classless and raceless family consumer unit of the suburbs. Other genres (comedy-variety, drama series, drama anthology, and westerns) remained popular, of course, but the new suburban sit-coms steadily gained among the very audience that it purported to represent.

This transition I have been describing, from radio to television networks, represents one of the crucial preconditions for the rise of rock 'n' roll. Its determining power concerns both the fate of radio and television during the fifties. Radio, losing possession of its national broadcast audience, gradually found its way into a new business of regional musical entertainment. Even as TV brought an end to network radio by appropriating its national advertising base, nonnetwork (independent) radio, as Reebee Garofalo observes,

> emerged as an effective medium for local advertisers, and it did so at a time when the number of radio stations in the United States had doubled from about 1,000 in 1946 to about 2,000 in 1948. Eventually the most successful independent radio outlets pushed aside the more staid network stations and cemented a reciprocal arrangement with record companies that has defined the music industry ever since: inexpensive programming in return for free promotion. (86)

This postwar arrangement between radio and record companies grew not only from the push of television, but also the pull of technological innovations in recording technology. In 1948, the year of the first full-scale national TV broadcasts, record companies developed the 33 and 45 rpm vinyl record formats. Far cheaper than the 78, and possessing much better sound quality, these new technologies made discs the first affordable medium for private ownership of recorded music.[11] In even less time than it took TV to supplant radio, the music industry made its own switch to this new commodity form. Whereas in the age of Tin Pan Alley, the music industry had sold sheet music, now it began to sell records, which, because of radio's rapidly evolving situation, it could increasingly promote on the air.

What I wish to emphasize is that, like network television, the new record/radio media alliance also hitched its fortunes to the suburban boom. Many writers have noted that, during the Second World War, numerous local radio stations opened up in city centers around the country (a fact I will return to in my discussion of rhythm and blues). Like the movie industry, whose theaters were also typically located downtown, radio faced a situation after the war in which white middle- and working-class people embarked on a mass exodus from the cities to the suburbs. The financial risk, however, was of a substantially different order for the two media. Movie theaters were directly threatened by the possibility that suburbanites might forego an excursion to town in favor of staying at home to watch "free" family entertainment on TV. As a broadcast medium, though, radio possessed the reach it needed to tap suburban audiences if it could only attract them with the right programming.

Radio succeeded in reaching a suburban audience in the fifties largely by pursuing avenues of interest and desire ruled out in the forms of TV entertainment. These avenues might be described in the following way. First, where network television defined its audience as national in scope—but at the same time conceived this nation as suburban from one end to the other—independent radio could profit from its local character, its broadcast radius's ability to define a differential regional geography that included a city center and outlying rural areas as well as the new suburbs. Radio, therefore, possessed a capacity (less possible on TV's national networks) to locate suburbs imaginatively in a relational context of geographical difference.

Speaking broadly, one might say that radio appealed to suburban interests that extended beyond dwelling at home or seeing oneself reflected in the suburban American family. If suburbia defined itself as a zone of unmarked domesticity that was neither rural nor urban, and that contained neither class nor racial difference, then radio potentially offered suburbanites access to other places that *were* rural or urban, that did contain class and racial difference, and that, from a suburban point of view, might sound nondomestic. Radio, to put this in other words, became a particularly promising medium for appealing to a dystopic, dissatisfied suburban imaginary that was eager to hear the sounds of places outside itself.

This approach to suburbanizing local radio programming was especially easy to realize in musical entertainment for the simple reason that the record companies with which new local radio stations began dealing had become increasingly diverse. The inexpensive sound media of the 33 rpm record and especially the 45 offered strong profits for start-up record companies while requiring comparatively low level of capitalization. As a result, the 1940s and 1950s saw considerable growth in small-label companies that avoided direct competition with the major labels (Columbia, Victor, and Decca) by recording what was then considered the "specialty music" of country and R & B. These companies grew increasingly eager to publicize their sounds on the radio just as local radio stations began to explore strategies for tapping suburban audiences (Garofalo, 84–85).

Unleashing Leisure: Youth and the Ideology of Free Time

As attested by the history of rock 'n' roll, it was to suburban teenagers that these sounds ultimately made their appeal. I will return shortly to the nature of these sounds, as well as how (and why) they came to signify for and in suburbia. But first, I want to consider why the dystopic side of suburbia's split vision, the one I will call the suburban counterimaginary, found its fullest expression within youth culture. The intimate connection between nondomestic visions of leisure and the tropes of youthful rebellion that are the subject of this book was no less important a condition for rock 'n' roll's historical possibility than television's takeover of radio's national network.

In chapter 1 I discussed the role of leisure in shaping the politics of postwar youth culture. Leisure, I noted, has long served as a means of negotiating the contradictions between the individual freedom of liberal modernity and the disciplining of labor under capitalism. The clash between the individual's right to liberty and capitalism's tendency to subordinate and discipline wage laborers achieved an ideological accommodation through the binarization of labor and leisure, or work and play. According to the logic of this structure, the workplace became the scene of economic necessity, of mandated toil and subjection where one must do as others tell you to do. The hours outside the workplace, in compensation, became elevated as the zone of liberated time—of leisure—in which the individual realizes him/herself through a personal pursuit of happiness.

This historic resolution, as I have suggested, became increasingly problematic with emergence of a Fordist system of mass consumption, which aimed to articulate leisure time with the commodities produced by the Taylorized factory. As Fordism increasingly subordinated leisure to the consumption of these standardized mass products, its viability as a zone of freedom diminished. This is not to say that consumerism as an ideology has not had considerable success in presenting shopping and consuming as a modern form of freedom. Rather, the point is that the standardization of Fordist capitalism's suburban commodities—hence the perception that freedom to buy the same things and live the same way might not be freedom after all—greatly undermined the reconciliation of liberalism and capitalism. The topic of this book is, in an important respect, about the age-based resolution to this postwar ideological dilemma. The Cold War, I have argued, by inciting youth culture to incorporate a thematics of rebellion, exempted teenage consumption from the stigma of deindividualization associated with standardized consumption. Presenting itself as an autonomous, and potentially dissenting mode of consumption—even within suburbia—youth culture gained ideological currency as a freer form of leisure than that found in parental suburban culture.

Rock criticism has implicitly concerned itself with this Fordist privileging of youthful leisure ever since Simon Frith first suggested in his groundbreaking book, *Sound Effects*, that youths (from the 1920s onward) have come to appear freer than adults. Frith suggested that youth has come to "symbolize leisure, to embody good times" in a way that renders young people as archetypical of the "problems of capitalist freedom and constraint" (201). The specifically Fordist problems of freedom and constraint, I would argue, played out in such a way that constraint became the chief issue surrounding adult consumption (was it not free enough?), while freedom became the concern regarding youthful consumption (did its autonomy go too far?). As suburbanization proceeded in the 1950s, "adult constraint," the ideological problem of standardized leisure, fell increasingly under the sign of domesticity, while youthful freedom, the complementary issue of nonstandard or rebellious leisure were conflated with the nondomestic, potentially wild pursuits of happiness—"entertainment" to the culture industry, and "kicks" in hipster lingo.

As I will show in the next chapter, this Fordist conflation of standardization and domestication played a major part in the ideological formations of postwar gender arrangements. For now, I want to focus on the point that it allowed youth—as a Cold War figure for dissent—to embody wildness—individual freedom from the constraints of standardized domestication. Adult consumption, located within the Fordist unit of the family and the space of the suburban home, came to be constituted as the domestic opposite of wilder forms of consumption, bonding youth to one another outside of home and family.

This binary of domestic versus youthful modes of consumption became an important means through which the split vision of suburbia was articulated. Familial happiness was closely associated with suburbia as a visionary hybrid of the city and the country. At the same time, suburbia also threatened to appear not as the achievement of personal happiness but rather as the fatal realization of mass values and consumer standardization. An alternative, youthful vision of happiness, propelled by a desire to be somewhere other than the wasteland of suburbia, both countered and exorcised this feared unfreedom of adult consumption. A young person, living in apparent dissatisfaction with suburban domesticity, fulfilled the desire of Cold War nationalism. Such a youth became the exemplary American individualist who refuses to submit to Fordist standardization. The rebellious thematics of suburban youth culture, in short, allowed suburbia, primarily a space of domesticity, to incorporate into itself a desire for the repudiation of domesticity—thereby creating its split vision—without ever having to dissolve itself.

For the same reasons that youth culture became identified with the dystopic side of suburbia's split vision, I would suggest that it also became identified with radio and its nondomestic possibilities, over and against television. I do not mean by this to say that young people did not watch plenty of television but rather that TV usually counted them as family members sharing the norms of the suburban imaginary. Radio, by contrast, created opportunities for teenagers to create a distinct youth culture. Both mobile and transistorized, radio offered entertainment to suburban youth enjoyable within the context of peer rather than family relations.

The one crucial exception to this tendency was found in the TV genre of the music show, itself usually directly adapted from a radio show. In the early to mid-fifties, during the early period of TV programming flux, this genre accommodated several successful regional teen dance and performance programs that would feed into the rock 'n' roll phenomenon: among them Alan Freed's *Big Beat* and Paul Whiteman's *TV-Teen Club*.[12] With the consolidation of national broadcasting by 1956, however, *American Bandstand* would displace these various local programs, to become perhaps the one remaining TV show where the countersuburban imaginary would reign supreme.

American Bandstand, though it proved successful, was marked by the difficulties of incorporating rock 'n' roll into the scene of national television. It was offered as a mainstream substitute for its more openly countersuburban predecessors, most especially the controversial Alan Freed show.

3. Dori and her friend watch Alan Freed's TV show *Big Beat* with Dad in *Rock! Rock! Rock!* (Vanguard, 1956).

To facilitate its acceptability to the entire family, host Dick Clark enforced strict rules of behavior on its teen dancers, including a conservative dress code and closely regulated dance movements.[13] In the end, *American Bandstand* would become a "segregated" space in the televisual landscape, the one tolerated locale where the sound of rock 'n' roll heard on the radio might be visually performed within the suburban home. By contrast, radio facilitated with relative ease the portable, nonfamilial spaces to be improvised by youth culture outdoors, in cars, garages, parks, at school, and elsewhere. By the mid-fifties then, developments in youth culture, radio, popular music, a countersuburban imaginary, and ideologies of undomesticated leisure were all converging on conditions that would make rock 'n' roll become possible.

Countersuburban Sounds: Rock 'n' Roll as the Imagined Elsewhere

If radio's reorganization as nondomestic medium was one precondition for rock 'n' roll, and youth's ideological claim on freedom yet another, then the final major precondition was the music available on the early fifties radio dial. Radio created opportunities for nonfamilial leisure in the suburbs; it linked undomesticity to youth culture in particular, but it accomplished all this by broadcasting sounds that evoked nonsuburban landscapes — either urban or rural — through which suburban youth might imaginatively displace themselves. Rock 'n' roll was less a distinct style than a naming process through which post-network radio condensed together different kinds of music, and repackaged them as the sound of suburban youth culture.

Earlier, I named rhythm and blues and country as the two most commonly cited musical sources for rock 'n' roll. I would suggest that these musics derived their potential for appropriation as — their appropriateness for — suburban culture from their relationships to mid-twentieth-century shifts in the labor/leisure binary.[14] Both "country" and "rhythm and blues," as it happens, were relatively new categories in the 1950s for the music industry. Rural, white working-class music had been supplied with a range of different names from the 1920s on, including folk, hillbilly, and country and western. *Billboard*, the music industry's trade magazine, began tracking this music in the mid-thirties on its disdainfully named "hillbilly chart," a popularity list added to the older "pop chart" that had always featured commercially mainstream Tin Pan Alley styles. In the forties, *Billboard* also added a so-called "race chart" for tracking the gamut of African American music. The origins of rock 'n' roll are often traced to what Philip Ennis has called the aligning of these "three streams" of postwar pop music, which he documents through the outburst of "crossover" songs in the mid-fifties, when hits from the two other charts found their way onto *Billboard*'s pop list.[15]

By then, *Billboard* had renamed its two newer charts for reasons reflecting changed conditions, both musical and extramusical. The term "rhythm and blues" had already begun to circulate during the wartime years, when a generation of blues musicians who had moved from south to north (and west) up-tempoed and even electrified their songs. By 1948, their music had become so popular among urbanizing African American audiences that, when *Billboard* finally renamed its "race chart," it chose "rhythm and blues" as the new title. Almost simultaneously, *Billboard* renamed its "hillbilly chart" the "country chart." Motivations for these two name changes are complex, but broadly speaking they concerned gains in practical and symbolic power that working-class and black people achieved during the war, a moment when the military effort could not take them for granted, leading the state to solicit their patriotism by promoting racial and class pride and self-respect. Too, the charts' new titles were influenced by the fact that both kinds of music were finding an increasingly diverse audience in the wake of rapid wartime population movements. The name changes worked both to acknowledge and accommodate this diversification.

The new names, "R & B" and "country," reflected not only gains in practical power for the black and white working-class people, nor just the broadening of each music's respective audiences, but also changes in musical styles that conveyed a greater confidence in their cultural capital. The event in country music leading up to the 1948 *Billboard* renaming was the emergence of honky-tonk, a style that led country away from a folk orientation and toward an electrified sound associated with roadhouse entertainment. Richard Peterson traces honky-tonk back to Prohibition-era roadhouses on county lines, where alcohol was less easily policed than in town. Crowded, noisy venues led bands to experiment with amplified sounds. Entertaining in a rowdy male space, the honky-tonk band also developed a graphic style of first-person narration far more tied to male sexual exploits than earlier modes of country music. Peterson notes that the traditional figures of the geezer and hillbilly, already fading since the 1920s, had been giving way to a more westernized image of the cowboy performer, such as Jimmie Rodgers or even Gene Autry (Peterson, 55–93). Honky-tonk only gained momentum during and after the war years, selling records to "juke joints" and winning larger audiences no longer necessarily restricted to rural regions. Its new cowboy figure, best exemplified by Hank Williams, now played speeded-up electric instruments and plied sexual innuendo in his songs, removing country music from stories of homestead nostalgia—of leisure at the scene of traditional domesticity—and cultivating instead the mobile, playful tales of the ramblin' man at the roadhouse.

A black, urban contemporary of honky-tonk, rhythm and blues similarly aimed to electrify and upbeat the (rural blues) music out of which it was emerging. Nelson George has even used the term "rhythm and blues" as an epochal label for the wartime and postwar African American condition, claiming that the term carried both a musical and a socioeconomic meaning. Regarding the former, George calls R & B "a synthesis of black musical genres—gospel, big-band swing, blues—that, along with a new technology, specifically the popularization of the electric bass, produced a propulsive, spirited brand of popular music" (xiii). In addition to George's sonal description here, we might also observe that rhythm and blues intensified the commodification of black popular culture. The new markets for African American pop music in northern and western cities became increasingly profitable during the forties, which in turn led to a proliferation of R & B recording labels (including Chess, Modern, and Imperial), record stores (especially following the advent of the 45 and 33), and local radio stations.

For George, R & B connoted the opportune wartime migration of African Americans "from the fields of the South for the factories of the North" as well as its aftermath in civil rights. R & B therefore delineates a period in African American history (from the forties till perhaps the seventies) marked by political optimism, energy, and hopefulness (George, xiii). Artists such as Muddy Waters, B. B. King, and Louis Jordan, but also Fats Domino (who began his career as an R & B musician, and only later became a rock 'n' roller), developed a new musical formation that helped to revise the meaning of blackness in a new, post-depression-era, urban commodity culture. R & B reworked a long-standing romantic role of music in African American culture, from slavery onward, as the symbolic expression of nighttime's freedom over and against the bondage of the day. Yet R & B is best understood less as a continuation than as a reappropriation of earlier moments in African American musical culture. Earlier forms of music (blues, shout, swing, and gospel) were made to speak to the new historical conditions, but only by a process of transformation in which their connotations were reassigned to a context of industrial wage labor and commodified leisure.

Developed in industrial centers, in places where money earned could be easily spent for entertainment as well as necessities, and during a world war in which mass unemployment had given way to the mass enlisting of the populace, R & B evoked an optimistic sense of expanding freedom through a specific set of ideologemes: signs with which it constituted an imaginative relationship to wartime social conditions. Deploying industrial binaries, such as necessary labor versus elective leisure and daily tedium versus nighttime entertainment, R & B generated celebrative stories about spending one's paycheck, enjoying the town on evenings and weekends, and thrilling to personal romances of love and lovemaking that replayed (as a story within a story) the framing romance of the freedom of leisure time itself. R & B, as I'm describing it here, invoked the context of a factory production system; it also strongly associated leisure with a form of commodity consumption and discretionary spending. However, the informing context for this consumption differed noticeably from the suburban mode that would emerge after the war. Most obviously, R & B leisure was not organized around domestic space or family life, but rather upon the entree of the individual (usually but not always a man) "stepping out" into the scene of urban nightlife. Its social network concerns friends and lovers (past, present, or future), rarely husbands, wives, parents, or children. The consumer items with which it is associated are not durable home goods but more transient commodities. The world in which it located itself was not private but public, not stationary but fluid and shifting.

The central ideologemes of R & B, in short, worked to imagine an urban (rather than a suburban) arena of industrial leisure. R & B may still be termed a quasi- or proto-Fordist musical form insofar as its social context was indebted to higher wages and employment due to the government's wartime intervention into the economy. Its entertainment value evoked a fantastic and utopic setting, a sensuous world of after-hour passions made possible by the revved-up economy. Yet, given that much of wartime production was geared toward the war effort, the mode of consumption that R & B celebrated was not (and did not need to be) matched to industrial output. Moreover, the wartime era was one of ongoing shortages for the working-class civilian population. No doubt, most fans of R & B lived arduous lives, sharing overpriced city apartments with their extended families. Still, wages did rise during the war in ways that encouraged an R & B imagination of free time as liberating the listener from these sorts of blues. The utopic imagination of R & B led its audience away from daytime worries and toward the thrilling joys and sorrows that the nighttime city had to offer.

I want to consider Fats Domino's version of this sound of leisure since, as someone who straddled the divide between R & B and rock 'n' roll, he produced a music that allows us to consider how the R & B fantasy of free time both facilitated rock 'n' roll and was in turn reworked by it. Domino was a musician whose style and career were clearly established in R & B. A creole Louisianan whose first name was actually Antoine and whose first language was French, Domino began playing boogie-woogie style piano in mid-forties New Orleans with the David Barthelemew Band. By 1949, Domino had won national success as an R & B artist on the independent Imperial label.

In both its playful energy and narrative codes, Fats Domino's music belongs squarely within the formation of R & B as I've described it. In songs such as "Blue Monday," for example, Domino sings about surviving the tedium of the week for the sake of the joys of the weekend. "Blue Monday, how I hate Blue Monday," Domino starts out, "Got to work like a slave all day" and all week long, until

> Saturday mornin', oh Saturday mornin'
> All my tiredness has gone away
> Got my money and my honey
> And I'm out on the stand to play.

Sunday is devoted to recovering from all the fun: "But I've got to get my rest / 'Cause Monday is a mess." In a song like "Blue Monday," that great time for which one lives might well be called "rhythm and blues," that stretch of the weekend where one can dance, spend, make love, and enjoy life, even if that joy takes the form of the blues, of love pain. Domino's famous rendition of "Blueberry Hill," for example, recalls the bittersweet memory of one magic night's "thrill," spent with his girl. And though her vows of fidelity were "never to be," Domino sings,

> You're part of me still
> For you were my thrill
> On Blueberry Hill.

Even in moments of pain or tedium, the singer of R & B carries these memories of thrill, fun, and freedom. More typically though, up-tempo rhythm and blues tended to sing about the actual high or "thrill" itself (and not just its memory), something Domino also took up in such songs as "I'm Ready [to Rock 'n' Roll All Night]" or "The Big Beat."

Though Domino might seem a quintessential rhythm-and-blues artist, nevertheless, in 1955, his music was reclassified by the musical marketplace as rock 'n' roll, about seven years after the suburban boom had begun in earnest. Unlike slightly younger musicians such as Little Richard or Presley, Domino, twenty-seven years old in that year and nicknamed the "Fat Man," was no obvious teen idol, nor had he obviously altered anything in his musical style to attract a youth audience.[16] Suburban teenagers, it seems, were interested in Domino's "straight-up" style of R & B. Before inquiring what difference the category of rock 'n' roll made, it is worth considering this initial suburban youth desire for the sound of rhythm and blues.

Earlier, I spoke of a split vision of suburbia, in which the dystopic vision of a sterile wasteland became increasingly aligned with youth culture. Whereas the utopic vision endorsed a standardized vision of domestic happiness, its dystopic negation tended to repudiate domestication as entrapment, expressing instead an antidomestic counterdesire for the extrasuburban. Within the countersuburban imaginary of a suburban teen audience, a song such as Fats Domino's "Blue Monday" conveyed an alternative to suburban family leisure that, by comparison, sounded like genuinely free time. In "Blue Monday" one finds freedom from work not at home but at the dance hall, "playing on the stand" with one's money and one's honey. As a place to rest up from all the fun, home is just fine in Domino's song. But for the singer, the weekend might be as blue as the workweek if one didn't leave home to seek out thrills (on Blueberry Hill, on the stand, or somewhere else).

In Domino's song, home is merely a way station between work and the fantasy space of play. To countersuburban ears, however, home became suburbia itself writ large, and Domino's play world a fantasy of leisure beyond family life. And to the extent that domestication became synonymous with staying at home, Domino intoned for suburbia a zone of freedom beyond domesticity. To put this another way, as R & B, Domino's music signified the energy of the upbeat black city enjoying its free time after work. As rock 'n' roll, the same music continued to signify the leisure of the black city, but now implicitly entered into a relation of difference from the white suburban home.

It is instructive to consider the broad similarities between how Domino's R & B and Bill Haley's country sounds were appropriated into rock 'n' roll. Rock 'n' roll's origin is often dated back to Bill Haley's "Rock around the Clock," which conquered the pop charts in 1955 only after it appeared in the film *Blackboard Jungle*. If so, then it is striking that the popularization of rock 'n' roll was triggered by the film's association of Haley's sound with juvenile delinquency (as the next chapter will discuss in detail). Haley, like Domino, was a performer whose career (as a "western swing" country bandleader) predates rock 'n' roll.[17] Like Domino's "Blue Monday," Haley's "Rock around the Clock" reached suburban teenagers by conveying a nondomestic, working-class form of leisure that could be appropriated by a countersuburban imaginary.[18] As George Lipsitz notes, Haley's song converts the clock governing blue-collar labor into an icon of leisure in which it measures out "doses of pleasure instead of units of labor" (113). To countersuburban ears, however, Haley's rocking timepiece might have contrasted with the clock at home, where one is stuck with nowhere to go and nothing to do. Unlike the slow-ticking, laborious pace of time in either the factory or the suburban home, when Haley and his listener rock, clock time whizzes by:

> One, two, three o'clock, four o'clock rock
> Five, six, seven o'clock, eight o'clock rock
> Nine, ten, eleven o'clock, twelve o'clock rock
> We're gonna rock around the clock tonight.

Haley expresses a wild-eyed fantasy about a cyclical, never-ending dance party, complete with a snare drum backbeat to punctuate the singer's rapid announcements. Neither hours at work, at home, nor even in sleep need intrude on the cyclical, self-enclosed universe of emancipated leisure that "Rock around the Clock" projects. Yet by leaving its grinding clock-time counterpart unnamed, "Rock around the Clock" invites the listener to choose their own location for the tedium against which the song poses its liberatory fantasy; the constraints of factory work or of suburban familial leisure function equally well as the opposite of rocking and rolling.

Though Haley mixed styles, drawing from R & B and even big band sounds, he was primarily an up-tempo country-and-western artist, evoking not so much the hop of the ethnic city as a western-swing country dance somewhere in Kansas or Texas. Yet, as the next chapter discusses, *Blackboard Jungle* linked "Rock around the Clock" to a multiracial cityscape in the Bronx. A considerable amount of slippage, one might say, took place in the early and mid-fifties between city and country as counterimaginary landscapes for suburbia. For all that one might expect popular music to maintain sharp distinctions between city and country sounds, in rock 'n' roll it seems one could scroll back and forth between them (and within them) as sheer variety of what I might call countersuburban sounds.[19] The R & B energy of the upbeat black city, therefore, was blurred in with the energy of other landscapes, such as those associated with the street talkers of black doo-wop, the midwestern and Texan big band sounds favored by Bill Haley, country guitar or honky-tonk piano, and so forth.

This fusing of sounds and spaces, especially across lines of race, was especially evident in the country strain of rock 'n' roll. Just as certain black artists remained largely identified with R & B (Muddy Waters and B. B. King, for instance) while others transitioned into rock 'n' rollers (Fats Domino, but also Little Richard and Chuck Berry), so too a distinction developed between country artists who crossed over into rock 'n' roll (Jerry Lee Lewis, Elvis Presley, Carl Perkins, for instance) and those who did not (Ernest Tubbs, Johnny Cash). Those who did were termed "rockabilly" artists, a name that expressed the insertion of "hillbilly" sounds and scenarios into an affectively charged topographic relationship with suburbia. Rockabilly artists also, however, drew heavily on R & B, blackening their music, often through evocations of wild male sexuality, that created tension between them and established country music.

Jerry Lee Lewis represents a particularly clear example of someone whose status as rock 'n' roll star was fashioned out of such a sexualized blending of honky-tonk and R & B sounds aimed at a youth audience. Born to a working-class Louisianan family (and nicknamed "the killer"), Lewis played the sound of wildness more vividly than any other early rocker, with the possible exception of Little Richard. Lewis consistently sings about desire as an uncontrollable (hence undomesticatable) force that he can only convey through his frenzied pacing. "Whole Lotta Shakin' Goin' On," in its famous couplet, "Well I said come over baby, we got chicken in the barn / Whose barn, what barn, my barn!!" turns the country farm into a place of double-entendres, blurring the idea of a barn party (and alluding perhaps to the nationwide radio barn dances of the 1930s and 1940s) into a sexual escapade:

> Now let's get real low one time now, Shake baby shake
> All you gotta do honey is kinda stand in one spot
> Wiggle around just a little bit

Meanwhile, "Great Balls of Fire" featured the seemingly innocent rural exclamation "Goodness gracious" only in order to describe the singer's thrill at being overwhelmed by passion:

> I chew my nails and I twiddle my thumbs
> I'm real nervous, but it sure is fun
> Come on baby, drive me crazy
> Goodness, gracious, great balls of fire!!

Lewis's songs succeeded in cutting across the various possible audiences—rural, urban, and suburban—perhaps more successfully than any other performer. Both "Whole Lotta Shakin'" and "Great Balls of Fire" hit number one on all three of the *Billboard* charts: pop, R & B, and country. Yet Lewis was rarely explicit about his ability to reach out from his base in country and R & B audiences to tap a suburban listenership. Only in the song "High School Confidential," does a Jerry Lee Lewis song fold its youth culture value back into itself, by relocating its blurring of sex and dancing into a high school party.[20] All the same, Lewis's sound deploys an erotics hillbilly wildness to stand outside and against suburban. In becoming a staple of suburban teen leisure activity, Lewis-style rock 'n' roll thereby invested (whether the songs acknowledged it or not) teen leisure with the codes of the honky-tonk sexcapade.

Little Richard, meanwhile, as an R & B counterpart to Jerry Lee Lewis, evoked a queerer sexual wildness in his exuberant, up-tempo sound, playfully costumed persona, and in his open lyrical celebration of sex. On the one hand, Little Richard's hits had one foot in the same R & B evocation of wartime leisure as the somewhat older Domino, though at an even greater speed. "Rip It Up," for example, is a fast-paced dance number premised on the same weekend fantasy as "Blue Monday":

> Saturday night and I just got paid
> I'm a fool about my money, don't try to save.
> My heart says "go go, have a time"
> Saturday night and I'm feelin' fine.

But in the chorus that follows, "Rip It Up" immediately turns toward the conflation of dance and sex for which rock 'n' roll (beginning with its name) became controversial:

> I'm gonna rock it up, *whoo*
> Rip it up
> I'm gonna shake it up
> Gonna ball it up.

The most flamboyant gender-bender of the early rockers, Little Richard consistently celebrated in his biggest hits ("Tutti-Frutti," "Good Golly, Miss Molly," and "Long Tall Sally," among others) the manic power of the sexual encounter as subversive fun, "rocking" and "balling" as a furtive, exhilarating escape from the sober expectations of family life often personified in his songs (by "Mama" in "Good Golly, Miss Molly," "Aunt Mary" in "Long Tall Sally"). As Glenn Altschuler notes, while Little Richard's feminized performance style connoted gay personality, it also thereby diffused the potential threat posed by a black man's openly sexual appeal to white girl fans (60–61). Little Richard comically staged sex as resistive play, but in various degrees of indirection. The original refrain "Tutti-Frutti, Good Booty," for instance, became in the recorded version of Richard's hit, "Tutti-Frutti, Aw-Rootie," while the bawdy lines "If it don't fit / don't force it. / You can grease it, / make it easy" became "I got a gal named Daisy. / She almost drive me crazy." The words were perhaps less important than the rawness of Richard's screaming voice. And if even this version was too forward, one could soon hear a thoroughly sanitized cover by Pat Boone

(Boone's recording quickly went gold, but this in turn spurred further sales of Little Richard's hit).[21] Even in its most cleaned-up versions, however, Little Richard's fantasy of sexual fun as antidomestic escape remained easy enough to discern and enjoy.

Little Richard, Fats Domino, Jerry Lee Lewis, Elvis Presley (to be discussed in chapter 5), and other performers in the R & B or rockabilly mode provided suburban youth culture with a palette of imaginary tableaus through which it could consolidate a sense of leisure quite distinct from the domestic model of family entertainment exemplified by TV. How exactly these extrasuburban fantasy spaces provided an appropriate structure for suburban teen leisure, however, needs clarification. Let me therefore work through the argument with some care. The fantasies of leisure that made their way into rock 'n' roll were drawn from musical forms embedded in a variety of historical conditions, but by and large they may all be called pre- or proto-Fordist. They are typically associated with agrarian (country) or industrial (city) landscapes, both of which organize life around manual labor while leaving leisure time open as an arena not fully articulated to the production system.[22] Country, R & B, black vocal group, and other styles tended to define the sound of leisure as "free time" and often (in Simon Frith's words) as an "implicit critique of work." Unlike the leisure of adult suburbia, the leisure defined by urban and country music's fantasies of play were not perceptibly driven by an external economic need to articulate mass consumption with mass production. The ideological value of country and R & B sounds to suburban youth culture therefore lay precisely in the fact that their fantasies of leisure (in narratives of entertainment) could be used to sound out an "other" to the Fordist consumption system.

If R & B and country music provide, in their feeling for leisure, an implicit critique of work, then their appropriation as rock 'n' roll allowed youth culture, in an analogous manner, to produce an implicit critique of suburbia expressed by the pleasure of being displaced from it. Through rock 'n' roll, black city nightlife, but also the country roadhouse, the barn dance, and even the city street corner (the setting favored by vocal harmony groups) now became recoded as fantastic scenes from beyond suburbia that could sonically evoke the emerging space of suburban youth culture itself.

The Elsewhere Is Right Here: Countersuburbanizing Rock 'n' Roll

For the first few years of its public existence, rock 'n' roll may be characterized as those sounds, broadcast into the suburbs on the radio that aurally transported suburban teenagers to either urban or rural fantasy spaces of free time. By 1957, however, rock 'n' roll had begun to develop—like the suburban ideal itself—a third space of leisure's liberation from suburbia, paradoxically enough in suburban youth culture itself. On the one hand, this youth culture bore a metonymic relation to suburbia as part of and contiguous with it. Aurally, however, its rock 'n' roll sound resonated with the decidedly nonsuburban tones of urban or rural playtime. Drawn into suburbia as a means of expressing a desire to be somewhere else, these sounds came to encode youth culture itself as an "elsewhere," a space where free time was lived and enjoyed in ways that contradicted the domestic norms of suburbia at large.

Richard Aquila, in his detailed reference book on early rock 'n' roll, proposes classifying the music into three major styles: "R & B rock, country rock, and pop rock."[23] The last of these, pop rock, combined musical and lyrical elements from R & B and country with Tin Pan Alley sounds, especially for its favorite genre, the love ballad. Pop rock, on the one hand, simply extended the centuries-old connection of youth with romantic love. Yet, in invoking the postwar category of the teenager per se, it brought both youth and romantic love into the orbit of suburban consumption, reflected first and foremost in the radio consumption of the songs themselves. Purist rock aficionados, to this day, still malign the pop rock artists of the fifties— Pat Boone, Ricky Nelson, Tab Hunter, Tommy Sand, and the like—for their cleaner-cut images and their commercial Tin Pan Alley sappiness, praising instead the more "authentic" sounds of R & B and country rockers. It was these pop rockers, however, who most openly declared youth culture a countersuburban space in identitarian terms, as an imagined sovereign territory within which teenage pleasures were emancipated from the tedium and constraint of the suburban quotidian.

Pop rock artists (themselves often teenage idols) rarely acknowledged an adult presence in everyday teenage life, but instead serenaded youth culture as a protected space where romance and fun should reign unimpeded.[24] In Tommy Sand's 1957 hit, "Teenage Crush," for instance, a boy woos his beloved by begging her not to accept what adults say about young love:

> They've forgotten when they were young
> And the way they tried to be free.
> All they say is "This young generation
> Is just not the way it used to be."

With the exception of his young voice, Sand's hit, with its slow-dance tempo and full string orchestration, sounds very much like prerock Tin Pan Alley hits. The singer's appeal, however, reveals something specific to rock 'n' roll. In a song that is otherwise about a crush, Sand's digression into generational misunderstanding makes explicit an implied alignment within pop rock between teen life, desire, the acting on desire, and freedom itself. These terms are then opposed to an adult world of muted or extinguished desire, where passionate pursuit of romantic happiness and freedom is lacking. The effect in Sand's ballad is to romanticize not only one particular young love, but a generational unit of young people that—in sharing these songs—creates for itself (in the face of an older generation's animosity) a universe of feeling and desire.

Celebrations of youth culture as a third scene of freedom from suburbia (alongside the rural and urban script) were even more frequent and explicit in doo-wop or (as Gillett calls it) black vocal group music (31–34). This strain of rock 'n' roll drew from a comic, a capella genre of African American music, often set on the street, that had often concerned a (usually male) protagonist thwarted through a lack of power, money, or opportunity. The vocal group's protagonist expressed defiance and resentment, often concerning access to consumer goods, in ways that proved tremendously attractive to suburban youth. As vocal group music transitioned into the doo-wop strain of rock 'n' roll, it often became the site for songs explicitly dealing with confrontations between delinquent teenagers and the adults who aimed to "normalize" them.

Few early rock 'n' roll groups narrated these conflicts more directly than the Coasters, a group based in L.A. and New York. In a scenario strongly echoing *Blackboard Jungle*, the Coasters' well-known "Charlie Brown" comically relates the story of a troublemaker who breaks the rules constraining student behavior. The world that Charlie Brown inhabits is never specified. On the one hand, the Coasters sing in a style easily identifiable as urban black English, and about a character whose name might signal his skin color. Yet his name could just as easily identify a delinquent version of the white, middle-class Charlie Brown who figures in Charles Schultz's *Peanuts*. Wherever he is, and whatever his color, Charlie Brown smokes in the auditorium, writes on the walls, throws spitballs, and generally goofs around.

The song plays on a call and response between a lead singer, who cleverly describes Charlie Brown's antics, and a chorus that names him to the accompaniment of a brassy band whose sound expresses the rebellious fun. In the final verse, the song even veers into a direct face-off with the teacher:

> Who walks in the classroom, cool and slow?
> Who calls the English teacher Daddy-O?
> Charlie Brown, he's a clown.

What's funny about Charlie Brown for the singer is presumably the frivolity of his resistance. For all his bravado, the bad boy must inevitably get in trouble, which he will then deny by feigning confusion in his low-pitched, wounded voice: "Why's everybody always picking on me?" Yet as a clown Charlie Brown adds the only life to what is otherwise a sterile institution devoted to the earnest ethics of work and study. His smoke, spitballs, and out-of-placeness distinguish him from his fellow students, much as the lead singer stands out against the chorus. Itself comedic, "Charlie Brown" draws on a desire to be the individualized clown who playfully declines the regimentation of school.

The conflict between a work and a play ethic is made even more explicit in "Yakkety Yak," another famous hit by the Coasters. This time, generational conflict centers not on teacher and student in school, but on parent and child at home:

> Take out the papers and the trash
> Or you don't get no spendin' cash.
> If you don't scrub that kitchen floor
> You ain't gonna rock and roll no more.
> Yakkety yak (don't talk back).

Here household chores become the opposite of rock 'n' roll, the leisure activity par excellence of a "spendin'" teenager with discretionary income. "Yakkety Yak" is sung satirically in the voice of the authoritarian father, who aims to inculcate in his kid a respect for hard work, and a sober sense that money must be earned. Yet the father's words swing to a fast-paced, playful rockin' rhythm that evokes the very fun to which his child hopes to escape. So too does the festive response of the sax to the father's admonitions, itself a stand-in for the teenager's backtalk. Paternal instruction thus unexpectedly returns one to rock 'n' roll, the object of the teenager's desire, the site of release from these chores, which the song moreover explicitly links to delinquent trouble:

Don't you give me no dirty looks.
Your father's hip; he knows what cooks.
Just tell your hoodlum friend outside
You ain't got time to take a ride.

Dad has the lingo down, meaning he knows what his kid does with his free time, what rock 'n' roll is all about, what this space of teen autonomy really means (defiance of the law, criminality). Since suburban dads were not exactly hipsters, likely to know "what cooks," "Yakkety Yak" suggests a setting far from suburbia, somewhere on the city street. Nevertheless, the familial home and its attendant chores were hardly unfamiliar to the song's suburban listeners. Like "Charlie Brown," "Yakkety Yak" achieved a certain blurring of locations that allowed suburban teenagers to be imaginatively partnered with inner-city youth as escapees from parental mandates. "Yakkety Yak" offers suburban teenagers a chance to be in on a secret, namely the imaginative collaboration of rock 'n' roll with illicit forms of freedom (the hoodlum friends) that would no doubt horrify their parents. Like the hapless "Charlie Brown," the kid in "Yakkety Yak" points the listener toward a desire to "talk back" even while humorously implying the foolishness of direct generational confrontation.

Compared to the other strains of rock 'n' roll, relatively few rockabilly artists sang self-consciously about teenage leisure in suburbia (working instead through their country settings). One significant exception, however, was Eddie Cochran, someone who, like the Coasters, possessed a comic sensibility. As someone whose family came from rural Oklahoma, but who moved to southern California as an adolescent, Cochran began his short career as a suburban teenager, using country music to develop a sound that could be marketed within the milieu of his upbringing. Cochran began his career as part of a "fraternal" duo, performing in the California country music circuit (at festivals with such names as Hometown Jamboree or Town Hall Party). Greatly impressed by the look and sound used by Elvis Presley to break out of country into the broad youth market, Cochran soon split up with his (more country-oriented) partner and began gearing his music to a rock 'n' roll market. Cochran adopted much of Presley's style, including a good dose of R & B. Far more explicitly than Presley himself, however, Cochran set the micronarratives of his songs within teen suburbia.

Where the setting of the dancing utopia is left ambiguous in Bill Haley's "Rock around the Clock," for instance, in Cochran's "Teenage Heaven" the space of pure happiness and freedom becomes directly a province of youth-culture imaginative passions. Somewhat self-mockingly, "Teenage Heaven" materializes the fantasy space of unimpeded youthful fun by way of a wish list implicit in much of fifties rock 'n' roll:

> I want a house with a pool
> Shorter hours in school
> And a room with my own vitaphone
> I want to stay up all night
> See the big city lights
> No more troubles, no more worries at home
> Just give me some time on my hands
> I want to make my own other plans
> Yah, I want my own coup de ville
> make my dad pay the bill
> Yah man that's heaven to me.

On first glance, it might not be clear what differentiates "teenage heaven" from the suburban vision of mainstream consumer culture. The singer's desires (true to Lawrence Grossberg's admonition) seem very much in line with postwar Fordism, aiming at suburban affluence in the form of a large home and fancy car. Yet there are moments when the song swerves away from these meanings toward a longing for something else. "Teenage Heaven," to begin with, is sung to a hipped-up version of the tune for "Home on the Range." Curiously, then, it quotes an old-school mode of country domesticity that poses an ironic contrast to the ostentatious home of "teenage heaven." Even setting aside Cochran's evident self-parody, it is important to see that his "teenage heaven" clings to a dual fantasy of escape, from both the suburban restrictions on adult and teen life respectively. To begin with, the heaven in question resembles an R & B world in which the singer is free to stay up all night long, playing in the city. Unlike the suburban vision of adult happiness, the singer's desires are not directed toward marriage, maturity, and a life of domestic bliss in his fancy home. Rather, the singer aspires to dodge the "troubles" and "worries" of home life, and pursue instead his "other plans" of playful nightlife. In this respect "teenage heaven" resembles not so much suburban adulthood as it does rocking around the clock with Bill Haley.

Moreover, "Teenage Heaven" implies an "actual existing" world of teen restraint that has summoned up this fantasy of heaven in the first place. By reading backward from the singer's "wants," it becomes evident how the song presumes the experience of teenhood: always fewer goodies than one wants, to be sure, but also too many hours in school, a restrictive bedtime, a general shortage of free time. A teenager also can't get to town, perhaps being stuck at home, where he or she apparently endures a barrage of familial troubles and worries. If youth culture expresses, in Cochran's song as in so many other songs, a dream of freedom, then it also attests to a considerable gap between that dream and the reality of its desiring teenager.

This posited gap between the dream of youth culture and the realities of teenhood serves the explicit subject of Cochran's single most famous rock 'n' roll song, "Summertime Blues." Sung from the perspective of a teenager who's "a-workin' all summer just a-trying to earn a dollar," "Summertime Blues" comically bemoans the singer's disappointments at trying to free up time for a date with his baby. Either the boss makes him work late, or his parents deny him the car. Denied time and transportation, the singer never finds what rock 'n' roll promises, namely his bit of teenage heaven, but is stuck instead with the plain old blues. In typical tongue-in-cheek, Cochran imagines politicizing this injustice:

> It's gonna take two weeks for I have my vacation,
> I'm gonna take my problem to the United Nations.
> Well I told my congressman and he said, quote:
> "I'd like to help you son but you're too young to vote"
> Sometimes I wonder what I'm a gonna do,
> But there ain't no cure for the Summertime Blues.

Playful though it is, "Summertime Blues" invests teenage leisure with ideological weight. Summertime is the equivalent of the R & B weekend or the country night at the roadhouse, yet this song presents its failure as a time of freely chosen pleasures. Instead, summer exacts extra hours of work, arbitrary parental restriction, and even a rebuff from one's deep-voiced political representative. In the world of this song, the singer's rights as a teenager (to enjoy summertime as a utopic space) cannot be secured precisely *because* a teenager's rights are not acknowledged. To the extent that these pleasures are thrilled to in other songs—by Little Richard, Jerry Lee Lewis, Elvis Presley, and so forth—they become, in Cochran's one big hit, illicit pleasures whose maintenance as right will require generational struggle: "I'm a-gonna raise a fuss I'm a-gonna raise a holler," advises the singer in the song's opening line.

School Day: The Cultural Work and Play of Rock 'n' Roll

For all their stylistic differences, the subgenres I have just described—pop rock, vocal group, and teenified rockabilly—shared a common mode of address. All three named their suburban teen audience, hailing them as the citizens of a utopically free and passionate youth culture. Eddie Cochran, the Coasters, and even Tommy Sand all invested youth culture with the sounds of desire for play and passion, over and against the drudgery of school, of home, of work, and more broadly of suburbia itself. If the setting and subject of this desire are new, its structure should already be familiar, for it reiterates the celebration of leisure time, based upon the proletarian binary of work and play, already found in the R & B and country rock of Fats Domino, Bill Haley, Jerry Lee Lewis, and others. These two sets of binaries are neither identical nor straightforwardly equivalent. They do, however, share a contingent resemblance whose basis needs to be spelled out.

I want to approach the question of their connection by way of one final case study, the music of Chuck Berry. Of all the rock 'n' rollers of the fifties nobody was more self-conscious or effective than Berry in scripting teen leisure according to country and R & B's dramas of free time. A close look at his work may therefore illuminate the valence of early rock 'n' roll's ideological work, regarding both its relationship to the musics out of which it was composed, as well as its imaginative position vis-à-vis suburbia. Berry is a performer whose music straddled the three styles of early rock 'n' roll offered by Aquila: R & B rock, country rock, and pop rock. Raised in a musically inclined middle-class black family, Berry had personal contact with both R & B and country music. He also grew up in an outlying neighborhood of St. Louis that anticipated the suburbs to be built after the war.[25] This peculiar confluence of biographical intimacies is reflected in the critical confusion that attends descriptions of Berry's music. Some critics—Richard Aquila, for instance—see Berry as "emerging from the rhythm and blues tradition" (178). Others, such as Reebee Garofalo, argue that Berry had more of a country sound, but that "there was simply no way to market a black man as a country singer" or else "Chuck Berry might well have had a very different career trajectory" (11).[26] No critics dispute Berry's singularity as an adult black man who authored the most notable songs of the decade to be written in the voice of suburban teenagers. How Berry actually reworked country and R & B music into rock 'n' roll, however, requires a closer examination of his music.

Of the many song trajectories that could be foregrounded, I have chosen to consider one that involves a somewhat unconventional R & B number, Berry's "Too Much Monkey Business," recorded in 1956. "Too Much Monkey Business" initially appears to be an R & B number emphasizing the tedious day instead of its antidote in the "rockin'" evening. Like many R & B songs, "Monkey Business" is sung in the first-person voice of a laborer, complaining about his low-paying job:

> Runnin' to-and-fro—hard workin' at the mill.
> Never fail in the mail—yeah, come a rotten bill!

Unlike most R & B songs, however, "Monkey Business" abandons the factory worker after the first verse, turning in each successive stanza to a new character's resentment of yet another site of entrapment.

Many of these sites specifically allude to the milieu of postwar consumer culture. Verse 2, for instance, protests the financial fetters of the installment plan:

> Salesman talkin' to me—tryin' to run me up a creek.
> Says you can buy now, gone try—you can pay me next week, ahh!

In verse three, a man berates domestication by women:

> Blond have good looks—tryin' to get me hooked.
> Want me to marry—get a home—settle down—write a book.

In the fourth stanza, Berry turns to the scenario of rock 'n' roll, adopting the frustrated voice of the dependent teenager:

> Same thing every day—gettin' up, goin' to school.
> No need for me to complain—my objection's overruled, ahh!

Played to a slow, repetitive rhythm that itself invokes coercion, "Monkey Business" constructs a chain of equivalencies between its successive characters and the settings they endure, each time echoing the same frustration (the "ahh!") with which the song began, namely a compulsory social discipline. If in the first verse the worker must submit to the boss's regimentation of work, this is substituted for by the salesman's repayment schedule in the second verse, the marital ties imposed by the blond in the third, and the rules of the school administration in the fourth. In each instance, an alien will pressures the singer into serving a powerful institution: the systems of factory, credit, family, and school respectively. Just as the factory produces workers as well as goods, so do the other settings respectively stamp out disciplined subjects: another consumer, another husband, or another student. "Monkey Business" thus spins off from the implicit critique of work in the R & B narrative, using assembly line drudgery as its master analog with which to critique other disciplinary arenas as so much more "monkey business."

Among these equivalent scenarios set up by "Monkey Business," the factory/school tandem stands out as the comparison that drives Berry's rock 'n' roll output, and arguably, much of rock 'n' roll in the fifties. Perhaps the most revealing point of translation from "Monkey Business" to Berry's rock oeuvre is his anthemic, and arguably his single most famous song, "School Days," released in the very next year. Like its predecessor, "School Days" begins with a forced march through a scene of grueling discipline:

> Up in the mornin' and out to school
> The teacher is teachin' the Golden Rule
> American history and practical math
> You studyin' hard and hopin' to pass
> Workin' your fingers right down to the bone
> And the guy behind you won't leave you alone.

Unlike "Monkey Business," which shifts from one disciplinary site to the next, "School Days" cleaves to the scenario of the studious teenager. Nevertheless, the narrative details of the teenager's day remain organized by the implicit metaphor of the factory, as revealed in the unlikely image of the student "Workin' your fingers right down to the bone." This substitution of school for factory becomes audible at several other points, if for instance, one juxtaposes the "studyin' hard" on a "School Days" with the "hard workin' at the mill" that launches the work day in "Monkey Business." So heard, "School Days" reveals a series of unremarked transpositions, for one's labor (in studying), the foreman (in the teacher), and the annoying coworker (in the "guy behind you").[27]

This doubling effect is musically reinforced by the electric guitar, which echoes each of Berry's lines, transposing its words into pure sonic form. Berry was of course famous as the great popularizer of the electric guitar as the great rock 'n' roll instrument, and for using it as a demonstration of immersion in the feeling of sound, most famously in his "duck walks." Here, the guitar functions almost as a second voice, ready to spin the tedium of labor into the joys of leisure. If the guitar begins "School Days" as a mere underscore for the voice, it will have become, by the end of the song, the pure sound of rock 'n' roll pleasure, which it is the voice's task to translate into words.

The song's second half, then, leaves the place of work far behind for the equivalent of the R & B weekend or the evening, the rhythm and blues of getting to spend one's paycheck in town. As in an R & B number, "School Days" marks the beginning of emancipation with the end of clock time, "Soon as three o'clock rolls around" when the listener leaves school to head into the nearest juke joint.

> Drop the coin right into the slot
> You're gotta hear somethin' that's really hot
> With the one you love, you're makin' romance
> All day long you been wantin' to dance
> Feeling the music from head to toe
> Round and round and round we go.

Just as the earlier verses transposed the work day into the school day, so here does the song carefully revise the worker's evening into the teenager's afternoon, and the dance hall into the juke joint. As the electric guitar gathers force, the song begins to deliver on the R & B promise of romance and energy, returning the fatigued, numbed body of the student to sensuous feeling.

R & B songs are often written in the first person, as evidenced by many of the ones I've discussed, from Domino's "Blue Monday, how I hate Blue Monday" or "I found my thrill on Blueberry Hill," to Berry's own "Too much monkey business for me to be involved in!" Pop rock songs too are frequently sung in the first person, as in Tommy Sand's "Teenage Crush":

> They call it a teen-age crush
> They don't know how I feel.

By employing a rare second-person voice, "School Days" makes an unusually self-conscious address to its listener. The singing "I" of the song remains unnamed, but through the voice of the adult artist, Berry, he invokes the working-class worlds of both R & B and country. It is not the singer but the implied listener who is the narrative figure of the song, however. This "you" is the suburban teenager whose story is given witness by the singer. The "I" of "School Days,"—as someone who understands the plight of "you," the listener, at school as well as the pleasures of the juke joint asserts both a gap and a likeness between the respective binaries of factory/nightclub and school/juke joint. "School Days" literally dramatizes the invention of rock 'n' roll when it stages its "I," drawn from the urban world of R & B, as someone who offers the sound with which the suburban "you" can imagine his or her own teenage existence.

In its final verse, when "School Days" celebrates its invention of rock 'n' roll, however, it paradoxically asserts a continuity with the musical past in an almost liturgical incantation:

> Hail, hail, rock and roll
> Deliver me from the days of old
> Long live rock and roll
> The beat of the drums, loud and bold
> Rock, rock, rock and roll
> The feelin' is there, body and soul.

As the song reaches its climactic end, the second-person voice disappears in favor of a simple first person, the "me" who prays to be "delivered from the days of old." Three possibilities exist for this first person. It might be the teenage "you" of the earlier stanzas who at last achieves an independent voice, taking up the song as his/her anthem of deliverance from school. It might also be the "I" of earlier verses, the singer who only now begins to speak about himself. Or, last, the "me" of this verse could represent a merging of the two subjects, a probable reading given that the scene has shifted so decisively away from a definite school day present into a timeless scene of emancipation.

In any of these cases, however, this last verse sets in motion a lineage of freedom and constraint. By alluding back to the title of the song, the singer's plea to be delivered from the "days of old" suggests, in a manner not unlike that of "Monkey Business" a chain of comparable day/night, work/play binaries. Now, however, a temporality has been added, for "School Days" names not simply another place of discipline, but the *newest* of such places, the latest addition to a series of oppressive days. Rock 'n' roll, in turn, becomes the latest incarnation of the "drums," the musical antidote to these oppressions. The final verse establishes an unending cycle of tension between submission and emancipation, fatigue and feeling, whose latest embodiment is found in the teenage "you." At the same time, the ahistorical collapse in this verse of the song's preceding "I" and the "you" drastically alters its subject of human emancipation, from the "hard-workin'" proletarian in the "days of old," eager to be freed from the workplace, to the "school day" teenager who escapes with friends and love interests into the romantic spaces of youth culture.

"School Days" establishes its implicit analogy of school to factory through two points of comparison. First, both serve as sites of exhausting labor and onerous discipline. Like the factory, Berry's school is a place for "Workin' your fingers right down to the bone." Both furthermore involve not simply exertion but also subjection, to bosses and teachers respectively. The student's chafing against adult authority is expressed even more baldly in "Monkey Business": "No need for me to complain—my objection's overruled, ahh!" In likening school to factory as subjectifying institutions, "School Days" establishes a correlative analogy between the juke joint and the R & B club. In R & B, the factory and the nightclub are inversely related working-class spaces, the respective worlds of constraint through labor and freedom through leisure. Likewise, in the rock 'n' roll of "School Days," school and juke joint are opposing teenage spaces. In school, teenagers work off their subjection to adults, while in the juke joint, they play in a realm of joyous autonomy. Through the force of Berry's analogy, then, school becomes a site of labor, discipline, and bondage, while the juke joint (and by extension youth culture) become an opposing site of leisure, freedom, and passionate pursuits, a respite from the arena of necessity.

This structure of comparison, discernible in "School Days," implicitly undergirds the rock 'n' roll of the fifties, though the site of labor in rock 'n' roll music must be broadened from school, its presentation in Berry's song, to project suburbia itself as a geography of subjection. R & B and country rock songs, like Fats Domino's, Bill Haley's, and Jerry Lee Lewis's, deploy an unreconstructed version of the labor/leisure binary, based upon the proletarian workday and weekend, that their teenage fans were apparently able to appropriate as a source of pleasurable imagination about their own suburban conditions. The analogical structure of "School Days" merely makes explicit a process by which teenage listeners of these songs could map labor and leisure directly onto suburbia and youth culture as their own arenas of constraint and freedom. Moreover, once their appropriative mechanism is recognized, rock 'n' roll songs that located themselves explicitly within youth culture may also be deciphered in terms of a suburban afterlife for the labor/leisure binary. To revisit earlier examples, "Yakkety Yak" invests teenage labor in the chores at home, and leisure in going for a ride with the "hoodlum friends." In "Summertime Blues," labor is literally assigned to the summer job, leisure to the date that the singer can never arrange. In "Teenage Crush," explaining oneself to adults (in a moral accounting) becomes labor, while wooing one's girl without impediment becomes teenage freedom. Over and over, in different ways and using divergent tones, early rock 'n' roll projected onto youth culture a desired realm of autonomy for teenagers, which it counterposed to the laboriousness of submitting as a teenager to the (familial, educational, or miscellaneously) adult disciplines of everyday suburban life.

Transcommodification: Pre-Fordist Leisure as Sonic Metaphor

To this point, I have suggested that rock 'n' roll created a popular music market among suburban teenagers by projecting the city, the country, and finally suburban youth culture itself, as fantasy spaces of emancipation from the laboriousness of suburbia. Recontextualized in this way, the rural and urban spaces sonically projected by R & B and country music substantively changed their meaning when they became adapted to a suburban youth market. Moreover, suburban youth culture, as a fantasy space that was musically elaborated only within rock 'n' roll itself, evinces a similar process at work. As Chuck Berry's music suggests, youth-addressed rock 'n' roll both implicitly depended upon, even as it substantively resignified, the binaries deployed in its musical sources.

It is all too easy to present this resignifying process as one that estranged an autochthonous and thus authentic music—of African Americans, of the working class, of city or country folk—from its origins, by commodifying it to the financial and ideological profit of postwar consumer culture. This approximates Lawrence Grossberg's thesis when he soberly links rock 'n' roll to the liberal consensus and its consumerist values. As a populist alternative to such pessimism, one might therefore also be tempted, like George Lipsitz, to defer the issue of commodification, and instead interpret the rise of rock 'n' roll as signaling suburban youth's growing identification with the values and worldview of African Americans or the working class. Both are misleading positions, however, and between them, they have promoted a hapless thumbs up/thumbs down debate over rock 'n' roll's alternately liberatory or pernicious political significance.

In coining the term "transcommodification," I offer a different analysis that acknowledges the commercial conditions attending rock 'n' roll's emergence, but does not take the music's commerciality to predetermine its ideological valence. It is not commerciality per se but rather its commercial specificities that distinguished rock 'n' roll from the other popular musics—R & B, country, and so forth—out of which it was composed. To understand how rock 'n' roll was differentiated from R & B, for instance, the historical relationship between them must be examined with an ear for how (why, when, and for whom) each music functioned as commercial entertainment.

I have already broached such an analysis by observing R & B's imbrication in an industrial world organized by urban nightlife and the wage laborer's paycheck. Rock 'n' roll organized its meaning in accordance with a radically different sort of world, one inhabited by suburban teenagers who used their small but highly discretionary incomes to escape familial domesticity. These vast differences notwithstanding, the core ideologemes supplied by R & B successfully hailed suburban youth, offering them definite imaginary relations to the conditions of their existence. The enabling conditions of this unlikely address, and the character of the resignifications it required, are the proper objects of analysis for an effective account of the "politics" of rock 'n' roll. And such an analysis requires the assistance of a theoretical concept like transcommodification.

What might it mean to transcommodify an object? In the simplest terms, it indicates that this object, previously distributed through the channels of one market, has become introduced to another market where it now enters into different exchanges with new consumers. Generally speaking, the success of any market depends upon bringing its goods within the physical and libidinal reach of a body of buyers. To the extent that the buyers in any particular market are therefore bound by some relation of contiguity (their spatial connection as "local market"), of similarity (their equivalence within a regime of taste) or both, the transcommodified object enters into the hands of consumers who are often "identifiable" in some way. Such "identifiability" is vital to the work of advertising in consumer cultures, where to "market" a product has traditionally meant first to "identify" and then to "appeal" to its likely consumers. This means, not so surprisingly, that "marketing" is at once an economic and a semiotic activity.

In *For a Critique of the Political Economy of the Sign*, Jean Baudrillard proposed what remains a useful model for approaching consumer culture along these lines, as at once an economic system of commodities and an ideological system of signs. Consumer items, Baudrillard argues, embody two forms of value at once. First, in accordance with Marx's theory of the commodity, they carry a definite (monetary) exchange value that is determined by the object's share in the total abstract labor power utilized by the system of production. Second, the commodity also bears what he calls a sign exchange value, which, in accordance with structural semiotics, Baudrillard defines as its systemic relation of difference to the signifieds of other consumer objects. Focusing on this latter form of (sign) value, Baudrillard explicitly compares the system of consumer objects to a linguistic system, and thus draws an analogy between the illusory freedom of the consumer and that of a speaker:

> A consumer is never isolated, any more than a speaker. . . . *Language cannot be explained by postulating an individual need to speak.* . . . Before such questions can even be put, there is, simply, language . . . a structure of exchange contemporaneous with meaning itself, and on which is articulated the individual intention of speech. Similarly consumption does not arise from an objective need of the consumer, a final intention of the subject towards the object; rather, there is social production, in a system of exchange, of a material of differences, a code of significations and invidious values. (75)

Implicit in Baudrillard's comparison here is the unity and the staticity of both language and object systems as formal systems of signs. Much like a language for Ferdinand de Saussure, consumer capitalism for Baudrillard (at least in this early book) comprises a singular "universe of consumption," a univocal code that organizes the entire system of sign/commodities through a web of fixed distinctions. For Baudrillard, these distinctions in the sphere of consumption express the hierarchical demarcations of social class that every commodity ultimately articulates.

The limitations of such a structuralist orthodoxy are fairly evident. While its explanatory power is considerable, as a model it must deny all dynamic processes or transformations within consumer codes. One cannot acknowledge change, slippage, or contradiction of any sort within the semiotics of consumer culture, including the sorts of movements that I am terming transcommodification. In place of Baudrillard's rigid structure, a more elastic understanding of consumer culture would analyze it instead as a historically shifting and semiotically incoherent formation, whose class distinctions are, at any moment, shot through and complicated by the only partial articulation of many commodity/sign subsystems that are themselves in continuously mutating relationships with one another. If reconceived along such lines, Baudrillard's semiologization of the commodity system has the potential to illuminate many of the key implications of "transcommodification."

First, just as a change in a product's (monetary) exchange value may occur when it is transcommodified, one might also expect a shift in its sign exchange value. When remarketed, a commodity is effectively drawn from one codified subsystem of objects and reinserted into another. A transcommodified object, in other words, most likely undergoes a process of transcoding. Its significance or sign value within consumer culture will be reassigned as it enters into fresh relations of difference with the objects of its new market. Moreover, these fresh relations lead not merely the object, but the entire subsystem of objects (the new market) to undergo at least some degree of reformulation. As an "alien" sign that must be incorporated into a preexisting code, the transcommodified object enacts a mutation that will rewrite the signifying relations among all the other objects.

At this level, a transcommodity such as rock 'n' roll functions much like a metaphor, a word that has been substituted from one category of discourse into another, thereby infusing it with new significance. In Paul Ricoeur's influential account, a metaphor results when a word is inserted into an unexpected linguistic context, one that seemingly contradicts its possible "literal" meanings. Under the hermeneutic pressure placed by this context, the reader momentarily invests the word with new signification. As Ricoeur notes, a more lasting "lexical" change can sometimes result from such a local "contextual" change (169). A successful enough metaphor, in other words, may eventually succeed in elevating itself into a new "literal" meaning of the word.

I have been placing the word "literal" in quotation marks here because the line between the "literal" and "figurative," as Derrida famously showed, is ultimately an untenable one.[28] As the very prospect of lexical change via metaphor demonstrates, a "literal" meaning of a word may represent nothing more than the fading of its "figurative" character. Generalizing from such instances to a broadly antireferential theory of language, Derrida presents the literal as an *effect* of the figurative by means of a wearing-away process he calls "usure" (210). This term, itself a numenistic metaphor for language, presents the "literalization" of words as akin to the gradual rubbing out of a coin face such that those who transact with it can no longer discern the figures to which its value was once attached. Derrida's monetary metaphor for the ineradicable (yet delible) figurative of language is an especially apt figure for the "transcommodity." Like a coin, the transcommodity is an object that carries both monetary and semiotic value through its transfiguration of an "elsewhere," another place in which it was minted and first exchanged. If the transcommodity, for a time, features its own transfiguration, over time this visage may become worn away. The "usure" of the transcommodity entails no necessary loss of its monetary value, yet it may be that the figure with which it began was once crucial in establishing its value, connoting as it does some place, time, or scenario into which its buyers had invested.

Rock 'n' roll, I propose, may be conceived a musical transcommodity in just this way. The medium through which the transposition of pop musical sound objects occurred would of course be radio. As I also noted, radio was no neutral medium of transposition, but one already structured in a relation of complementary alternativity to the domestic medium of television. As such, radio already worked to revise the meaning of the music it imported, from the commercial markets of the city for example, by aligning it with a non- or even antidomestic imagining of suburbia. Heard against the suburban consumer culture of domesticity with which it was now surrounded, the sounds of R & B or country tended, in Ricoeur's terms, to make no "literal" sense within its new contexts. What, after all, could a song about breaking from factory work to hit the town possibly mean in relation to the consumer objects of the new housing tracts: the automobile, refrigerator, TV? As Ricoeur would surely suggest, such a song would take on fleeting metaphorical meanings, though here it must be considered how and why these meanings were highly potent for a youth culture that was consolidating itself as both within and yet alternative to the suburban norm.[29]

In a song such as "School Days," what begins as overt metaphor can be witnessed wearing itself away through what Ricoeur might call the "literalization" of rock 'n' roll. The generic sign of rock 'n' roll, in other words, at first a metaphor supplied by other musical lexicons, developed quickly into a new suburban musical lexicon that could no longer be treated as some "fleeting" generation of meaning. "School Days" therefore exemplifies the Derridean notion of "usure," for the figure of R & B (the scenario of the worker in/out of the factory) has faded in the process of rock 'n' roll's "literalization," until it is hardly visible at all. Nonetheless, the literality of a narrative about a suburban teenager only achieves its seeming transparency by relying upon the figurative elements that R & B provided. Only the transfigures of the tired worker, the oppressive factory, the emancipating nightclub, and the joyous sounds of R & B, in other words, made possible a certain literal imagining of youth culture within the confines of suburbia. Rock 'n' roll as a transcommodity appropriated R & B, country, and other sounds as metaphor, transforming them into the countersuburban currency of the new youth culture.

More needs to be said, however, regarding *why* R & B and the other sounds on the suburban radio proved themselves such potent metaphors for teen life. Standard R & B binaries, such as the factory versus the club, or clock time versus free time, after all, described a working-class organization of space and time that hardly reflected the situation of teenagers. Indeed, as the "literal" complement of labor, leisure, understood as one's freely chosen pursuits of pleasure outside of the workplace, does not even apply to the lives of teenagers *as teenagers*.[30] Such contradictions between context and literal meaning, however, are the very stuff of metaphor. The question at hand is how to explain the aptness of this contradiction, what unexpected resemblances rock 'n' roll revealed in the shock of its inappropriateness.

Clearly, what survived the translation of these other musics into rock 'n' roll was an underlying binary relation of freedom and unfreedom, though now dispersed onto a variety of different sites. Freedom continued to be linked to leisure, but "leisure" now became a figurative term broadly attached to a passionate engagement with suburban youth culture itself, in juke joints and dance parties, but also in automobile chases, romantic dates, and so forth. Unfreedom too migrated to new tableaus, still to include the workplace, but with school and home now taking precedence as that which counts as labor. In the crudest sense, then, we might say that the binaries of freedom/unfreedom in R & B became core metaphors for a similar relation felt to structure suburban teenage life. Early in this chapter I cited Roger Silverstone's claim that suburbia figures alternately as dream and nightmare, as paradise and as wasteland. Rock 'n' roll, it would seem, drew upon the "unfree" side of R & B's binaries to constitute the latter imaginary. Rock 'n' roll mapped suburbia as a sterile wasteland by association with the factory or the deadening job of its musical predecessors. In turn, the "free" side of those same binaries allowed rock 'n' roll to present itself—and youth culture in general—as the respite, the escape, the zone of leisure within suburbia that young people might flee to as an escape from its dreary counterpart.

In what respect, however, might the working-class job possibly have served as an appropriate metaphor for suburbia, a place after all associated with home rather than workplace, and with leisure rather than labor? It is this paradox that drives the suburban counterimaginary, so it is important to trace its logic. Rock 'n' roll's analogy between work and suburbia depended for its intelligibility precisely on the standardization of the suburban home world. The obligatory nature of participating in a consumerized version of domestic leisure allowed rock 'n' roll to compare personal life in suburbia with the logic of the assembly line. Rock 'n' roll, in this respect, iterated a view of suburbia akin to the Frankfurt school analysis of mass culture, as well as a range of widely discussed liberal self-criticism in which the "conformity" of suburbia was critiqued as subordinating the individual to the imperatives of a production system. Unlike either liberal or Frankfurt school texts, however, rock 'n' roll also offered, in opposition to the labor of suburbia, a compensatory utopic arena constructed through the transfiguration of working-class leisure. Its logic, in short, was rather like that discussed in the preceding chapter between figure and ground in American "identity" criticism, only here rock 'n' roll expressed the spirit of, or became the "soundtrack" for, the free persona, set against the stultifying landscape of conformist necessity.

It is vital to see that, by appropriating working-class leisure as a metaphor for its "identity" as the sound of suburban youth, rock 'n' roll stood on its head the utopic suburban imaginary with which I began this chapter. The suburban imaginary, I suggested, established suburbia as an arena of leisure, separated off from the laborious worlds of work and public life in the city. The consumer culture out of which suburbia was constituted, therefore (the homes, automobiles, refrigerators, televisions, barbecues, and what have you) worked to signify suburbia as a realm of private freedom and leisure against the city. Rock 'n' roll, however, reversed their signification. Like suburban consumer culture, it operated through binaries of constraint and freedom. But its metaphorical usage of working-class scenarios mapped suburbia onto the side of labor rather than leisure. In turn, leisure became the purview of all that was *not* suburbia. Leisure was projected back onto the city, or onto the country, onto black or hillbilly culture, as well as onto youth culture itself, which became an internal "outside" to suburbia. In short, rock 'n' roll, as transcommodity, transvalued suburbia, constituting in the process the aural center of what I earlier termed the suburban counterimaginary, the view of suburbia as a nightmare, a place as sterile to human happiness as a factory floor, and just as in need of emancipatory alternatives.

In the rock 'n' roll imagination, a teenager in the new world of postwar suburbia lived two parallel lives, ones that could be compared to the laboring and the leisuring existences of the factory worker. In the first of these, the teenager lived at home, worked small jobs, and went to school, always under the tutelage and guidance of adults, who aimed in the process to bring youth into a sense of adult maturity and responsibility. This, for rock 'n' roll, was the necessary labor of growing up. In the second life, however, teenagers played among themselves, hanging out, enjoying their music, dancing and romancing while adults were kept at bay. These two lives correlate precisely with the two historically distinct categories of youth that I considered in chapter 1. The first of these lives approximated the idea of adolescence, a transitional category between childhood and adulthood tied to a pedagogical narrative, a social bildungsroman that emplotted one's maturation into national responsibility. In the fifties, however, this domain of "adolescence" subjection itself became transcoded as the drab domain of "conformity," in which a youth needed to meet the expectations of adults in an "organizational" setting. By contrast, the second life corresponded closely to the new, politicized category of the teenager, a subject occupying a space of autonomous identity, in which free play became an alternative pedagogy, a means of achieving self-determination for a democratic future through a transitional period of independence. This realm of freedom was the space of identity's emergence, the place allotted to youth where they could imaginatively refuse conformity. In establishing the former, adolescent conformity, as the labor of one's youth, and the latter, teen life, as its leisure, the freedom of identity, rock 'n' roll established itself, in a broadly though diffused sense, as oppositional anthem of identity. It projected the utopic sound of youth as they imagined their psychopolitical liberation from a Fordist matrix, the very matrix that (paradoxically enough) had given rise to the teenager and his/her music in the first place.

IDENTITY HITS THE SCREEN: TEENPICS AND THE BOYING OF REBELLION

Any juvenile seeing it would have to have a feeling of disgust for the bad boy.
—Ronald Reagan, in defense of *Blackboard Jungle*

When the titles flashed, Bill Haley and His Comets started lurching, "One . . . Two . . . Three O'Clock . . . Four O'Clock Rock . . ." it was the loudest sound kids had ever heard at that time. . . . Bill Haley was playing the teenage national anthem and he was LOUD. I was jumping up and down. *Blackboard Jungle*, not even considering that it had the old people winning in the end, represented a strange act of "endorsement" of the teenage cause.
—Frank Zappa, quoted in Richard Aquila, *That Old Time Rock & Roll*

Like radio, the film industry had thrived in the 1930s and 1940s, only to experience the postwar years as a period of severe crisis. In effect, the prewar film industry had already long been organized along Fordist lines. The "dream factory" of the classical studio system possessed not only a finely tuned "assembly line" process but also direct ownership of movie theaters, where its products found ready mass exhibition. In 1948, however, an antitrust court ruling known as the Paramount Decision closed the door on the so-called studio system. Declaring the industry's successful alignment of mass production and consumption to be an illegal vertical monopoly, the courts ordered studios to sell off their movie houses. Compounding this major blow, the Paramount decision also forbade the movie industry from competing with national radio for control over the developing medium of television, whose programming needs might have provided an alternative forum for exhibition (Schatz, 432–435).

As if this were not enough bad news for the industry, the rise of the postwar suburbs intensified the ongoing impact of the Paramount decision. Box office receipts began to dwindle as many of Hollywood's traditional moviegoers—city-dwelling working- and middle-class families—relocated far from the urban movie theaters. Unlike radio, which could still transmit its signals from downtown stations to the new suburbs, the movie palaces stood helpless while their audiences thinned. With ticket sales shrinking, the newly independent theater chains grew increasingly selective about what films to exhibit, creating the dismal prospect of a Hollywood "bomb."

Hollywood's cultivation of the teen market, as Thomas Doherty shows in his lucid history *Teenagers and Teenpics*, derives from this postwar crisis. In its search for new means to a reliable box office, the industry developed two very different sorts of movies: the blockbuster and the exploitation film (29–37). The blockbuster, defined by its state-of-the-art production values, wide-screen technologies, a cast of Hollywood's most luminous stars, and maximal advertising, aimed by dint of sheer market force to reconstitute the prewar mass audience on a highly lucrative one-time basis. The exploitation film took exactly the opposite approach. Characterized by its combination of special interest topics and low production costs, it aimed for a narrow but steadfast audience that could bring a modest but reliable profit.

The drive-in theater promised another partial solution to the industry's problems. Cheaper to construct than a brick-and-mortar theater, built on affordable land adjacent to the new suburban developments, drive-in theaters exploited the new automobile culture to draw at least some suburbanites back to the movies. Finally, Hollywood also began to analyze the profile of its core moviegoers, and discovered it to be composed largely of adolescents, seeking forms of entertainment that (as in the case of rock 'n' roll radio) drew them outside and away from the family-centered entertainment increasingly dominated by television (Doherty, 61–66).

By the late 1950s, the youth audience, the exploitation film, and the drive-in venue would be brought together into the coherent marketing strategy of the "teenpic," a specialty picture for teenagers that came in a range of genres and styles. In the ensuing effort to discover the images, stories, sounds, or themes that might actually "exploit" youth's potential as a new market, moreover, Hollywood found two early answers: the figure of the rebel and the countersuburban imaginary of rock 'n' roll. The rebel offered a character whose oppositional narrative helped to establish a difference between the teen and adult markets. Often the teen rebel appeared as a juvenile version of the Hollywood gangster, casting the antagonism of cop and robber in specifically generational terms.[1] Rock 'n' roll's counter-imaginary, meanwhile, expressed the exuberance of youth autonomy, offering an emotional justification for a distinct teen film culture that operated outside the traditional codes of Hollywood scoring.

The first film to unite these two motifs was *Blackboard Jungle* of 1955, which tells the story of a white teacher named Richard Dadier (Glenn Ford) —just out of the navy and newly recruited by all-male, inner-city North Manual Trades High School—as he struggles to wrest the allegiance of a black student, Gregory Miller (Sidney Poitier), away from an interracial gang of juvenile delinquents led by an Irish boy, Artie West (Vic Morrow). *Blackboard* is most famous for having helped to launch the rock 'n' roll "revolution." The song often celebrated as the first rock hit, Bill Haley's "Rock around the Clock," climbed the charts only after it appeared as the movie's title song. Strictly speaking, however, *Blackboard* was not a teen-pic, for it was marketed primarily to adults as a "social problem film" about the scourge of juvenile delinquency and the heroism required of teachers who would overcome it. The film succeeded with this audience, but it was unexpectedly embraced by teenagers as well, and in ways that adults found deeply troubling. The concern with young viewers began even before the film's release, when a New York City teacher was stabbed to death by a student (McGee and Robertson, 31). This incident immediately foregrounded the basic question that would consume adult debates over the film. Would *Blackboard Jungle* help the public to tackle juvenile delinquency by telling the truth about it, as MGM claimed, or would the depiction of youth violence on screen simply exacerbate the problem? Even though the murderer could not yet have seen the film, his crime's uncanny parallel to *Blackboard*'s final scene, in which Artie slashes and threatens to kill Mr. Dadier in their Bronx high school classroom, provided ammunition for those critics of the film who believed in the deleterious effects of screening such subject matter.

As James Gilbert notes, the makers of the film were quite pleased to discover that their feature had found an unanticipated, secondary audience: "Attending a preview of the film, producer Brooks was surprised, and obviously delighted, when young members of the audience began dancing in the aisles to the rock and roll music. This occurred repeatedly in showings after the film opened" (Gilbert, 184–185). Other adults, however, were less than thrilled to learn that teenagers were erupting wildly as soon as the film's prefatory comments on the "social problem" of juvenile delinquency gave way to "Rock around the Clock." Their suspicions were further confirmed by "other reactions [that] were more threatening. For example in Rochester, New York, there were reports that 'young hoodlums cheered the beatings and methods of terror inflicted upon a teacher by a gang of boys' pictured in the film" (Gilbert, 184–185).[2] One Toronto alderman, upon witnessing local teenagers' response to a showing of *Blackboard Jungle*, told a local newspaper that "Hollywood has succeeded, as usual, in glorifying in the minds of teenagers just the things it claims to attack. [Alderman] Dennison claimed he would lead in the ban efforts. . . . He said the great applause in the film came when a 'tough guy' pupil told a teacher to 'go to hell' and then drew a knife and stabbed the teacher" (*Variety*, "Toronto Hubbub"). In the weeks following the film's release, the press also reported several scattered incidents of juvenile delinquency allegedly linked to the film. In a column titled "Police Seek to Finger 'Blackboard Jungle' as Root of Hooliganism," for example, *Variety* reported that the film "was blamed by Schenectady police for prompting several teen-agers last week to form a gang, which proposed to wage a battle with an Albany group. Other juvenile outbreaks were [also] attributed to the motion picture. . . . Sergeants Joseph Monaco and Patricia Wellman of the Youth Aid bureau said that several teenagers, picked up by police for questioning, 'admitted' they banded together after seeing *Blackboard Jungle*." Even in Memphis, where the film was licensed on an "adults only" basis, teenage girls gathered after the movie to burn down a local barn. According to the *Motion Picture Daily*, a local juvenile court judge had determined that "the leader of the group, organized just a few hours before the fire, is a 14-year-old who said she got the idea after seeing *Blackboard Jungle* which finished a three-week run at Loew's state here on Thursday. She [Judge McCain] said the girls said, 'We wanted to be tough like those kids in that picture.' The leader said, although the picture was labeled 'for adults only,' she and her date had no difficulty gaining admittance and that there were others there even younger than she." Incidents such as these only deepened public concern that young people were seeking out *Blackboard Jungle* because it encouraged misreadings that glorified teenage violence and terrorism.[3]

Nevertheless, MGM, the studio responsible for *Blackboard*, could hardly afford to pull the film from distribution, since the box office receipts quickly revealed it to be a smash hit by any measurement (Gilbert, 185). Within one year of its release, *Blackboard Jungle* had grossed nearly $7 million, "holding over for a third week in some areas where a one-week run is normal" and becoming "the company's top money-making new film of nearly the past couple of years" (*Variety*, "Blackboard Jungle").

MGM was further reassured by the fact that, though the film was under attack in some publications and even banned in certain cities, it also had well respected defenders who were satisfied by the film's professed intentions, and by what they believed to be the moral force of its message. Most notable of the film's proponents was then Screen Actors Guild president Ronald Reagan, who at the Kefauver hearings on delinquency, lauded the positive role model presented by Mr. Dadier, and the indisputable villainy of Artie West: "Any juvenile seeing it would have to have a feeling of disgust for the bad boy," Reagan told the committee. "And I got something else out of it. I found in it a great tribute to a group of persons who seldom get much credit—the schoolteachers of this country" (McGee, 47). For the most part, adult institutional voices agreed with Reagan. As *Variety* reported, "Nine of the twelve civic, religioso and parents-teachers groups which appraise films in the so-called green sheet praised *Jungle*, rating it 'outstanding' for a pic of its type" (*Variety*, "Blackboard Jungle").

In the end, *Blackboard Jungle* survived the onslaught of criticism to become a smashing commercial success and eventually the model for an entire subgenre of delinquent teenpics. Within a year, in fact, the first genuine teenpic, *Rock around the Clock*, would flagrantly try to pull in the same teen audience by recycling the Bill Haley song used to such success in *Blackboard Jungle*, and this effort was quickly followed by dozens of other low-budget teen-oriented films featuring rock artists and rebel dramas of teen life.

How to Read Oppositionally

Precisely because *Blackboard* succeeded as a traditional Hollywood social problem film, but also as a prototeenpic, it illuminates key points of contact between mainstream motifs of culture and the "subcultural" themes that would become the mainstay of the new youth market. It is in the tension between these two receptions, as we shall see, that identity discourse and the bad boy as its attendant figure made their way into the codes of Hollywood cinema. Stuart Hall's foundational essay "Encoding/Decoding" offers a powerful vocabulary that, ever since its publication, has guided cultural studies critics in their basic approach to the polyvalence of popular reception, and especially so in acutely contested instances such as *Black-*

board's. In invoking Hall's terms, however, I will also be commenting on cultural studies' own unacknowledged relationship to the history of identity discourse provided here. Cultural studies terms apply so very well to *Blackboard Jungle* because it was this precise sort of text, with its trope of the masculine youth rebel, that made cultural studies possible in the first place. In its founding theories of audience agency—resistance through ritual—cultural studies celebrated resistive identity through the very figure of the bad boy that *Blackboard* offers up for analysis. In rereading *Blackboard* as the moment of transition into the teenpic, therefore, I will be revisiting at a theoretical level the tacit origins of cultural studies itself in the notion of identity. Both the reception of *Blackboard* and the cultural studies theory of resistance, as we shall see, bring into focus the problematic role of masculinity in early identity discourse, and particularly in its conflation with the ideal of rebellious agency.

Reading Like an Adult: From Delinquency to Development

In "Encoding/Decoding," Stuart Hall first made the immensely influential argument that power differentials within or between audiences will fissure a popular text's meanings along political lines. Mapping a Marxist understanding of ideology onto reader response criticism, Hall proposed a working analytic distinction between three types of popular reading: dominant, oppositional, and negotiated.[4] A dominant reading will identify and decode a popular text's preferred meanings, by which Hall means those interpretive results that both "have the institutional/political/ideological order imprinted in them" and "have themselves become institutionalized" (134).

By contrast, an oppositional reading of a popular text occurs only when a viewer systematically "refuses" the meanings preferred by dominant ideology and instead "decode(s) the message in a globally contrary way. He/she detotalizes the message in the preferred code in order to retotalize the message within some alternative framework of reference. This is the case of the viewer who listens to a debate on the need to limit wages but 'reads' every mention of the 'national interest' as 'class interest'" (137–138).

Between these two extremes lies the negotiated reading. Typically performed by viewers or readers who are ambiguously situated within power relations, negotiated readings accept a popular text's preferred meanings at the general level, but modify them "at a more restricted situational (situated) level," often by positing exceptions and local alternatives (137).[5] Today, the dominant/oppositional polarity deployed in Hall's 1979 essay may seem somewhat mechanical. Nevertheless, as a corrective to *Screen*'s "ideological apparatus" approach to pop culture as well as to the Frankfurt school's "culture industry" model, the reception-directed argument of "Encoding/Decoding" became a guide for much of subsequent popular culture studies.[6]

Insofar as *Blackboard* possesses a "dominant reading" in Hall's sense, it was one that reflected the generic codes of the "social problem" film, refracted through the ideological pressures of the early moment. As previously noted, *Blackboard* tells the story of a white teacher, Mr. Dadier, pitting his authority against the delinquent solidarity of an interracial gang led by the Irish boy, Artie Shaw. Triangulated between them is Gregory Miller, a smart black boy. While Dadier wields his status in the classroom, Artie employs various covert forms of attack: avenging his friend by beating up Dadier (and another teacher) in a dark alley, anonymously accusing him of using racist epithets in class, and even sending unsigned notes to his pregnant wife, Anne, accusing her husband of cheating on her with another teacher, Miss Hammond.

In the end Dadier wins Gregory over from the gang, though before he does, the teacher must himself be taught a lesson in the racial politics of liberal democracy. Dadier had overhastily assumed that the black student, Gregory, was his anonymous accuser and learns to regret this mistake. When he apologizes to Gregory, Dadier proves his commitment to the democratic principle of racial justice. Only near the end of the film does Dadier (along with the viewer) learn for certain that Artie was the real culprit. In the climactic scene, as Artie pulls a switchblade on Dadier during class, Gregory finally sides with the teacher, towing all but one of the other boys along with him.

In narrating a white man's effort to shoulder the burden of civilizing a denizen of the "blackboard jungle," the film depicts a cross-racial identification (of a black boy with a white man) that serves ideological interests very much along the lines of what, in chapter 2, I termed the developmental narrative. Gregory here stands in for the majority of Dadier's ethnically and racially diverse students, who will "grow up" to join Gregory in finally rallying to his side against Artie and his one remaining crony, Belazi. As Peter Biskind has argued, this ending sacrifices the two genuine "bad apples" so that the film's other boys can be redeemed into a liberal intergenerational consensus on the need for students to cooperate with an understanding school system (216). Implicitly too, then, this cooperation concerns "development" in the sense of class mobility, for it will embark the students upon the road to occupational self-improvement. The developmental lesson that Dadier teaches Gregory and the other boys, however, also has to be understood through the motif of masculinity: when a boy abandons his infantile loyalty to the gang and learns to side with the adult values of the educational system, he becomes a man worthy of respect—and employment—by other men.

Much like the "new image" of America demanded of intellectuals by *Partisan Review*, *Blackboard* appears to express a patriotic loyalty to the American way of life. A recent veteran of the Second World War, Dadier must now fight a new war in the trenches of the inner city that seems no less important to the country's future. His moments of doubt are overcome by reiterations of national duty: a chanting of the Pledge of Allegiance that he witnesses at another, more middle-class school, or an American flag with which the bad apple Artie Shaw will be pinned helplessly toward the end of the film. Delinquency will be vanquished, in the end, when Dadier and the students unite as dutiful Americans.

The developmental reading of *Blackboard*, in which delinquency is a "social problem" to be solved, is strongly encouraged by certain structures in the text itself, which take great pains to provide normative guidelines for reception. Perhaps the most explicit and powerful of these guidelines is the bombastic, discursive preface that rolls up the screen before the film begins, declaring *Blackboard Jungle*'s socially responsible and patriotic purpose of informing citizens. As this preface reminds the viewer, "We, in the United States, are fortunate to have a school system that is a tribute to our communities and to our faith in American youth." It then continues, "today we are concerned with juvenile delinquency—its causes—and its effects." This concern justifies the film's content, according to this preface because, "we believe that public awareness is a first step toward a remedy for any problem." Not private profit then but public welfare, not exploitation but education, motivates the graphic depiction of teen criminality.

The preface's clever slide in the subject position of the personal pronoun, from its explicit "We-the-citizens-of-the-United-States" to its implicit "We-who-have-produced-this-film" rhetorically align, the film's producers and viewers as equally responsible Cold War citizen-subjects: both take seriously their public duty to inform and become informed about political questions of the day. Within this preface at least, the implied producers and viewers are also unmistakably adults. The film is not for youth, but only about them.

In this respect, the film claims for itself the same pedagogical value as does the Evan Hunter novel upon which it is based; both texts aim to provide adults with the social knowledge they require in order to tackle the problem of juvenile delinquency effectively. However, Hunter's naturalistic novel actually sticks far more closely than the film to its professed informational function. Depicting teacher Rick Dadier's harrowing first semester on the job at Manual High in the Bronx, the novel documents for its reader an urban ecology of the blackboard jungle. It methodically analyzes the desperate situation of those who live in the "trash can of the school system," explains why they behave as they do, and demonstrates the naïveté of middle-class faith in the public educational system as an engine for social mobility. In so doing, the sensationalism of Hunter's novel actually subverts comfortable American assumptions about prospects for economic uplift among the urban underclass.

By contrast, the film might appear to serve Cold War ideological interests far more loyally than the novel, whose grim thematics of political economy it replaces with a moral economy, in which the reformable delinquents are actually saved in the end while the unredeemable are treated to their just deserts. Unlike the novel's more ambiguous ending, in which Dadier wins only a limited victory against the worst of the delinquents, the film version concludes with Dadier's triumphant transformation of Manual High, showing its viewer how the integrity and dedication of a single good teacher can save the educational system.

The film reveals its ideological divergence from the novel with particular clarity in one of the few scenes appended to Hunter's original narrative. After enduring a series of setbacks, the downcast Rick Dadier finds new inspiration by visiting Professor A. R. Kraal, the man who had once trained him to teach. Professor Kraal, now a high school principal, takes Dadier on a tour of his shiny, suburban school, an image of the educational norm from which Manual High so strikingly deviates. On this campus, a lily-white student body obediently studies Latin, practices chemistry, and proudly sings the national anthem. Reinspired by this vision, Mr. Dadier returns to Manual High, puts his shoulder back to the wheel, and single-handedly succeeds in steering his kids onto the right track.

Brown versus the Blackboard of Education

The contrast sketched between Kraal's school and Manual High is only a brief addition to Hunter's narrative of 1954, but it indicates a sharpening of the story's engagement with perhaps the most unavoidable of all politi-

4. Professor Kraal's all-white, coed school is a vision of suburban order in *Blackboard Jungle* (MGM, 1955).

cal contexts of its day: racial desegregation. The film's release in March of 1955 came some ten months after the Supreme Court's first ruling in its landmark *Brown v. Board of Education* case on the unconstitutionality of segregated schools, and only two months prior to a widely anticipated second decision in which the Court determined that desegregation must be implemented "with all deliberate speed" (Oakley, 191–193).

Brown v. Board of Education can be usefully contextualized within the geopolitical model of the "age of three worlds." The Supreme Court's verdict favoring desegregation made vital sense in the competition with the Soviet Union for the "hearts and minds" of Africa and Asia's new nations, who were all too aware of the United State's white supremacist racial order. Yet, even for white moderates and liberals building this evolving hegemony, the legal decision offered an acceptable political goal only under very specific terms and conditions. By and large, even the most liberal whites could only affirm racial integration by imagining interracial schooling taking place through the piecemeal admission and assimilation of nonwhites to primarily white and white-staffed schools. A "minority majority" or nonassimilationist integrated education seemed tantamount to accept-

5. Integrated, all-boy Manual High is in utter chaos in *Blackboard Jungle* (MGM, 1955).

ing the collapse of the racial order. "It's all very well to talk about school integration—if you remember that you may also be talking about social disintegration," President Eisenhower himself remarked privately in 1956, one year before reluctantly ordering the use of federal troops to escort nine black students to all-white Central High School in Little Rock Arkansas (Oakley, 194).

The portrayal of a "wild," fully integrated high school student body in both the film and book versions of *Blackboard* engaged these racial fears directly, collapsing juvenile delinquency and desegregation into the representation of a singular "social problem." The film version of *Blackboard Jungle*, however, marks its racial position even more explicitly by stressing the contrast between Kraal's school and Manual High. The former becomes a model institution that Manual High must emulate if Dadier is to make integrated schooling a positive success rather than a debacle. In Kraal's school, students are patriotic, obedient, and loyal to the white, middle-class American values modeled by teachers and the principal. At Manual High, racial integration initially seems to signal the death of patriotism, obedience, and social order. Manual's white students (with the exception of one

IDENTITY HITS THE SCREEN 145

cowed good boy) are in fact as unruly and disrespectful as their nonwhite peers. Artie, the worst of these bad white boys, even expresses his open contempt for patriotism, explaining proudly how he will refuse to play the sap if called upon to fight for his country.

Though Kraal tempts Dadier with a job offer at his school, Dadier reluctantly turns it down, feeling that his students deserve opportunity too, and that his duty therefore lies with them. By the end of the film, that duty has been discharged. Through his perseverance, Mr. Dadier manages to convert his integrated classroom's attitude and behavior into something very much akin to Kraal's all-white classrooms. The moment of truth, of course, comes in the final scene when all but one student abandon Artie as he brandishes his knife at Mr. Dadier. Indeed, the fate of the one exception, Belazi, is coded symbolically to reflect the school's shift toward obedience and patriotism. As Belazi makes a move to join Artie's attack on Mr. Dadier, another student grabs an American flag and rams Belazi against the blackboard with it. With this act, the reign of juvenile delinquency ends at Manual High, and the school is reborn as a successful democratic experiment in integration, institutional proof that the white teacher's authority can survive in a multiracial classroom, just as America's geopolitical authority can survive in a multiracial age of global decolonization.

Blackboard Jungle: *Reading Like a Teenager*

If *Blackboard*'s significance had been exhausted by these "social problem" meanings, however, then it would never have become a textual prototype for the teenpic. Although, as I have suggested, *Blackboard* resolves its narrative by vanquishing the widely feared multiracial "delinquency" problem and reestablishing white adult authority, the film's original teenage audiences seem to have pointedly ignored the moral of the story, revoking in the process the premature closure between implied producer and viewer asserted in the film's preface. Through what meanings and pleasures, then, might teenage viewers have been enjoying this film?

Curiously, the text of *Blackboard Jungle* seems to comment on this very question by proposing a model for its own subversive uses. In a film-within-a-film scene, *Blackboard* explicitly depicts a fragmentary moment of "oppositional" youth reading. When he first arrives on the job at Manual, Mr. Dadier employs tough tactics in an effort to coerce discipline from his sullen, rebellious students. When the stick fails, Dadier tries a carrot instead, attempting to win their interest by bringing a tape recorder into class. Artie and the other students mischievously manage to subvert the taping session, so Dadier tries again by screening an animated cartoon of *Jack and the Beanstalk*. This time, Dadier succeeds. The students enjoy watching the movie and afterward are pleased to discuss it.

Over the course of their discussion, Dadier proposes a reading consonant with his own liberal paternalism. He wants the students to identify with Jack, but on very specific terms. The giant from whom Jack steals the harp and goose, as it so happens, had himself killed Jack's father long ago. As a loyal son who slays his father's murderer, Jack is judged by Dadier to be a laudable figure. However, in keeping with his liberal notion of racial tolerance, Dadier increasingly stresses that it must not be the giant's *difference* that excuses Jack's violence; an attack on someone justified through prejudice alone is immoral.

Gregory, meanwhile, is reluctant to identify with Jack. To begin with, Jack is lazy and inconsiderate of his poor mother, thoughtlessly selling the family cow for a "mess of beans." But even more importantly, Gregory is disturbed by the fact that Jack kills without any knowledge—let alone proof—that the giant is his father's murderer. Recognizing the absence of any formal procedure for ascertaining the giant's guilt, Gregory grows somewhat skeptical that the giant got only what he deserved, suspecting that he was scapegoated merely because of his physical difference.

Though he distrusts Dadier's reading, Gregory's eventual desertion of the gang for the educational system is portended by the broad possibilities for cooptation built into his own reading: if Jack's laziness alienates Gregory, then Gregory is grasping firmly onto a masculine breadwinner ethos, something Dadier actually encourages as a way of getting Gregory to buckle down in the classroom. If Gregory wants a trial, he is calling for liberal judgment, the putative impartiality of which legitimates institutional violence, as it will by the end of the film, when the revelation of Artie's guilt sanctions Dadier's right to smash the delinquent boy repeatedly against the blackboard. Indeed, if Jack has managed to avenge his father, then by the end of the cartoon he has begun to take on his father's own masculine responsibility. Gregory's reading thus portends the implication by the end of the film that, with this change of heart, Gregory is now following in Dadier's footsteps and will someday himself become the new bearer of paternal authority.[7]

While Gregory is quicker than Dadier to ascribe the giant's death to a moral logic that rests ultimately upon his otherness, he ultimately accepts Dadier's insistence that Jack's deed would be ethical if the giant's crimi-

6. Artie is left out of the fun when Dadier screens *Jack and the Beanstalk* in *Blackboard Jungle* (MGM, 1955).

nality could be proven. Gregory, in his concern for the possible victim of a racial injustice, flirts with the giant, but ultimately accepts Jack as the proper object of identification. In Hall's terms, Gregory's reading is a paradigmatically negotiated one, disinclined to accept dominant ideology in local situations when it victimizes him in terms of his racial position but inclined to play along at a more global level.

Artie West's reading, however, is very different. At first, Artie, the boy who turns out to be the villainous gang leader, refuses to join the other boys in enjoying the movie (an anticipation of his eventual isolation). He recognizes that Dadier is trying to shift the class's identification with *Jack and the Beanstalk*. Any pleasure they take is ultimately not theirs, but Dadier's. "It's a phony," he snarls. To enjoy the cartoon is already to be coopted by the teacher's game, to accept the hierarchy of white/professional/adult/teacher over nonwhite/poor/young/student. For one brief instant, however, Artie does something else, announcing to the class that (like Dadier) he identifies with Jack. Unlike Dadier, however, Artie likes him because Jack proves that crime pays, getting away with both theft and murder. His response directly parallels that which adults feared teenagers were engaging in with *Blackboard Jungle*, namely identifying with Artie rather than with Dadier.

Dadier's effort to win sympathy for the giant as a possible victim of intolerance is as much a response to Artie's generational threat as it is a moral lesson on racism. Jack, after all, is a boy who victimizes a giant man, a juvenile delinquent who kills an oversized adult. "Is it right to dislike somebody because he's different?" asks Dadier. "There are a lot of us right here in this classroom who are different than anyone else." In fact, Dadier is the only one who is marked as different from *everyone* else; he is the only adult in a room full of boys, and for that matter an adult whom the students have treated unfairly: for merely handing over the would-be rapist to the authorities, the class not only gives him the cold shoulder, but some of them actually retaliate by beating him up in an alley under cover of darkness.

The fairy-tale cartoon conveniently speaks to Dadier's experience, since the giant pursues Jack only after he has stolen the magic harp, which is personified as a woman screaming for help. Should Dadier be attacked simply because he is an adult who tried to stop a juvenile rapist? In its generational register, Dadier is reacting to what he fears is a real possibility that Artie's reading may be embraced by his classmates.[8] Gregory, for one, is deeply affected by Dadier's plea, turning half toward Artie and half toward Dadier after class to warn, "That giant, if he done wrong, at least I think he should've had a trial."

Dadier's discursive maneuver in this scene parallels that of adults to *Blackboard Jungle* itself. Acknowledging both the dominant meanings preferred by the text, but also the fact that these were not the meanings that teenagers seemed to derive, Senator Estes Kefauver's congressional committee report, *Motion Pictures and Juvenile Delinquency*, articulated the conflicted reading that many adults had negotiated with *Blackboard Jungle*:

> While the committee recognizes and appreciates the artistic excellence of this film, it feels there are valid reasons for concluding that the film will have effects on youth other than the beneficial ones described by its producers. . . . It is felt that many of the type of delinquents portrayed in this picture will derive satisfaction, support, and sanction from having made society sit up and take notice of them. Although the tough individual portrayed by Artie West is used to show the crime-does-not-pay requirement by the end of the film, even the producer . . . agreed that the type of individual portrayed by Artie West upon viewing this film will in no way receive the message purportedly presented

in the picture and would identify with him no matter what the outcome of the film. (United State Congress, 46–47)

Artie's reading of *Jack and the Beanstalk*, that crime *does* pay, the committee suspects, threatens to overwhelm the preferred reading of criminality in *Blackboard Jungle*, namely that it *does not*. Of course the rather small number of violent juvenile delinquents were not the committee's only concern any more than Artie represents Dadier's sole concern. The rowdy success of the film with a wide teenage audience fed an even deeper anxiety, namely, that alienated but heretofore obedient teenagers might also choose to identify with Artie and his gang.

The Blackness of the Board:
Cross-Racial Identification and Oppositional Reading

In addition to identifying with Jack both as juvenile and as delinquent, Artie takes his pleasure in a way that also has submerged crossracial implications, though they may not be obvious at first glance. Race, as we saw in Dadier and Gregory's readings, is a central issue in the class's discussion of *Jack and the Beanstalk*. Artie's identification with Jack, however, would seem also to imply his identification with whiteness. In fact, this is not so simple. If Artie's Jack is a thief, then so is the giant: both of them steal the goose. And if his Jack is a murderer, then so again is the giant, who killed Jack's father. If criminality, if taking what one wants and getting away with it, is the basis of Artie's identification, then the giant is as promising a candidate as Jack. Jack in fact follows in the giant's footsteps, much as the "hipster" would emulate the "Negro" in Norman Mailer's hotly debated essay "The White Negro."

Originally just "half a page about what I thought of integration in the schools," Mailer's essay on the "whys" and "hows" of the postwar hipster subculture grew out of his contention that "the white loathes the idea of the Negro attaining equality in the classroom because the white feels that the Negro already enjoys sensual superiority" (299). For Mailer, the "White Negro" is anyone who, in a suffocating postwar age that demands stringent conformity at the same time that it threatens nuclear annihilation, has chosen to drop out of the white race and become a hipster. The hipster, abandoning the sterile privilege of white "classroom superiority," self-consciously models his life on the "Negro," pursuing instead the black man's "sensual superiority." The "Negro," in turn, serves as a figure whose

7. The multiraced boys of Manual High rock together in *Blackboard Jungle* (MGM, 1955).

racial marginalization and terrorization has long led him to adopt an existential, even psychopathic, creed of acting on his desires without regard to the law. Mailer, ironically enough, given the original intent of his essay, thus ends up accepting mainstream white concern with juvenile delinquency as a potential consequence of racial integration, only he valorizes rather than condemns that result.[9] Like Jack for Artie, the white negro for Mailer is someone who proves to the world that crime does indeed pay, most of all in a conformist era like the fifties.

By scrutinizing *Blackboard Jungle*, we can find possibilities for white negro modes of criminal identification similar to those Artie West picks out in *Jack and the Beanstalk*. For example, by using Bill Haley's anthem "Rock around the Clock" to fade from the film titles (superimposed on a blackboard) into a diagetic use of the same music in the opening shot of delinquent students dancing in the schoolyard, *Blackboard Jungle* could interpellate its youth-cultured spectator into their rebellion, drawing an explicit identification between such general youth-cultural forms as rock 'n' roll, the increasingly preferred music of *Blackboard*'s actual youth audience, and the film's depiction of black, Puerto-Rican, and white youth's unified antagonism toward the white, adult-controlled educational institution. The

IDENTITY HITS THE SCREEN 151

musical reference is oblique, requiring an inference similar to Artie's in the case of the cartoon. Bill Haley and the Comets, like Elvis or Jerry Lee Lewis, are white. Yet their rock 'n' roll music was clearly intelligible in the fifties as an appropriation of black culture, along the complex lines noted in the preceding chapter. The use of the title song thus indirectly solicits a white youth spectator to identify not with the white adult Mr. Dadier, but with the racially mixed and threatening body of students.

Up to this point, I have used primarily textual evidence to reconstruct an oppositional reading, a strategy that, by locating structures of meaning agreeable to youth rebelliousness, helps to explain why *Blackboard Jungle* was so amenable to appropriation as a proto-teenpic. That these meanings were so readily activated by teen moviegoers, however, indicates that they were already entering into general discursive circulation. That is why Mailer's "The White Negro," which explicitly calls the new hipster sensibility a "ménage à trois" between the bohemian, the juvenile delinquent, and the Negro, proves so helpful in elucidating the racial dimension of Artie's identification with Jack (305–306). In effect, Mailer's essay restates and affirms the same mode of rebellion—linked through Robert Lindner to the wider discourse of identity—that *Blackboard Jungle* mobilized for teenagers.

As a way of confirming that these oppositional youth pleasures and meanings were growing in power and importance from the mid-fifties onward, I offer two additional intertexts from the late sixties. Both were widely read essays that, like Mailer's, explicitly theorize cross-racial identifications among white youth. Mailer had already discussed the oppositionality of the white negro in terms of generational conflict, arguing that the language of hip is one "most adolescents can understand instinctively, for the hipster's intense view of existence matches their experience and their desire to rebel" (308–309). By 1968, an essay from Eldridge Cleaver's *Soul on Ice* would foreground such a generational conflict even more prominently. The bestseller of the Black Power movement, *Soul on Ice* was published by Dell as a mass-market paperback which sold two million copies within four years, particularly among young people involved in the counterculture and the New Left.

In the essay entitled "The White Race and Its Heroes," Cleaver begins by referring to himself as an "Ofay Watcher," one of the colored people of the world who view their white oppressors from the shadows of colonialism. Since entering Folsom Prison in 1954, only one year prior to *Blackboard*'s release, Cleaver tells us he has witnessed a remarkable development among young Ofays, "who are experiencing the great psychic pain of waking into consciousness to find their inherited heroes turned by events into villains. Communication and understanding between the older and younger generations of whites has entered a crisis.... So thoroughgoing is the revolution in the psyches of white youth that the traditional tolerance which every older generation has found it necessary to display is quickly exhausted, leaving a gulf of fear, hostility, mutual misunderstanding, and contempt" (72–73). Cleaver suggests that white adults cannot admit that young people no longer deify such heroic father figures of the race as George Washington and Thomas Jefferson, who for all their high-sounding rhetoric owned hundreds of slaves and were thus important players in the crimes of colonialism:

> The elders do not like to give these youngsters credit for being able to understand what is going on and what has gone on. When speaking of juvenile delinquency, or the rebellious attitude of today's youth, the elders employ a glib rhetoric. They speak of the "alienation of youth," the desire of the young to be independent, the problem of "the father image" and "the mother image" and their effect upon growing children who lack sound models upon which to pattern themselves. But they consider it bad form to connect the problem of the youth with the central event of our era—the national liberation movements abroad and the Negro revolution at home. (74)

Cleaver's words here seem to speak almost directly to the preface of *Blackboard Jungle* discussed earlier, whose assertion that "today we are concerned with the problem of juvenile delinquency," decenters racism as the film's social problem even as it implicitly connects the two issues. As Cleaver's argument suggests, the film's dominant meanings repudiate the possibility that racial oppression (as opposed to racial mixing) could motivate juvenile delinquency. Indeed, the narrative structure itself, in which it is a white youngster, Artie, who is the embittered, adversarial, delinquent leader, and not Gregory, also serves to undercut the valorization of youth criminality as an appropriate response to white racism. Instead, the film presents Dadier as a champion of liberal values and stigmatizes Artie as an opportunist who cynically uses the issue of racism to create a wedge between Dadier and his other students.

But while this particular structuring of the characters in the film bolsters the dominant reading, it cannot entirely repress the semiological alternatives. Cleaver notes in the same essay that America has always had two conflicting images of itself, images that are effectively captured by Frederick Douglass's famous speech "What to the American Slave Is the Fourth of July?" Cleaver quotes Douglass: "To him your celebration is a sham; your boasted liberty, an unholy license; your national greatness, swelling vanity; your sounds of rejoicing are empty and heartless; your denunciation of tyrants, brass-fronted impudence; your shouts of liberty and equality, hollow mockery" (78). From the perspective of a racially oppositional reading of *Blackboard Jungle*, Douglass's "you" could well be referring to Dadier and his liberal rhetoric. In fact, the film gives no indication that the students have experienced any racial tensions among themselves at all until Dadier attempts to instruct them in liberal tolerance. In other words, the film permits a reading that reverses Artie and Dadier's moral standing in the dominant reading: it is *Dadier* who cynically exploits racism, using it to divide the students who have united against him.

Cleaver argues that "because there is no common ground between these contradictory images of America, they had to be kept apart" (79). Of course, in *Blackboard Jungle* it is precisely these images that are *not* kept apart but instead allowed to coexist textually. Depending on how one reads, Dadier is either a heroic father figure or a racist tyrant. The school system is an institution serving either democracy or white supremacy. And Artie West is either a savage criminal or one of the emerging new breed of Ofays described by Cleaver, born in the fallout of *Brown vs. Board of Education*, who prefers to identify, and even to organize, with his racially oppressed cohorts rather than with their colonizers, and who in exactly this way have formulated for themselves an identity independent of their elders (177). Little wonder that to overcome these threatening meanings it has set in motion, *Blackboard Jungle* must break the alliance between Artie and Gregory, particularly via racial antagonism, so that Gregory can freely choose to assist Dadier in defeating the threat of the juvenile gang.

A second intertext from the late sixties adds another dimension to the argument: Jerry Farber's widely circulated essay "The Student as Nigger." Like Cleaver's *Soul on Ice*, Farber's essay, a radical political text, was quickly picked up by a mass market paperback company, Pocket Books, and proved highly influential in the generational political thinking of young sixties radicals, especially on high school campuses. The book's popularity, as Farber himself noted, was due in no small measure to its central analogy between white/black and teacher/student hierarchy, a comparison that, as he explains, "embodied ideas and feelings that had been around for a long time, but were by then working their way rapidly to the surface" (13). Farber's essay begins with a series of specific observations: the separate but unequal student dining facilities, the policing of student sexuality, the encouragement in students of obsequious deference and obedience. He concludes:

> What school amounts to, then, for white and black alike, is a 12-year course in how to be slaves. What else could explain what I see in a freshman class? They've got that slave mentality: obliging and ingratiating on the surface but hostile and resistant underneath.
>
> As do black slaves, students vary in their awareness of what's going on. Some recognize their own put-on for what it is and even let their rebellion break through to the surface now and then. Others—including most of the "good students"—have been more deeply brainwashed. They swallow the bullshit with greedy mouths. (93)

While Cleaver assumes that white youth actually step beyond their own privileged interests, disidentifying with their elders in order to form a shared identity with their colored peers, Farber draws an analogy between white supremacy and the psychopolitical subordination (the enforced slave mentality) of all students, including white ones, within adult-controlled institutions.

However problematic, Farber's analogy provides a heuristic explanation for the initial solidarity of the students at Manual High, and does so without attributing transcendent ideals to the white students. The oppositional viewer need not consider Artie's lead in the classroom rebellion to be inspired by some implausible vision of a beloved community. Rather, Artie has merely gathered together his classmates, who are disciplined in school as "niggers," regardless of their race. In the scene where Dadier attempts to win the class's cooperation by bringing a tape recorder to school, for example, Artie and the class cleverly insist that Dadier give the microphone to Morales because they discern that the teacher's tactic, which requires obedience to institutional language, cannot tolerate Morales's repeated use of the word "stinking" (or "f-cking" in the novel) to comment on how he spent his morning. Dadier tries to declaim their amusement as a racist abuse of Morales rather than an attack on his own authority. "I can see you're really good friends to Morales," he scolds. But the students know better. As even Gregory puts it, "Sure are, too bad you can't say the same, Teach."

Dadier, whose liberal understanding of racism as personal intolerance disallows a "Student as Nigger" analogy, cannot imagine this incident as a metaphor for institutional subordination. Hence his profound offense when the principal tells Dadier that an anonymous student has accused him of using racist language in the classroom. Dadier justifies his use of racial epithets, "spic," "mic," and of course "nigger," as part of a lesson in the need for tolerance in an integrated classroom. For Artie, who reported him, however, they function to splinter the class's generational solidarity along racial lines, and thereby make it easier for Dadier to reimpose the teacher/student hierarchy.

Bad Boyhood in Blackboard:
The Masculinist Negotiation of "Oppositional" Reading

There was thus a second possible way of reading *Blackboard Jungle*. Marked by an adversarial relation to the increasingly powerful liberal ideology of assimilationist integration, this reading celebrated student resistance to the teacher's authority, especially in the name of their interracial identity as subjected youths. As a rebel gang animated by the countersuburban sound of rock 'n' roll, the students in *Blackboard* implicitly became, in this reading, surrogates for the general identity claims of youth. But one must qualify the sense in which this reading was in fact a fully "oppositional" one in Stuart Hall's sense. Early identity discourse, as I have argued, found its hegemonic figure in the bad boy, who masculinized its core ideal of personal sovereignty. In this regard, what one might be tempted to call the "oppositional" teen reading of *Blackboard* was no exception.

Let us return for a moment to Farber's "student as nigger." After drawing the racial/generational analogy, he tries to explain why it is that teachers would treat their students like "niggers" turning to yet another analogy, that between subjection and emasculation:

> Their [teachers'] most striking characteristic is timidity. They're short on balls.... In California state colleges, the faculties are screwed regularly and vigorously by the Governor and Legislature and yet they still won't offer any solid resistance. They lie flat on their stomachs with their pants down, mumbling catch phrases like "professional dignity" and "meaningful dialogue."... [T]he classroom offers an artificial and protected environment in which they can exercise their will to power. Your neighbor may drive a better car; gas station attendants may intimidate you; your wife may dominate you; the State legislature may

shit on you; but in the classroom, by God, students do what you say—or else. (95)

In the "oppositional" reading of *Blackboard*, the students' resistance finds authorization in a similarly misogynistic and homophobic logic of phallic male sovereignty. There are numerous reasons to find Rick Dadier's manhood suspect. He is soft-spoken; his wife has lost a baby; he lacks sufficient sexual interest in his attractive colleague, Miss Hammond. At several points, the students question his heterosexuality, a suspicion that Dadier inadvertently confirms with such banter as "I came back to school today because I missed you so much, Artie." Also, the day after Artie's boys successfully beat Dadier up in a dark alley, Gregory teases Dadier in class for using makeup to hide the bruises: "That's okay Teach, I know lots of men who wear makeup." Even his role as disciplinarian raises doubts. Dadier received his teaching accreditation at a women's college. His mission is clearly to convert Manual High (an all-boys' school) into something like the suburban ideal represented by the coed high school administered by Professor Kraal. Dadier's duty thus seems to involve importing the feminine and its castrated obedience to Manual.

If Dadier is emasculated in the "oppositional" version of *Blackboard Jungle*, then what of the students themselves? Returning to Farber on this question:

> The less trained and the less socialized a person is, the more he constitutes a sexual threat and the more he will be subjugated by institutions, such as penitentiaries and schools. Many of us are aware by now of the sexual neurosis which makes white men so fearful of integrated schools and neighborhoods, and which makes the castration of Negroes a deeply entrenched Southern folkway. We should recognize a similar pattern in education. There is a kind of castration that goes on in schools. It begins before school years with parents' first encroachments on their children's free unashamed sexuality and continues right up to the day when they hand you your doctoral diploma with a bleeding, shriveled pair of testicles stapled to the parchment. (96)

To rebel against the school system, hence, is to ward off this threat of castration, to stand up to the teacher's efforts at domination and emasculation, which for Farber are analogous terms.

Keeping Farber's phallic mode of rebellion in mind, let us return to the opening scene of the film, in which students dance in the schoolyard to Bill

8. The boys hoot from behind bars at a passing woman in *Blackboard Jungle* (MGM, 1955).

Haley's "Rock around the Clock." I suggested that this scene has the oppositional potential of interpellating a young white spectator into interracial rebellion against his elders. Indeed, the rock 'n' roll soundtrack makes this scene one of the most subversive in the film, a moment when the implied viewer is most clearly a youth who rocks to the music of delinquency. Teen-pic meanings are here most privileged over "developmental" ones.[10] From a long shot of the schoolyard dancing, however, the camera pans along the sidewalk to a group of delinquent boys behind the "bars" of the schoolyard, crudely appreciating a woman who walks by.

This masculinization of opposition, I argue, is itself a compromise, a negotiation with the era's dominant gender ideologies of the era that qualifies and problematizes the scene's potential oppositionality. How is this so? First, it is significant that the students dancing together in the opening scene are all boys. This opening scene, like several others that follow, makes available an unusually explicit homoerotic (third) reading where boys take sensual pleasure in one another. Guided by the tropes of heterosexualized and masculinized youth rebellion, in which the students of Manual High do not want to be "screwed" by Dadier, however, the film cannot tolerate any implication that they may indeed want to be "screwed" by one another.

158 CHAPTER FOUR

The threatened eruption of homoerotic meaning is repressed by extending the shot so that it concludes with a crass image of the delinquents' heterosexual desire. The shot thereby restores phallic oppositionality to the boys: their desire to "screw" marks them as rebellious, as refusing to submit to the school authority that intends to castrate them.

In general, the rebellious, integrated schoolboys of Manual High tend to control the heterosexual male gaze of the camera throughout the film. In addition to the opening sequence, for example, another scene soon follows in the auditorium, where all the boys at the school orientation meeting whistle at Miss Hammond. The camera dwells with emphasis on the faces of color staring at her legs, then cuts to their point of view, following her legs tightly as she climbs the stairs to the podium. This scene is soon followed by the attempted rape itself. While the boy who tries to rape Miss Hammond is white, the racially marked shots preceding it tinge the incident with the American myth of the black rapist.[11]

In the dominant reading, Dadier's fortunate interruption of the rape attempt establishes his credibility as a role model. The delinquent's expression of uncontrolled, violent desire is criminal, requiring Dadier's intervention as agent of institutional law. The narrative is thus structured along lines parallel to American racial mythology, where the lust of black men for white women requires the political dominance and vigilance of white men. And in this scene, that white man is Dadier. However soft-spoken and not quite classically heroic he may be, Dadier is man enough to stop a crazed delinquent from sexually assaulting a respectable white woman.

This lesson is not only for the viewer's benefit but also for the students within the film, who must respect Dadier's ability to fight, however furious they are at the consequences for their prison-bound friend. No mere organization man like his fellow teachers, Dadier remains a capable soldier for the new wartime conditions. When they take revenge on Dadier later by ambushing him and another teacher in an alley, Artie's gang will be sure to outnumber them by three or four to one. Dadier, in other words, is rendered as a genuine Hollywood hero fighting against enormous odds. Ultimately he must win because, though the street toughs he takes on may put on a macho front, they are actually cowards who fight only when the odds favor them. In the final scene, when he can square off one-on-one with Artie, Dadier proves himself more of a man than the delinquent punk who has tormented him.

In the oppositional reading of the attempted rape scene, however, the delinquent's sexual violence finds legitimacy as an act of rebellion against

9. Dadier watches the boys eyeing Miss Hammond in *Blackboard Jungle* (MGM, 1955).

10. But it's a white boy who tries to rape Miss Hammond in *Blackboard Jungle* (MGM, 1955).

the repressive domination of school authority; Dadier's interference becomes an act of institutional violence that martyrs the boy. Here, normative (i.e., adult-identified) reading strategies have been reversed, interpellating the spectator into an alliance with the (masculine) rapist and against the female victim's (desexualized) male defender. These oppositional meanings are unmistakably a threat to the dominant gender regime of the fifties as represented by Dadier, a strong yet domesticated man, and his wife, Anne (more on this regime in the next chapter). Yet this oppositionality is conveyed through a logic of intensified misogyny and sexual rivalry, conceiving women as property of the men who represent the oppressive institution, and whose abuse by the boys thus serves as means of expressing their defiance.

Cultural Studies and the Masculinist Heroics of Youth Resistance

What does this pair of readings tell us? In narrower theoretical terms, *Blackboard* provides a detailed case study of how, in order to perform any "oppositional" reading at all, other oppositional meanings must be repressed or denied. This point is somewhat analogous to Gayatri Spivak's argument that the subaltern cannot speak, because in order to do so, some other axis of alterity, such as that of woman, must be silenced. Likewise, any "oppositional" reading is premised upon the denial of other oppositional readings, that any counterhegemonic practice is founded upon the repression of political difference. *Blackboard Jungle*, Frank Zappa notes, was experienced by young postwar viewers like himself as a thrilling endorsement of the "teenage cause." Notwithstanding the fact that it had "the old people winning in the end," the film featured Bill Haley "playing the Teenage national anthem and he was LOUD" (Aquila, 8). What specific readings, however, might have been foreclosed by the prototeenpic reading that he and other teenagers performed?

The opening scene cited by Zappa, in which possible homoerotic meanings to rock 'n' roll dancing must be repressed, is potentially revealing here. One might easily detect the strong potential for a queer reading of *Blackboard Jungle* in which homosexual desire threatens both the institutional authority of the school and the machismo of the gang. As Dadier and Artie struggle for influence, they occasionally act out their aggression in scattered moments of unmistakable sexual banter, as in a scene where Dadier publicly jokes about keeping Artie late after class, saying, "I miss you, Artie," to which one of the boys whistles, "Oooh, Dadier!" The struggle between Dadier and Artie, moreover, is played out most directly through a battle for the affections of Gregory, and thus as a tale of homoerotic triangulation. Like *Catcher in the Rye* and (as the next chapter considers) *Rebel without a Cause*, *Blackboard Jungle* is a text that is open to a gay male appropriation of youth rebellion, and yet these meanings seem to have remained very much in the "celluloid closet," even among the film's vociferous critics.

Alternatively, one could elaborate another possible reading also denied by the oppositional youth reading, this time centering on Anne Dadier. Dadier's pregnant wife appears almost entirely in scenes that are spatially and narratively separated from the conflict at school. Trapped for the most part at home in the family apartment or later in the maternity ward at the hospital, Anne enters the conflict primarily as yet another, off-site object of struggle between her husband and Artie, who sends her letters asserting her husband's infidelity. Given that her isolation is what allows her to be emotionally devastated by the letters, Anne's story suggests other meanings, critical of the gendered boundary between public and private, that could enable another kind of oppositional reading. Both the gay and feminist readings, however, are buried by the masculinist oppositional reading, which requires that the film serve as an assertion of the rebel boy as hegemonic representative of what Frank Zappa termed the "teenage cause."

This leads us to a more historical observation, however, about the influential patterns of early identity discourse. It is no coincidence that the oppositional reading of *Blackboard Jungle*, which made the film into a prolific model for subsequent teenpics, so closely resembles the exemplary figures of resistance in the tradition of cultural studies. As Angela McRobbie once persuasively argued, British cultural studies was born through its own love affair with masculinist youth culture, romanticizing the tough rebelliousness of working-class boys: the mod, rocker, teddy boy, and punk heroes of books such as Stuart Hall and Tony Jefferson's *Resistance through Ritual* or Dick Hebdige's *Subculture*.[12] McRobbie might well have taken note of another evident exclusion in these books: that of gay youth.

Yet, before inquiring as to why girls and gay youth were excluded from their analyses of resistance, one might well ask the still more basic question as to why cultural studies staged resistance on the terrain of youth culture at all. Youth's privileged status as the subject of resistance, I would argue, was delivered to cultural studies courtesy of the discourse of identity itself, where from its inception in Erikson's work, youth had served as the life stage associated with agonistic identity formation. The oppositional reading of *Blackboard Jungle* was shaped by the discourse of identity, which then made its way into the youth movements of the 1960s, as witnessed by the continuities I have noted with the writings of Eldridge Cleaver and Jerry Farber. Cultural studies was itself born out of the New Left of the sixties, and the centrality of its concern with resistant youth cultures can be traced back quite compellingly to the identitarian cast that was given to the era's generational antagonisms as they played out in both the United States and Britain during the fifties. Cultural studies' own repertoire of oppositional images, in other words, draws heavily from the likes of Artie West, and this genealogy has everything to do with the discourse of identity that can be traced between them.

British cultural studies is usually understood as a movement rooted in class analysis in the British socialist tradition, though emphasizing the cultural as well as the economic determinants of class. As the opening essay in *Resistance through Ritual* (the seminal 1976 anthology edited by Stuart Hall and Tony Jefferson) reveals, however, cultural studies was saturated and guided by identity discourse from the start. This in fact helps to explain why cultural studies was so readily assimilated by subsequent American critics. In the opening essay, the word "identity" appears repeatedly, and most often when tracing the resistive unity of the youth subculture, in contrast to a more quiescent working-class "parent culture" that does not take arms in the conformist fifties against a subordinating hegemonic culture. The "generational experience of the young," Hall and his coauthors argue, should be privileged because youth encounters the structures of domination at "crucially different points in its biographical careers" than its parent culture. What they mean, in essence, is something like Erikson's concept of the moratorium, in which youth represents a moment of delay, prior to adulthood, when one may explore and evaluate social roles and self-conceptions. Should youth choose to resist the prospect of its insertion into the adult space of subjugation, it will develop rituals with which to fashion an oppositional identity voicing its own refusal, much like Erikson's drama of America's freeborn "rebel sons." A subculture crystallizes "an expressive form, which then defines the group's public identity. This 'internal coherence' moreover acts as 'a kind of implied opposition to (where it was not an active and conscious contradiction of) other groups against which its identity was defined'" (57). This lodging of "identity" in the space of the oppositional youth group finds its symbolic protoype in the boy gang of

Blackboard Jungle. The case of *Blackboard*'s prototeenpic meanings should therefore have a special poignancy for cultural studies practitioners, for they presage their own identitarian accounts of youth culture.

The submerged history of these strongly racialized and gendered encodings of rebel identity deserve further scholarly excavation, since today the young people of the fifties are largely remembered as the conservative elder siblings of sixties rebels. While youth in the fifties, mainstream pop history tells us, accepted the social complacency of their parents, it was only the next decade that witnessed a rupture in generational harmony. However, as the case of *Blackboard Jungle* indicates, generational rifts accompanying the rise of identity discourse came noticeably earlier. Specifically, *Blackboard* reveals how the historical moment of *Brown v. Board of Education* posed the cultural possibility of youth identity being defined against whiteness, and in solidarity with racial difference. The film thereby anticipates not only the anti–white-supremacist politics of identity that animated the black and brown power movements, but also the political activism of certain young whites in the sixties who would enthusiastically support the efforts of the Student Non-Violent Coordinating Committee (SNCC), form SDS (Students for a Democratic Society), volunteer to go south for Freedom Summer, and join Berkeley's free speech movement (itself born out of student solidarity work for southern civil rights). It also anticipates the writing of a book like Hebdige's *Subculture*, with its deep interest in the references and allusions of punk style to black culture.

At the same time, this tradition of racial and generational radicalism frequently articulated its rebellion against white adult power as a phallic sexuality against an emasculating social order. These masculinist tropes, evident in *Blackboard*'s prototeenpic reception, form a postwar trajectory discernible, to various degrees, in rock 'n' roll itself, the hipster subculture, and in such popular analyses as Mailer's "The White Negro" and Paul Goodman's *Growing Up Absurd*.[13] In the sixties, this phallic mode of protest was carried forward by figures such as Farber, who programmatically called for a youth politics "with balls," and Cleaver, who advocated the "rape-on-principle" of white women and denounced James Baldwin as a sexual traitor to his race. The generational and racial radicalism made available by *Blackboard Jungle*, then, structured into its opposition a tendency toward misogynistic and homophobic modes of protest.

As subsequent chapters will elaborate, certain countertendencies existed such that both female and queer protest also remained possible within the general political domain of youth identity. At the same time, this dominant code of masculinized rebellion would become oppressive enough by the late sixties to help to precipitate a splintering of the youth movement into the larger array of activisms that we have come to call identity politics.[14] Yet the questions with which this chapter began remains open: Why did identitarian opposition take so masculinist a form? What were the ideological stakes involved in the drama of the bad boy? To answer these questions, we must return to the gendered space of the suburban family.

5

OEDIPUS IN SUBURBIA:

BAD BOYS AND THE FORDIST

FAMILY DRAMA

In her original attributes, then, the American woman was a fitting and heroic companion to the post-revolutionary man, who was possessed with the idea of freedom from any man's autocracy and haunted by the fear that the nostalgia for some homeland and the surrender to some king could ever make him give in to political slavery. Mother became "Mom" only when Father became "Pop" under the impact of the identical historical discontinuities.
—Erik Erikson, *Childhood and Society*

How is a man to know who he is today? By what does he identify himself? Not by a relationship to the soil on which he was born. . . . Nor can a person find his identity in the family—for that institution is breaking down. . . . The sudden equality of the sexes creates tension in both men and women as they realize their old roles are destroyed but are uncertain what their new ones should be.
—David McReynolds, "Hipsters Unleashed"

I never look for trouble
But I never ran
I don't take no kind of orders
From no kind of man
I'm only made out
Of flesh, blood, and bone
But if you gonna start a rumble
Don't you try it alone
Well, I'm evil
So don't mess around with me.
—Elvis Presley, "Trouble," from *King Creole*

As I have argued, Cold War culture advanced contradictory perspectives on American life. On the one hand, the United States was celebrated as the archetypal democratic nation, championing the freedom of its individual members. And yet, the sovereign *individuality* of an American appeared elusive in an era that also heralded the standardization of life in the new suburbs. The allegedly declining autonomy of the typical American became an especially vehement topic when brought to bear on the figure of the sovereign male citizen, understood as the individual atom of a free "American people" that defied mass mentalities. This is the context that accounts for the influence of William Whyte's attack on the postwar "organization man" and his capitulatory "social ethic." It also informs *The Lonely Crowd*'s grim narrative of the transition from America's great "inner-directed" men—its founding fathers, pioneers, and self-made heroes—to a new "glad-handing" American, driven by his social image rather than personal conviction. Manhood, in short, came to measure the dangers that the mass culture of Fordism posed to the sovereign personality—and thus to the positive identity—of the American people.

Advocating the view that the dangers to American manhood were being fully realized, Paul Goodman's influential *Growing Up Absurd* argued that the nation's "youth problems" could only be meaningfully understood alongside the dissolution of "excellence and manliness" perpetrated by the "conformity of the organization" (x). Published at the end of the fifties, when the "juvenile delinquent," the "beat generation," and the teen "rebel" had already become central motifs in the media landscape, Goodman's book brought together the various strands of anti-Fordist critique, arguing that America's youth problem did not stem from its boys' failure to get a clear message about how to grow into men. Rather, they had understood the organized society's instructions all too well, and had rejected them. Any boy who obediently "adjusted" himself to the demeaning roles of organizational manhood, and thereby forfeited his "manly independence," was simply "growing up absurd." It should not be so surprising, therefore, that so many boys declined to do so. Writ small, Goodman's national narrative of "absurd development" dramatized nothing less than the son of the Fordist suburbs refusing to become like his father.

Such stories about a bad boy in conflict with suburban manhood loosely constitute an oedipal drama, playing out as they do the son's aggressive feelings toward his father. Yet it is not identical to Freud's oedipal drama for several reasons. The son does not wish to replace the father so as to gain possession of the mother. Rather, in this drama, the son *refuses* to replace the father, and often precisely because he does not want to be *possessed by* the mother as is his father. This oedipal drama of the suburbs worked explicitly within the Cold War "momist" tradition, most vehemently represented by Philip Wylie in *A Generation of Vipers*, in which a castrating wife's demands underscore her husband's loss of agency. Erikson, while sympathetically "explaining" the historical basis for her domineering character, likewise cited "Mom" as a key threat to contemporary "American identity" because she exposed young American psyches to an "emotional and political short circuit" that jeopardized nation's "dynamic potential" (287).[1] In the resulting drama, the son does not desire "mom" (or her younger counterparts) so much as he fears the threat of impotence she brings. The suburban Oedipus, therefore, was no small child caught in the moment of the Freudian sexual drama. Rather, he was an adolescent or teenager, caught in the quite different (and later) moment of an Eriksonian drama. What looks like an oedipal crisis is in fact a staging of Erikson's single most famous scenario: the identity crisis. Because his father has failed him as a model of sovereign male personality, the son must move through what Erikson called "disidentification" or "negative identification," a rejection of the flawed paternal role. Sexuality remains at issue in this drama, but less as a matter of the son's object choice than as an expression of the erotics of (his) identity.[2]

Hollywood and the New Rebel Hero

It is worth recalling that, in *The Catcher in the Rye*, Holden Caulfield singled out Hollywood movies as the phoniest of all media for the telling of stories. When it comes to the "character" of its men, Holden vigorously denounces the unflappable Hollywood "tough guy," who shows neither fear nor vulnerability. By the mid-fifties, however, Hollywood films had begun to image a different sort of male star, whose sensibility approximated Holden's own, thanks to the growing influence of Lee Strasberg's Actors Studio and its brand of method acting. Typically projecting such qualities as emotional vulnerability, disaffected inner isolation, and eroticized sensitivity, the new method acting stars such as Marlon Brando, James Dean, and Montgomery Clift, as Virginia Wexman observes, were often labeled rebel heroes, "a new breed of neurotic, alienated men, reckless and nonconforming both on-screen and off [whose] alienation centered on their sense of themselves as male" (169).

As Wexman notes, these rebel heroes also seemed to embody an uncertain relationship to heterosexual masculinity. Though their films still might thematize a romantic plot, they differed sharply from traditional Hollywood love stories where a courtship was threatened by external obstacles. As Wexman puts it, "In the films of these new stars . . . love came to be seen as a relationship in which the woman ministered to the internal conflicts of a neurotic male who was unsure of his masculine identity" (170). This male heterosexual uncertainy, Wexman argues, was closely associated with prolonged adolescence, and an inability or unwillingness of the protagonist to mature. It is no surprise that in describing Salinger's appeal to youth readers, one of *Catcher*'s critics of the fifties, David Leitch, explicitly associated the style of James Dean's character in *Rebel without a Cause* with Salinger's Holden: "Jim [James Dean's character], like 'the catcher,' is a big brother and protector. In his mannerisms—the disconnected, hesitating speech, his slouching walk and unexpected, whimsy gestures—he expresses a childish uncertainty and confusion similar to that suggested by Holden through language" (76).

Few films prior to 1955 actually deployed this new "Holdenesque" acting sensibility of Hollywood's younger stars in order to represent "youth problems." Yet the first two films to do so—*The Wild One* and *Rebel without a Cause*—had a huge impact, singlehandedly breaking with prior cinematic traditions of adolescent representation, which had divided fairly neatly between narratives of young toughs from the slums in need of adult help and spiritual redemption (exemplified in the Dead End Kid films of the thirties) and those of relatively untroubled middle-class kids (such as the Andy Hardy films of the forties starring Mickey Rooney).

I have already discussed how *Blackboard Jungle*'s use of the rock 'n' roll's countersuburban imaginary became a blueprint for Hollywood's designs on a teen market. Brando and Dean also made an immense contribution to the rise of the teenpic through their pioneering iconizations of the bad boy as a cinematic type. *Wild One*, *Rebel*, and *Blackboard Jungle* were soon followed by numerous (often lower budget) films starring other young actors—Elvis Presley, Sal Mineo, Steve McQueen, Michael Landon, John Saxon, John Cassavetes, and others. Almost overnight the teenpic was born as the preeminent narrative medium through which the bad boy circulated.

The postwar films most closely associated with method performance, as Wexman also notes, often concerned "the rebel hero's difficulty defining himself in relation to a father figure" (170). This "difficulty," as we shall see, stands in for the Eriksonian moment of "identity crisis," as it confronts a suburban manhood that embodies an identitarian crisis of agency and personal sovereignty. In this chapter, I consider two method-inspired films that staged the ideological tensions shaping the rebel boy's oedipal drama of identity: *Rebel without a Cause*, starring James Dean, and *King Creole*, starring Elvis Presley. In both films, the "struggle for identity" was conflated with the reconsolidation of sovereign masculinity, an articulation that bore deeply conservative implications. At the same time, they also pit the rebel's boyhood against his father's manhood by borrowing strategically from various codes of blackness, working-classness, gayness, and even (paradoxically) femininity. Despite its apparent gender conservatism, the oedipal rebel drama thereby carved out space for a much wider appropriation of identity discourse.

The Domesticated Male: Boon or Bane?

In the popular imagination, we usually associate the fifties with a cult of domesticity, but many of the period's oedipal identity dramas, *Rebel without a Cause* and *King Creole* included, suggest that domesticity was actually a deeply embattled postwar value. If domesticity finds its binary opposite in wildness, then certainly there were moments in the 1950s when wildness was preferable, as we saw in the positive reading of the delinquents inhabiting the "blackboard jungle," or even in the "wild" antisuburban energies of rock 'n' roll. Domesticity, after all, conjured up the lifestyle of the Fordist suburbs, and these suburbs—as we have seen—took on both a utopic and a dystopic set of meanings. Domesticity, like the "organization," expressed the impulse to a Fordist standardization of culture that was often seen as problematic from the emerging viewpoint of identity discourse.

Manhood held a special place in the contestation of domesticity, much as it did for public doubts about the "organization," as one can see from a pictorial article that appeared in the January 1954 issue of *Life*. Entitled "A Boon to the Household and a Boom for Industry: The New American Domesticated Male," this playful article's sequence of cartoon frames depicts the domesticated male's many advantages as a modern and progressive type of husband and father (4). No longer a mere breadwinner who lives largely in the outside world and plays little role at home beyond enforcing discipline, the new domesticated male finds himself primarily as an integral family member and consumer. *Life*'s article projects a past when men had understood themselves primarily as producer—psychically oriented around a life at work—and when women had been responsible for conducting the ancillary business of household consumption for their men. Now, however, the article suggests, times had changed for the better. Men too have become creatures of the private sphere, their wives' domestic partners in a child-centered family life organized by purchase and consumption of commodities. *Life* of course touts this development as a "boom for industry," a key element in stimulating consumption for the Fordist economy. But more striking is its alleged "boon for the household," since wives and children were held to appreciate men's increased participation in the domestic sphere.

This Fordist celebration of male domesticity dovetailed with certain prominent Cold War interests. To begin with, shifting the terrain of definition for masculinity from production to consumption worked to undermine the forms of male worker-identity upon which the spectrum of thirties leftwing culture—from the New Deal to the Communist Party of the U.S.A.—had been based. Touting the American male's move from producerist to consumerist identity served the rhetorical purpose of showing that American men had implicitly repudiated "divisive" class politics in favor of a universal sharing of the fruits of American capitalism. These ideological implications often became explicitly part of Cold War propaganda, given that a domestic lifestyle of mass consumption was held to demonstrate the American way of life's superiority over Soviet communism. For example, as Elaine May points out, in the famous "Kitchen Debate" with Nikita Khrushchev, Vice President Nixon rhapsodized the affluent living standards of the new American suburbs as a model for all nations (16–19). Domesticity for men as well as for women therefore aligned with Cold War interests insofar as the lure of suburban mass consumption aided in both the international and the domestic attacks on communism.

By and large, however, it was his "boon to the household" that made the domesticated male a sometimes Cold War hero, anchoring as he did an egalitarian and consensual family structure that better reflected American democratic values. Postwar celebrations of domesticity, of course, also abetted the rapid demobilization of women in the workforce as World War II veterans returned home. Paradoxically, however, women's domestication was *equated* with their wartime employment. As Elaine Tyler May notes: "Experts called upon women to embrace domesticity in service to the nation, in the same spirit that they had come to the country's aid by taking wartime jobs. To meet the challenge of the postwar era, women were to marshall their energies into a 'New Family Type for the Space Age.' Women's domestic roles needed to be infused with a sense of national purpose" (102).

This "New Family Type" required not merely the domestication of women, however, but also of men, who were expected to relinquish patriarchal status and become "equal" partners with their wives. This shift bears important psychopolitical connotations that trace back to popular arguments (elaborated by Wilhelm Reich and the Frankfurt school writers) concerning fascism's origins in hierarchical family relations (20). Already by 1945, this argument had received a full articulation in a *Parents* magazine article entitled, "How *Not* To Raise Our Children." In it the author, Harriet Davis, warns readers to take heed of the lesson Germany offered because, despite the unconscious admiration some Americans hold for the efficiency of fascist regimes, Germany's political values are in every respect opposite of those esteemed in America: "submission, not self-reliance ... authority not justice ... power, not principle ... status, not equality ... obedience, not achievement" (122). While Davis's dichotomous binaries were meant to distinguish liberal democracy from fascist authoritarianism, in a few short years they would be widely applied to the rival characters of the American and Soviet systems, the former geared toward nourishing the "identity" of its citizens, the latter toward dissolving them into mass subjection.

The fascist power to dissolve personal sovereignty, Davis explains, begins with a child's acclimation to her or his own subjection within a patriarchal family:

> The German father reigned supreme in the home; his wife bowed to his will, and his presence was a source of potential fear to the children. Their first duty, like their mother's, was submission to his authority. . . . [T]o complete the bewilderment, a child saw his father, the domestic god, whose word was law at home, change into a quite different creature, bowing and scraping to his superiors the moment he stepped over his own doorsill. The stern frown became an ingratiating smile; the erstwhile tyrant clicked his heels and bowed. . . . Father's own childhood obedience carried inevitably over into unquestioning adult submission to authority. (122–124)

As Davis's argument shows, the identitarian ideal of the young self emerging into sovereignty out of "childhood obedience" was closely tied to conceptions of the American family as the primary setting for inculcating psychopolitical rights. Specifically, sovereign personality becomes an ideal to be defended against the protofascistic authoritarianism of the old world patriarchal family. In its place, Davis advocates a new world, liberal family system that remains consistent with modern democratic values:

> Our democratic ideals are standing the test of war as well of peace, proving the strong and healthy endurance of American "culture." . . . A sound inner core of strength should grow from our American ideal of parent-partnership, both father and mother strong, both kind, both standing for the same principles. . . . Any mother who longs in a weak moment for the kind of husband who exerts old-fashioned discipline may well ask herself how she would enjoy seeing her children cringe in their father's presence and how long she could submit to the masculine arrogance which accompanies such a family system. (122)

The autonomy of the young (i.e., the ability of children *not* to cringe in their father's presence) thus depends integrally upon nonpatriarchal arrangements of equal power and shared interests between mothers and fathers. As the war against fascism gave way to the war against communism, liberal discourse continued to emphasize this ideal of achieving a democratic family capable of raising children as autonomous liberal subjects who would preserve the independence of the American mind, while immunizing it from communist worship of the state. *Parents* in particular continued to invoke the familial ideology outlined by Davis, publishing new articles such as "You're Practicing Democracy at Home When the Children Help Make Decisions in Family Council" and related parental pledges such as "Help Make Democracy Live" (10).

Davis's vision rewrites the popular postwar version of the Freudian drama—whereby the father represents authority (morality, the law, the superego) and the mother desire (affection, satisfaction, the id object)—so as to incorporate women's wartime sense of empowerment, displacing it, however, from the workplace to the family. In tacit compensation for women's return to the home, Davis's model family type requires marital equality. Even as Davis urges women to become wives and mothers, she also encourages their self-assertion as strong family leaders who avoid "weak moments" of capitulation to their husbands. Men, while restored to the status of breadwinner, must renounce the "masculine arrogance" of patriarchal prerogative to become equal partners with women, sometimes even children, in the domestic sphere of American democracy.[3]

All of these Cold War credentials notwithstanding, the domestication of the American male came in for considerable criticism. Even *Life*'s own cartoon strip depiction of the "New American Domesticated Male," though inflected positively, employs a tongue-in-cheek tone suggesting that something was amiss in a world where men were expected to become so thoroughly creatures of domestic life. Conservative writers and critics objected more bluntly, arguing that the so-called modern, new, or democratic suburban family only diluted men's self-esteem when it blurred the distinctions between fathering and mothering. Boys raised in such a family would surely find themselves without adequate masculine role models. Bruno Bettleheim, in a typical article titled "Fathers Shouldn't Try to Be Mothers," wistfully described the recent decline in "the old-fashioned family [where] the father, through his work, provided for the family's physical existence and, he hoped, its emotional well-being. He set an example for standards of behavior and enforced them. He was the protector and the breadwinner—in a time when the bread was harder to win and the family knew it" (40). Lamentably, postwar affluence had already diminished the father's stature as breadwinner, but the "democratic" family only exacerbated this situation by requiring him to participate in the feminine tasks of childrearing and domestic upkeep: "When he tries to find greater fulfillment of his fatherhood by doing more for the child along the lines only mothers used to follow, the result is that he finds less rather than more fulfillment, not only for his fatherhood, but also for his manhood. The completion of womanhood is largely through motherhood, but fulfillment of manhood is achieved [not] through fatherhood . . . [but] by making a contribution to society as a whole, an impulse which is quickened when a responsible man becomes a father" (126). As Bettleheim and other gender conservatives warned, men who followed *Life*'s advice by defining themselves through their domestic roles rather than their work lives would soon find their masculine position within the family supplanted by a grotesque mimicry of motherhood.

Like Davis's liberal agenda for the family, Bettleheim's conservative program also justified itself within a wider field of Cold War discourse. The liberal democratization of the family, claimed conservatives, far from constituting an institutional bulwark against communist authoritarianism, placed America at grave risk. The abdication of patriarchal authority, like the abandonment of religion, could lead only to softness, moral decay, and loss of the masculine virtues so sorely needed for the struggle against world communism. J. Edgar Hoover's 1956 speech "The Twin Enemies of Freedom: Crime and Communism," for instance, blamed youth's susceptibility to both juvenile delinquency and communism squarely on parental unwillingness to "administer discipline," "provide firm moral backing," or even teach the distinct "spiritual and civic responsibilities of manhood and womanhood" (105).

In a similar pronouncement, noted Princeton economist Mark Jones concurred that the nation's youth problems stemmed from liberal parenting philosophy:

> We are saturated with equalitarian sophistries and hell bent for the impossible in the form of repealing the basic laws of nature which give us individual differences. We seek earnestly for some way to realize our wishful thinking. . . . We would like to have individuals with a hard fiber, but produce them by soft methods. . . . Turning from the utterly unrealistic spirit of majority sentiment toward reality, we find first that we are deep in the throes of Socialism. While we have been diverted with equalitarian wishful thinking, the stagehands have completely changed the set behind the iron curtain, and we are more than halfway back toward slavery. (662)

Hoover's and Jones's polemics point to the profound conflicts between the Fordist suburban family vision and more conservative elements in Cold War discourse. *Life*'s "Domesticated Male" served well as the egalitarian father of Davis's democratic family, but he most certainly did not evince the "hard fiber" called for by conservative anticommunists.

Life itself printed a commentary on these fault lines between Fordist family life and Cold War conservatism in its next issue, where a strongly worded editorial letter denounced the new masculinity that the magazine had effectively praised: "Sirs: The new American domesticated male makes me sick. No culture worth a damn ever raised a race of comfort-seekers, puttering like women. If this pot-bellied 'male' replaces our adventurers, our explorers, our rebels, it will be at great cost to our great nation. Signed, R. Sperry."

Like Hoover and Jones, Sperry used a rhetoric that mobilizes a binary of soft/effeminate versus hard/masculine, in this case mapped onto an opposition posed between suburban consumerism and national heroism. Sperry's attack on the emasculation of the domesticated father-husband sheds light on the gendered character of the bad boy, a figure who embodied everything for which Sperry wished. If father would no longer be the adventurer, explorer, and rebel, then at least the son wished to take his place. If postwar manhood was found lacking in masculine sovereignty (as we also saw in *Blackboard Jungle*), perhaps it could be located instead in postwar boyhood.

The "identity crisis" dramatized by the Hollywood "rebel movie" captures this precise ambivalence toward male domesticity. As we shall see, films such as *Rebel without a Cause* and *King Creole* incorporated both liberal and conservative discourses on domesticated males and the family. Like gender conservatives, Hollywood's bad boy cringed in his dad's presence, not because he was the "erstwhile tyrant" described by Davis in *Parents* magazine, but rather because he was the "potbellied 'male'" maligned by R. Sperry, a figure who would "bow and scrape" no less pathetically than Davis's "authoritarian German father." All the same, the bad boy was no aspiring patriarch. In these films, the bad boy's love interests—sometimes a girl who overtly eroticizes him, sometimes another boy who homoeroticizes him—point toward gendered futures that were anything but conservative for their time. So too with the bad boy's general quest for identity, which draws not on the "traditionalist" codes of the great white patriarch, but rather on blackness, working-classness, ethnic, sexual, and even gender difference to establish a countersuburban authority.

The Rebel's Causes

Among the numerous bad boys of the fifties, James Dean in *Rebel without a Cause* has probably become the single most famous and lasting avatar. As Graham McCann puts it, Dean projected an image of being "the middle-class boy from the Midwest who dropped out (before there was any 'counterculture' to drop into), the 'first American teenager'" (21). Dean posed continually during his short career as a bohemian, a lover of fast cars and late nights, a player of bongo drums, and an aficionado of nearly every signifier of rebel youth. Moreover, Dean's sudden death in a car crash, at the age of twenty-four, while en route to a racing event uncannily echoed the close call experienced by his character in *Rebel without a Cause*, Jim Stark, while participating in a "chickie run." Though in the public eye for no more than a year, in death Dean became a cult figure for young Americans, who would devote to him an endless stream of fanzines, clubs, documentaries, and books. Dean's romanticized end solidified his reputation as the preeminent figure of the suburban American teenage boy as a natural-born rebel.

Yet Dean's image rests on numerous historical contingencies without which he would never have so fully signified the fifties bad boy. To begin with, Dean's primary film vehicle, *Rebel*, had important sources in director Nicholas Ray's personal history. Forty-four years old when *Rebel* was released in 1955, Ray had once been active in the radical theater of the thirties, working as a member of the leftwing Theater of Action troupe in New York City. Even at this early stage, Ray's interest in the political motif of youth was already evidenced in a play he performed called *The Young Go First*. Collectively written by members of the troupe, the play criticized the paramilitary structure of the New Deal's Youth Conservation Corp, while dramatizing the exploitation of youth by adults for military purposes (Eisenschitz, 22–32).

In 1948, Ray began working in Hollywood. One of his earliest and most explicitly political films, *Knock on Any Door* (1949), was a naturalistic courtroom drama in which a lawyer (Humphrey Bogart) defends a poor Italian boy named Nick Romano (played by John Derek) against a murder charge, pleading with the court to consider the corrosive effects of the boy's personal hardships growing up in the slums. One of Nick Romano's badboy slogans, "Live fast, die young, leave a beautiful corpse," would later be famously repeated by James Dean himself, in an eerie predictive interpretation of his own death as an expression of youthful defiance.

Shortly after the release of *Knock on Any Door*, the House Un-American Activities Committee launched its campaign against Hollywood leftists in earnest, and Ray later claimed that he was only saved from blacklisting by the personal intervention of Howard Hughes, then owner of RKO Studios, this despite refusing Hughes's request that he direct the red-baiting film project *I Married a Communist*. Ray's 1954 film, *Johnny Guitar*, which dealt with a hostile town's collective effort to scapegoat and destroy the livelihood of a saloon owner (Joan Crawford), can in fact be read as a veiled indictment of the McCarthy witch hunts. When Ray returned to the theme of youth, six years after *Knock*, with *Rebel without a Cause*, his new project bore hardly a trace of the traditional sociological discourse of leftwing or progressive politics. Unlike Nick Romano in *Knock on Any Door*, whose badness constitutes a response to poverty and social injustice, Jim Stark of *Rebel without a Cause* would lack any economic basis for his rebellion, which took instead the psychopolitical form of an oedipal conflict. Nevertheless, the thematic of youth rebellion in *Rebel* might be understood to have preserved for Ray an expression of dissent against an inhuman and repressive social order, however depoliticized in Old Left terms.

Dean's consummate bad-boy status also derived from *Rebel*'s proximity to the very heart of identity discourse. It was Robert Lindner who provided Ray's film project with its name when, in 1944, he published a case study with the title *Rebel without a Cause*. In it Lindner describes his clinical work with Harold, a boy whose early deprivation and abuse by a tyrannical father had "stunted" his superego and left him with a pyschopathic personality. Harold's upbringing closely resembles that of the child in the German authoritarian family described by Harriet Davis, and Lindner indeed considered the importance of Harold's case to lie in the fact that "the psychopath is not only a criminal; he is the embryonic Storm-Trooper," the personality type that serves the fascist leader (16).

Very little of Lindner's original text actually survives in the Hollywood film, with the exception of its basic premise that adolescent troubles primarily derive from dysfunctional family relations. A series of writers, including Irving Schulman, perhaps the most popular postwar novelist of juvenile delinquency, were hired by Warner Brothers to translate Lindner's study into a screenplay. After 1944 meanwhile, Lindner went on to publish several new studies in which he continued to revise his psychopolitical argument about youth rebellion.

In 1955, nearly simultaneously with the production of Ray's film, Lindner put out his most controversial book, *Must You Conform?*, an essay collection arguing that demands on individuals to conform in an increasingly massified society had reached a dangerous level. Rebellion, Lindner argued, is an invaluable instinct that leads humans to reject and change their environmental status quo with the aim of improving the quality of civilized life. Breaking with mainstream American psychiatry, Lindner fiercely attacked "adjustment" as the "Big Lie" used in modern conformist societies to stifle this instinct. Such "adjustment," he warned, leads inexorably to various forms of deviant and socially *unuseful* rebellion among the young, including fascistic or communistic mass politics, juvenile delinquency, and even homosexuality. Whether or not Ray was explicitly influenced by these ideas, it is evident that the film version of *Rebel* adopts the basic premise of Lindner's later work, namedly that conformist pressures have forced youth into dangerous acts of rebellion.[4] Indirectly then, Dean's image as a countersuburban rebel is heavily indebted to Lindner.

The fortuitous convergence of these variables—Ray's leftist background, Lindner's identitarian psychiatry, and Dean's own version of method acting—conferred upon the bad-boy figure in *Rebel without a Cause* a star status with tremendous oppositional possibilities. In the film, however,

OEDIPUS IN SUBURBIA 179

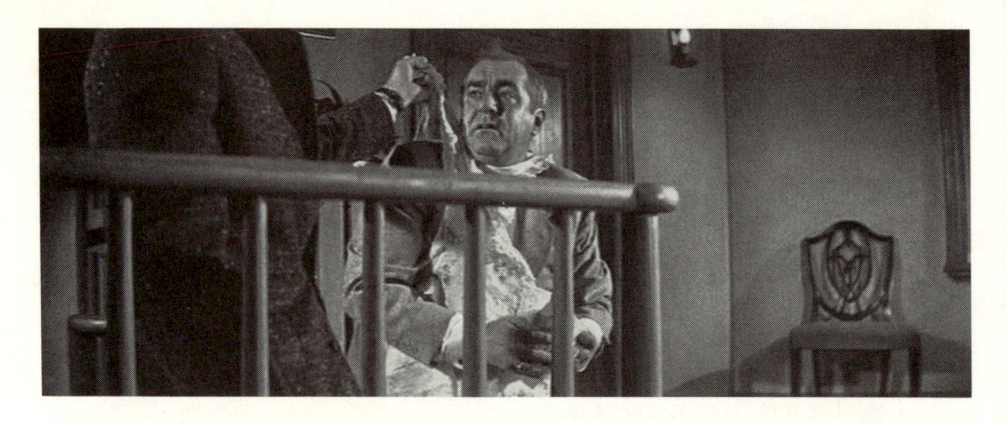

11. Mr. Stark as the "Domesticated Male" in *Rebel without a Cause* (Warner Brothers, 1955).

these historical determinants of the rebel give way to a more proximate narrative cause: the domesticated father who must be rejected by the son seeking his identity. "I'll tell you one thing," proclaims the film's otherwise confused teenage protagonist Jim Stark, gesturing toward his father, "I don't ever want to become like that!" Jim's disidentification is powerfully captured in a memorable scene when, hearing a crash at home, Jim looks down the stairs only to find his aproned, kneeling father cleaning up a spilled tray of food intended for mother. As his father mumbles, "Better clean it up before she sees it," Jim, sickened like R. Sperry at the sight of a "pot-bellied" domesticated male, stutters: "Let her see it. What can happen? Dad... stand... don't... you shouldn't... what're you...?" In *Rebel*, Jim's dilemma is premised on a series of equivalences: a father's domestication equals his feminization, which equals his loss of authority, which equals his symbolic castration. It is significant that this scene is very much about pain in the son's gaze upon his father. *Rebel*, I suggest, is organized visually in a way that constructs a male spectator position different from, but in a specifiable relation to, the conventional male spectator associated with classical Hollywood cinema.

The Rebel's Plight

Rebel without a Cause, it is commonly noted, is a middle-class juvenile delinquency film. Founded on Lindner's ideas, it makes considerable use of popular psychiatric discourse to explicate its "social problem" as a by-product of dysfunctional families. Three troubled teenagers, whom we meet in an opening scene at the police station, serve as the film's protagonists. Jim Stark is the new teenager in the neighborhood, a kid completely at odds with his parents. Jim initially lacks even an acquaintance at school, but quickly befriends a social pariah nicknamed Plato (played by Sal Mineo). Jim also becomes interested in Judy (played by Natalie Wood), a local teenage girl who is dating Buzz, leader of a local gang.

Always eager for kicks, the gang encourages Buzz to challenge Jim, first to knife fight and then to a chickie run with stolen cars. When Buzz dies accidentally during the run, the gang flees, leaving Jim, Judy, and Plato together. The three outcasts grow close, eventually forming a fictive nuclear family, with Jim and Judy as parents and Plato as the son. But in a scene at an abandoned house, while Jim and Judy have momentarily left the sleeping Plato so as to be alone together, the vengeful gang shows up and terrorizes him. Plato, who has brought a gun with him, fires at one of the gang members and runs away, tearfully berating Jim for failing him as a father. Jim and Judy pursue Plato, as do the police. Following him into the local planetarium where he has holed up, Jim nearly persuades Plato to surrender. At the last moment, however, the police mistakenly open fire and Plato is killed. Frank Stark, who by now is on the scene (with his wife too), promises his son that henceforth he will try to be stronger. Jim sadly introduces his parents to Judy, and the movie then ends as everyone leaves in a funeral-like procession of cars.

Rebel quickly reveals its three protagonists as the unwilling victims of various forms of parental failure. In the opening scene, each teenager has been separately hauled in to the local police station for a minor act of delinquency. There the chief police officer, Ray, teases out a lay psychiatric exposition of each of the youth's home problems. As it happens, these problems largely revolve around the inadequacies of their respective fathers. Plato, caught shooting puppies, is a child abandoned by both his parents to the care of their black maid, but Plato's tragedy is epitomized in a late scene by the painful discovery of his absent father's monthly support check. Judy consorts with a gang of hoodlums because her father is unable or unwilling to express his affection for her. In both cases, Plato and Judy's parents deny their children something vital to their maturity. Plato needs the most basic care from his parents, and responds to its absence by showing cruelty toward the young. Judy requires a physical affection from her father that will ease her way into mature heterosexual romance.

Jim's own family problems become clear when his parents and grandmother arrive to pick him up at the station. Mother and mother-in-law begin trading shrewish accusations as to who is at fault for their boy's delinquent tendencies, with father hesitantly joining in the hectoring exchange. Listening to the three as they swap their inconsistent arguments, Jim finally yells in exasperation, "You're tearing me apart. You. You say one thing. He says another, and everyone changes back again." This interchangeability horrifies Jim as a child of the domesticated male, and a victim of the so-called modern democratic family in which the father has granted "Mom" too much authority. The oedipal drama set in motion inverts the Freudian scenario: in lieu of a son who competes with his father for his mother, Jim must compete with his mother for meaningful access to his father.

Significantly, the bad boy's visual positioning is made explicit when Jim enters Officer Ray's private office. Ray represents everything that Jim's father lacks—authority, confidence, and even the strength to strike Jim when he gets too troublesome. Ray in short proves his mettle as the kind of man that Jim might want as a father. What the state can supply, however, Jim's modern family cannot. As Ray asks about his situation at home, Jim peers through the keyhole at his parents. From a Freudian perspective, father and mother should be the objects through which a male child establishes his respective relations of identification and desire; Jim's view of the parents would therefore ideally unite into one gaze what Laura Mulvey calls narcissistic gratification (the father as ego ideal) and scopophilic gratification (the mother as the originary object of desire). But Jim's act of voyeurism is anything but productive of pleasure. Though the character's, spectator's, and camera's points of view have been perfectly aligned, invoking the suturing technique of classic Hollywood cinema, Jim's gaze produces, not visual pleasure, but instead a painful confrontation with castration anxiety, though one in which the parental character roles have been perversely switched. Turning away from the keyhole, Jim announces his mother's mastery of his father to be the source of his problems: "I don't know what to do anymore, except die. Maybe if he had the guts to knock Mom cold once, then maybe she'd be happy and then she'd stop picking on him, because they make mush out of him, you know? Just mush. Now, I'll tell you one thing. I don't ever want to be like him." The codes of the classical gaze so well described by Laura Mulvey, though in play, are made to signify an atypical message. Jim's father, far from representing the imaginary male self, the more perfect image in the mirror who can serve as an ego ideal, represents instead a degraded self, the visual prospect of emasculation. Neither does mother serve as a primary object upon whom Jim

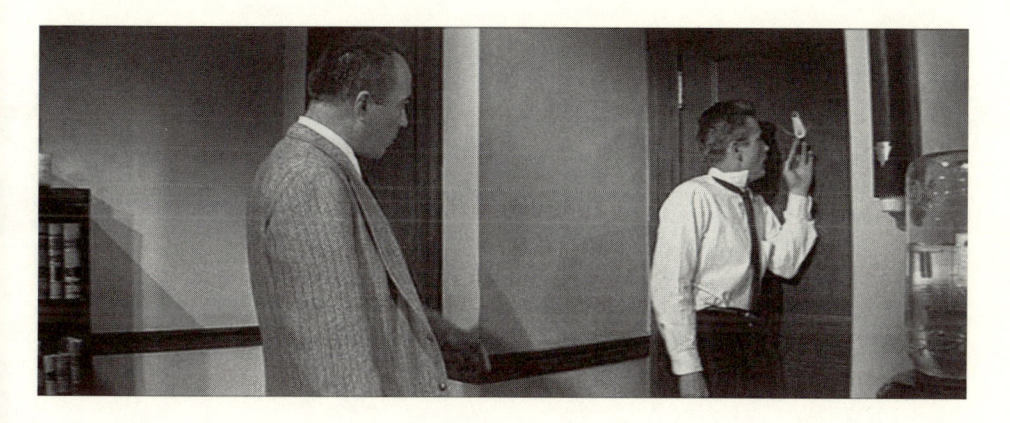

12. Jim looks painfully through the keyhole in *Rebel without a Cause* (Warner Brothers, 1955).

might model his subsequent erotic interests. In the Stark family, it is not the mother who implicitly represents the castrated subject, and the father the potential castrator. Rather, it is the mother who *explicitly* castrates, and the father who is evidently castrated, and with whom the son therefore must avoid any identification. This refusal to identify is repeatedly represented in Jim's pained gaze. *Rebel* is replete with shots of Jim with his eyes closed, or looking down and to the side, especially at those moments when his father overtly fails him. In turning away from this "stark" version of the father in the modern family, Jim's narrative moves instead toward an exploration of various "deviant" alternatives.

Ganging up on Masculinity: Straight Stories

If what makes Frank Stark painful to behold is his inability to master his own wife, one might expect a phallic masculinity, as embodied in a voyeuristic male gaze, to represent the option that Jim seeks. In *Blackboard Jungle*, as we saw, it was just such a phallic connotation of the gang's rebelliousness that activated that film's "oppositional reading." *Rebel* likewise presents phallic boyhood as a rebellious alternative to domesticated manhood. Early in the film, Jim achieves a degree of voyeuristic mastery through the mediation of the macho delinquent gang led by Buzz. As Jim realizes that Judy, to whom he is attracted, is Buzz's girlfriend, a love triangle takes shape in which Jim joins Buzz as a classic bearer of the male look, while Judy appears as the image to be looked at.

This status, however, is only activated upon personal danger. Follow-

13. Buzz's knife caresses the tire of Jim's car in *Rebel without a Cause* (Warner Brothers, 1955).

ing a field trip to the local planetarium, the mischievous gang tries to goad Jim into a confrontation. As they surround his car, Judy sits on the hood, smiling dangerously at Jim and making herself up in a hand mirror. The camera cuts to Buzz's point of view as he looks down at Judy's legs dangling next to the tire. Buzz then looks back up at Jim, and the camera cuts to a close-up of his face; Jim has been caught sharing Buzz's gaze at his girlfriend's legs. As though in response, Buzz takes out his knife and slides it toward them. For a moment it seems that the target might be Judy's legs, but instead Buzz punctures the tire. As it caresses the tire in this particular shot, the knife is painfully overstated as a violent, phallic symbol for the gang. Equally overstated is the implied masochistic pleasure Judy takes from her position in the gang's sexual system. The gang allows her to occupy a feminized position of sexual exhibition, something to which her father is extremely hostile. Both Hollywood's male gaze and its female image, apparently disabled by the suburban family, are thus recaptured with the help of the gang.

The gang's promise of phallic erotic power is emplotted as a failure, however, in that it demands a regressive immaturity. Both Jim and Judy explore juvenile delinquency, after all, because their families have failed to provide them with adequate oedipal resolutions to adult masculinity and femininity. The gang attracts both of them because it provides an apparent option. Jim can be macho, desiring Judy, fighting Buzz with knives, then racing in a chickie run. Similarly, Judy can be feminine and feel desired by her boyfriend and by Jim too when he competes for her. But, as both Jim

184 CHAPTER FIVE

14. Jim serves as Judy's erotic object in *Rebel without a Cause* (Warner Brothers, 1955).

and Judy come to see, this requires unsustainable performative antics (like knife fights and chickie runs) that culminate in disaster.

When Buzz dies during the chickie run, the gang's appeal evaporates for both Jim and Judy, and so too do its looking relations. Jim and Judy begin to cultivate a different sort of heterosexual relationship that culminates in a late scene where they leave Plato to find time alone in the upstairs of an abandoned house. Looking relations are reversed as Judy now contemplates *Jim* as an erotic object. As she lies on top, gazing at him while his eyes flutter open and closed, Judy asks Jim what kind of person he thinks a girl wants. It is significant that Judy quite carefully avoids asking "what kind of man" and Jim, apparently surprised by her ambiguity, responds that of course a girl wants "a man." Judy does not deny this, but qualifies his answer: "Yes, but a man who can be gentle and sweet, like you are . . . and someone who doesn't run away when you want them. Like being Plato's friend when no one else liked him. That's being strong." These conventionally feminine qualities—gentleness, sweetness, but especially nurturance—are converted into masculine ones by Judy, who claims that they signal strength. However, this image of masculinity closely resembles, and thus shares the ideological precariousness of *Life*'s "American domesticated male." Like her pleasure in an earlier scene when she observes that Jim's "lips are soft," Judy's attraction to Jim threatens to feminize him. "All this time I've been looking for someone to love *me*," Judy tells the prone Jim, "and now *I* love somebody. And it's so easy. Why is it easy now?"

No longer troubled by her father's erotic refusal, Judy has discovered,

OEDIPUS IN SUBURBIA 185

through Jim, that her sensual life need not take a passive form. Unlike her failed attempt to be loved by her father, with Jim she is able herself to love, to gaze rather than to be gazed at. Once again, however, the narrative turns in a way that foregrounds the risks implied for the male position. Even while Judy and Jim share this private moment, as Joan Mellen has observed, the gang is busy stalking and terrorizing Jim and Judy's "son," Plato, punishing Jim for his passivity and forcing him back into an active narrative role (214).

Between Boys: Homoeroticizing the Rebel

While Judy represents a clear heterosexual alternative to Jim's oedipally dysfunctional family, Plato's role in the film has led some critics to claim *Rebel without a Cause* as a queer text. Plato's status as a closeted figure in the film finds numerous forms of confirmation, whether in assertions to that effect by the screenwriter (including one famously featured in the documentary film *The Celluloid Closet*), or in textual cues that range from the most general (Sal Mineo's delicate features) to the specific (scenes where Plato has a male pinup in his locker, or most explicitly when he invites Jim to spend the night). What this subtext connotes, however, is somewhat less clear. In one compelling reading, Christopher Castiglia has argued that *Rebel* is organized around a rivalry between Frank Stark (the father) and Plato (the lover) for Jim's allegiance. Castiglia suggests that, unlike the homosocial triangles discussed by Eve Sedgwick in *Between Men*, triangles involving three men may destabilize patriarchal masculinity by suggesting a queer alternative to its heterosexual norms. In choosing between the authority figure of the father and a man who threatens that authority (the homosexual), the son as protagonist must negotiate between the patriarchal privilege offered by his father (and consequently heterosexual convention) and the otherness, the alienation from male heterosexual privilege, embodied in the son's potential acceptance of a homosexual lover, signifying an acknowledgment of his own homosexuality (208).

This is the same sort of triangle that, as I previously argued, enables a queer reading of *Blackboard Jungle* centered upon Gregory and Artie's bonds within the gang and their common stance against the teacher's paternal authority. In Castiglia's reading of *Rebel*, however, Judy short-circuits this possibility by providing the heterosexual object choice of a boy-meets-girl narrative that ushers in a conventional oedipal resolution. At the end of the film, Plato's death and Jim's introduction of Judy to his parents are both necessary elements in Jim's reconciliation with his remasculinized father.

This reading traces a persistent (if usually disavowed) homoerotic dimension to the male rebel figure of the 1950s. Male homoerotic affiliation represented one important way to articulate youth's rejection of domesticated suburban manhood. As my discussion of the beat generation will elaborate, the homoeroticism of bad-boy rebellion became particularly vexed at moments when relations between boys were elevated to the status of a unified generational outlook. In *Rebel without a Cause*, however, Jim's revolt is overdetermined on several fronts, so that the "crisis of identity" he dramatizes evokes, but cannot be reduced to, gay identity. To begin with, one can only privilege the homoerotic triangle of Frank Stark, Jim Stark, and Plato by decentering other triangles that also drive the narrative. Buzz and the gang, for example, are hardly mentioned in Castiglia's analysis, yet this too is an important triangle, a homosocial one in which the struggle between Frank Stark (the father) and Buzz (the gang leader) for Jim's allegiance constitutes a rather different binary of domesticity versus juvenile delinquency. Whereas the Plato/Frank contest involves contest between heterosexual privilege and a homoerotic allure, in the case of Buzz versus Frank, Jim's decision seems to lie between bourgeois privilege and respectability versus a promise of phallic erotic mastery. Here the crisis of Frank's authority lies not in sexuality alone, but more generally in that he is too conformist, forever worrying about what other people think, and as a result unwilling to take action. To use David Riesman's terminology, Frank Stark's "other-directed" personality lacks the "moral gyroscope" of the traditionally individuated American. His bourgeois privilege thus proves paradoxically disempowering when compared to Buzz's existential confidence.

Judy, Frank, and Jim also constitute a dramatic triangle. In this instance, the ideological battle appears to line up between adult marriage and teenage romance. Although the former alleges to offer public companionship and (again) respectability, in actuality it has led to a loveless, squabbling coupledom that contrasts poorly to what Judy and Jim are finding in each other. Castiglia assumes that Judy largely functions as a surrogate for Frank, that she is the girl whom Jim must choose in order to opt for his father (and straightness) over Plato (and gayness). This dismisses Judy's importance as a rebellious figure in her own right, however, something Castiglia himself acknowledges in passing when he writes that "the color red, associated with Judy's 'wild' sexuality, is quite significant in the film. In the initial sequence at the police station, Judy (who has been brought in for wandering the streets alone late at night) wears a red coat. And it is her bright lipstick that ensures her alienation from her father, who calls her a tramp. When Jim dons his flaming red jacket [late in the film] then, he exchanges his traditional garb for one that subtly links him to Judy and her defiant femininity" (210). Castiglia reads Judy's "femininity" solely for how it is semiotically transferred to Jim, which he then takes as a sign that homosexualizes Jim. If we take Judy's defiance as meaningful on its own terms, however, then we can see her as representative of an antisuburban genre of romance that allows her sexual agency vis-à-vis Jim. She demonstrates that the bad boy is not the only possible type of teen rebel. Judy represents what in chapter 7 I will call the sexual bad girl of the fifties, a female figure for identity with her own specific trajectory of possibilities and limitations. For now, however, it is worth stressing that, as Judy becomes more active in their heterosexual relation, Jim becomes more passive in order to become her companionate equal. Because this development seems to echo liberal Fordist family arrangements, it represents exactly the sort of gender deviance that, from a conservative perspective, must be squelched. And indeed, the terms of Jim and Judy's relationship are implicitly erased as a prelude to Jim's reconciliation with his parents. Though Judy is not literally killed off, as are Buzz and Plato, by subordinating herself to Jim's heroism she is converted into the properly deferential girlfriend whom Jim can publicly avow to his parents in the closing scene.

The Erotics of Rebel Identity

What relation do these various erotic triangles bear to one another? Perhaps these distinct movements of *Rebel*'s narrative are best viewed as variations on a larger triangle in which Jim is caught, a contest between an "absurd" adult world (in Goodman's sense) and a regressive teenage peer culture that offers several ways to satisfy a sense of identity, but at the apparent price of arrested development. The various alternatives embedded within that peer culture become disentangled from one another only gradually. Buzz's delinquent gang initially seems to subsume Judy and Plato. When Buzz dies, however, Judy and Plato become distinct options in their own right, and ones to which the "rump" gang is hostile. Juvenile delinquency, egalitarian heterosexual romance, and homoerotic partnership thus all become alternate modes of rebellion enabled by a dissident peer youth culture.

Castiglia deems Plato and Jim's relationship a homoerotic rebellion against what he calls the "regime of the norm," by which he more specifically means "the traditional domesticity of white, middle-class suburbia" (208). This thesis, though useful, needs to be complicated in several ways. Firstly, the domestic regime of the postwar suburbs was in no sense "traditional," though it certainly presented itself as such. Rather, the Fordist suburbs had rapidly brought into existence a drastically new mode of everyday life, anchored by the new family system that serves for Castiglia as the "norm." It is more useful, therefore, to think of the deviant meaning ascribable to Plato and Jim's relationship as produced alongside the suburban "regime of the norm," and by the same forces. It becomes, that is, a particular sort of countersuburban imaginary, like rock 'n' roll directed outward and away from suburban domesticity, but in this instance focused on an emphatic deviation from its heteronormativity.

The postwar codes of sexual deviance bore a complex imaginative relation to the new suburban norms. In the fifties, certain strains in mainstream psychiatry were raising doubts about the "democratic" suburban family system through their medicalization of homosexuality.[5] In this respect, psychiatry, contrary to its reputation as a liberal institution, was often closely aligned with conservative attacks on liberal family visions such as Harriet Wilson's or Fordist ones such as *Life* magazine's. For example, in an overview of male homosexuality and the "disintegrated family," the sociologist Hendrik Ruitenbeek described a homosexual epidemic among American boys who had been pushed into a "flight from masculinity" by three related failures of the modern liberal family (22). Ruitenbeek might well have had Jim Stark tacitly in mind as he listed them: the decline of paternal authority, the castrating power of mothers, and growing sexual demands from girls. Read against Ruitenbeek's typology, the effeminate and nervous Plato, with an absent father and a fretting mammy substituting for his mother, seems only further along the "flight from masculinity"; his desire to make Jim into his guardian and father figure would have been easily readable by psychiatry of the day as a strategy for escaping the pressures from his "disintegrated family" and from sexualized girls like Judy.

While Ruitenbeek certainly meant to pathologize the homosexual "flight from masculinity," when read against the grain, homosexual "flight" could also be affirmed as a creative and legitimate turn away from the unappealing fate of a sexless domesticated manhood. It represented, in other words, one way that a boy might refuse to "grow up absurd." In the psychiatric world, nobody in fact made this point more strenuously than

Robert Lindner, the originator of the rebel without a cause. Within a "sex-rejective, sex-repressive society" like ours, Lindner argued, homosexuality should be understood as "a form of rebellion, and the homosexual as a non-conformist" (Must, 40–41). This view, in Lindner's quite radical estimation, "cuts through much of the debris of prejudice and pretense which ordinarily interfere with intelligent discussion of the problem" (Must, 41). It is the sexlessness of mass manhood, in short, that constitutes the proper political context for homosexuality, which Lindner describes as "another minority . . . discovering itself, and beginning to struggle for what it regards as its rights" (Must, 73). Homosexuality's antithetical politicized relationship to the liberal suburban family could thus play in either conservative or radical protoidentitarian directions. In the former case, the homosexual became, like the communist, a threat to national security propogated by the soft family system. In the radical version, however, the homosexual became the erotic figure of revolt against the suburban conformity typified by sexless, castrated domesticated males, expressive of what Rob Corber has called an "oppositional consciousness" critical of Fordist masculinity (*Homosexuality*, 4).

In the scenes that establish Plato and Jim as young nonconformists in *Rebel without a Cause*, one finds just such a political undertow. In the opening shots at Jim's new high school, for example, Plato marks himself as a disruption by crashing his scooter into the curb at the exact moment that the high school attendant fires a gun to signal the hoisting of the school flag. The buzz of voices stops and all the students other than Jim and Plato stand respectfully while Old Glory is hoisted. Immediately following this show of patriotism, Jim unknowingly treads upon the school emblem, a social transgression that elicits cold stares and warnings from the witnessing students. Initially, therefore, national loyalty seems associated with an oppressive "schoolyard" conformity, to which the rebels Jim and Plato cannot be reconciled. Though brief, this scene taints the deviancies that Jim will later entertain (delinquency, egalitarian romance, and homoerotic relations) with a connotation of political dissent.

In one sense, this early tilt in favor of otherness will not last. Whereas Jim initially shares Plato's sullen attitude toward the police and his discomfort at school, by the end of the film, he will be cooperating with Officer Ray to woo Plato out of the observatory, thereby demonstrating his acceptance of the law and its security forces. Ray's contrast to Mr. Stark offers Jim the model of manhood that he can ask his father to live up to. Nevertheless, Plato as the most excluded and alienated of the youths in the film remains a sympathetic character right through to the tragic end, when he is fired on by the police and killed. As I showed earlier by way of the response to *Catcher in the Rye*, the bad boy represented America, but as the nation's rebel character he also defied the nation's current normativities. For what it is worth, later in the film Jim ends up wearing the patriotic colors of red, white, and blue: his jacket, T-shirt, and jeans respectively. Red might (as Castiglia claims) signify sexual "wildness," but even more obviously in the fifties it connoted the "red menace." Brightly colored jackets were, moreover, widely associated with juvenile delinquency in the fifties. If we therefore take red to signify the otherness internal to the national colors (whether the Cold War enemy, delinquency, or sexual deviance), then it is noteworthy that Jim manages to divest himself of the red jacket in the film's penultimate scene at the observatory, giving it to Plato as a gesture of trust. When Jim's father then sees the red-clad Plato shot and killed by the police, he momentarily assumes that his son was the victim. Thankful that it was not his son, Frank finds the resolve to promise Jim a new strength of character, to "stand up" for him in the manner that Officer Ray, agent of the state, has already demonstrated.

James Dean's famed red jacket is a paradigmatically overdetermined signifier, but this overdetermination merely reiterates the way in which *Rebel* brings together connotations of sexual, political, and criminal otherness in the figure of the bad boy. What made James Dean such an iconic bad boy in *Rebel without a Cause*? Perhaps it was the moment of existential delinquency that his character shares with Buzz, or perhaps it was his soft eroticism as he draws out Judy's sexual passion, or perhaps it was the homoerotic promise of his wistful tenderness for Plato. Yet all three dimensions of James Dean's performance share in a certain antisuburban eroticism. Each glamorizes the sexiness of a boy whose struggle for identity leads him away from the asexual, impotent drabness that would otherwise await him in his father's domesticated form of manhood.

The Bad Boy as Creole King

If in *Rebel* the flight from domesticated masculinity is principally articulated via the bad boy's ambiguous sexual positioning, then in *King Creole* his escape is also signified on the axes of race and class. This difference has everything to do with Elvis Presley's specificity as a postwar icon. In what remains the finest cultural study of Presley, *Elvis*, David Marsh chronicles Presley's rapid rise to stardom in 1955 and 1956 as the most visible jolt in the cultural earthquake set off by the rise of rock 'n' roll in popular music. Following a long tradition of critics before him, Marsh suggests that rock 'n' roll's dramatic impact derived from its unabashed mixing of differently raced and classed musical forms. Presley, in many respects, became emblematic of this aggressively marketed hybridization. Born to a dirt poor family in Tupelo, Mississippi, and working as a truck driver before his musical career began, Elvis Presley represented the lowest possible class of person out of the most stigmatized region of the country. His career began in country music, a style that had long been segregated onto its own pop chart, and which, prior to the 1940s, had in fact been derogatorily titled the "hillbilly" chart (a parallel to the dismissively titled "race" chart that was later renamed "rhythm and blues").[6] Presley's star image thus openly connoted his origins in rural southern poverty.

Moreover, as his critics unfailingly note, Presley's music (like the other artists at Sun Records) also incorporated black gospel and rhythm and blues styles in ways that drew ire within purist (and often racist) country music circles. Many music critics have singled out Presley as the most infamous of all white performers to steal black musical styles, and the debate over whether Presley was exploiter or exploited in his career is not one that this chapter will engage (although my earlier discussion of rock 'n' roll makes clear enough how I tend to approach questions of "appropriation" in consumer culture). Yet Marsh makes this powerful (if polemical) point:

> If Elvis had simply stolen rhythm and blues from Negro culture as pop-music ignoramuses have for years maintained, there would have been no reason for Southern outrage over his new music. (No one complained about Benny Goodman's or Johnnie Ray's expropriations of black styles.) But Elvis did something more daring and dangerous: He not only "sounded like a nigger," [something Presley's first promoter Sam Phillips later claimed he had been looking for in a white performer] he was actively and clearly engaged in race-mixing. The crime of Elvis' rock & roll was that he proved that black and white tendencies could coexist and that the product of their coexistence was not just palatable but thrilling. (47)

Presley, in Marsh's view, was a figure for integration, and one might extend this to say that he injected both class and racial ambiguity into his performance of identity: black in his whiteness, poor in his wealth and appeal to middle-class youth, rural and urban at once in his presence within the new suburbs. Indeed, it is these symbolic conflations that made Presley grow more controversial with every gain in the youth market. As Trent Hill indicates,

> At first, he [Presley] seemed to be merely the grotesque punchline to a cultural joke that people were taking too seriously. The 30 April 1956 issue of *Life* called him "A Howling Hillbilly Success" and suggested that his music was a travesty of the traditional male role; his music had "a sob around every note." But as his popularity increased and his appearances multiplied, the opposition stiffened. *Life* claimed in an issue later that year that Presley was "A Different Kind of Idol," one who set potentially dangerous precedents, who legitimated both the personal style and sexual expressiveness of delinquents (or of blacks), whose career was pushing the boundaries of American acceptability perhaps farther than it should be allowed to go. (55)

Earlier I suggested that race and class, city and country, became the basis for rock 'n' roll's suburban counterimaginary, and it is thus clear that Elvis embodied this imaginary with a vengeance. In the reading that follows, I want to focus on how Presley's suspension between races and classes took on countersuburban meanings through their oedipalization. For Marsh, Presley's Hollywood films are a shameful travesty of his deeper cultural meanings. Already, in his early television appearances on the Dorsey Brothers show, the Milton Berle show, and finally the Ed Sullivan show, the respective emcees had expressed what Marsh shows to be a contemptuous bourgeois view that the "hillbilly culture he [Presley] symbolized had no place in American life" (106). Hollywood, Marsh believes, aimed to further contain Elvis's explosive meaning, by showing that his character, "a rebel at the outset, can be assimilated into what passes for the good life, his dreams bought off by mere material success and the ability to keep to his place" (116).

Presley's Hollywood products, nonetheless, should not be so quickly dismissed. As I noted earlier in this chapter, the rise of the method-acting star had a radical impact on the style of masculinity that could be performed in Hollywood film, namely one whose image could be overtly eroticized in ways traditionally limited to female stars. As Trent Hill notes, such a tendency was already implicit in Presley's musical performance styles, and a major source of the objections to him:

> Perhaps the most common complaint in the demonography of Elvis is that he was a marginally literate pedagogue whose chief lesson was

> sexual confusion. The writer for *Life* and Jack Gould of the *New York Times* both agreed that Elvis's signature stage mannerism—his wild, grinding, abandoned hip movements—were not so much suggestive of a new masculine sexuality as they were reminders of the old spectacular presentations of female sex: the burlesque, the bump-and-grind, the hoochy-koochy. And Gould implied, that was the only reason (or excuse) for his fame. (55)

Though his films were less prestigious than Dean's or Brando's, in translating his musical personae onto the screen, Presley played a crucial role in popularizing the eroticized male screen image. Noting Rudolph Valentino and James Dean as possible precursors, David Shumway even goes so far as to claim that "in the history of mass culture, Elvis is the first male star to display his body as an overt sexual object" (126). As I will show, Elvis's eroticization of the male star image cannot be separated from his rearticulation of that image as a rebellious bad boy. Self-eroticization, in other words, became one means by which the bad boy could figure dissident identity.

Presley made only four films during the 1950s, after which he was inducted into the army and effectively removed from the scene of American popular culture for several years.[7] In each of these four films, however, Presley's image was shaped progressively in the "method" direction of the alienated but emotional male rebel who is unsure how to perform his masculinity. In *Love Me Tender*, his first film, Presley plays a sensitive young cowboy. In *Loving You*, he plays a character more directly aligned with his rock star image, a young country singer who becomes an overnight sensation because of his popularity with youth, a popularity in turn resented and challenged by adults. Though gentle, in this film he carries a bitter psychic wound associated with being abandoned by his parents at an early age, something his girlfriend must contend with if their relationship is to succeed. By the making of *Jailhouse Rock*, Presley has moved decisively in the direction of the vulnerable but angry young man. Imprisoned for a crime he did not intend to commit, Presley becomes hardened in prison, and, even as he becomes a musical celebrity in the remainder of the film, vacillates between amoral cynicism and an on-again, off-again passion for the woman who jumpstarted his career. The very idea of "jailhouse rock" implies making the most of one's imprisonment, of getting one's kicks while under confinement, and it alludes also to a criminal male world of cross-class and cross-racial companionship.

However, in *King Creole*, his last Hollywood project before departing for military duty, Presley made a thoroughgoing youth rebel movie. The film was directed by Michael Curtiz, who, like Nicholas Ray, had displayed Old Left affinities with his antifascist classic *Casablanca* and the avidly pro-Soviet *Mission to Moscow*.[8] Curtiz, also like Ray, had recently dealt with the theme of troubled youth, employing the Dead End Kids for his well-received courtroom delinquency melodrama, *Angels with Dirty Faces*. In *King Creole*, Presley plays a young man, Danny, who is kicked out of school in the first fifteen minutes of the film, burglarizes a department store with a gang of juvenile delinquents (led by Vic Morrow as Shark, a reprise of his role in *Blackboard Jungle*), and gets in way over his head with a local crime lord. Presley's songs in *King Creole* also tend to be more hard-edged than in his previous films, with more rhythm and blues and rock 'n' roll, and with fewer ballads. Most important, this was the first film to translate Presley's racial and class connotations onto the screen. Thus in *King Creole*, Presley at last captured on film something of his rock star, bad-boy image.

As I noted earlier, Marsh is highly critical of Hollywood's use of Presley, and *King Creole* is no exception. "Elvis Presley was not a down-and-out refugee of the middle class, like Danny in *King Creole*," Marsh complains about the social background ascribed to his character, Danny: "In that film, we are asked to believe not only that Presley's father could be the parson-like Dean Jagger, the incarnation of the pursed lip, milquetoast Yankee, but that Elvis could be the son of a pharmacist" (116). As we shall see, this objection takes the narrative far too literally, particularly given Marsh's skill in otherwise acknowledging and addressing Presley's status as a *symbolic* figure. It is true that, superficially, *King Creole* tells a strikingly similar story to *Rebel without a Cause*. It too is an oedipal drama in which a troubled (but handsome) son, played by a major teen icon, refuses to grow up to be like his impotent, middle-class father. Yet the differences are also telling.

In *King Creole*, Presley stars as a young boy named Danny Fisher who will become a rock 'n' roll singer in his hometown of New Orleans. Danny's family, we learn, grew up outside of town, in a suburban home by the river. After losing his wife, Danny's father lost his nerve, and with it his job as a pharmacist. In a striking reversal from his role in *Rebel without a Cause*, Jagger now plays precisely the domesticated male to which (in the role of Officer Ray) he had previously stood as the manly alternative. This difference, as Marsh inadvertently lets us know, has much to do with Jagger's middle-class star persona, which provides an appropriate foil for manhood vis-à-vis the no less middle-class character of Jim Stark, but fails to do so against Elvis's distinctly non-middle-class character.

Early on in *King Creole*, we are made to understand that the father's paralysis is once again due to the mother's excessive importance within the family. As Danny's sister, Mimi, puts it in the opening minutes of the film, "It's a terrible thing to lean on someone so hard you don't know you're leaning. Never finding out till suddenly she isn't there anymore. It's been like stumbling around the dark [for Pop] ever since." As far as Danny is concerned, his father is a quitter. When his high school principal accuses him of becoming a hoodlum, Danny objects: "I'm not a hoodlum. A hustler I've had to be, because of my old man. You see, when my mother died in an accident three years ago, it may as well have taken the old man too, because he took himself right out of it. He quit cold. He lost the drugstore, the house, and his few jobs since then."

Danny must therefore shoulder the responsibility of breadwinner for the family; lacking faith that his father is up to the task. More important, though, Mr. Fisher's chronic unemployment is itself a symptom of his emasculation, a fate to which Danny refuses to resign himself. In one of many angry exchanges, Danny tells his father: "I don't wanna crawl.... You crawl, you've got no choice, they got you on the run early," but "that's not gonna happen to me." The film repeatedly confirms Danny's perspective. Even when he does get hired as a pharmacist's assistant, Mr. Fisher's tentativeness and unwillingness to stand up against his sullen manager keeps putting his job at risk.

For all the similarities between this opening narrative gambit and *Rebel*'s, however, significant differences are already evident, particularly in terms of the film's class assumptions. The simple fact that Mr. Stark's emasculation comes at the hands of his wife while Mr. Fisher's is felt through his boss suggests that work as well as domesticity is at issue in *King Creole*. Whereas Jim Stark's alienation takes place within a securely affluent suburban setting, Danny's involves harsh and involuntary downward mobility, something Marsh downplays when he calls him a middle-class refugee. Danny's father's job troubles have cost the family its old home off the river. Instead, Danny, Mimi, and their father now live in a cramped apartment in a seedy neighborhood of New Orleans that is largely peopled by prostitutes, drunkards, and street gangs.

If one steps back from the literalist portrayal of a father-son relationship to view the story as a symbolic oedipalization of two class positions, then one can begin to grasp *King Creole* as staging an ideological conflict between a "paternalized" professional middle-class position embodied in Dean Jagger—the consummate other-directed Organization Man—and

15. As in *Rebel without a Cause*, Danny finds his father painful to behold in *King Creole* (Paramount, 1958).

the "teening" of a different social position associated with a background of poverty, raciality, and urban life. *King Creole* shapes into an oedipal struggle between a white, middle-class, suburban manhood—figured as castrated, as in *Rebel*—and a not-quite-white, working-class, urban boyhood that is valorized because it takes seriously the search for masculine agency—the work of sovereign identity formation.

The film opens with the Fisher family—father, Danny, and his sister, Mimi—living in a cramped apartment in a poor neighborhood of town. Unemployed, Mr. Fisher nonetheless pushes Danny to graduate high school and enter a profession, but Danny lacks the patience and desire to follow in his father's failed footsteps. Already supporting the family as a busboy at a local nightclub, Danny exhibits a strong attraction to the energy and excitement of city life. It's significant that *King Creole* is set in perhaps the one part of the country where, in keeping with a French rather than a British colonial legacy, the black/white color line has remained somewhat permeable. Louisana creole designates not so much black as blackened culture, a confluence of African American, French, and native traditions whose adherents cut across legal racial categories. New Orleans, therefore, provides an alibi for the racialization of Presley's character. The film opens with a singing trio of black street sellers hawking creole foods, including gumbo, the stew medley that has become a symbol of creolization. Following the credits, the camera returns to the street, where it picks

16. Danny jokes with the prostitutes across the street in *King Creole* (Paramount, 1958).

up another food seller, a beautiful young black woman selling crawfish. Only then does the camera climb up the building to introduce us to Danny, who joins the woman below in a sensuous duet about "crawfish." Through this duet, Danny's connection is established, across the color line, to the blackened culture of New Orleans. His partner, whom we periodically see passing under Danny's window, serves less as a realized character than as emblem for the creole rhythm that Danny has acquired from the streets. Danny's creolization involves, not simply racialization, but also his sexualization. In sharing a song that savors the flavors of creole cooking, the duet revel in their sexy youthfulness, in their shared openness to the sensual. This joy, however, simultaneously becomes associated with the financial woes of the creole streets, a place where everyone needs to sell something. As the song ends, Danny glances across the street to a bordello, where the prostitutes make a play at him. "Oh no, you've gotta pay me!" Danny boisterously replies, a joke that implicitly references his commonality with the prostitutes as a purveyor of his own eroticism. Elvis, as I noted, was in many ways a pioneer in the commodification of male sexuality, both appreciated and condemned as one of the very first male stars to overtly sexualize his image. Yet sexual self-commodification is here presented as a risky business, one that, as the film will later suggest, endangers one's independence.

This sequence is also placed in an immediate tense relation to Danny's father. Danny's sister, Mimi, calls out, "Don't let Pop catch you talking to

198 CHAPTER FIVE

that," to which Danny replies irritably, "Why not? I'm just being neighborly, and he picked the neighborhood," immediately making clear that his father is to blame for losing the old house and the middle-class life it promised. On the one hand, father is opposed to the street life. He despises it, and wants Danny to have nothing to do with its low lives. Danny, however, holds his father responsible for having brought him into such a world. Mr. Fisher therefore has no right to complain about Danny's involvement with the poor, with blacks, with prostitutes.

The exact nature of Danny's feelings for and connections to this world, however, are ambiguous. The duet with the salesgirl seems pleasing to both of them, and his exchange with the prostitutes friendly. But is it a flirting erotic play or a social identification with these women that we are witnessing? Both possibilities seem ideologically troubling for a Hollywood film of the 1950s. If a love affair, then the flow of Danny's erotic energy is dangerously inappropriate. From a romantic point of view, this first flash of Danny's rebellion against his father suggests that he might come to desire a girl like one of these. If the relation is one of identification, then it is important that it is not only blackness or low-classness with which Danny is being identified, but also female hustling. Both the crawfish girl and the prostitutes are trying to sell something through the exchange of their own erotic image. Will a world of poverty and desperation lead Danny, like these girls, to have to sell himself to some moneyed man? When Danny says, "Oh no, you gotta pay me," he is playing a simple game of sexual conceit, but he is at the same time expressing the principle by which he will try to get ahead in the film.

Danny works at a nightclub, the Blue Shade. The next morning, before school, when he goes there to work, he meets Ronnie, a jaded prostitute whom he saves from harassment at the hands of a drunken john. Ronnie becomes the character who most centrally embodies Danny's dual relationship to the street as I described it above. She is someone who also once did well in school (graduated with honors, she tells Danny) and hoped to make a career for herself as a singer in the New Orleans night club circuit. At first, she worked for Charlie LeGrande, the amiable owner of the King Creole club. Eventually, however, she fell into the grasp of Maxie Fields, a local crime lord (played by Walter Matthau), who owns virtually every other establishment in town. Though left deeply cynical by her experience, Ronnie is nevertheless attracted to the youth and vitality of Danny. Likewise, Danny is attracted to Ronnie.

Like his bond with the prostitutes and the crawfish woman, Danny's

17. Danny looks for a "hot accident" with Ronnie in *King Creole* (Paramount, 1958).

growing connection to Ronnie lies somewhere ambiguously between desire and identification. Attracted to Ronnie, Danny quickly adopts an aggressive erotic swagger, telling her about the hot "accident" they're going to have when they finally get together. His looks at her are also the moments when he appears most in control of a Mulveyan male gaze.

Danny's phallic mastery and toughness function within the narrative in accordance with his developing musical persona as a King Creole, a virile, energetic rock 'n' roll singer from the streets of New Orleans in possession of his own erotic power, his career, and his destiny. The scene that, in fact, launches Danny as a rocking bad boy comes early on, when Maxie, the club owner, with the intent to humiliate Danny, coerces him into singing a number. Projecting both unexpected talent and defiance, Danny offers up the playfully aggressive "Trouble" number, backed up by a band of black R & B musicians. In this number, Danny publicly demonstrates that creolization has taught him a lesson in masculine self-respect, which might make him evil from his weak-willed father's perspective, but which he requires if he is to withstand the likes of Maxie Fields. Paradoxically, given its machismo, however, this performance affiliates Danny with Ronnie in a more dangerous way, not through sexual interest but instead through a risky cross-gendered identification. In refusing to trace his father's footsteps, Danny emulates Ronnie's instead. Hoping for a show business career, he begins, like Ronnie, with the likeable Charlie LeGrande, who signs him immediately after the number. But, also like Ronnie, Danny is an act that Maxie

200 CHAPTER FIVE

18. Danny sings "Trouble" in *King Creole* (Paramount, 1958).

Fields intends to own. "Looks like I got to him first," Le Grande informs Fields, who replies, "You always do Charlie, but I wind up with them sooner or later," then explains to Danny, "He handled Ronnie when she was a singer, now I do." The threat, of course, is that the same will happen with Danny, and much of the narrative develops around Fields's various stratagems for getting Danny in debt to him.

At a structural level, then *King Creole*'s narrative is organized through Danny's negotiation of a path between two equally emasculating options. On one side, Danny refuses to end up like his father, a man whose white, professional respectability invariably rubs away to reveal his shameful impotence. By refusing to be like the old man, Danny has acquired the means to stand up and talk back, to make trouble for those who would control or domesticate him. Yet, in rebelling against his father to become a singer, Danny must take care not to end up like Ronnie, a has-been street performer, now a prostitute in the clutches of a petty tyrant. Between the respective fates of Ronnie and his father, Danny tries to sing his way along a third path—that of a King Creole.

The very notion of "king" is crucial here, for it expresses what Danny seeks: identity as an ideal that names the privilege of a masculine sovereignty, as distinguished from another masculinity marked precisely by its lack of sovereignty, its state of subjection and dependence. What launches Danny's story of rebellion is his father's abdication as a "king of his own castle." The figure of the "King Creole," celebrated in Presley's title song

OEDIPUS IN SUBURBIA 201

performance, is of course aligned with his own famous nickname, "the King," and his multiple coronations as the "King of rock 'n' roll." For Presley to have escaped his crushing background as "poor white trash" is to have become a king, a self-made master of his own destiny as well as of the music for which he is famous. Yet, Presley's career was also famous for the many attempts by others to control and manipulate him, beginning with Sam Philips (or even his mother), but most notoriously with his manager at RCA/Victor, Colonel Parker.[9] Presley's films strangely echo this public narrative by including characters that try to steal away his protagonist's autonomy. In *King Creole*, Maxie Fields is that figure, and it is likewise significant that in the first meeting between Danny and Fields, each is warned about the other using that term. Ronnie, when asked who this kid is, tells Fields, "The king of Yugoslavia, how should I know?" Just seconds later, Shark warns Danny to watch out for Fields, saying, "He's the king of everything around here!" This is the same scene I cited earlier, in which Danny sings the song "Trouble," also quoted in the epigraph. Danny brags, "I was born standing up, and talking back," implicitly challenging Fields to just try to push him around. Fields rises to the challenge, and tries to "lord" it over Danny for the remainder of the film. Kingship as the royalized reference to a sovereign personhood, understood as male, becomes both end and problem in this film.

Danny's identification as creole is vital in this context. To become a king again, to recapture the sovereign masculinity forfeited by his father, Danny must in effect leave suburbia behind for the city. If suburbia domesticates men, then the rough-and-tumble streets of New Orleans promises to wild them, to make them tough and keep them on their toes. It is by introjecting an urban blackness, then, by becoming King Creole, that Danny may grow up as the kind of man that his father also needs to become.

The Bad Boy as Teddy Bear

Generally aligned with the dangers associated with his father is Danny's second love interest, Nellie. After he is expelled from school, but before he starts to sing for Charlie LeGrande in *King Creole*, Danny briefly joins Shark's street gang. They decide to burglarize a department store, with Danny serving as the decoy by walking into the store playing a guitar. One of the store girls, Nellie, notices the heist, but, entranced by Danny, decides not to give them away. At first, Danny, in another macho moment, tries to take sexual advantage of Nellie, using a phony name and leading her to a

19. Danny sings "Lover Doll" in *King Creole* (Paramount, 1958).

motel room while claiming to be taking her to a party. At the moment of truth, however, Nellie's response takes him by surprise. She neither simply goes along with him, as a "tramp" like Ronnie might, nor angrily storms away. Instead, she begins to cry in confusion over how to deal with her real passion for him in the midst of what is otherwise an empty life: "I've never been to a place like this before. But I want to see you again. Is this the way? I've been looking at the door of that lousy five and dime for over a year. And today when you walked in I thought . . . [crying] . . . I like you, that's the reason I'm crying. I like you better than anyone I know, and I don't even know you." Shaken by her honesty, Danny calls the whole thing off, but continues to maintain a connection to Nellie. If Danny's relationship with Ronnie echoes that of Jim and Judy early in *Rebel*, when Jim appropriates Judy's eroticized image through a phallic association with Buzz and the gang, Danny's relationship to Nellie resembles that which Judy and Jim achieve later in *Rebel*, when Jim becomes erotically passive in the face of Judy's sexual agency. As I noted, Nellie falls for Danny when he comes into the department store, displaying himself as a cute, soft balladeer (he sings "Lover Doll"), posing before the gaze of all the women in the store. This is a differently eroticized Elvis, not the bad boy but the cute boy, whose songs express male tenderness, not sexual threats.

As in *Rebel*, this sort of heterosexuality gets linked to the very dynamics that led to rebellion in the first place. It resembles, that is, the "egalitarian marriage" that leads to the impotent, domesticated father, which the male

20. Danny as the uncomfortable object of Nellie's gaze in *King Creole* (Paramount, 1958).

rebel is trying to escape. If in *Rebel* Judy needs to be resubordinated to Jim's heroics, then, in *King Creole* Danny holds Nellie at bay all the way through the film. In one scene, he takes her for a boat ride to show her the old home where he and Mimi grew up. This scene captures Danny's nostalgia and longing for the old domestic arrangements of the middle-class nuclear family he once had: "Pa bought it when I was about eight years old. . . . We sure had lots of happy times there. I'm gonna buy that house back someday, or one just like it. And I guarantee, nobody's gonna take it away from ME." This desire, however, is in tension with what is happening aboard the boat. In the shot, Danny faces the camera in the foreground, but looks bashfully down or away, while behind him, in a position of visual control, Nellie is gazing adoringly at Danny, much as Judy does to Jim in *Rebel*.

Afraid to meet the desire in Nellie's eyes, Danny's sense of virility seems shaky. His confidence that nobody can take anything away from him appears threatened by Nellie's overly forward interest. When she at last asks him if he's ever going to kiss her tonight, Danny answers: "Nellie, don't fall in love with me. Love means getting married and having kids. I don't even know who I am yet." "Who do you have to be?" she asks him. His answer is, "I don't wanna be like my old man. Love, marriage, having kids, I wanna be somebody first." The struggle for identity, for secure and sovereign personhood, requires boys to be bad, to defer marriage and suburban life until they can devise an alternative to the domestication of their fathers.

Being somebody, having an identity in terms of the music of the film,

204 CHAPTER FIVE

seems to involve the hard rock or blues songs like "Trouble" (someone who can defend himself), "Dixieland Rock" (a sense of geographic belonging that includes loyalty to one's own kicks), and "King Creole" itself (the figure of the racial hybrid rock star). Sexuality, in these songs is all about a "masculine" vision of sex rather than a "feminine" vision of romantic love, and about the likes of Ronnie than those of Nellie, as in

> You'll never know what heaven means
> Till you been down to New Orleans
> With the black-eyed babies by the old Bayou
> It makes you awful glad that you were born a man.

These songs contrast with the ballads that Danny also sings, not only "Lover Doll" in the department store, but also "Young Dreams" and the closing number, "As Long as I Have You." If the rock numbers are strongly racialized, the ballads are strongly associated with the white Tin Pan Alley style of pop crooning. And rather than being sung about an individual who disperses his erotic energy and pleasure across the creole landscape, the ballads are always concerned with a heterosexual couple, a romantic number that promises to end in domestic bliss. Even Danny's identity as a musical performer, then, is split down the middle between the two love interests, the two worlds, and the two options.

This division lines up with Presley's performances outside of the film, the larger split between the Elvis who sang love songs like "Love Me Tender" and "Loving You," as opposed to the tough defiant Elvis of "Blue Suede Shoes" and "Jailhouse Rock," who sang rockabilly and R & B tunes in regional dialect. In a short meditation on the meaning of her own Elvis fandom as a young girl, Sue Wise proposes as names for these two personae "Elvis the Butch God" and "Elvis the Teddy Bear." The former represents the dominant representation of Elvis as macho hero. The latter, however, was "her Elvis," the one who lovingly kept her company as a lonely young girl, and who never let her down. However downplayed in rock 'n' roll histories, this side of Elvis was certainly no less popular than his rock 'n' roll persona.

King Creole exhibits this divided meaning of Presley's star image, and in a way that illuminates their ideological relationship to each other. The "Teddy Bear" Elvis is meaningful and compelling for Nellie, yet it is frightening for Danny to occupy that position because it threatens to recapitulate his father's emasculation. On the other hand, the King Creole world of the rockin' streets also seems to risk eventual subordination to Maxie Fields, who is forever scheming for a way to become Danny's pimp. A threat of emasculation exists here too, in which Danny's sex appeal may become Maxie's property and in which Danny will become, not simply a weak man but, even worse, a kept man.

Danny's sexual attraction to Ronnie is quite literally exploited by Fields, late in the film, when she is set up to seduce him in Fields's house. Danny refuses, but this sets off the final struggle, as Danny slugs Fields, and Fields retaliates by sending Shark and the rest of the gang (now working for him) to kill Danny. In the confrontation with Shark, Danny is wounded, but Ronnie finds him and secrets him away to her hidden retreat, a small home somewhere on the bayou. The terms of their relationship, however, change radically in this scene. The wounded Danny has become vulnerable and weak, a man in need of a helping woman's care, impotent like his father. Ronnie, meanwhile, has come clean. No longer cynical and world-weary, she has now rebelled herself against Maxie Fields's hold over her, and for the sake of a romantic love that resembles the one desired by the younger Nellie. "You look like a kid," Danny tells her. Ronnie tells him how she imagined all sorts of magical happy endings to her life, marrying the first respectable man she met: "I don't have much pride left. I know what can be and can't be. But do you think for a little while you could make it the way I dreamed it, that you could love me, and that my dream could come true?" What Ronnie is asking Danny for is exactly what Danny asks for in his ballads as opposed to his rock 'n' roll numbers, for a sweet girl he can love and care for, and make happy. She asks him, in effect, to be her "teddy bear," and Danny replies affirmatively, "It wouldn't be hard to love you."

This romantic union, however, is not the one that resolves the narrative. Moments later Maxie Fields finds their hideout, and in the ensuing shootout, both Ronnie and Maxie are killed. Nor is the relevant reconciliation between Nellie and Danny, for even at the very end, Danny holds Nellie at bay, insisting that he is not yet ready to begin a life with her. In the final act at the King Creole club, Danny sings a love ballad, seemingly directed at Nellie, in which he appears to imply that he has moved beyond Ronnie, his first love, to a last and more mature love. As the song reaches its climax, however, the final object of Danny's affection shifts:

> Let's think of the future
> Forget the past
> You're not my first love
> But you're my last

21. Danny sings "As Long as I Have You" to his father in *King Creole* (Paramount, 1958).

> Take the love that I bring
> Then I'll have everything
> As long as I have you.

Nellie is in the audience, listening in rapture to this song that seems addressed to her. But on the last reprise, on the words "As long as I have you," Danny's father walks into the club. As in *Rebel*, the film closes with a final gesture of acceptance and reconciliation between father and son, and one in which the surviving heterosexual love interest (Nellie and Judy respectively) are subordinated to that reconciliation. Danny's song expresses at once his love for Nellie and his love for his father, yet both of them are a love he has had to come to by way of a different love, one that he has somehow left behind.

As in *Rebel*, reconciliation requires a concession from both sides. Danny will remain a nightclub singer, but he ends the film no longer singing the racially and sexually rebellious creole sounds of rock 'n' roll. Ronnie's own eleventh-hour fantasy transformation from a street girl into a good woman has enabled Danny to start winding his way back toward his father's professional, white suburb. Even so, the film does not allow Ronnie to survive. As someone who first embodied all of Danny's rebellious aspirations, his badness, then later his atonement and desire to be good again, Ronnie serves as a classical scapegoat. She clears the path to Danny's anticipated union with Nellie, just as Plato must die in *Rebel* so as to bring Jim and

Judy into their closing union. And yet, as in *Rebel*, *King Creole* acknowledges the traumatic price of this resolution. Danny postpones indefinitely his romance with Nellie, still in mourning for Ronnie and the radical possibility she represented: a countersuburban, antidomestic romance, animated by cross-class and cross-race desire as well as by cross-gender identification. If both films end with ideological closure of the sort obligatory in Hollywood films, they refuse to do so without preserving the desire for a kind of bad boy whose desires grant him a dissident identity: as racial, as classed, as gay, or even as transgendered. The rebel may have to be a boy, but his rebellion against suburban masculinity pulls in directions strikingly familiar from the hindsight of identity politics.

Bad Boys and Weak Fathers: Analyzing the Fordist Oedipus

The ideological dynamics of *Rebel* and *King Creole* are highly complex. Both end in moments of reconciliation that conclude the son's struggles against the father. Two questions therefore need to be posed. First, how can one summarize the stakes of these revolts? What do the poles of these father-son conflicts actually represent? Second, and no less crucially, what sort of terms provide for their final reconciliations? What must be yielded by each in order for these films to achieve ideological closure, and what does that "yielding" tell us?

The first point that needs to be reiterated is that the bad boy's oedipal revolt against the father is narrated through the latter's patriarchal failings. Once domesticated, the "man" of the house seems no longer capable of remaining its master. In this respect, the bad boy seems to be a conservative as opposed to a liberal figure, someone who resists the new Fordist family arrangements on behalf of the male privilege they are held to have dismantled. Seen from this perspective, the rebel figure seems irretrievably tied to a reactionary sexual politics in which rebellion against existing social arrangements aims to recuperate men's authority. Certainly, a traditionalist rhetoric of manhood suffuses these films, in Dean's disgust at his father in an apron, and in Presley's disgust for his father as someone "who crawls" and forever "turns the other cheek." Moreover, the mode of masculinity they desire often seems tied to violence, as when Jim wishes dad would "knock her cold once in a while" or Danny, whose bitterest memory of his father recollects his refusal to punch back at another man. *Rebel* and *King Creole* are both stories about sons who want fathers that are willing to fight back.

208 CHAPTER FIVE

At a deeper level, however, these oedipal desires lead in more open-ended directions, if only because they refuse Fordism's social rigidities in the name of an unspecified identitarian self-determination. Although this rebellion is often framed in the terms of patriarchal nostalgia, its exploration actually occurs across much broader avenues. Some of these are certainly phallic paths, as in the delinquent gangs of both films or in the King Creole persona performed by Presley. Yet even these routes can function as powerful decenterings of Fordist suburban norms. Becoming a delinquent is a very different way of achieving phallic mastery than becoming a patriarch. Moreover, Presley's mode also draws in racial and class otherness explicitly as modes of resistance to the suburban norms. The idea of masculinity in the modality of an urban, street-based creole identity was not easily reconciled to the Fordist suburban imaginary, nor did it reiterate conservative family arrangements. These are macho rebellions, in other words, articulated in response to alleged "patriarchal failure," but it is far from clear whether they themselves (rather than the narrative resolutions by which they are foreclosed) aim at patriarchy's restoration. If *Rebel* ends with such a restoration, for instance, it comes at the *price* of Dean's rebel personae.

Moreover, other avenues of rebellion in these films seem emphatically not nostalgic for patriarchy, but seem instead to lead elsewhere. Consider, for instance, the girl-centered heterosexuality that develops through Judy in *Rebel* and Nellie in *King Creole*. If these relationships often reinvoke the very failure of patriarchy that launched bad-boy rebellion to begin with, they nonetheless are presented as attractive in their own right, and as possessing some sort of utopian possibility that escapes male castration *tout court*. Some notion of male rebellion resides here that involves a passive erotic yielding to a girl, and thus must be considered a break of sorts with conventional modes of masculinity. This particular mode of male rebellion, moreover, seems bound to a vital promise of female empowerment. For both Judy and Nellie, the experience and expression of erotic desire seems liberating. Judy is released from the feminine need to "be loved" that is repeatedly thwarted by her father. Nellie in turn escapes the tedium of her alienated life at the shop. Suspended in these moments from the bad-boy narrative are feminist possibilities to which I will return in chapter 7.

Finally, *Rebel* and *King Creole* each offer particularly radical possibilities for youth rebellion by way of the identification of their rebel protagonists with the narrative scapegoats in each film. In *Rebel*, Plato points to a queer mode of bad-boy rebellion that can in no way be readily reconciled to patriarchy. Here, Dean's movement away from his father leads somewhere that could radically undermine the basic heteronormativity that underwrites *any* family system, conservative or liberal. In *King Creole*, Ronnie becomes the crucial figure. Her body is made to signal male castration, which at first glance might simply seem to confirm Laura Mulvey's analysis of the role of the female image in patriarchal libidinal economies. However, these issues are so explicitly thematized in the narrative that they open up highly unconventional readings. If *King Creole* tells the story of Danny's struggle to avoid castration, and if Ronnie becomes the figure whose fate he must try to escape, then "castration" becomes something worth battling against for both characters; in no way does the film belittle Ronnie's wish to avoid "crawling" and being "used." A feminist resistance to the position of woman as "castrated," in other words, constitutes Ronnie's character in the narrative, something made explicit as an identity project when she finally rebels against Maxie Fields herself, yelling, "No, you don't own me. You bought me, you don't own me, I meant to tell you that. I hate you." Given a man's name, Ronnie herself momentarily shares and regenders Danny's status as bad boy, pointing toward a tomboy mode of female masculine rebellion that will also be explored in chapter 7.

Despite all of these textual and spectatorial openings, however, it must be acknowledged that at its most schematic level, the oedipal narrative of the bad boy rendered youth rebellion as a distinctly male privilege and responsibility fueled by the emasculated meaning of the suburb's "domesticated male." It is this surface meaning, moreover, that first carried over into the social movements of the following decade. Consider, for instance, Jerry Rubin's 1968 yippie manifesto, *Do It!*, which places Elvis as the origin of "the sixties," extending *King Creole*'s oedipal conflict one step further with the arresting claim: "Elvis Presley killed Ike Eisenhower." Despite the apparent calm of the father figure Eisenhower fifties, where Dad beamed proudly at his suburban house, car, and manicured lawn, Rubin writes that "under the surface, silent people railed at the chains upon their souls. A latent drama of repression and discontent." With driving rhythms that aroused their "repressed passions," Elvis gave music that brought America's youth together and liberated them from the suburban grip, leading them to the free spirit of the sixties (18). The New Left challenge to "Amerika," Rubin thus flamboyantly proclaims, "sprang, a predestined pissed-off child, from Elvis' gyrating pelvis" (17).

The very fact that Rubin begins with Elvis in his missionizing manifesto suggests the rhetorical authority that the postwar narrative of the identitarian rebel would grant the new social movements. Rubin, in citing Elvis, sets himself up as a direct descendant, the bad boy of the sixties who carries on the liberationist work of the bad boy of the fifties. Equally significant, however, is Rubin's crude expression of the same Cold War containment thesis that many scholars of the fifties still reiterate. The Cold War era, that is, was a drama of repression from which Elvis, or Jerry Rubin's New Left, or the subsequent social movements of identity politics, came to liberate us. But where did these movements, or the New Left, or Elvis, actually come from? Did they emerge ex nihilo, as a spontaneous expression of discontent? To appropriate Rubin's own miniversion of the oedipal bad-boy narrative, I want to suggest that Daddy Eisenhower and rebellious son Elvis were mutually constitutive figures. Presley clearly required Eisenhower as a father figure whom he could disobey and thereby demonstrate his independence. But it must also be understood that, within the terms of the Cold War, Eisenhower also needed Presley. As the leader of the so-called free world, the president relied not only on rebel images like Presley's, but also James Dean's, Holden Caulfield's, Jack Kerouac's, and so forth, to embody young Americans' ability and inclination to dissent from impending conformities and homogenizations. They demonstrated that Cold War America, despite its suburbanization, remained a free nation whose people decide their own futures rather than being inserted, as in totalitarian societies, into predetermined positions in preexisting social structures.

Two absences in Rubin's mini-oedipal narrative must also be noted: first, its complete neglect of the racial and class connotations of Elvis's rebellion; second, its silence on the rebel's masculinization. As these absences in Rubin's narrative attest, mainstream Cold War culture tended to invest the rebellion it needed in narratives featuring white male and heterosexual figures of youth. Nevertheless, as both *Rebel* and *King Creole* demonstrate, the bad boy's oedipal rejection of his father also constituted a rejection of his whiteness, his middle-classness, and his suburban brand of manhood. In many representations, the bad boy openly adopted signs of blackness, the working classes, and women, as badges of his countercultural identity. The narrative of the bad boy therefore tended to align blackness and working-classness especially, but also, in sometimes remarkably open ways, sexualized femininity and queerness with an intrinsic character of rebellion against suburban conformity. This created ripe conditions for much broader appropriations of the rebel narrative on behalf of many different social and cultural movements. Instead of a bad boy, the identitarian basis of the rebel figure could eventually yield up the bad black, the bad girl, the bad queer, or, coming full circle, the bad creole, as a pantheon of identitarian figures whose dissent was authorized by a Cold War promise of liberation from social conformity.

Such appropriations were not only a latent possibility waiting to be realized in the sixties, but already manifested in the fifties. I want to end by sketching one last oedipal bad-boy narrative of the fifties, a rather obscure film *Take a Giant Step*. Like *Rebel*, this is a film about a boy growing up in an affluent suburb who defies what he considers the other-directed mendacity and weakness of his parents, and especially his father. The difference, however, is that in this film both the boy and his parents are black. *Take a Giant Step*, the decade's only film about a black teenager to be marketed as a teen-pic, was tagged "Sometimes Teenage is spelled T.N.T.!!" in a direct appeal to the young teen rebel tradition.

The film starred Johnny Nash, a rhythm and blues singer from Houston, Texas, who would move to Jamaica in the late sixties and end up working with Bob Marley in the world of reggae music production. In *Take a Giant Step*, Nash plays Spencer Scott, a nineteen-year-old boy whom we meet in the opening precredit shot, standing up angrily in defiance of his teacher and peers, the only black boy in a classroom full of white students. When he returns home it becomes clear that Spencer has problems, not only at school but with his parents as well. Like Jim Stark, what Spencer finds objectionable at home is that his parents care more about pleasing their neighbors than in doing the right thing, that is, in defying the everyday racism that shapes their suburban community. When it comes to racial self-assertion, Spencer finds that his parents actually have less gumption than his grandmother, who lives with them yet seems entirely out of place in the suburbs, representative of an earlier era less driven by social conformity. In frustration, Spencer runs away to the other side of town, where he spends an afternoon seeking out a poorer (but hopefully less domesticated) grade of black people.

As with the protagonists of *Rebel* and *King Creole*, Spencer's identity formation is also intertwined with his sexual awakening. The new tensions he feels with his former white friends at school stems from their reluctance to socialize with him now that they have begun to date girls. Since Spencer is precluded by local racism from romancing any of the neighborhood girls, his erstwhile friends have no way to include him. For the first time, Spencer feels acutely his racial exclusion, but this comes at the precise moment that he too has begun to search a romantically appropriate girl companion, someone who must also be black but who hopefully

22. Black teenpic movie poster for *Take a Giant Step* (United Artists, 1959).

will share his antipathy toward his parents' servility toward white suburbia. In the end, Spencer comes closest to finding such a girl in Christine, his own family's maid, played by Ruby Dee. A slightly older black girl from the South, and therefore in no way mistakable as an aspiring suburbanite, Christine nonetheless wisely encourages Johnny to "take a giant step" by reaching out to his weak-willed but well-intentioned parents. Feeling she has crossed a line of propriety in the process (and in the play upon which the film is based, their relation becomes more openly sexual), Christine quits her job. Johnny's parents, recognizing at last that Spencer has "good" cause to be "bad," meet him halfway, declaring that they will try to stand up more strongly for their identity because that is evidently what their son needs to achieve his own. Exactly like *Rebel* and *King Creole*, then, a resolution takes place in which the bad boy will forego his rebelliousness if its cause is addressed, and if his father can begin to reclaim something of his own personal autonomy.

It is crucial to see how openly a psychopolitics of black identity is formulated in the oedipal drama of *Take a Giant Step*. What the film denounces, at a basic level, is the "domestication" of blackness by the suburbs, its colonization by a Fordist conformity saturated with white expectations about the servility of blackness. What his dad promises Spencer by the end of the film amounts to a greater racial self-assertiveness, so that the demand one finds in *Rebel* and *King Creole* for a father who "stands up" or won't "crawl" suddenly appears to have very real political teeth. *Take a Giant Step* was not a famous film. Nonetheless, as the oedipal struggles of its black teen rebel demonstrate, it did not take long for the discourse of identity to begin serving as an authorizing force in the politics of race. The bad boy of Cold War culture must therefore be seen in all his ideological contradiction. His most famous incarnations gave identity a predominantly white male face, yet his countersuburban messages relied so heavily on the codes of race, class, gender, and sexuality that they bestowed upon the faces and stories of Fordism's various possible "outsiders" a growing political importance and claim to power.

214 CHAPTER FIVE

6

BEAT FRATERNITY AND

THE GENERATION OF IDENTITY

In the last chapter, the bad boy appeared as a solitary figure, a son rejecting his father's servility as a means of realizing his own sovereign identity. The identity concept would have displayed little political potency, however, if the sovereignty of the individual did not also stand in for the collectivity's. Even the loner bad boys portrayed by James Dean or Elvis gained their legitimacy as rebels only as proxies for youth's general right to establish an identity independent of that foisted upon them by a Fordist world of conforming adults. By 1957, this collective representation of young rebel identity had secured a public name: the beat generation.

"Generation" is obviously a far older social concept than "identity," with a genealogy tracing back to the Bible.[1] Yet there is a specifically modern discourse of generations, closely allied to romanticism, in which a generation is valued, less for preserving a received tradition than for articulating a historically new outlook. Such a modern generation takes a name (lost, beat, silent, X) that is meant to distinguish its cohort's situation or predicament from those of its predecessors. Because these predicaments (let alone one's attitude toward them) are subject to many possible articulations, representation plays a critical role in the formation of a modern generation. To be sure, this role is often disavowed; people of the same age are presumed to share a unique and therefore self-evident synchronization of their lifespan with ongoing historical developments. The classic sociological thinker Karl Mannheim called this synchronization a "social location," arguing that age groups, like social classes, endow "the individuals sharing them with a common location in the social and historical process, and thereby limit them to a specific range of potential experience, predisposing them for a certain characteristic mode of thought and experience, and a characteristic type of historically relevant action" (291).

Yet a common age is hardly sufficient to ensure a unified generational perspective. Even if large-scale events (wars, depressions, revolutions, and so forth) provide an age group with a shared frame of reference within history, its members will cut across so many social axes (regional, religious, racial, ethnic, gendered, sexuality, and class, to name but a few) that the received meaning and significance of their shared temporal coordinates is bound to vary enormously. What does it mean to be born during the depression, to grow up during the Second World War, and then to reach adulthood under the nuclear threat of a cold war? No doubt quite a bit, and yet to reduce it to any single thing, one must willfully dismiss the mediating role of ideology in placing us imaginatively at our temporal coordinates.[2]

Nevertheless, the ideological work of a generational name is precisely to *make* it mean one thing, to narrate a common destiny as shared by *all* people demographically defined at that moment as young. Like other collectivities then, a generation can only be produced via a hegemonizing act of representation. We might say then that a generation comes into existence if and only if a sufficiently powerful, vocal, and influential historic bloc within the age group has come to recognize itself—and begun to act upon—a generational representation. To paraphrase Marx, a generation is not an age group *in* itself, but an age group *for* itself, though it is crucial to remember that the implied self-image, the "itself," may actually have been produced by someone who falls outside the age group.

This indispensable moment of representation helps account for popular literature's prominent role in the naming of generations. Because the naming of generations represents an attempt to articulate and direct what Mannheim calls the "continuous emergence of new participants in the cultural process," the window of opportunity, so to speak, when that hegemonizing move can be made may open quite suddenly. Relative to other forms of collective nomination, a "generation" (precisely because of its temporal designation) is often born of strategic moments that favor an imaginative position seen in relation to new historical situations and events. Louis Althusser's theoretical narrative of interpellation (which describes how persons are inserted into an ideology as its subject) recapitulates just such an occasion. Interpellation occurs at moments when one is hailed by some name to which one then responds. Within Althusser's framework, appellation (being named) would appear to be a prerequisite for interpellation (recognizing oneself). One must after all be addressed as somebody in particular. Novels—and potentially films or popular texts of any sort—that step in at the opportune historical moment to hail young people as members of a particular generation are therefore in a strong position to define their significance as a collective subject in history.

The Beat Generation as the Generation of Identity

In 1955 editor Evelyn Levine wrote a glowing report for Viking Press on a manuscript submission by Jack Kerouac that was then titled *The Beat Generation*. This novel, Levine wrote, needed to be published even if it proved a financial failure, for it represented a great deal more than the updating of some other decade's "flaming youth": "I think it's essentially about young people trying to find their identity (and true, a subject of many past and current novels). . . . There is a great deal of (what might be called) immorality in the book—use of narcotics, drinking, immoral sexual relationships. I don't think that author is exaggerating too much—in searching for their identity, they're also trying to live to the fullest; protesting against the older generations and society's rules" (quoted in Theado, 159). On the strength of this endorsement, the novel would be published two years later under the title *On the Road*. The draft title and Levine's identitarian reading of it would survive, however, on the original dust jacket, which described a postwar cohort "roaming America in a wild, desperate search for identity and purpose, [that] became known as 'The Beat Generation.' Jack Kerouac is the voice of this group and this is his novel" (Theado, 166).

While Kerouac had originally written *On the Road* in 1951, by the time of its release in 1957 the concept of identity had diffused widely across multiple sectors of postwar culture. Social science had adopted the term wholesale. Consumer youth culture, in these intervening years, had learned to mass-produce images of the bad boy with enormous financial and cultural success. Rock 'n' roll had taken over radio, Hollywood teenpics were making enormous profits for an otherwise declining movie industry, and figures such as Brando, Dean, and Presley had rapidly become dominant icons of the American teenager as rebel. In the literary domain too, the rise of mass-market books was already well under way, and it was in paperback form that *On the Road* (much like *The Catcher in the Rye*) would make its impact.[3] What the beat texts succeeded in doing was to lay claim on the identity narrative of fifties youth culture, and to name its audience the "beat generation."

Today, by and large, the referential ambiguity of the "beat generation" is remembered only weakly, and the name is usually taken to designate only the handful of writers who called themselves beats, and perhaps another handful of writers with whom the self-named "beats" associated. Even when it was used in this restricted sense, however, the "beat generation" alluded to a second, more expansive meaning. Paul Goodman, for example, confessed that the beat generation was "socially important out of proportion to its numbers . . . [since] they act out a critique of the organized system that everybody in some sense agrees with" (170). Assuming this consensus of feeling among the young especially, the term "beat generation" was also often taken during the 1950s to connote the entire cadre of young Americans who lived out their teen and young adult years (roughly speaking) between 1945 and 1960, and who presumably shared the social position embodied by the beats. In his celebratory study of the beats, Bruce Cook recalls his response to reading *On the Road*: "I soon came to regard the Beats as my generation. I felt the same keen sense of identification with them that thousands of others my age did. . . . It is difficult, separated as we are by time and temper from that period, to convey the liberating effect that *On the Road* had on young people all over America. There was a sort of instantaneous flash of recognition that seemed to send thousands of them out into the streets, proclaiming that Kerouac had written their story, that *On the Road* was their book" (3).

Though today this second usage of the word "generation" has largely fallen out of use, a certain ambiguity persists. The latest reprint of Jack Kerouac's *On the Road*, for example, proclaims itself on the back cover to be "The Novel That Defined a Generation," a claim that is also reiterated in a blurb by Gilbert Millstein drawn from an early review of the novel: "A historic occasion . . . the most beautifully executed, the clearest and the most important utterance yet made by the generation Kerouac himself named years ago as 'beat,' and whose principal avatar he is." In a similar vein, Gary Snyder's blurb for Viking Press's recently released *Portable Beat Reader* calls the volume "a deft and definitive collection. It catches the flavor of playful, serious defiance of the whole generation." In recent examples like these, the more extensive meaning of "beat generation" still survives, affirming the so-called beat writers as literary representatives of the rebellious impulse shared by all young Americans in the fifties.

This residual ambiguity of the "beat generation's" referent is the legacy of a victory these writers won in the field of postwar youth representation. Against considerable cultural competition (including such rival designations as a "generation of esthetes," the "luckiest generation," the "explosive generation," the "silent generation," and the "shook-up generation") the "beat generation" proclaimed in the literary works of the beats won out to become the standard by which the historic situation and attitudes of young Americans became measurable to adults, and against which they would measure themselves when making generational claims.[4]

The beat writers did not achieve this representational victory overnight. As most surveys of modern American literature attest, the beats were a small circle of men who embraced an alternative hipster lifestyle in the forties, and began writing about their ideas and experiences by the late forties and early fifties, but were only discovered by mainstream American culture in the late fifties. Allen Ginsberg and Jack Kerouac, both students at Columbia, met William Burroughs in 1944 through his wife, Joan Burroughs (also a student), and were initiated by him into New York's growing postwar bohemian/drug/criminal subcultures. John Clellon Holmes, also a Columbia student in the forties, befriended Kerouac and Ginsberg shortly thereafter. All three were powerfully affected (in different ways) by their encounter with Neal Cassady, a handsome, frenetic, former juvenile delinquent from Denver. In 1950 Ginsberg also introduced Gregory Corso into the beat circle.

It is around this time that the term "beat generation" first made its modest way into public discourse on youth. In 1952 John Clellon Holmes published his modestly successful novel, *Go*, itself a *roman à clef* about the New York beat circle in the late forties. Encouraged by his publisher, Holmes also published an article later that year for the *New York Times Magazine*. Titled "This Is the Beat Generation," it described what Holmes took to be a paradoxical spirit of rebellious affirmation and religiosity among young Americans. As Holmes recalls, the piece "caused a ripple of curiosity, prompted a few hundred letters, and then it was forgotten" (*Passionate Opinions* 55).

Several of the beats gradually drifted away from New York in the early fifties, resettling by mid-decade in San Francisco's North Beach district, where they participated in the burgeoning literary scene now known as the San Francisco renaissance. The breakthrough of "beat generation" as a standard name for young Americans came only after this relocation to the West Coast, and on the heels of the emerging mass youth subculture. In 1956, Allen Ginsberg published his first poetry collection, *Howl and Other Poems*, with City Lights Bookstore in San Francisco. The obscenity trial that followed the police seizure of the book brought widespread media attention to Ginsberg's account in the long title poem of what he explicitly referred to as his generation's exploits (again drawn almost exclusively out of the personal histories of the beats). This encouraged Viking Press to go ahead in 1957 with the publication of Jack Kerouac's breakthrough novel *On the Road*, yet another fictionalized telling of beat adventures taken to be representative of a whole generation of young Americans. In the wake of the enormous attention lavished by critics and readers on *On the Road*, John Clellon Holmes wrote a second article, this time for *Esquire*, titled "The Philosophy of the Beat Generation," claiming Elvis Presley, James Dean, and youth culture generally as the province of the beat generation. Kerouac himself followed suit with "The Origins of the Beat Generation," which appeared in *Playboy*.

These are the principal texts by which the beats inaugurated a furious round of public discourse on young Americans, now suddenly premised on their "beatness." Beginning in 1957, articles on the beat generation appeared regularly in popular magazines and newspapers, Herb Caen of the *San Francisco Chronicle* coined the derogatory variant "beatnik," and other (i.e., non-beat) writers and critics, including Norman Podhoretz, Paul Goodman, Norman Mailer, and Kenneth Rexroth, proposed their own varying interpretations of its sociocultural implications of "beat" novels and films circulated in growing numbers, while bohemian subculture itself was renamed as the locus of a new beat youth.[5] By 1959 when Gregory Corso published his own poem on beatness, "Variations on a Generation," he would choose to cast it in the form of a by then ubiquitous media interview.

Ginsberg roughly chronologizes the development of the beats like this: "We'd already had, by '48, some sort of alteration of our own private consciousness; by '55 we had made some kind of public articulation of it; by '58 it had spread sufficiently so that the mass media were coming around for information" (quoted in Knight, 234). By "the mass media," Ginsberg is referring to the later representations of beatness by other writers and cultural producers, which he derides as "the exploitation of the Beats—the Beat [self] discovery is '52 or something. I'm talking about the mass media spread and exploitation, actually, in the stereotype characterization, the Frankenstein image that they put down" (quoted in Knight, 235).

However, Ginsberg conveniently diminishes the popular achievements of the beats themselves in promoting their own mass-mediated self-images. Their mainstream magazine articles, best-selling novels, pocketbook poetry collections, and even appearances on prime-time national tele-

23. Original cover design for the paperback edition of *On the Road* (1957).

vision, should make us wary of taking Ginsberg at his word. The beats were not powerless figures watching helplessly as the media buried their true selves under the false, damning stereotype of the beatnik.[6] If anything, the beats utilized the media (and especially print media) to wage an impressively successful campaign affirming their own version of what a "beat generation" of young Americans meant. In an important sense, one can say that the beats used the media to build for themselves a reputation as the legitimate representatives of the young, and that their texts therefore took on uniquely authorized status.

So far I have suggested how the beats laid claim on their special authority to *name* a generation of young Americans, but nothing about how that name signified and inflected the normative principle of identity. Just who or what was this allegedly beat generation? As we shall see, the signification of being beat actually varies quite a bit from text to text. Nevertheless, at its most general, to be "beat" typically meant some combination of three things. First, it implied that this generation was "beat" in the sense of fatigued or even defeated. Its "search for identity" was thus an exhaustive, uphill battle. Second, it could suggest that this generation was "beat" in the sense of beatific, that is, saintly or holy. Its search for identity was spiritually motivated or sanctioned, and thus appeared as a countervalue to Fordist materialism. Finally, it could refer to a generation that has a "beat," meaning a sense of rhythm, or a rhythmic sense of life, or even a "life rhythm" as in a heartbeat. To have a "beat" was thus to possess a unique living identity, and one that was presumably out of synch with the deadened absence of rhythm in the square world.

All three of these connotations, finally, converged in the image of an age group that clashes with mainstream America, and whose social position leads naturally to rebellion. As beat critic-cheerleader Bruce Cook put it, "If the beats meant anything to complacent, conformist Eisenhower America, it was change" (4). The generation's presumed defeat or exhaustion alluded to a relentless oppression or even aggression exerted upon it by mainstream American life ("Howl," for example, depicts this pressure as a war against the young that they can only lose). In this respect, "beatness" becomes, as Cook suggests, the privileged binary opposite in the fifties to "conformity" or "squareness," suggestively invoking the wearied determination of an outmatched and yet defiant generation.[7] At the same time, however, "beatness" in the sense of holiness or saintliness suggests that the young are not so much defeated as elevated through their embrace of a possible martyrdom. In refusing conformity, the young transcend a spiritually impoverished America, and in their beatness they come to embody a renewed commitment to identitarian values above and beyond those connected with America's consumer and/or militaristic culture. Finally, "beatness" in the sense of rhythm suggests a passion for meaning and for life that presumably has been deserted by the mainstream, but could perhaps be recovered by embracing the primitive, as in Kerouac's romantic sense of kinship with the "Fellahin," the "natural" peoples of the third world, presumably unconstrained by any regime of Fordist regimentation.

These various senses of beat oppositionality have all contributed to a remarkable fetishization of the relevant writers whose self-presentation was ultimately so successful that today they continue to be celebrated as though they were the one small island of rebellious consciousness in a vast ocean of decade-long conformity. Paradoxically, their consciousness is presumed to have informed that of all young Americans belonging to their generation, even if youth were not always willing to act on it, or were not even quite fully aware of it.

Kerouac, Ginsberg, and Burroughs make up the traditional beat triumvirate, but of these three writers Burroughs in fact had very little interest in such promoting of the beat generation. He was older than his compatriots (decisively outside the defined span of the beat cohort), queerer in his practice and theories of sexuality, and most important, profoundly skeptical of any identitarian narrative professing liberation from a regime he presumed all but invincible given the so-called algebra of need, a calculus of addiction that enfolded hip and square, organization man and junkie alike. Whereas Ginsberg became a major public figure and advocate of beat ideals, and whereas Kerouac too (shyness notwithstanding) would write definitional magazine articles and appear on television, Burroughs absented himself from the United States for much of the 1950s, first relocating to Mexico City, then to Tangiers. His first novel, *Naked Lunch*, was not published in the United States until 1966, well after the beat era had given way to something else.

Though a less renowned writer than Burroughs, John Clellon Holmes was, in the fifties, perhaps the single most passionate beat exponent. Not only did he publish the first self-designated beat generation novel in 1951, but he also wrote (as previously noted) two of its most influential manifestos: "This Is the Beat Generation" in 1951 for the *New York Times Magazine* and "The Philosophy of the Beat Generation" for *Esquire* in 1958. Along with Kerouac and Ginsberg, Holmes must therefore be counted as a principal architect of beat claims upon the collective identity of American youth.

All three writers advanced these claims through an effective use of literary genres grounded in fictionalized autobiography, particularly the *roman à clef* and the confessional poem. On the one hand fictional, the characters portrayed in the novels and poems could function as definitive representations of American youth. Because they were recognizable as autobiography, these texts also celebrated their authors as real-life counterparts of their fictional protagonists. This then further authorized the beats as generational "insiders" to speak on behalf of their nonliterary peers to "outsiders" (i.e., their elders) in widely read popular magazine essays.

Beat Identity as a Homosocial Desire

If the beat generation were (as sometimes claimed) an already existing universal age position merely awaiting its literary expression, one might expect to find in the autobiographical fictions of the beats an equivalence between protagonist, author, and generation, in which each "beat" character substitutes for any other. As I have argued, however, the beat generation was not a collectivity there to be discovered, but one that needed to be produced as the movement of identity. Specifically, American youth needed to be persuaded that the beat "search for identity" reflected their own condition growing up under Cold War conditions.

Insofar as they worked to do this, the beat texts that I will be discussing are paradigmatic instances of performative language, following precisely along the lines delineated in Judith Butler's general analysis of identity: they retroactively call into being that which they name. Of course, many young Americans looked, thought, and said nothing like the beats or the characters in their fictions.[8] Nevertheless, the beat generation became culturally viable as a common identity because the relevant texts and the popular responses to them made it plausible that young Americans *wished* they measured up, or at any rate *would wish* it if only they began to recognize their shared coming of age in the postwar historical moment. To achieve that end, the beat texts needed to provide a rhetorically persuasive historical roadmap to the development of that generational identity, navigating their readers to the unequivocal conclusion that anyone growing up in the United States at this moment would, ultimately, have to feel beat.[9]

To this end, the chains of identification between young people one might expect to find imagined in beat texts are in fact not simple givens but instead depicted as links they desire to forge with one another. To put it another way, the story told by the beat texts is not that of a generation as a fait accompli but, on the contrary, the difficult struggle to bring one into being, the embattled process of young people's enlistment into the beat generation, understood as the common identity project of their time. Typically, a subjective gap separates the narrator from another character who more fully incarnates the beat generation.[10] Over the course of the novel or poem, the narrator tries to act on his desire to identify with that character, and the bond that develops between them becomes a synecdoche for the bonds that hold together the entire generation.

Actual readers who resisted immediate identification with the beat generation were likely better served by such texts, which begin with similarly hesitant narrators. But this in turn created an ideological problem for beat texts, in that each of them needed to explain why a gap of identification would exist at all between these two members of a generational cohort. Why, that is, would two young Americans not naturally and immediately see I to I (as it were) if they belong to the same historically beat subject?

If in a beat narrative, one is gradually won over to one's authentic generational identity, then the narrative must also account for the obstacles that apparently inhibit the forging of that identification.

The ideology of the beat project was crucially defined by these obstacles, for who the beat generation alleged itself to be was deeply influenced by whom or what it held up as its impediments, its opposites, or its adversaries. To be beat was to refuse conformity in the name of identity. In some important sense, then, it was "conformity" per se that expressed the obstacles and adversaries of beatness. Like rebellion, however, "conformity" is a transitive verb disguised as a noun. The very concept presupposes some external norm. To characterize beatness as the privileging of rebellion over conformity thus begs the most important question: just what are the norms of conformity that beat texts represent as the source of their generation's rebellion?

Any persuasive answer to this question must return to the gendered issues raised by the bad-boy figure, for the resistant, young narrator of a beat text, whether Paul Hobbes in Holmes's *Go*, Ginsberg's "I" in "Howl," or Sal Paradise in Kerouac's *On the Road*, is always a man. And likewise, the authentic beat with whom that narrator struggles fiercely to identify, whether Holmes's Hart Kennedy, Ginsberg's Carl Solomon, or Kerouac's Dean Moriarty, is also invariably male. In each of the canonical beat texts that so influenced fifties culture, the synecdochic generational bond between narrator and representative beat is *always a bond between two men*.

Nonsexualized yet intense male bonds in literature are, of course, the subject of Eve Sedgwick's classic study *Between Men*. Though "homosociality" is the term she reserves to characterize such nonsexualized relations (in contradistinction to "homosexuality"), Sedgwick's innovation was to analyze them nevertheless as relations of desire, no less libidinal for their lack of a specifically sexual articulation. For Sedgwick, the effect of pulling homosociality, "back into the orbit of 'desire,' of the potentially erotic . . . is to hypothesize the potential unbrokenness of a continuum between homosocial and homosexual—a continuum whose visibility, for men, in our society, is radically disrupted" (1–2). Only in certain epochs like our own, Sedgwick observes, has "men loving men" been considered something radically different from, and perhaps threatening to "men promoting the interests of men" (3).[11] Sedgwick's analysis of modern homosociality begins with the narrative form of the erotic triangle, which connects two heterosexual, male rivals for a woman's affection. Various male interests, Sedgwick shows, can be promoted in these typically competitive, but always passionate, male-male social relations. But by locating specifically sexual desire on the axes represented by the *other* sides of the triangle, the male-male relations can always be distinguished as nonsexual relations guaranteed through the exchange of the woman.

Despite the protection afforded by the heterosexual sides of the erotic triangle, however, male homosocial desire brings with it bouts of homophobic paranoia. Sedgwick argues that, particularly since the eighteenth-century secularization of sexual discourse, homosocial relations have become vulnerable to "sexual blackmail" by other men, or even to uninstigated homosexual panic among the participants themselves:

> To put it in twentieth-century American terms, the fact that what goes on at football games, in fraternities, at the Bohemian Grove, and at climactic moments in war novels can look, with only a slight shift of optic, quite startlingly "homosexual," is not most importantly an expression of the psychic origin of these institutions in a repressed or sublimated homosexual genitality. Instead it is the coming to visibility of the normally implicit terms of a coercive double bind. . . . For a man to be a man's man is separated only by an invisible, carefully blurred, always-already-crossed line from being "interested in men." Those terms, those congruences are by now endemic and perhaps ineradicable in our culture. The question of who is to be free to define, manipulate, and profit from the resultant double bind is no less a site of struggle today than in the eighteenth century, however. (89–90)

In Sedgwick's account, men desire masculinity precisely for the privileges it affords, and yet because this desire often appears as a homosocial passion for other men, it threatens to represent its subjects (even to themselves) as homosexual in a homophobic society. This double bind means that political struggles within and between groups of men along axes such as class, race, and (though Sedgwick never explicitly suggests it) generation, can gain powerful leverage through homosexual blackmail.

Several beat writers, most prominently Ginsberg, were openly gay, and even those who were not had close relations with those who were. As a result, it is generally supposed that the beats were sexual heroes who defied the homophobia of their day. As we shall see, the story is more complex. It is true that in many beat texts, homosexuality figures prominently at the level of theme, plot, or character, and that its political force had everything to do with the beat generation's passionate opposition to the coercive heteronorms of suburban domesticity. Nevertheless, the sexuality of beat rebellion becomes particularly fraught in the declarative textual statements of generational identity, which sought their referent not merely in the literary circle of their authors, but in the general condition of America's youth. These texts, regardless of the sexual orientations or politics of their authors, needed to manage a homophobic threat to their popular interpellative project in precisely the form that Sedgwick terms homosexual blackmail. As John D'Emilio has noted, "The association of homosexuality and the beat scene in North Beach was so commonplace that defenders of the new bohemians felt compelled to disprove the charges" (180). As we shall see, the most public textual statements of the beat generation were likewise compelled to "disprove the charges." How both the homosexual charges and their rebuttals were effectively incorporated into the identity narrative that shaped the beat generation, constitutes an underlying concern of this chapter.

In all three of the respective breakthrough texts by Kerouac, Holmes, and Ginsberg—*On the Road*, *Go*, and "Howl"—beat-generational identity appears as an affective chain, the archetypal link of which becomes their protagonists' desire to identify and consort with another young man embodying beatness. The homosocial bonds at the narrative center of these texts therefore represent the beat generation as a masculine community. If Sedgwick's underlying argument is that homosociality is a mechanism closely associated with the reproduction of male privilege, however, then the beats here present an apparent paradox, for they present their male community, not as the site of privilege, but as the site of identity formation, which requires a revolt against the dominant regime of suburban "conformity." For the beats, the homosocially constituted cohort stands in youthful opposition to the normative authority of "maturity." The question for assessing the oppositional gestures of the beat generation therefore becomes, how and why did its texts pose male homosociality as the very substance of youth's identity, understood as a defiant alternative to the maturity of elder generations? We can begin to pursue an answer to this question by starting with the observation that homosociality in the principal texts of the beat generation does not follow the form of the classic erotic triangle but operates along a quite different pattern. To discover this form, we must turn to the texts themselves.

Western Kinsmen of the Sun

One would be hard pressed to find a work of fiction more unequivocally driven by male homosocial desire than Jack Kerouac's *On the Road*. An intimate confession of one man's undying passion for another, it opens with Sal Paradise meeting Dean Moriarty for the first time on the latter's trip to New York City. Narrative momentum builds as Sal and Dean struggle to establish a fraternal fidelity to one another. The novel climaxes with the last and most painful of Dean's betrayals of Sal on a last road trip to Mexico City. And it ends in a reversal, when in the final pages Sal turns his back on Dean.

Without ever intimating any sexual interest between the two men, *On the Road* nevertheless mimics the language of romantic love in conveying their relationship. Sal, the narrator, describes his first encounter with Dean in terms that many readers might find familiar: the new love interest who inspires an emotional rebound from the doldrums of recent romantic failure: "I first met Dean not long after my wife and I split up. I had just gotten over a serious illness that I won't bother to talk about, except that it had something to do with the miserably weary split-up and my feeling that everything was dead. With the coming of Dean Moriarty began the part of my life you could call my life on the road" (3). Sal's fascination with this "young Gene Autry—trim, thin-hipped, blue-eyed, with a real Oklahoma accent—a sideburned hero of the snowy West," is never openly sexualized (5). Instead, Sal has a different way of explaining his attraction to Dean:

> Somehow, in spite of our difference in character, he reminded me of some long-lost brother, the sight of his suffering bony face with the long sideburns and his straining muscular sweating neck made me remember my boyhood in those dye-dumps and swim-holes and the riversides of Paterson and the Passaic. . . . And in his excited way of speaking I heard again the voices of old companions and brothers under the bridge, among the motorcycles, along with the wash-lined neighborhood and drowsy doorsteps of afternoon where boys played guitars while their older brothers worked in the mills. (10)

Sal's loving attention to the details of Dean's physical presence, the "suffering bony face" and the "straining muscular sweating neck," recalls Sedgwick's observation that male homosocial desire "can look, with only a slight shift of optic, quite startlingly 'homosexual.'" Yet the desire that is here cathected onto Dean manifestly concerns a return from marital adulthood to the fraternity shared by small-town American boys. Yet Sal's desire to join with Dean in that "wild yea-saying overburst of American joy" will not be easily fulfilled, largely because Dean's fraternal loyalty proves fickle (10). Sal acknowledges the naïveté of his early enthusiasm for this "western Kinsman of the sun," admitting that

> Although my aunt warned me that he would get me in trouble, I could hear a new call and see a new horizon, and believe it at my young age; and a little bit of trouble or even Dean's eventual rejection of me as a buddy, putting me down, as he would later, on starving sidewalks and sickbeds—what did it matter? I was a young writer and I wanted to take off.
>
> Somewhere along the line I knew there'd be girls, visions, everything; somewhere along the line the pearl would be handed to me. (10–11)

It is because the pearl promised to every beat-generational hero proves so elusive that Sal must admit he is only "slowly joining" those "sordid hipsters of America, a new beat generation" (54). The reasons provided by Sal for this slowness represent the narrative material to be worked through by the novel.

On the Road's narrative development is belied by the repetition of its numerous cross-country road trips. Inspired by Dean's initial departure from New York, Sal makes the first of these journeys, hitchhiking to Dean's hometown, Denver, in pursuit of his hoped-for "buddy." There he discovers Dean already overextended, running back and forth between his first wife, Mary Lou; a new woman, Camille (whom Dean will also marry); and a mutual friend, Carlo (the novel's Allen Ginsberg character). Growing bored and impatient, Sal leaves Denver for San Francisco. From there, Sal returns to New York, where Dean comes to visit him. Sal and Dean then leave, together with Dean's first wife (Mary Lou), for San Francisco. When they both abandon him there, Sal leaves for Denver, but soon visits Dean again in San Francisco, where he is now living with Camille. When she throws them out of the house, they travel together to New York, where Dean meets and marries his third wife, Inez. Sal returns to Denver, but Dean soon catches up with him, and they leave on their most ambitious road trip of all, through Mexico. When Sal becomes deathly sick in Mexico City at the end of the trip, Dean deserts him, returning to New York alone. Sal, deeply hurt, makes his own painful way back to New York. There he falls in love with a woman, and in a closing moment, when Dean unexpectedly accosts them on a cold Manhattan night, it is finally Sal who abandons Dean on the street.

This narrative of geographical oscillation, in which Sal and Dean are forever coming and going, seeking, abandoning, or escaping each other, appears at first to embody a libidinally symmetrical relationship of mutual pursuit and rejection. Dean runs after Sal about as often as Sal chases down Dean. Yet, regardless of who heads where, until the reversal of the final scene Sal is always the needier partner, the one more easily wounded, and therefore the more desperate for a pledge of devotion. More than anything, Sal's story in *On the Road* is a tale of sad frustration at Dean's incapacity to commit to Sal as a brother. Sal's first trip to Denver, where Dean is absorbed by three other relationships, proves prophetic. Dean reciprocates Sal's fraternal love only fleetingly, forever leaving him behind in order to indulge a renewed obsession with one of the three women he has ended up marrying across the country.

Significantly, Dean's lack of fidelity to Sal is mirrored by the experiences of Dean's three wives. For Mary Lou, Camille, and Inez, this betrayal is compounded by their loss of Dean's material assistance as a provider and parent to their children. For a few months at a time, Dean will settle down with one of them. Eventually, however, Sal or one of the other boys will arrive, once again inspiring Dean to desert their home. Typical is Sal's description of arriving at Camille and Dean's home in San Francisco: "Dean and I began talking excitedly in the kitchen downstairs, which brought forth sobs from upstairs. Everything I said to Dean was answered with a wild whispering, shuddering '*Yes!*' Camille knew what was going to happen. Apparently Dean had been quiet for a few months; now the angel had arrived and he was going mad again" (183). In insistently describing this "madness" as something that develops between men, and at women's expense, Sal genders the meaning of beatness itself. A beat boy is a youthful angel who descends on his young male friends and sweeps them away from the trap of their married homes. As in *Rebel without a Cause* or *King Creole*, domesticated manhood is the fate to be avoided. In *On the Road*, however, the revolt against domesticity becomes a homosocial project of boys together.

The ideal of beat homosociality is made explicit in a late scene when a "sewing circle" of wives confronts Dean with his irresponsible treatment

230 CHAPTER SIX

of his families. Watching and inwardly commenting on the row, Sal blames the dispute on a sea change in the women's attitudes since Dean's adolescence, which he associates with marriage: "There were earlier days in Denver when Dean had everybody sit in the dark with the girls and just talked, and talked, and talked, with a voice that was once hypnotic and strange and was said to make the girls come across by sheer force of persuasion and the content of what he said. This was when he was fifteen, sixteen. Now his disciples were married and the wives of his disciples had him on the carpet for the sexuality and the life he had helped bring into being" (194). In light of how his relationship to Dean actually functions, Sal should have every reason to identify with these women, one of whom tells Dean, "For years now . . . you've done so many awful things I don't know what to say to you" (194). Indeed, just a few pages earlier in the novel, on their arrival in San Francisco, Dean had simultaneously deserted Sal and one of his wives, Mary Lou, unceremoniously dumping them both on the street: "Suddenly Dean was saying good-by. He was bursting to see Camille and find out what had happened. Marylou and I stood dumbly in the street and watched him drive away. 'You see what a bastard he is?' said Marylou. 'Dean will leave you out in the cold any time it's in his interest.' 'I know,' I said, and I looked back east and sighed" (170).

Far from affirming their point, however, Sal takes Dean's side in the quarrel. In so doing, he acts out of an implicit romantic self-interest, competing fiercely as he is with Dean's wives for their husband's attention. Sal's only hope to capture Dean as a comrade, after all, rests on the latter's irresponsibility as a husband and father. And indeed, it is only after Camille throws Dean out of the house that he and Sal at last go "to a bar down on Market Street and decided everything—that we would stick together and be buddies till we died" (190).

Sal justifies his self-interested defense of Dean by sanctifying their relationship as the one that forges the bonds of the beat generation, by contrast to the "square" demands of the women: "He [Dean] was BEAT—the root, the soul of beatific. What was he knowing? He tried in all his pores to tell me what he was knowing, and they [the women] envied that about me, my position at his side, defending him and drinking him in as they once tried to do" (195). As Sal would have it, these women were also once attracted to Dean's auratic beatness, but, being women, they inevitably grew frustrated by its incompatibility with marital domesticity and fidelity. As a young man who desires only a fraternal bond with Dean, however, Sal's appreciation for Dean's youthful madness remains constant, allowing him to see that the women's accusations are "not true":

> I knew better and I could have told them all. I didn't see any sense in trying it. I longed to go and put my arm around Dean and say, Now look here, all of you, remember just one thing: this guy has his troubles too, and another thing; he never complains and he's given all of you a damned good time *just being himself* [emphasis added], and if that isn't enough for you then send him to the firing squad, that's apparently what you're itching to do anyway. (194)

In these scenes, the signification of the "beat generation" gains some clarity. Not only does Sal desire Dean for his youthfulness, but the desire *itself* appears as a youthful desire; it is one boy's wish that another boy rebel against "settling down," so as to stay his buddy for life. In so doing, Sal's desire for Dean becomes a synecdoche for the desire of an entire generation of boys who, approaching manhood, refuse to abandon their fraternal community for the dubious "mature" substitute of marriage.[12]

In *On the Road*, two principal obstacles prevent the success of this rebellion, one obvious, the other less so. The first is of course the "sewing circle" of women itself, which might in the end coerce the beat boys to abandon their search for a collective identity forged out of homosocial community. The emotional toll of staying on the move makes for an overpowering temptation to just settle down. Indeed, the fatigue of Kerouac's boys as they resist the lure of domesticity is perhaps the most important sense in which they are becoming a beat generation. As Sal confesses to Dean,

> "I want to marry a girl," I told them [Dean and Marylou], "so I can rest my soul with her till we both get old. This can't go on all the time—all this franticness and jumping around. We've got to go someplace, find something."
>
> "Ah now, man," said Dean, "I've been digging you for years about the *home* and marriage and all those fine wonderful things about your soul." It was a sad night; it was also a merry night. (116)

The night remains merry because, as Sal and Dean both know, they are never quite overwhelmed by their weariness. When early in the novel, Sal falls in love with Terry, a young Mexican woman, he spends weeks role-playing as a domesticated man (97). But eventually, just as Dean abandons his wives, so Sal leaves Terry with no other words than, "Well, lackadaddy, I was on the road again" (101). The toll of the road is well worth the freedom from commitment. After abandoning Lucille, yet another marital prospect, Sal complains: "She wanted me to be *her way* . . . and the whole thing was hopeless, besides which Lucille would never understand me because I like too many things and get all confused and hung-up running from one falling star to another till I drop. This is the night, what it does to you. I had nothing to offer anybody except my own confusion" (126). Confusing as the beat life of constant movement may be, it nevertheless remains vastly preferable to remaining stationary in a single home, which in *On the Road* signifies doing things "*her way.*"

As narrator, Sal privileges relationships between men by implying that, unlike those between men and women, they express a desire to free your brother rather than to control or be controlled by him. Transcending the petty power struggles found in merely sexual relations, the fraternal love between Sal and Dean, "two broken-down heroes of the Western night" (190), presumably escapes any wish to domesticate each other as their women do. Brothers do not jeopardize the utopian character of their bond by trying to manipulate one another through jealousy, dishonesty, and emotional unpleasantness.

Beyond the threat of heterosexual marriage, however, *On the Road* also suggests grave doubts regarding the sustainability of the altruistic fraternal bonds it celebrates, precisely because, in the final instance, the boys' desires may not be so purely homosocial. At several points, Sal seems panicked by the nerve-wracking similarity of his brotherly feelings for Dean to romantic love. In perhaps the riskiest moment in the novel, Sal offers to commit himself to Dean after they are both thrown out of Camille's house. This poignant moment, ostensibly about a friendship, seems nothing less than a proposal of marriage, precisely the domestic trap they have both worked so hard to avoid:

> I looked back at him and blushed. Resolutely and firmly I repeated what I said—"Come to New York with me; I've got the money." I looked at him; my eyes were watering with embarrassment and tears. Still he stared at me. Now his eyes were blank and looking through me. It was probably the pivotal point of our friendship when he realized I had actually spent some hours thinking about him and his troubles, and he was trying to place that in his tremendously involved and tormented mental categories. Something clicked in both of us. In me it was suddenly concern for a man who was five years younger than I, and whose fate was wound with mine across the passage of the recent

years; in him it was a matter that I can ascertain only from what he did afterward. He became extremely joyful and said everything was settled.... "Well," said Dean in a very shy and sweet voice, "shall we go?" (189–190)

Though their vow of brotherly commitment to each other should be the happiest moment in their friendship, Sal confesses that they "both felt perplexed and uncertain of something." As they stand indecisively, a line of Greek men and women emerge from a nearby house where another set of vows have just been exchanged, at a wedding party held for one of their daughters.

In the scenes that immediately follow, Sal and Dean are dogged by a sexual undertow that threatens their fraternal aspirations. Sal and Dean head out of town, hitching a ride with a "fag" who represents (as Dean explains) just the sort of person who needs "to worry and betray time with urgencies false and otherwise, purely anxious and whiny" (208). When the "fag" propositions them later, Dean scares him off by responding with a professional hustle. Hungry, Sal and Dean stop at a restaurant where they use the john. When Sal puts on a go-and-stop show for Dean, peeing first in one urinal and then continuing at a second, Dean warns him about the "awful kidney miseries" this will give him in old age. Sal responds furiously, "'Ah,' I said, 'you're always making cracks about my age. I'm no old fag like that fag, you don't have to warn me about *my* kidneys'" (212). Sal's reference to himself as a "fag" is entirely unsolicited, and yet it is highly motivated. "Every one of these things I said was a knife at myself. Everything I had ever secretly held against my brother was coming out: how ugly I was and what filth I was discovering in the depths of my own impure psychologies" (213). Having declared themselves a couple of sorts, Dean and Sal begin to face the emotional insecurities and power plays found in an "impure" sexual relationship, the very antithesis of the fraternal love rhapsodized by Sal as the sacred bond of his generation.

In *On the Road*, fraternal and sexual love appear irreconcilable, and it is the grave threat that the second poses to the first that animates Sal's ongoing aggression toward gay men. It likewise motivates the novel's studious desexualization of all beat relationships. Whatever the methodological limits of appeals to biographical facts, it is striking that *On the Road* translates even Allen Ginsberg's lengthy romantic relationship with Neal Cassady into a strictly platonic relationship. In so doing, the novel elevates Dean's relationship with Carlo above the pettiness of merely sexual relationships, such as those with two women that Dean is also pursuing at that moment. When Sal first arrives in Denver, he meets up with Carlo, who describes to him Dean's daily itinerary:

> "Dean is in Denver. Let me tell you." And he [Carlo] told me that Dean was making love to two girls at the same time, they being Marylou, his first wife, who waited for him in a hotel room, and Camille, a new girl, who waited for him in a hotel room. "Between the two of them he rushes to me for our own unfinished business."
>
> "And what business is that?"
>
> "Dean and I are embarked on a tremendous season together. We're trying to communicate with absolute honesty and absolute completeness everything on our minds." (42)

The subtext of suspicion that one can read into Sal's interjection, "'And what business is that?'" recalls Sedgwick's theory of homophobia, explained in terms of the *formal* similarity of the homosocial and homosexual, which is in turn grounded in the continuum of male desire. In *On the Road*, however, what actually makes the formal similarity of homosociality and homosexuality frightening is the *substantive* similarity of the homosexual and the heterosexual, both of which are equally nonutopian (because sexual) forms of desire. If Dean's business with Carlo is really no different from his business with Mary Lou or Camille, then beat-generational bonds are ultimately no different from the marital relations of adult women and men anywhere in America. That is, they are sexual and thus domesticating. The moments in *On the Road* celebrated by Sal as emblematic of generational fraternity, and hence of fullest generational identification, are ironically also moments of the greatest sexual peril, threatening to undo that rebellious community by exposing it as no different from the adult social institution of marital domesticity that it defies. *On the Road* is written from the perspective of a homophobic narrator, to be sure. Yet Sal admirably admits discomfort with his own homophobia, and a wish to be more tolerant. Compounding Sal's fear is something else, a terror of sexual desire for his brothers that is not merely homophobic, but what should in all fairness be called maritophobic, since heterosexual marriage models the erasure of identity to which the domesticating effects of all sexual relations must eventually lead.

The Boy Gang That Mustn't Bang

Though Kerouac became the vastly more famous novelist, John Clellon Holmes was a far more ardent promoter of the beat generation, someone who in a 1958 article would actually redefine the entire domain of "rebellious" youth culture, from rock 'n' roll to James Dean, as so many expressions of beatness ("Philosophy"). To consider Holmes's version of generational identity, then, is to consider the most rhetorically extensive version advanced by any beat writer. In many ways, Holmes's novel *Go* (published six years before Kerouac's) anticipates *On the Road*'s structural opposition between a rebellious beat fraternity and (heterosexual) marriage. Holmes originally titled his novel *The Daybreak Boys*, after a nineteenth-century New York waterfront gang. In a 1976 introduction to the reissue of the novel, Holmes states, "I felt that it [*The Daybreak Boys*] was an appropriate title for a book about a new underground of young people, pioneering the search for what lay 'at the end of the night'" (a phrase of Kerouac's) (xxi). Holmes's preference for this title might have seemed peculiar to readers of the novel, which features several important women characters and devotes infinitely more attention to the heterosexual relationships within the beat social circle than does *On the Road*. In her beat era memoirs, Joyce Johnson recalls that "in a 'Dream Letter' from John Clellon Holmes recorded by Allen Ginsberg in 1954 are the words: 'The social organization which is most true of itself to the artist is the boy gang.' To which Allen, awakening, writing in his journal, added sternly, 'Not society's perfum'd marriage'" (76). This image of the artistically committed boy gang, as offered by the phantom Holmes of Ginsberg's dream, supplies an interesting rationale for Holmes's preferred title. In turn, Johnson's memoir, *Minor Characters*, suggests through its title a reproach to the "Dream Letter," which by enshrining the fraternal relations between boy artists as the essence of beat identity, reduces women to bit players whose place in the generational saga can only be as minor impediments to the literary heroism of the men. Ginsberg's addendum implicitly justifies this artistic attention to fraternity by asserting its social rebelliousness. It is "society" that demands attention to marriage, while the beats' commitment to art, their literary duties as generational spokesmen, require them to defy the representational norm, to portray instead a boy gang. Beat rebellion, both Holmes and Ginsberg imply, is embodied in its against-the-grain emphasis on homosocial (as opposed to heterosexual) narration.

Though Holmes's publisher did not allow him to use this title, in Britain the novel was released as *The Beat Boys*, to more or less the same exclusionary effect. In the United States, however, Holmes's novel was simply published as *Go*, a regular imperative in the novel that, as it recurs, takes on an increasingly gendered quality. It first appears in the novel innocuously, buried in a paragraph describing the beat scene that writer-protagonist Paul Hobbes (the fictionalized John Holmes) encounters as he strikes up a friendship with David Stofsky (the Allen Ginsberg character) and Gene Pasternak (the Jack Kerouac character).

> He [Hobbes] came to know their [Stofsky and Pasternak's] world at first only indirectly.... It was inhabited by people "hungup" with drugs and other habits, searching out a new degree of craziness and connected by the invisible threads of need, petty crimes of long ago, or a strange recognition of affinity. They kept *going* [emphasis added] all the time, living by night, rushing around to "make contact," suddenly disappearing into jail or on the road only to turn up again and search one another out. They had a view of life that was underground, mysterious, and they seemed unaware of anything outside the realities of deals, a pad to stay in, "digging the frantic jazz," and keeping everything *going* [emphasis added]. (36)

This passage sets up "go" as a signifier for the qualities that attract these men to one another as generational compatriots. "Go" condenses youth, activity, physicality, newness, and excitement into a single imperative. Yet Hobbes is only slowly won over to this directive. Initially, as we are told, "Hobbes ventured into the outskirts of this world suspiciously, even fearfully, but unable to quell his immediate fascination for he had been among older, less active, and more mental people for too long, and needed something new and exciting" (36). The narrative voice, closely identified with Hobbes's point of view, thus offers us a typically resistant "prebeat" protagonist, one who will only gradually achieve his own "strange recognition of affinity" with his generational peers. Stofsky and Pasternak serve, in turn, as incarnations of beatness, much as Dean Moriarty does in *On the Road*. This is "their world," their "view of life." They are the ones who have remained true to their youthful values, while it is Paul who must find his way back from among "older, less active, and more mental people."

The word "go," then, begins as a characterization of Stofsky and Pasternak that expresses Hobbes's desire to join in the dynamic identity of their generation. The beat generation is the one that "goes," and as Hobbes increasingly comes to understand them, admire them, and finally join them, he too begins to "go," to move within a dynamic community of men. This dynamism, moreover is associated with the sort of virility they possess:

> He spoke of them to others as being "badly educated" but at least not "emotionally impotent" like so many young men who had come out of the war. . . . They operated on feelings, sudden reactions, expanding these far out of perspective to see in them profundities which Hobbes was certain they could not define if put to it. But they accepted him, came to him with their troubles because he would always listen. They thought of him, he decided, as a regrettable intellectual, but acted as though they believed he was not completely "impotent." (35–36)

In this passage the word "beat" possesses the same referential ambiguity I discussed earlier in conjunction with the generation itself for it serves to characterize both a literary circle and an entire cohort of young Americans. Insofar as it signifies defeat, the word would seem to apply to the *majority* of "young men who had come out of the war" and who had ended up, in Hobbes's words, "emotionally impotent." At times, the novel concerns itself with this general sense of a postwar beat generation, perhaps most overtly in a late scene when Hobbes and a young woman, Estelle, see a young man so worn down and passionless that Hobbes begins to "tell her about the 'beat generation,' tell her that though he did not know that it existed, somehow he sensed that it was there, tell her things . . . the 'cool' man and his own heightened concern about the evening had thrown into relief in his mind. He talked steadily, gravely, about the war and how it had wounded everyone" (211). Though at this moment, Hobbes counts the gang as typical, among the wounded, telling Estelle about "Hart [Kennedy] and Stofsky and Pasternak and Agatson, of their faithlessness and his recognition of a similar discontent inside himself," usually the generational identity of the gang that Hobbes comes to embrace seems not representatively cool, but indeed exceptionally hot. It is characterized by the *potency* of its members' passion for activity (211).[13]

This apparent contradiction between Hobbes's circle and youth in general is ultimately sublated. The daybreak boys are indeed representatively wounded, like all other young men, but they also differ from most in that they have begun to transcend their defeat. Hobbes respects not the majority of young men, who are merely beat like the "cool man," but rather those like Stofsky and Pasternak who have nevertheless found the will to keep going. In this sense, rebellion is a vital ingredient for an affirmative beat-generational identity. It is as a homosocial community refusing to be defeated by its own exhaustion that Hobbes comes to admire the gang, much as he might respect the "virile" tenacity of a band of long-distance runners. In an important sense, then, the daybreak boys are not representative of their generation *as it is*, so much as they are representative of *what it can potentially become*. They are, as Ginsberg will put it in "Howl," the "best minds" of their generation, whose exceptional status merely realizes an incipient rebelliousness that is already present among the young at large.

This sense of the beats, as those who fulfill the inner possibility of their cohort, is most strongly conveyed in section 2 of *Go*. Titled "Children in the Markets," it alludes to a passage in the Gospel of St. Matthew:

> But whereunto shall I liken this generation? It is like unto children sitting in the markets, and calling unto their fellows,
>   And saying, We have piped unto you, and ye have not danced; we have mourned unto you, and ye have not lamented.
>   —Matthew 11:16, 17

In this passage from the Gospel, the generation is not *identical* to the children who pipe and mourn in the market, but it can be *likened* to them through an act of representation. In a similar fashion, the boys in Hobbes's circle provide a novelistic portrait to which an entire beat generation can be likened, even if that generation as a whole has not yet actually called and piped and mourned. This relationship of resemblance between the beat boys and their generation is appealed to early in section 2. The word "go" that characterizes Hobbes's circle has now become the name of a bar on Times Square, the Go Hole, a place which in turn serves as a spatial metaphor for the historical moment of a generation's revolt:

> The Go Hole was where all the high schools, the swing bands, and the roadhouses of their lives had led these young people; and above all it was the result of their vision of a wartime America as a monstrous danceland, extending from coast to coast, roofed by a starless night, with hot bands propelling thousands of lonely couples with an accelerating, Saturday-night intensity. In this modern jazz, they hear something rebel and nameless that spoke for them, and their lives knew a gospel for the first time. It was more than a music; it became an attitude toward life, a way of walking, a language and a costume; and these introverted kids (emotional outcasts of a war they had been too young to join, or in which they had lost their innocence), who had never belonged anywhere before, now felt somewhere at last. (161)[14]

Although the sense of belonging attributed to the young derives from their shared location in history, their interpellation into that generational collectivity also requires jazz, the sound that evokes a refusal of their historical moment. Jazz, like *Go* itself, can interpellate the young as beat by enabling them to recognize their woundedness as a cause for insurgency. In this respect, it also plays the same role as rock 'n' roll will play in a few short years, as the sound of a counterimaginary around which youth can consolidate an antisuburban and antidomestic identity. The urban space of the Go Hole functions much like the dance hall does in "Rock around the Clock" or the juke joint in "School Days."

At the Go Hole, a seemingly defeated generation is transformed into a defiant one willing to seek its identity in spite of its historical adversity. In their instinctive recognition through jazz of the need to "go," the entire generation of young Americans can be likened to the most "potent" of all the characters in the novel, Hart Kennedy. More fully representative of beatness than even Stofsky or Pasternak, Kennedy (the Neal Cassady character) arrives from Denver with his wife, Dinah, to capture the imagination of Paul Hobbes's circle of bohemian friends. Like the kids at the Go Hole, Kennedy expresses his beatness through his obsession with bop music, thereby making himself into a visionary spectacle for the boy gang:

> His [Kennedy's] hands clapped before him, his head bobbed up and down, propelled, as the music got louder, in ever greater arcs, while his mouth came grotesquely agape as he mumbled, "Go! Go!"
>
> Hobbes wandered about nervously, feeling he should not stare at Hart, but when he saw Stofsky looking at the agitated figure with an adoring solemnity, he stared frankly with him, remembering Ketcham's description:
>
> "This Hart is phenomenal. I've never seen such enormous nervous energy, and Gene [Pasternak] gets just like him, in a kind of way." (115)

Once again, though attracted to Kennedy's affirmative energy, Hobbes cannot bring himself to embrace it as readily as the other members of the boy gang. Though "not completely impotent," as Hobbes himself puts it, he is not altogether potent either.

> Hobbes found Pasternak beside him, saying eagerly: "Isn't Hart [Kennedy] terrific? And he's like that all the time! He doesn't care about anything! He yells 'go!' to everything, everything!"

> "Sure, Gene, but the word for *that* is 'come!' not 'go!' Hah-ha! . . . Come!"
>
> If this was the wrong sort of answer, Pasternak gave no explanations, but lurched immediately away. (135)

Situated midway between defeat and defiance, beaten and beatific, Hobbes's indecision stands in for the problematically uneven process of generational identification itself. What makes Hobbes resist Kennedy's kinetic response to defeat? What thwarts him yet spares Stofsky or Pasternak? The decisive clue may be found in Hobbes's pun, which expresses a doubt that is wrapped up in his acknowledgment of Kennedy's sexual prowess.

Like *On the Road*, *Go* locates the obstacle to homosocial community in the men's heterosexual relationships. Hobbes's solidarity with the gang is largely curbed by his wife, Kathryn, who resents Hobbes's increasing involvement with the boys while she works to support his novel writing. Kathryn's complaints express the chronic conflict in beat fiction between "society's perfum'd marriage" and the "boy gang":

> "You care more for your crazy friends than you do for me! No, it's the truth! . . . But why do you want to see them, anyway? They're just a lot of loafers, parasites! Oh, it's all very well for them to run around and stay up all night, they don't work. They can go home whenever they're tired, and sleep for three days if it suits them! They're just lazy, but you won't admit it!" She, too, was exaggerating her real feeling, and though they both knew this it made no difference and was not mentioned. (40)

Hobbes, it turns out, is not alone to face this obstacle to beat solidarity. Rather, he just faces it to a greater degree. Kathryn makes greater demands on his loyalties than do most of the other women, and Hobbes is more inclined than the other men to accommodate. As a result, heterosexuality exerts a greater pull on Hobbes than on most of the beat boys.

Kathryn's complaints, however, go beyond those expressed by the women in Kerouac's fiction. Unlike *On the Road*, in *Go* the men do not merely prefer their homosocial affairs to the heterosexual commitments. Holmes's men actually exploit their heterosexual relationships to sustain the homosocial community. Like other beat men in the novel, Paul does not work.[15] Kathryn's recriminations against his friends (loafers, parasites) therefore also implicitly apply to him; Paul's potential for "going" is predicated on her support.

Though Kathryn's accusations are somewhat softened by the narrator, they are also confirmed by other women characters who feel similarly exploited. Pasternak, while, not financially dependent on a woman, takes sexual advantage of an unhappily married woman, Christine, whose family life limits her interference with his primary ties to the boys in the gang. Hart's ability to "go," meanwhile, clearly comes at Dinah's financial expense. Upon their arrival in New York it is Dinah who finds a job and Hart who, in Kathryn's word, "loafs." As one minor character, Ketcham, describes a day in their routine:

> "At Stofsky's last night . . . they were all high, and at about five o'clock, just before they all went to sleep, Hart came out of the bedroom and told Ed to be sure to wake Dinah up at eight-thirty so she could get to her job on time. 'You get her up and drive her down, that's the most important thing! Don't let her oversleep now!' Then he went inside again and didn't wake up till twelve himself. And she'd been up all night, taking tea and drinking beer with Ben."
>
> "Sure," Kathryn said sardonically. "He doesn't want to lose her salary. Oh, he cares about those things, no matter what he *says*! But does he get a job? It's been two weeks and I'll bet he hasn't even been looking. That's the *Beat Generation* for you!" And she looked at Hobbes. (166)

Repeatedly through the novel, the dependency of the men's beatness on their exploitation of women explodes as a disruptive force in the midst of the men's solidarity. But while the heterosexual relationships pose limits to a full realization of the homosocial ones, they are also structurally necessary to them. Here *Go* parts companies with *On the Road*, which presents beat homosociality as opposed to domesticity, but never as parasitically dependent upon it. In *Go*, without "society's perfum'd marriage" the boy gang would not exist, because, ironically, it rests upon women's support.

If *Go* depicts a symbiotic relationship between the boy gang and "society's perfum'd marriages," it places a third possibility, the gay male relationship, into an eerie limbo. Unlike Kerouac in his novel, Holmes frankly presents its Allen Ginsberg character, David Stofsky, as gay. At no point, however, does he become sexually involved with another man. This absence spares the novel from a difficult representational decision: either to depict a gay sexual relationship between two of the daybreak boys, or alternatively to place it outside the gang as equivalent to a "perfum'd marriage," by partnering Stofsky to a man outside the gang who satisfies his financial and sexual needs so that he could devote himself to "going" with the other boys. Instead, the novel leaves Stofsky's sexual desire nearly unvoiced, implicitly understood by all but only rarely articulated. If, however, this half-open closet is meant to bypass homosexuality as a desire that might disrupt the beat tandem of heterosexual marriage and homosocial boy gang, then it falls. Stofsky simply becomes the novel's only sexually frustrated character, the one whose unrequited desire turns jealous and destructive.

Stofsky's sexual threat to the boy gang appears most explicitly in a scene that turns on his desire for Hart Kennedy. Kennedy, having botched the seduction of another woman earlier that day, makes the fatal mistake of telling the story (an errant act of male bonding) to the secretly jealous Stofsky: "His [Stofsky's] laugh was edged with a vicious playfulness; and looking at Hart [Kennedy], to whom he was so attracted and with whom he liked to play the confounding oracle most of all, he wondered why he felt glad for a moment" (168). When Kennedy's wife, Dinah, arrives, Stofsky goads him into the foolhardy move of telling *her* the story. Exhausted by his unending adulteries, Dinah cannot accept this latest betrayal. She fights with Kennedy and leaves New York the next day. Having thereby lost both his lover and provider, Kennedy himself departs shortly thereafter. Stofsky's misplaced sexual jealousy, in short, robs the daybreak boys of their ideal rebel by destroying his marriage.

Though his motivation is suggested more subtly, Stofsky effects a similar disaster for Paul. One late night at a party, Kathryn finally departs for a tryst with Pasternak, to whom she has been attracted for some time. Stofsky in turn propositions Hobbes, who refuses. Several evenings later, Stofsky encourages Kathryn to look through Hobbes's desk for a personal journal. What she discovers instead are love letters he has written to another woman (a phantom relationship as it so happens) that signify to her Hobbes's distaste for their marriage and his disrespect for all that she has endured for his sake:

> "Listen," and she ruffled through the sheets of paper hurriedly. "'Our marriages go wrong . . . and we have our affairs,' or this, 'one feels trapped' . . ."
>
> She slammed the sheet down abruptly. "I didn't think I was trapping you. I didn't know it had been so terrible for you all along."
>
> "But . . . but it hasn't. That wasn't written about us. I mean, I was just speaking generally . . . about everyone. . . . Although that doesn't matter, and I don't want to argue about it." (226)

Kathryn isn't mollified by Hobbes's explanation, because regardless of whether the affair actually occurred, she now recognizes she has forfeited everything to provide her husband with his boyish freedom:

> "Did it matter that I had nothing else [but the marriage]? . . . But even without *her*, you had your work, your friends, the kind of life *you* wanted to live. But . . . but what did I have? What? . . . I was the ignorant little wop you married, the peasant and the *wop*! The fool, the drag on everyone! . . . But why did you marry me? Why did you, Paul? So you could hurt me? Is that why? . . . I don't understand it, I don't understand . . . the way you do things . . . all of you." (230)

Once again the novel grants Kathryn a strong voice with which to attack her exploitation by a beat ethos of fraternity. Still, it is Stofsky's erotic impulses that have brought the structural tension between heterosexual marriage and the homosocial gang to a crisis point. *Go*'s apparent sympathy for the beat women thus serves to stave off "homosexual panic" of a variety far more conventional than *On the Road*'s. Kerouac's novel manifested a homophobia closely and surprisingly related to fear of heterosexual marriage. Holmes's novel acknowledges the beat generation's reliance on heterosexual marriage only to deploy this dependence as an argument against sexualizing the boy gang.

In 1950 Holmes wrote an anonymous article titled "The Sexual Gentleman's Agreement" that openly expresses the homophobic anxieties he would submerge in the novel. The article bluntly attacks the mainstream's alleged toleration of closeted homosexuality in the arts. Using the "Mr. Belvedere" movies as evidence for an ostensible decline in America's "accurate or ideal representations" of itself, Holmes warns:

> Something has happened to the America that once saw itself as a tall, silent man who was tough, resourceful, and possessed of an enviable know-how, or as an average home-and-wife-loving citizen who kept up with the Joneses. . . . If we can so easily take the fictional Belvedere to our breasts when we have been led to believe that his fact-counterpart, the urban homosexual, is, next to the Jew of the liberal newspapers, the most constantly sinned-against outcast in modern society, something has certainly been happening under our cultural noses, and it's time to take a longer look. (102–103)

Fictions like the Belvedere films, Holmes believes, indicate that there is a gentleman's agreement not to speak of the "homosexualization" of American art and culture. Holmes considers this a serious danger because, above and beyond replacing masculine heroes with effeminate ones, in homosexual art "symbolic or actual love between men would be idealized," while "women would probably come off badly as sexual objects" (105). Holmes is primarily concerned with the second of these qualities, which he also calls the "typical homosexual case against women" (106). "The Sexual Gentleman's Agreement" poses as a defense of women against the allegedly ubiquitous, misogynistic homosexual art whose sexual agenda (i.e., turning men away from women as sexual partners) Americans have tacitly agreed to ignore.

The essay's concern, however, lies not simply with the artistic slanders against women, but its effects, namely with the disease of gender conflict that they presumably spread. Holmes asks:

> Can women continually see members of their sex destroyed, mocked, isolated, and humiliated; pictured as shrews, whores, idiots, and mantraps, and retain any self-confidence or sense of personal worth? And can non-homosexual men swallow the same amount without eventually coming to think that their wives, sweethearts, sisters, and mothers have something of the "menacing, aggressive Poles" about them? To say "no," is to conclude that art has no effect whatsoever on the people who give their attention to it. We know this is not true, and if propaganda can bring whole nations to war, why should the sexes be immune? (107)

This potential war of the sexes, attributed in "The Sexual Gentleman's Agreement" to the tolerance of closeted homosexuality, also haunts Holmes's novel. As we have seen, when conflict does erupt in *Go*, between Kennedy and Dinah, and between Hobbes and Kathryn, it is catalyzed by the closeted homosexual desire of David Stofsky, who subconsciously wishes to disrupt the other men's heterosexual relations.

Like his "fact-counterpart" Allen Ginsberg, Stofsky is a seer who experiences visions illuminating both the loveless postwar world and the beat answer of seeking and prophesying love. Looking down upon the desolate city, which to Stofsky appears invaded by some malevolent spirit,

> it was as though the very pumping, physical heart of all humans was being remorselessly atomized by the machine of a gigantic mind, over which hovered the sky, a dumb mushroom-head of smoke.
>
> Then this was the sick rose, he thought! This, the heart itself, was

the dying blossom through which love drifted unheeded, and which hung, as the clouds hung in that night, lifeless and rotting on a wintry vine.

Sitting there, naked and chilly, he longed for something certain and close beside him, for the love that he wanted to cry out to everyone lay just below their trembling masks. (90)

Though the prophet of love, Stofsky's own passions only bring trouble, however. As Kathryn complains: "I wish he'd just leave us alone, that's all. Why doesn't he stop interfering with everyone all the time? Look what he did with Hart and Dinah! His own friends! . . . And he's always talking about love" (296).

But being gay, Stofsky's personal love is for men, and here lies the central problematic in Holmes's novel. If the social organization that is truest to itself for the artist is the boy gang, a generation of young beat men bonded by their mutual fraternal love, then Stofsky threatens the beat generation even more profoundly than do the women. Indeed, his threat *produces* their threat. So long as beat identity remains merely a *social* desire that does not compete with marriage, the women's inevitable jealousy of their men can be managed. Should sex infiltrate the fraternal bonds, however, their very survival becomes jeopardized. In *Go*, ironically, the very potency of the boy gang as a bonded collective identity depends upon its desexualization.

Crazy Shepherds of Rebellion

If *Go* deploys homophobia as a strategy for interpellating its readers into a homosocially produced generational identity, then the work of Allen Ginsberg would seem to present a quite antithetical approach. Ginsberg is often cited as a political precursor and point of reference for gay movements since the 1970s. His graphically erotic poetry is considered an important milestone in gay literary self-exploration, and his progressive politics are considered to bridge the political radicalism of the Old Left with the sexual and cultural radicalisms of the late New Left. Ginsberg, to put it simply, is not a writer one would typically consider homophobic, nor will I argue that he is. Indeed, Ginsberg's canonically beat text, his epic poem "Howl," became instantly famous by way of an obscenity trial concerning its graphic depictions of sex, particularly between men, and most of all in one "notorious" line in which the poet describes how the "best minds" of his generation "let themselves be fucked in the ass by saintly motorcyclists, and screamed with joy." Pointing out that its trial made "Howl" a bestseller in San Francisco, John D'Emilio has argued that the poem's "description of gay male sexuality as joyous, delightful, and indeed even holy turned contemporary stereotypes of homosexuality upside down" (181). Nevertheless, as I will show, "Howl" too excludes gay sex as a beat-generational bond, celebrating generational relations as a fundamentally homo*social* practice of shared identity.

Whereas *Go* presents a beat generation that pipes and laments in an adult marketplace, "Howl" purports to *be* that pipe and lament, voicing directly a generation's despair while crushed by the Fordist monolith of postwar America, but also its joy as it struggles to survive. The poem is divided into four sections. In section 1, which takes up nearly two-thirds of the poem's overall length, the poet's generation recounts the shocking exploits that convey its philosophical, political, and sensual search for identity. Section 2 depicts the mad generation's adversary, Moloch, whose aggression makes generational unity necessary. Section 3 builds upon that necessity through a declaration of embattled solidarity with Carl Solomon, a young man Ginsberg met in Rockland Mental Hospital, and the person to whom the poem is dedicated. The fourth and last section, titled "Footnote to Howl," proclaims the holiness of the world that at once motivates and sanctifies the generational struggle.

As in other principal beat texts, "Howl"'s narrator-protagonist only gradually comes to identify with a figure who incarnates the "madman bum and angel Beat in Time" (67). In "Howl," however, the triangulation of the desire for collective identity is made fully explicit. The narrating "I," who appears in the first line of the poem, reappears a few more times in the first and second sections, but only becomes fully present in section 3. His generation, meanwhile, is described as a "they." Mediating between them is the generation's representative figure, Carl Solomon, designated by "you." In section 1, the "I" bears witness to the damage wreaked upon the generation he shared with "you," Carl Solomon. In section 2, he comes to understand the nature of their enemy, Moloch. In section 3, the "I" swears his allegiance and commitment to both "you" and implicitly to "they" in their generational struggle. By allowing the you-in-the-world (i.e., the reader) to occupy the position of the you-in-the-text (Carl Solomon), "Howl" offers up Ginsberg's flattering identification with the reader as incentive for the reader's identification with the mad generation. In the end, both the "I" and the "you" are to be merged into "they" (the best minds of the generation), implicitly completing the interpellative production of an "us": the beat generation.

Like *Go* and *On the Road*, the lengthy first section of "Howl" takes the form of fictional autobiography. Beginning sensationistically, "I saw the best minds of my generation destroyed by madness" (62), "Howl" promises a dramatic story that will deliver an answer to the question raised by this opening line: why would madness be striking down the best and the brightest of America's young? As the mad generation enacts yet another verb in a new locale with each successive line (they are always the ones "who ***ed"), a frenzied sense of movement gathers, much like the youthful "going" described by Holmes or the "madness to live" as testified by Kerouac.[16] This relentless activity always takes the form of a quest, though its object continually changes. Of these, sex and sexuality are among the most important, and it is notable that the first sexual adventures to be enumerated are the gay ones, in which the best minds

> let themselves be fucked in the ass by saintly motorcyclists, and
> screamed with joy,
> who blew and were blown by those human seraphim, the sailors,
> caresses of Atlantic and Caribbean love. (64)

The vivid naming of the mad generation's sexual partners is an important feature of the poem, for at all times it seems that these "best minds" are sleeping with someone else ("saintly motorcyclists," "sailors," and even "whomever come who may"), but never one another. This pattern continues as the poet moves into heterosexual territory, describing his generation as those

> who sweetened the snatches of a million girls trembling in the
> sunset, and were red eyed in the morning but prepared to
> sweeten the snatch of the sunrise, flashing buttocks under barns
> and naked in the lake
> who sent out whoring through Colorado in myriad stolen night-cars,
> N.C. secret hero of these poems, cocksman and Adonis of
> Denver—joy to the memory of his innumerable lays of girls in
> empty lots & diner backyards, moviehouses' rickety rows, on
> mountaintops in caves or with gaunt waitresses in familiar
> roadside lonely petticoat upliftings & especially secret gas-station
> solipsisms of johns, & hometown alleys too. (64–65)

During this part of section 1, when the beat generation's youthful energy becomes specifically sexual activity (or as Paul Hobbes put it in *Go*, when going becomes coming), N.C. or Neal Cassady reappears once more as the generational hero. Yet N.C. returns only in time to be commemorated for his heterosexual virility, *after* the gay sexual scenes. As Oliver Harris notes, lines proclaiming the poet's own sexual activities ("Holy the Cock in my mouth / Holy the Cock in my asshole") as well as his lengthy sexual relationship with the secret hero, "our long old love" (230) were excised from the published edition of "Howl." In Harris's view, these deletions sacrificed the poem's value as an explicitly gay sexual statement for the sake of a vaguer celebration of the "principle of adhesiveness" between men, one that Ginsberg well knew "would sell better at some distance from the particulars of cock-sucking" (230). Yet, as we have seen, "Howl" shows no such reticence concerning the generation's anonymous encounters with sailors and motorcyclists. The lines scrupulously edited out of the generational record by "Howl," I suggest, are the ones that threaten to sexualize the *identity* of the "best minds" as a beat generation.

Consider that the lines deleted by Ginsberg would have diluted the underlying grammatical structure of section 1, which promotes the identity of a plural (but male) protagonist, the ones "who blew and were blown," "who balled," or "who copulated." As previously noted, the best minds' transitive sexual acts are always directed outside their collectivity, toward "saintly motorcyclists" or "sailors," "a sweetheart" or "gaunt waitresses." As the "best minds" are grammatically assembled into one subject, "Howl" materializes a generational collectivity that is founded upon mutual identity rather than on mutual sexual attraction. Instead of the best minds *wanting* one another, a relation that would distribute some of them as objects at least some of the time, the best minds are in some crucial sense supposed to *be* one another, subjectively speaking, standing in for one another's "minds" through their shared identity.

While in section 1 the poet's generation encounters numerous others, the much briefer section 2 concerns only one other: that "sphinx of cement and aluminum [who] bashed open their skulls and ate up their brains and imagination" (68). In each succeeding line, this opponent, "Moloch," is re-invoked through a new set of images that materialize a national juggernaut out of the military-industrial landmarks of Fordist America:

> Moloch whose eyes are a thousand blind windows! Moloch whose skyscrapers stand in the long streets like endless Jehovahs!

> Moloch whose factories dream and croak in the fog! Moloch whose smokestacks and antennae crown the cities!
>
> Moloch whose love is endless oil and stone! Moloch whose soul is electricity and banks! Moloch whose poverty is the specter of genius! Moloch whose fate is a cloud of sexless hydrogen! Moloch whose name is the Mind! (68)

Moloch appears, not only as a bodily monolith but also as a mental one, a totalitarian mass mind that continues to absorb the multiple "minds" who inhabit the land into its despotic unity. In a doubled national allegory much like the one associated with *The Catcher in the Rye*, "Howl" projects a rebel identity narrative in which the beat generation incarnates a free American character defending its personality against an especially pernicious variant of the American "age of conformity." The beat generation is figure to Moloch's landscape, but Moloch is also obviously a personality, a bloodthirsty deity built from the sinews of the nation's industrial, financial, and military units, who demands the human sacrifice of his worshipers' firstborn. "Moloch" thereby becomes a paternal figure gone awry, a murderous father who devours his best and brightest sons.

Moloch is repeatedly described as "loveless," whether parentally or romantically, his fate "a cloud of sexless hydrogen" (68). To be trapped within Moloch, the poet cries, is to be robbed of both sexual and social contact: "Moloch in whom I sit lonely! Moloch in whom I dream of Angels! Crazy in Moloch! Cocksucker in Moloch! Lacklove and manless in Moloch!" (68). Perhaps more than any other stanza in "Howl," this one risks blurring the line between the lonely poet's homosocial desire (for generational identity) and his sexual desire. His dream of angels refers back to the best minds of his generation as he first described them in the earliest lines of the poem: "angelheaded hipsters burning for the ancient heavenly connection to the starry dynamo in the machinery of night" (62). Since the poet is a "Cocksucker in Moloch," alone and desperately desiring a male lover, one might readily take his dream of the angels as lovers who will liberate him from his "lacklove" and "manless" subjection to Moloch. Still, "Howl" words this desire reticently, leaving unspecified whether the angels will liberate the poet through sexual communion or the sharing of identity. In stark contrast to the dictatorial unity of Moloch, this sacrificial generation of young Americans remains a plurality, a group of individuals who rally around the value of sensual and spiritual pursuit. To join the angels is therefore to gain an identity that includes erotic agency, to become part of a generation that loves in a loveless world, and that differentiates its common personality against the landscape by doing so, thereby becoming part of a group or people that in itself brings individual isolation to an end.

In this way, the mad generation's sexual adventures also become part of a guerrilla war waged against Moloch, for if Moloch is loveless and sexless, then their sexual passion can easily attract others "lonely in Moloch" who, in returning the love of the poet's generation, demonstrate that they too desire more than a passionless life, that they are sympathetic fellow travelers who appreciate this quixotic rebellion, even if they are not (yet) part of it. This structuring element gives us a dynamic in beat writing that comes closest to a Sedgwickian erotic triangle, for in some sense the struggle between Moloch and the poet's generation is triangulated through these sexual partners in a manner that resembles cuckolding. The poet's generation seduces others, both men and women, who are nominally the possessions of Moloch, but are secretly attracted to the sensual beats and accept their advances. Moloch and the beats are thus engaged in an erotic rivalry, which happens to be the one arena in which the beats have an advantage over the "loveless" Moloch. Sexuality therefore promises to be a most potent weapon in the mad generation's arsenal. And it is here that once again the erotics of identity—the significance of the bad boy's sexiness—becomes evident. Nevertheless, the effectivity of this rhetoric once again depends on cathecting beat sexuality, not inwardly among themselves, but outwardly, toward Moloch's ambivalent subjects.[17]

By section 3, however, any triangulated sense of sexual rivalry gives way to a binary drama of armed struggle. The section begins with the poet's pledge of allegiance to his generational hero, "Carl Solomon! I'm with you in Rockland where you're madder than I am" (69). Every subsequent line in the section begins by repeating, "I'm with you in Rockland." Read literally, the phrase suggests that the poet is with Carl Solomon inside the Molochian madhouse. Taken figuratively, it also expresses the poet's solidarity with Carl in his struggle against Rockland/Moloch. The two senses work together to solidify their generational bonds. Carl and the narrator share both a common experience of repression that leads Carl to demand a common struggle:

> I'm with you in Rockland,
> where you bang on the catatonic piano the soul is innocent and
>   immortal it should never die ungodly in an armed
>   madhouse. (70)

This line is a call to arms, and precipitates the vision of warfare mounted by the mad generation against the inhumanity of Rockland/Moloch:

> I'm with you in Rockland
> where we wake up electrified out of the coma by our own souls'
> airplanes roaring over the roof they've come to drop angelic
> bombs the hospital illuminates itself imaginary walls collapse
> O skinny legions run outside O starry-spangled shock of mercy
> the eternal war is here O victory forget your underwear we're
> free. (70)

A long deferred pronoun appears in the closing lines of section 3, namely the first use of "we," which serves to unify not only "I," the poet, and "you," Carl Solomon, but also "they," the best minds of their generation, a collective subject into which both "you" and "I" are now merged. The identitarian gap between narrator, hero, and generation closes here at last. It does so, however, through the image of closing ranks, of pulling together for a holy war against the "fascist national Golgotha" (70). When the collectivity of the generation at last becomes imaginable, it is not as a lover but as a warrior, as a committed troop of "mad comrades" or "skinny legions" revolting against Moloch.

The final stanza of section 3 draws back again from the collectivity for a private, sentimental moment between the poet and Carl:

> I'm with you in Rockland
> in my dreams you walk dripping from a sea-journey on the highway
> across America in tears to the door of my cottage in the Western
> night. (70)

As does *On the Road* in its opening pages, "Howl" here employs deeply romantic language to convey the poet's desire for intimate connection with this other man. And yet here too, one finds nothing sexually explicit. Carl is the young man who has brought the poet to generational consciousness, and for whom the poet expresses a special affection that nonetheless remains within the domain of the homosocial. Insofar as the "you" associates "Howl"'s reader with Carl Solomon, the poetic "I" insinuates a similar affection for the reader, one that passionately credits him in advance as a generational hero, but which the reader need not take (or homophobically fear) as expressing sexual desire for him.

"Footnote to Howl," often read as a final, fourth section of the poem, recapitulates the spiritual sense of the world honored and defended by the poet's mad generation. At the same time, this section reconfirms generational identification as a solidarity achieved as partners in a struggle rather than as lovers in a romance. Condensing the figurations of "Howl," "Footnote" pithily announces, "Holy the Angel in Moloch!" the mad generation within the madhouse of postwar America, while also introducing a final image for the triangular rivalry between Moloch and the beat generation over the "lamb" of middle-class Fordist America: "Holy the lone juggernaut! Holy the vast lamb of the middleclass! Holy the crazy shepherds of rebellion!" But who exactly is the Angel in Moloch? Who are the crazy shepherds of rebellion? Only in the "Footnote" are names finally named:

> Holy Peter holy Allen holy Solomon holy Lucien holy Kerouac holy Huncke holy Burroughs holy Cassady holy the unknown buggered and suffering beggars holy the hideous human angels! (71)

Everyone is holy, according to "Footnote." But in this stanza the holy angels themselves, the generation's "best minds," are all revealed as Allen Ginsberg's male compatriots, that most familiar fraternal gang of boy comrades, here elevated by "Howl" 's epic holy war into the self-appointed champions of American youth.

It is worth spelling out how "Howl" both resembles and differs from *Go* and *On the Road* in the sexual dynamic of its generational project. Neither Kerouac nor Holmes allows homosexual desire to play any celebratory role in the rebel heroism of the beat generation. Indeed, for both authors, gay desire menaces the homosocial bonds through which they figure generational solidarity. Gay desire can do so either directly by provoking jealousy between the men (Kerouac) or indirectly because that jealousy will then instigate secondary conflicts between the men and their women (Holmes).

In "Howl" by contrast, male-male sex expresses the virility of the beat search for identity. The boundless libido of the beat generation, as represented by their sexual access to both women and men, becomes an explicit challenge to Moloch's loveless world. Even in "Howl," however, beat homosexuality never turns inward, because in this comparatively homophilic text, generational unity is based on what one might call the "oneness" of identity, rather than the "twoness" of sexual desire. In "Howl" sex becomes part of the narrative movement through which the beat generation meet others (and then leave them behind). It is a fleeting activity, however special, that expresses and enacts the generational rebellion of the "mad comrades" against a Moloch-worshiping America. The poet's bond with his generation, however, must not be left behind, but must steadily deepen. Fraternal love cannot be one more instance of what Sal in *On the Road* called "all this franticness and jumping around" (116), but must grow as a sort of solidarity with one's own generational soul.

Fraternally Yours

In all three of these works—*Go, On the Road*, and "Howl"—the beat generation constitutes a group of "boys" who bond over their shared desire to be mutually identified. This is, of course, a homosocial desire as distinguished from either a heterosexual or homosexual one. As Sedgwick's study showed, however, homosocial desire has driven a wide range of narrative projects, ranging from comic dramas about cuckolding to gothic expressions of homophobic terror at submitting to another man. With the beat generation, homosocial desire took that particular, politically charged form that Catherine Stimpson has described as "a radiant vision of psychic, literary, and national brotherhood" (376) in which "men together can support, in each other, an enhancement of sensation, action and politics" (375).[18] This description, which strikingly echoes the appeal of gay liberation for queer men and feminism for women, suggests a paradoxical truth about the beat generation. On the one hand, it excluded women from its celebrated "boy gang" and homosex from that gang's constitutive bonds. At the same time, however, it articulated the desire for a gendered collectivity of rebels that eventually proved adaptable to a feminist movement rooted in the identity of women and a gay movement centered upon the identity of gay men. To understand this, we must analyze the desire for a beat generation as the iteration of a fraternal ideal.

Like "generation," "fraternity" was an important conceptual prototype for imagining the "identity" of collectivities. Erikson's discussion of American identity, for instance, begins with the revolt by the nation's "freeborn sons" against political despotism. As this allusion to the American revolution also suggests, the Cold War gender politics of identity drew on fraternity for precisely its legacy as a great post-Enlightenment ideal. As Carole Pateman argues in her classic study *The Sexual Contract*, the ethos of "fraternity" was vital to the reorientation of male political power by the revolutionary liberal ideas of the late seventeenth and eighteenth centuries. To be schematic, traditional patriarchy, previously linked to monarchism as legitimated by the rule of the father, was reformulated and made ideologically compatible to the political liberty of the sons: "The revolution in which the slogan 'liberté, egalité, fraternité' was proclaimed began in 1789, but the alliance between the three elements was forged much earlier. Modern patriarchy is fraternal in form and the original [social] contract is a fraternal pact" (77). The philosophical origin myth of modern democracy rests in a grand revolutionary narrative in which sons, collaborating to overthrow the despotic rule of their father(s), form a social contract amongst themselves guaranteeing their status as political equals and formalizing their brotherly ties.

Always implicit but usually submerged in the various retellings of this narrative, Pateman argues, is the sons' agreement to a complementary sexual contract preserving male rights over women.[19] Even as the father's political right over his sons was overthrown and replaced by the egalitarian social contract, his conjugal right as a husband to women's sexuality was preserved in the sexual contract, which dispersed it among all the sons. Roughly speaking, Pateman argues that these two contracts (social and sexual) function in tandem as a modern origin myth that structures the respective political logics of the public and private spheres in liberal democratic societies. Male authority survives, but the familial basis of men's rights to rule women are transformed from a paternal to a fraternal logic.

Homosociality, as it was first broached in queer theory by Sedgwick, and fraternity as here analyzed in feminist political theory may be thought together very productively. As Pateman's appeal to the slogan of the French Revolution reminds us, the notion of universal brotherhood is a central tenet of modern politics that valorizes and idealizes affective (but nonsexual) bonds between men. Fraternity may therefore represent a historically nuanced and politically potent mode of homosociality that bears a close connection to the articulation of male privilege. Conversely, locating Pateman's concept of fraternity within the framework of homosocial desire allows it to be considered not only as political ideal but also as libidinal investment. Though never treated as such by Pateman, fraternity functions as an *erotic* category in exactly that broad sense Sedgwick attributes to homosociality, for fraternity appeals to men's *brotherly love* or to their *love of one's fellow man*. It represents the desire for communion with other men based on liberty (consent) and equality (reciprocity).

The bonds of the beat generation were built out of just this sort of fraternal desire. As my readings suggest, the growing sense of identification felt by the protagonists of these texts for the authentically beat character is cast as a passion for someone whom the protagonist comes to perceive as his brother. His interpellation into a beat generation—and by extension the reader's as well—takes the form of a recognition that he belongs to a brotherhood. Pateman's insight that fraternity is imagined to originate in the revolutionary struggle against the father, moreover, allows us to consider rebellion as the central drama of beat brotherhood. In the principal texts, the beat generation is never an empowered brotherhood but always an embattled one, disobedient and in struggle against demands that they conform to the wishes of an older generation's authority. The beat generation is not yet a democracy of brothers, that is, but rather a *democratic revolution in progress*. "Howl" portrays that revolution directly, announcing itself as the epic tale of the sons' uprising against Moloch, their struggle to defeat the father-king-tyrant figure of Cold War Fordism. *On the Road* and *Go* are more indirect, focusing as it were on the story that takes place behind the trenches, the struggle to attain brotherhood or establish a boy gang rather than the struggle of that unstable fraternity to win its generational war. Both struggles take place simultaneously, for the generational identity that the beat texts work to produce is equated with the solidarity of revolutionaries. Not untypical is the conclusion of John Clellon Holmes's "This Is the Beat Generation," where he explicitly compares the beat generation to the progenitors of the Russian revolution, who also began by asking the "eternal question," and ended by meeting in cellars to plan the overthrow of the tsar (64). Like all the beats, Holmes explicitly nationalizes the generational conflict. This is a generation of young Americans whose movement toward revolutionary values reiterates the American revolutionary past. Whether routed through Dean Moriarty, Kerouac's "sideburned hero of the snowy West," Ginsberg's best minds, who "blew the suffering of America's naked mind," or Holmes's young Americans, who see wartime America as a "monstrous wasteland," the fraternal rebellion of the beat generation aptly cites a nationalized tradition of political rhetoric that Jay Fliegelmann has celebrated as "the American revolution against patriarchal authority," but that Dana Nelson has aptly critiqued as a false masculinist egalitarianism that has historically served in the United States to accommodate men to both the capitalist marketplace and white supremacy.[20] Fraternity, in short, is a revolutionary slogan of the Enlightenment that (like liberty and equality) bears a dialectical political meaning.

During the Cold War, identity discourse was closely allied with this fraternal motif, whose citation of the American Revolution against Britain helped to recast the twentieth-century United States as a role model for new decolonizing nations seeking their own popular sovereignty. As Jerry Griswold has shown: "America's [eighteenth-century] writers and thinkers consistently understood and presented the Revolution as the story of a child who had grown older and entered into a period of oedipal rebellion. The argument between George III and his colonists was constantly portrayed as a family squabble between an intractable father and deserving sons. Declaring themselves independent, the Sons of Liberty came together in a fraternal struggle against the tyranny and despotism of the patriarch" (14).

As the United States gained geopolitical power during the nineteenth century, the revolutionary rhetoric of oedipal revolt gave way to a "revised myth that defined America not in terms of its youthful antagonism toward Europe, but as a mature nation-state taking its place among the 'family of nations'" (94). During the Cold War, however, a partial reversal occurred as national self-representation split between these two modalities. On the one hand, the image of a mature, developed society was retained through its association with industrial Fordism, but on the other, the discourse of identity revived the motif of a young revolutionary America claiming its sovereignty. Thus the split maps precisely onto the figure/ground relation of the national allegory that I discussed in chapter 2. The ideoliterary project of the beat generation combined these images in a telling way, portraying the "mature" or "developed" America as the despotic patriarch against which the beat generation became the youthful, fraternal revolt. This generational battle, as Allen Ginsberg described in an article originally published by *Village Voice* in 1959, was one between "an America gone mad with materialism, a police-state America, a sexless and soulless America prepared to battle the world in defense of a false image of its authority" and the beat generation's own "wild and beautiful America of the comrades of Whitman... the historic America of Blake and Thoreau where the spiritual independence of each individual was an America" ("Poetry," 26–27). Victory over the military-industrial Fordist tyranny, Ginsberg also observed, would bring America back into the democratic fold with the young Asian and African nations of the third world:

> Now Detroit has built a million automobiles of rubber trees
> and phantoms
> but I walk, I walk, and the Orient walks with me, and all
> Africa walks
> and sooner or later North America will walk
> for as we have driven the Chinese Angel from our door he
> will drive us from the Golden Door of the future. ("Death," 150)

The beat rejuvenation of America's youthful passion for independence—as foretold by Whitman, Blake, and Thoreau—was synonymous with the recuperation of identity itself for both the nation and the individuals who comprised its fraternal promise.

Sisterhood Is Powerful

The continuities between the beat politics of identity and those of second-wave feminism of the 1960s and 1970s are simultaneously elided by, yet readable through, the embrace of the term "patriarchy" as feminism's principal category for the analysis of power relations between women and men. The concept of patriarchy helped to cast "women" collectively as the young rebel protagonist raising her consciousness of oppression by a paternal tyranny. "Men" were thus collectively cast as the given antagonist of women's struggle for identity, and as the beneficiaries of the despotic parent culture against which the movement waged its revolt. Like the rebel boys battling against the suburban father, or the best minds of Ginsberg's generation warring with Moloch, women became sisters pooling their resources ("Sisterhood Is Powerful!") in a struggle against the patriarch(s).

Feminist representations of male power were paternalized in the process, even as sexual politics implicitly took a generational form. Like the beat generation, second-wave feminism also interpellated its subjects by way of homosocial desire, though a female one drawing on sisterly affections and solidarities as "women together" confronted the patriarchy. In this respect, second-wave feminism finds its identitarian origins reflected in an inverted image by the beats' gender politics of fraternity: a cadre of brothers (rather than sisters) waging war against a tyrannical patriarch who uses a strict system of gender conformity to disempower his progeny (though here by way of a sexless, impotent, domesticated masculinity).

If the women's liberation movement drew one kind of inspiration from the fraternal beat revolt against Moloch, namely as a prototype for narrating feminist sisterhood, it drew a different kind from the manifest sexual inequality of the beat generation. The stark contradiction between the beat rhetoric of equality (restricted to the fraternal world of beat men) and the equally legendary beat devaluation of women as an auxiliary to the movement was only the first of many similar subsequent contradictions (within Students for a Democratic Society [SDS], the Student Non-Violent Coordinating Committee [SNCC], the counterculture, and so forth) that would itself be incorporated into the rebel identity narrative of women's liberation. "Consciousness raising," meant to foster collective identity, became both a literary and a political strategy, as it had for the beats.[21]

This split significance of the beat generation for feminists is explored vividly in Alix Kates Shulman's *Burning Questions: A Novel*, one of the most successful novels of the movement. Fictionalized as an identity memoir entitled "My Life as a Rebel," Shulman's novel is written in the first-person voice of its protagonist, Zane IndyAnna, who recounts her political journey from the 1950s to the 1970s. Zane's story takes place in three main locations; she grows up in the stultifying suburb of Middletown, Indiana, leaves for the vibrant beat scene in Greenwich Village, then drops out in order to marry and have children, only at last to join a radical feminist group known as the Third Street Circle in the late sixties. In spatial terms, Zane thus travels gradually from a scene of Fordist conformity to a space of psychopolitical self-emancipation. Middletown is repeatedly called a postwar "Babylon, representative of an other-directed America in which each person aims (per H. L. Mencken) to appear as much as possible like his fellows—to act like them in all situations and to think like them whenever his powers of thought are challenged. What the people of Middletown fear above all things is oddness" (36). By contrast to a "square" life in Middletown, the beat scene on MacDougal Street feels like liberation, but where women are concerned it quickly reveals itself as yet another space of conformity, where they are expected to meekly accept their place as "chicks." Taking up with Marshall Braines, a successful beat writer, Zane discovers that she has no place in his inner circle of beat men. When this becomes a source of tension between them, Marshall abandons her by hitting the road to San Francisco. When he returns, it is with another woman in tow. Zane, quitting the scene in disgust, marries a conservative professional man and raises three children over the ensuing decade. Late in the tumultuous sixties, however, she attends a women's consciousness-raising session that leads her to join the Third Street Circle, a radical feminist sisterhood whose militant struggle for women's liberation offers her the revolutionary freedom, equality, and comradeship that she had failed to find among the beats.[22] Explicitly dialectical in her personal philosophy, Zane presents the beat generation as exemplary in its contradictions for women, promising them freedom, equality, and comradeship, but disenfranchising them because these ideals are reserved for the fraternity alone. All the same, the beat scene proves paradoxically inspirational, expressing to Zane even in its sexist failure what feminism will finally deliver.

To All Gay Brothers

By contrast to the women's movement, gay liberation would draw more easily on the beat vision, accessing the boy gang as a prototype with which to imagine collective gay identity. Indeed, the gay liberation movement would go on to canonize the beat writers (or at least the manifestly queer ones) as forerunners or even elder brothers of the movement precisely because the beat generation had preached a sexual revolt against heteronormative suburban domesticity. One might just as easily have expected gay liberation to critique beat fraternity as a homosocial ruse, however, given its emphatic exclusion of homosexuality. Consider, for instance, an angry essay by Nick Benton in *The Gay Liberation Book* (a 1973 movement compendium) entitled "Don't Call Me a Brother." Though Benton expresses special irritation with the so-called (straight) men's liberation movement, his essay generally indicts *all* nongay models of fraternity, contending that "as a gay male one of the most oppressive terms which has been used on me in my life is the term 'brother.' 'Hey, there, brother, how ya doin'!' (Slap, slap) Pounding me on the back or on my ass, the straight man has always tried to include me on his team by seducing me with the term 'brother'" (181). Benton notes the unspoken erotic element in such heterofraternities, whose "brother" hits him on the ass and tries to "seduce" him into joining his collectivity. "This type of bonding is what men have done since the dawn of time," warns Benton, and its animating fear is effeminacy, which "is synonymous with the loss of power, synonymous with what it means to be gay" (182). It is striking that Benton's objection to straight "brotherhood" is virtually identical to Catherine Stimpson's critique of the sexual politics of the beats, who despite their paneroticism, clung tenaciously to a rigid code of gender value that valorized masculine agency while devaluing passivity as a feminine weakness. The "fag" or "queen" is always an invective figure among the beats, even for Allen Ginsberg, who, as late as a 1974 *Gay Sunshine* interview, would persist in calling himself gay only in the "heartfelt, populist, humanist, quasi-heterosexual, Whitmanic, bohemian, free-love, homosexual tradition, as you find it in Sherwood Anderson, Whitman, or maybe Genet, a little, *versus* the privileged, exaggeratedly effeminate, gossipy, moneyed, money-style-clothing-conscious, near-hysterical queen" (16). Nevertheless, the very same *Gay Liberation Book* that includes Benton's critique of brotherhood also begins with an editorial note describing itself as "a tribute to all gay brothers" (11) and concludes with a transcript of Allen Ginsberg's remarks at the Chicago 7 Trial (the very same one regarding which Tom Hayden would assert that "our crime was our identity"). Asked in the transcript to explain a graphic sexual scene from his "Love Poem on Theme by Whitman," Ginsberg replies by describing Whitman's political vision along lines dear to gay liberation:

> We have many loves, many of which are denied, many of which we deny to ourselves. He [Whitman] said that the reclaiming of those loves and the becoming aware of those loves was the only way that this nation could save itself and become a democratic and spiritual republic. . . . And he defined that tenderness between the citizens as, in his words, adhesiveness, a natural tenderness flowing between all citizens, not only men and women but also a tenderness between men and men as part of our democratic heritage, part of the adhesiveness which would make the democracy function. (201–202)

Even here, Ginsberg's word choice remains carefully ambiguous: "love," "tenderness," "adhesiveness," all of these are words whose erotic content could well remain on the social side of the social/sexual divide.

The logic that structures Ginsberg's caution, and that indeed guided all of the homosexual censorship in the works of the beat generation has become an important topic in contemporary queer studies, for it concerns the status of sex in the public sphere. The fraternity that the beats celebrated, after all, was intended as an incipient public sphere, a revolutionary collectivity of insurrectional citizens who aim to renew the democratic spirit and restore the identity of the American nation. Yet the public sphere, as Eric Clarke reminds us, is itself a historiconormative construct that, from Kant's time onward, has relied upon what he calls a "subjunctive mood," in two key senses. First, it presents itself as if it were fully inclusionary, when in fact it is premised upon exclusions from civic participation. Second, these exclusions occur because publicity only arranges inclusions by treating personal vices (private interests) as if they could be translated into public virtues. Yet this process requires a kind of "sanitation" of particular interests so as to make them conform with a public ideal. As a result, "Even as excluded groups are brought into the fold, so to speak, the homogenization of interests and representations demanded by inclusion also indicates that it requires deferred and demonized remainders; queer persons and interests that would doubtless seem slightly out of place on a city council or in an Ikea commercial" (7). The beat generation, as this chapter approaches it, was just such an exercise in publicity, both in the sense that its principal texts aimed to create "publicity" for themselves, drawing new persons into the fold, and also because they conceived the beat fraternity itself as a radicalized counterpublic aiming to rejuvenate American democracy.

It is in this context that we must understand the beat generation's careful management of homosexuality. As Clarke explains, sexuality is a particular vexed domain for the public sphere, precisely because it is presupposed as a space of intersubjectivity that would always already preclude the desire to treat others as objects (rather than as ends in themselves). Because it suggests the objectification and instrumentalization of bodies, sex becomes a counterfactual threat to the imaginative composition of a public sphere as made up of free and equal citizens who do not treat one another as a means. In Clarke's reading (which relies heavily on unpublished lectures by Kant), sex and the reciprocal equality of subjects have historically been deemed compatible only within contractual, companionate marriage, leaving queer sex as a demonized remainder (111–116).

This argument can be placed in dialogue with the no less historically important masculinization of the public sphere, which (as Carol Pateman shows) elevated fraternal bonds into the social glue of the democratic public. Two consequences emerge. First, since the fraternal model of the public aims to represent itself as the social contract (between brothers), while expelling the marriage contract (between a brother and the woman he marries), even marital sex has historically appeared (Kant notwithstanding) as a form of unilateral possession (i.e., so long as men represent their women in the public, they can possess them in private). The beat generation recapitulates this pattern through its devaluation of (unequal) marriage as a bond inferior to those of its brotherhood, yet indispensable to it as a sign of fraternal virility.

The masculinized public sphere has yet another consequence. Fraternal relations—built as they are out of homosocial desire—always risk becoming sexualized and thereby threaten to reintroduce objectification and instrumentalization into the very space from which it was supposedly banished. In calling for tenderness and adhesiveness between male citizens, Ginsberg characteristically played it both ways, expressing himself in a way that was meant to stave off the fear of a homosexualized inequality, but that could also be taken by the gay liberation movement as a call to public sexual solidarity. Ginsberg's language transfigures homoerotic desire into the stuff of identity itself, a sense of free and equally shared belonging and personhood necessary for building public good. By delimiting sex to something a brother does with people *outside* the fraternity (whether women or other men), Ginsberg and his fellow writers also established for the beat generation its own subjunctive mood, imagining its existence *as if* it constituted a free and equal boy gang whose members would never instrumentalize one another.

Read closely, however, one can see that fraternal equality is more elusive in beat texts than the rhetoric would suggest. Its elusiveness, moreover, derives from exactly the issues that would concern women's and gay liberation respectively: the *actual* sexual relations of the beat men with women, and the *possible* sexual relations with one another. While the beats replicated what Pateman calls the "sexual contact," coupling the social equality of brothers with sexual control over women, they dealt with this right quite anxiously. On the one hand, they tend to celebrate the sexual access of the beat hero as a sign of his virility. "Howl" calls N.C. the "cocksman and Adonis of Denver—joy to his innumerable lays of girls" (65). At the same time, sexual access may distract beat men from the fraternal community, for it means becoming embroiled in what are openly admitted to be power relations marked by domination and subordination, battles between husbands and wives, or boyfriends and girlfriends in which—empirically—women were not without power since, in beat circles the men were often financially dependent on the women. Under all circumstances, moreover, the public world of fraternity was supposed to be freed of such struggles, for its idealization depends upon its claim to embody a noninstrumentalizing equality.

The Inequality of Collective Identity

Even within its celebratory representation of fraternity, however, the beat generation did not present a symmetrical identity of equals. In its declaratory texts the beat generation always has a center, embodied in figures such as Neal Cassady, which even young men can only poorly approximate. The beat texts struggle with this contradiction quite openly, exploring even the frustrations of their narrators, whose initial hope to achieve a true brotherly equality with the man (or men) they so desire is never fulfilled. Much of the poignancy of the beat texts derives from this sense of fraternal failure: Sal Paradise's grieving silence in *On the Road* after the last and most painful of Dean's departures, "Okay, old Dean, I'll say nothing" (302–303), or implicitly in the recession of generational unity in the final stanza of "Howl," when Carl Solomon arrives in tears at the door of the poet's cottage. This undercurrent of failure, however, remains just that, a flow of contrary meaning that remains submerged beneath the aspirations and solicitations of these texts to produce a political fraternity of bad boys. The beat generation articulated youth as a rebellious generation committed to the revitalization of America's revolutionary democratic principles. This is not the place to evaluate in any final way the beat politics of identity, which would be reflected back over time in the unequal sisterhoods of feminism or in the unequal brotherhoods of queer politics. What I want to stress here and now is the double-edgedness that accompanied the politics of identity as a collective enterprise, bearing a radical side whose democratic imperative can be deeply politicizing to those whom it interpellates, but also a subjunctive side, an "as if" quality to its politics of membership and inclusion whose disavowals of inequality have continued to haunt the politics of identity.

WHERE THE GIRLS WERE:

FIGURING THE FEMALE REBEL

Naturally, we fell in love with men who were rebels. We fell very quickly, believing they would take us along on their journeys and adventures. We did not expect to be rebels all by ourselves; we did not count on loneliness. . . . But we knew we had done something brave, practically historic. We were the ones who had dared to leave home.
—Joyce Johnson, preface to *Minor Characters*

With oedipal revolt and generational fraternity both presiding over early identity discourse, did girls have a place as iconic rebels in the 1950s? Certainly, one would be hard pressed to name a female icon for identity who received attention comparable to that trained upon James Dean, Elvis Presley, or Jack Kerouac. In part, this absence reflects the gender pattern of bad-boy narratives, in which girls often embodied the domestication that the boy repudiates.[1] Rebellion and conformity often mapped tightly onto masculinity and femininity respectively, so that the badness of boys might draw definition in contrast to the goodness of girls. Yet it is not difficult to show that this gendering of the rebel narrative belied the actual imaginative life of many postwar girls, even the ones most closely identified with domesticity. In *Young, White, and Miserable*, a monograph that carefully studies the vicissitudes of growing up female in the 1950s, Wini Breines offers ample evidence that white, middle-class girls—the very ones expected to move happily along into suburban marriages and motherhood—actually experienced great trepidation about such a future. Yet in her consideration of the decade's youth culture, Breines concludes that these doubts found little room for representation, existing mostly as a hidden groundswell of incipient revolt.

Rebel girls, I will argue, actually played a much larger imaginative role in postwar American culture than Breines might grant. Many of the decade's principal bad-boy narratives, after all, also featured an (admittedly overshadowed) rebellious girl who acts as the bad boy's female counterpart and romantic partner. These girls (Natalie Wood's Judy in *Rebel*, Ronnie in *King Creole*, Mary Lou in *On the Road*) form a subplot in the bad-boy narrative that became important in two ways. First, her romantic interest established the bad boy as a romantic figure, but second—and more interestingly—the rebellious girl acted as the female supplement to his status as representative of a generation in crisis. These roles were usually linked, making two things usually true about the rebel girl found in the bad-boy narrative. First, she is attracted to his style of masculinity; it is her appreciative eyes that bring the boy into an erotic focus, magnifying his glamorous appeal. Second, the rebellious girl aspires not to domesticate the bad boy, but, precisely because she finds his rebelliousness attractive, hopes instead to enjoin his defiance of their domesticated parent culture.

This latter quality, I shall suggest, possessed a tremendous potency in opening up narrative and symbolic agency for female revolt. Because women's obligations under the Cold War were primarily associated with being strong wives and mothers, suburban living was seen as a foundation for, and not a threat to, normative femininity. This situation contrasts markedly with the suburban "crisis of masculinity" that validated bad boys like Dean or Presley. And yet, insofar as bad boys needed to differ from their fathers, their love interests also needed to differ from their mothers. The masculine crisis of the bad boy thus produced, as an unanticipated consequence, the need for antidomestic girls who repudiated the suburban gender system. Cold War culture thus called not only for the "lady" but also the "tramp," to use the terms Alan Nadel borrows from Disney (118). There were, however, at least two important variants of the antidomestic rebel girl.

In one of the few studies to consider rebellious girls as significant characters on the representational stage of postwar culture, Rachel Devlin has excavated the discourses of female juvenile delinquency for evidence that challenges "most chroniclers of the period [who] describe female rebellion as only incipient in nature and largely hidden from view" (85). Devlin suggests instead that the female delinquent functioned as an important figure around whom condensed considerable "cultural anxiety about the family generally and of fathers specifically" (84). Psychiatrists, who dominated the diagnosis of the female delinquent, attributed her deviance to the romantic failure of her father, either because he withholds from her the erotic interest she needs to achieve heterosexual maturity, or conversely because he expresses excessive interest by jealously overmonitoring her relationship to her boyfriends. Three things are of particular interest here. First, like the bad boy the female delinquent represented an adolescent in the process of forming her identity. Second, according to the oedipal analysis of her delinquency the rebel girl was motivated by her urge to romance a different kind of man from her inadequate father. Her identity, in short, took shape through her refusal of the "role expectation" that she prove herself a "good girl" by marrying a "good boy." Finally, as Devlin notes, the girl's oedipal impasse could lead toward two opposite forms of deviance. Either she might seek a substitute for her father, pursuing a man with whom she could engage in a compensatory form of "precocious sexuality and promiscuity." Or, alternatively, the girl might choose to assume the masculine role herself, thereby fleeing the oedipal impasse entirely.

These two possibilities correspond closely with a pair of gendered figures through which young female rebels were typologized in the 1950s: the "bad girl" and the "tomboy." The "bad girl" refused to be good by adopting an antidomestic, sexualized femininity. The other figure, the "tomboy," rebelled instead by consolidating a female masculinity modeled upon the bad boy. Both types were widely represented and discussed in postwar culture. Both also took on narrative lives of their own, sometimes becoming the principal of their own rebel story. Admittedly, even here they rarely did do so outside of a presupposed romantic relation to bad-boy rebellion. This corollary status, however, should not tempt us to dismiss the bad girls and tomboys of the fifties as coopted figures; their capacity to represent, and to champion, antidomestic female identity serves as an important precedent for the explicitly feminist and queer politics of female identity that would arise in the decades to follow.

Introducing the Story of a Bad Girl

> The problems I want to discuss in this book belong primarily, in our society, to the boys: how to be useful and make something of oneself. A girl does not have to, she is not expected to, "make something" of herself. . . . Correspondingly, our "youth troubles"

are boys' troubles—female delinquency is sexual: "incorrigibility" and unmarried pregnancy.—Paul Goodman, *Growing Up Absurd*

So commented Paul Goodman in his 1960 best seller, a book that, as we have seen, powerfully champions a youth revolt against the organized society, yet here urges his readers not to concern themselves overmuch with female rebellion. Motherhood and marriage are entirely "self-justifying," explained Goodman. Hence, girls do not suffer the evacuation of identity that boys face in the organized society, with its meaningless work and hollowed-out community. In her work on fifties "bad girls," Wini Breines has cited this same infamous passage by Goodman to illustrate that the rebellious impulses felt by postwar girls were not allowed expression. Still, Goodman at least acknowledged her existence, however grudgingly: there she is, unmarried and "incorrigible," waiting to be taken seriously. Breines's analysis of fifties bad girls is itself a sort of revisionist commentary on Goodman's weak nod to the sexually delinquent girl, a figure Breines essentially reads as a female response to "growing up absurd." The young postwar woman, after all, might find her suburban home life as purposeless and alienating as her husband did the organization, as Betty Friedan demonstrated only four years after the publication of Goodman's book.

For those growing up female in the 1950s, promiscuity was a powerful stigma. "The fear of being known as a 'bad girl' loomed as terrible punishment for girls," Breines observes (113). Yet badness for girls possessed a glamour not entirely unlike that associated with badness for boys. At the outset, it is clear that being a bad girl had a certain kind of political charge, for it involved the claiming of sexual agency outside of a marital teleology. In the fifties, a girl could be sexually active and perhaps still be "good" if she confined her activities to the one boy she (eventually) intended to marry. Outside these limits, sex potentially signified her rejection of both suburban marriage as a life goal and chastity as its complementary feminine ideal. While such transgressions always threatened to appear as "delinquency," in positive iterations they also expressed in sexual terms a girl's psychopolitical independence. Like the bad boy, moreover, the bad girl drew strongly from the codes of blackness and working-classness to signify her resistance to white, heteronormative domesticity. If not poor or black herself, which she in fact often was, the bad girl at the very least served as a surrogate for those who were.

Like her male counterpart, the bad girl became a particular staple of the

Hollywood teenpic, as several prominent actresses—Natalie Wood, Sandra Dee, and Debbie Reynolds, among others—developed sexually rebellious teen star images. The most unabashedly explicit bad girl of the Hollywood teenpic, however, was Mamie Van Doren. Although she never broke into the top tier of big-budget or high-visibility projects, laboring for the most part at the low, exploitation end of the teenpic world, Van Doren successfully established herself as a tough-talking, cigarette-smoking, busty teen girl out for herself and her personal pleasure. Van Doren's greatest bad-girl hit, *Girls Town*, though poorly remembered today, can be usefully compared to such bad-boy movies as *Blackboard Jungle*, *Rebel*, or *King Creole* for its expression of justified youth revolt against a repressive parent culture. Like *Blackboard Jungle*, *Girls Town* employs rock 'n' roll as the defiant sound of a gang of lower-class (girl) delinquents resisting adults' calls for obedience. Like *Rebel*, it justifies youth rebellion as a response to parental failure, and like *King Creole*, it concerns a protagonist who asserts her personal sovereignty. All of these similarities, however, are also made different by the female character of Van Doren's rebellion.

In *Girls Town* Van Doren plays a tough, sneering, orphan girl named Silver, whose tender-heartedness is only slowly revealed during her confinement at a Catholic reformatory on the (mistaken) suspicion of having pushed her boyfriend over a cliff at Lover's Lane. Its rock 'n' roll appeal involves the cinematic debut of the young Paul Anka, who performs several of his best known songs, including his breakthrough hit "Lonely Boy." *Girls Town* also casts young jazz singer Mel Torme as its principal villain, although he does not perform as a singer in the film. Finally, as a further draw for music fans, the film includes a vintage performance by the Platters, perhaps the most popular of rock 'n' roll's early black vocal groups.

Girls Town's narrative of redemption from badness is borrowed directly from *Boys Town*, the depression-era juvenile delinquent film upon which it is loosely based.[2] However, unlike Whitey, the boy character played by Mickey Rooney in that earlier film, whose criminality concerns petty theft and minor illegality, Silver's female brand of delinquency, very much in line with Paul Goodman's characterization, concerns sexual incorrigibility. Silver is a bad girl in large part because of her freewheeling eroticism. To be sure, we also learn early in the film that Silver has recently been charged with striking her teacher ("She hit me first," insists Silver). And, obviously enough, she is perceived as capable enough of violence to be easily suspected of killing her lover, Chip. Silver's main crime, however, is that she dates boys without regard for proper modesty. Not only has she apparently

24. Silver defies both the police chief and Chip's father in *Girls Town* (MGM, 1959).

been dating a rich boy (Chip) unlikely to marry her, but we first meet her when she has stood him up to go out with yet another boy to a make-out party thrown by a completely different gang. Silver's feistiness is directly tied to her confident sexual directness and to the power over boys that it grants her. When Chip's father, a wealthy businessman, insults the low-class Silver at the police station by exclaiming, "I don't know what my son saw in you," Silver defiantly responds by shifting in her seat, throwing her bust into profile for the camera as she snarls through a drag on her cigarette, "Oh, yah?"

In my discussion of *King Creole*, I observed that Elvis Presley's character Danny Fisher becomes vulnerable insofar as he risks falling into the same condition of servitude to the tyrannical Maxie Fields as Ronnie, the bad girl of that film. Ronnie's captivity, the film implies, grew precisely out of her sexual rebellion as a bad girl. Because she played her eroticism in order to aim for something beyond marriage and motherhood, Ronnie's sexuality became open to exploitation and predation by an immoral rich man. *Girls Town* associates bad girls with the exact same vulnerability. Silver's sexual rebelliousness appears initially as a source of strength, but the film makes it equally clear that when girls play the sex card they leave themselves exposed to dangerous boys. This is established early in the film, when the prologue depicts an anonymous girl nearly raped by a boy at Lover's Point. In his struggle to subdue her, the boy (who will soon be revealed as the hapless Chip) inadvertently slips over the edge of the cliff to his death. The still sobbing girl jumps into a car and drives off, at which point the title sequence begins, while the camera adopts her position behind the steering wheel. As the car careens dangerously past one vehicle after another, the bluesy title number (sung by Paul Anka) offers what amounts to a punchy address to the bad girl. It begins with a peon to modesty ("Listen to me, girl, / Watch your ps and qs, / Or you'll be singing the Girls Town blues"). The song then fixes the origins of female delinquency in neglect ("Many girls need love, / Many girls need care, / And if they're unattended then there's trouble everywhere"), and lastly presents the reformatory as the cure to the ill:

> Some of them seem bad,
> I don't know why they should,
> 'Cause when they leave there they all seem good.
> You go to Girls Town,
> You'll always find
> You come out with peace of mind
> From Girls Town.

As a commentary on the preceding rape scene, the title song seems to lay the blame on the girl, warning that whenever girls forsake the etiquette of sexual modesty, they risk some serious blues. The title visuals of her reckless driving further reinforce this disapproving view of the bad girl as a reckless agent, heedlessly driving her life at a pace that risks a major crash. Who can say when she will collide with a boy who will make her pay for her sexual forwardness? At the same time, however, the snappy R & B quality of the song militates against the grain of the song's lyrical content, as does the colloquial tone of the language. A definite erotic energy suffuses the number that conveys the bad girl's admirable hipness and vitality. Moreover, the viewer's perspectival placement in the bad girl's position behind the wheel actively solicits our identification with the thrills of her ride and the energy of the song. *Girls Town* will move back and forth between the poles of disapprobation and ebullience, underlining the costs of female sexual delinquency even while acknowledging the potency that it invests in girls to move agentially through the world.

Two principal narrative lines lead out from the prefatory failed rape scene. First, because it turns out that Silver was Chip's scheduled date on the fateful day, she is hauled into the police station as the principal suspect in his death. Although Silver maintains the strong alibi that she never kept the date but went instead to a party, the police chief uses her spotty record as an excuse to sentence her to the Girls Town reformatory in order to placate Chip's wealthy, politically powerful father. In the second narrative line, it is revealed that it was Mary Lee, Silver's younger, precocious sister who went in Silver's stead on the date, and who thus was the one struggling with Chip when he slipped over the edge. Another wealthy, amoral boy, Chip's friend Fred, who witnessed the event from a distance, eventually recognizes Mary Lee, and blackmails her, first just for kicks (making her ride as his partner in a dangerous drag race), but later in order to prostitute her in Mexico as a way of making money to repair his car.

Silver's and Mary Lee's stories initially convey opposing views of the bad girl. While Mary Lee's sexuality establishes her vulnerability to the villainous Fred, Silver manages to use sex as the source for her defiant strength. Like *Rebel without a Cause*, *Girls Town* makes use of its early scene at the police station to establish sympathy for its youth rebel as a misunderstood delinquent. Here, Silver's social recalcitrance calls into question the norms enforced by a corrupt juridical order. Like *Blackboard Jungle*, *Girl Town* presents us with a rebel who rebukes the law's complicity with an unjust class system, one that demands her appreciative docility even as it conspires to frame her as undeserving of the social privileges that accompany bourgeois normality. The fact that Silver is poor and has no parents predetermines her guilt. Even though Silver can claim multiple witnesses who will attest that she was nowhere near Chip when he died, the police chief acts, not on the evidence of the case, but instead on Silver's questionable character as vindictively insisted upon by Chip's angry father. Silver's sullen retorts when he is allowed, unbelievably, into the scene of her interrogation, her defiant cigarette smoking, her hip insults, and her aggressive sexual double entendres, are all strongly endorsed as understandable responses to a travesty of justice. "What's my crime, Dad?" Silver cries in disbelief when the police chief sends her to Girls Town, in effect condemning and sentencing her without a trial. "Not having as much money as this jerk? Or my mom wasn't in the social register?"

Silver's tough-chick performance serves as an acting-out of these angry accusations throughout the film. Later, when the exasperated head of Girls Town, Mother Veronica, who offers nothing but kindness to Silver, exclaims, "I don't know what gets into you young people. It's more than rebellion," she inadvertently reminds us and Silver that her defiance is legitimate, leading the bad girl to retort, "You old folks made such a great world for us. Too bad we don't appreciate it." Like the bad boys in their narratives,

Silver's rebellion actually does have cause: she refuses to meekly accede to a fundamentally unacceptable world.

Silver's sexual delinquency is not only justified on principle, but even makes a kind of strategic sense. It is miserable enough that Silver must struggle to keep herself and her sister alive, without money or parental support, but, adding insult to injury, she must then suffer adults who harrass her for the "immorality" she exhibits with these efforts. Silver here resembles a teenage version of the Sadean woman as described by Angela Carter. Building upon the Marquis de Sade's philosophy of sex as portrayed in the stories of Justine and Juliette, Carter suggests the profile of a poor woman who hits upon the realization that she cannot afford virtue, which will only lead her into weakness and degradation. Instead, by embracing her erotic appeal to men, the poor girl can convert her sex into the coin of power and wealth. So too in *Girls Town,* Silver represents a girl who has rejected the social etiquette of modesty, chastity, and all around goodness, and instead employs her sexual charisma on behalf of her own pleasure and advantage.

Once Silver enters Girls Town, however, she is slowly converted to the view that, in this new setting at least, she cannot afford to be bad. Girls Town does not deserve the kind of defiance that Silver shows the outside world, for, as we quickly learn, it is a compassionate institution that protects and nurtures its wards as foster daughters. Though many of the other girls are just as tough as Silver, no doubt her equals in delinquency on the outside, they resent her flaunting of Girls Town's rules, particularly the ones that concern sexual conduct. At one point, the other girls even place Silver on trial for sneaking out on a date. "You kids know we've got a pretty good thing going here," observes Vida, the girl prosecutor who becomes Silver's chief rival at Girls Town: "There's no walls around us, we're not caged up like a bunch of monkeys, and the sisters treat us real human. So what does this flea-brain do? She sasses the sisters, smokes in the room, and last night she breaks out and goes nightclubbing. Now, if the law finds out about that, how long do you figure they'll let us stay here?"

In explicitly contrasting the rules of Girls Town to the abusiveness of the law, Vida validates the former as a means of arranging for a female mutuality that allows the sisters to care for the girls while the girls look out for one another. In Girls Town, Silver's rebellious stance serves, no longer as sound strategy, but instead as self-defeating concession of her access to sisterly solidarity. Even the sexual self-determination that Silver at first seems to claim by nightclubbing proves quickly to be its opposite. Not only does the delivery man whom she dates prove so sexually aggressive as to make her feel harrassed, but Silver further discovers that he is nothing other than a detective, hired by Chip Gardner's father in an effort to incriminate her. Sexual delinquency inside of Girls Town, it seems, leads a girl not to freedom but to the troubles that plague the vulnerable and friendless.

Once Silver moves in the direction of these conclusions, she begins to absorb the lessons derivable from Mary Lee's plight. Just a few years behind her older sister Silver as a bad girl, Mary Lee's horrific encounter with Chip, and her resulting vulnerability to the other rich bad boy, Fred, seems to lead further and further down the road of sexual servitude. As the one soft spot in her otherwise tough, unsentimental personality, Silver's love for her younger sister becomes the occasion for her spiritual transformation. The film repeatedly casts Silver's concern for Mary Lee as maternal in nature; "She's just a baby," pleads Silver in trying to win help for her rescue effort. Not suprisingly, once she turns to saving Mary Lee, Silver finds herself unable to maintain her rebellious loner pose, learning instead that she must accept any and all benevolent offers of assistance that Girls Town has to offer. The actual catalyst for Silver's transformation, however, is neither one of the other girls nor one of the nuns, but a former bad boy turned good.

Jimmy Parlow, a pop teen idol played by Paul Anka, enters the scene early on in *Girls Town* as a celebrity obsession of one of the delinquent girls, Sarafina, who clings to a delusion that she and Jimmy are madly in love with each other. When, shortly after her arrival at Girls Town, Silver adopts Sarafina, calling her her "henchman," she sets in motion a triangular relationship in which she and Jimmy implicitly become Sarafina's common guardians. Two things must happen, however, to facilitate this relationship. First, Silver must overcome the class rage that feeds her bitter distrust of Jimmy. Second, Jimmy must succeed in deeroticizing Sarafina's longing for him. Silver's knee-jerk anger at Jimmy stems from her perception that, like Chip or Fred, he is another spoiled rich boy who could never understand the plight of the girl who is infatuated with him. Accusing him of offering "meaningless charity" to "poor little low girls," she asks, "What has a cat like you with all that gold know about a kid without a buck in the world, no old lady, no old man?" Though chagrined by her anger, Jimmy turns out to possess a past resembling those of the Girls Town wards. "I've been a kid without a buck in the world, no old lady, no old man. You should've seen the neighborhood I grew up in," he exclaims, and recounts for her a time when he broke into a pool hall for a mere forty dollars. Jimmy under-

25. Jimmy wins Silver's trust in *Girls Town* (MGM, 1959).

stands the rage she feels and her reasons for rebellion. Wealthy and famous though he may now be, Jimmy as a former juvenile delinquent bad boy can be counted on to empathize with Silver, Sarafina, and the other girls of Girls Town.

Jimmy performs a crucial compound alchemy in *Girls Town*, transmuting male experience into female experience, wealth into poverty, badness into sweetness, and romantic love into familial tenderness. With the exception of the bluesy title number, Jimmy's songs are neither rock 'n' roll numbers nor conventional romantic ballads. Instead, they wistfully express his feelings of sadness, loneliness, and lovelessness. In his first number, performed in the nightclub to which Silver goes on the ill-fated date with the detective, Paul Anka plays his breakthrough hit, "Lonely Boy," sung in the voice of a sad boy hungry for affection. "I'm just a lonely boy, lonely and blue," Anka sings, forlornly describing himself as "waiting for someone to give him her love." "Lonely Boy" was well known in the 1950s as the song that Anka wrote after his mother's death. Along with "When You're Sad and Lonely," Anka's other number in the film, it equates romantic loneliness with the lovelessness of the orphan, setting up Jimmy as a figure of direct identification for the girls at *Girls Town*. No rich teen idol here who might seduce and exploit the girls, Jimmy instead offers himself as a mirror to his girl fans, the image of the poor, orphaned, and vulnerable.

In *Girls Town*, Jimmy sings, in other words, *as* one of the girls rather than as a boy who *wants* them. It becomes increasingly clear that Jimmy will become, not a suitor for Silver, Sarafina, or one of the other girls, but instead a brother. *Girls Town* is careful to close off the heterosexual option in favor of a heterosocial sibling relation that hinges upon his male femininity, his capacity for nurturance. For instance, when Sarafina awakens from an attempted suicide with sleeping pills, Jimmy tells her how alone he was growing up as a boy, how often he wished that his parents had also given birth to a girl. If you were my little sister, he explains, "We couldn't be sweethearts, but we could make awful good friends." With these words, Jimmy successfully urges Sarafina to desexualize her attachment to him, stripping it of its potential for sexual revolt so that it becomes instead a familial affection marked by sisterly tenderness and goodness.

Even Silver eventually finds herself won over by Jimmy's brotherly relation to the girls. And once she stops perceiving him as a rich kid just toying with the poor, lonely girls of *Girls Town*, once she trusts his shared concern for Sarafina, Silver quickly finds it in her to plea for his help in saving Mary Lee. "You wanna do some good? How about going down to the station and getting my sister a lawyer? She isn't even sixteen, she's just a baby!" Moments later, she joins Jimmy in the chapel where he sings the Ave Maria, including the key line: "Ave Maria, listen to my children's plea, thou canst save amid despair." Silver burst into tears, her anger and antagonism melted in the warmth of such tender maternal mercy. Silver's new and less belligerent spirit comes not a moment too soon, for only through a new attitude of cooperation can her younger sister be saved. When Mary Lee is abducted by Fred toward the end of the film, Silver's toughness is revealed as entirely impotent, as only provoking the other girls into mistrusting her and preventing her from taking action. When, instead of defying the other girls, Silver turns to pray at the altar of Saint Jude (the patron saint of lost causes), the other girls conclude that Silver is "for real," and offer to help her out. Together, the girls track down Fred, defeat him, and free Mary Lee.

In some respects, this scene of victory carries the potential of a protofeminist sisterhood. It presents a scene of poor and singly powerless girls uniting against the cruel intent of a wealthy and powerful male community that includes would-be bad boys (Fred), businessmen (Chip's father), and the law. The implication, in this reading, is that girls who defend their own interests through a kind of rebellious sexual individualism put themselves at risk, while those who unite socially (like the beats on a familial rather than a sexual basis) can act protectively and caringly. As a feminine boy

26. It takes a sisterhood to defeat Fred in *Girls Town* (MGM, 1959).

who also treats the girls as sisters, Jimmy becomes an honorary member of the Girls Town sisterhood. Likewise, the nuns, as celibate adult sisters, become a powerful model for the community of girls. Silver's trajectory in *Girls Town* moves from that of the defiant and sexy bad girl to a chaste older sister who protects her younger sibling by joining with their other sisters.[3]

On the surface, the sisterhood of the film's climax suggests that Silver's conversion primarily concerns her transformed relationship to other women, both laterally in her new alliance with the other girls but also vertically through her acceptance of maternal responsibility for both Sarafina and Mary Lee. From the viewpoint of family romance, *Girls Town* appears to thematize mother-daughter relations, narrating how a girl who at first refuses a mother figure eventually comes to identify with her. Whereas on her arrival at Girls Town Silver had refused to refer to Veronica as "Mother," explaining that "'mother' 's a dirty word to me," by the end of the film, when a newly arriving bad girl parrots her old line exactly, Silver responds by telling her, "You'll learn." And when she speaks her final goodbyes to Veronica, she pauses meaningfully before calling her "Mother."

Silver's conversion involves boys far more closely than this apparent emphasis on mothers and daughters might suggest, however. She began the film as a bad girl precisely because she did not expect boys or men to offer her anything not explicitly paid for in the coin of sex. She becomes a good

27. Silver reconstitutes her nuclear family in *Girls Town* (MGM, 1959).

mother by learning otherwise. Jimmy's importance to the film rests precisely on the fact that he stands as an exception to this rule, and as such is the only character who can win her heart. A bad boy who has turned good and also a poor person who has become rich, Jimmy understands from personal experience Silver's rebelliousness, yet he also has the capacity to aid her from a position of wealth and power. This in effect allows Silver to join Jimmy in grace, to repeat the conversion experience that he once underwent. Silver turns from bad to good, and, as the final shot suggests when they drive off together in Jimmy's fancy car, with Mary Lee in the back seat, she may well be leaving behind poverty for access to affluence.

Together, Jimmy and Silver prefigure a new nuclear family, one that has absorbed the lesson of rebellion but has matured enough to take on adult responsibility ("You'll learn," as she says to the new, unreformed bad girl before driving off). Making sure that Mary Lee learns too will now become Silver and Jimmy's responsibility, but unlike domesticated couples who have never actually felt the imperative to rebel, they will understand what drives Mary Lee and be stronger parental figures for it. For all its focus on girls and women, *Girls Town* closes by confirming the bad girl primarily through her compatibility with the bad boy once both of them had outgrown rebellion. The strength they exhibited in their badness now can serve the making of family and the parenting of children.

As a narrative about Silver's conversion, from a sexualized bad girl in revolt against adults into a chaste good woman who loves her girls in a motherly fashion, *Girls Town* recounts a story of Silver's domestication. To the extent that Silver begins by believing that maternity is nothing but rhetoric, a pretense that some people actually care about anybody else, she comes to embrace maternity herself as real possibility that she has learned at Girls Town. Together, Jimmy, Silver, and Mary Lee represent a nuclear family (much as Jim, Judy, and Plato briefly do in *Rebel without a Cause*), but this one involves no apparent romantic or sexual relationship between Silver and Jimmy. Rather, they seem to bear a domestic relationship based solely on their joint guardianship of Mary Lee, one in which the wealthy Jimmy Parlow provides for the material needs (earlier he supplied Mary Lee with her lawyer; here he supplies the car). The final shot in *Girls Town*, in short, represents not sisterhood but a nuclear family modeled on breadwinning paternity and nurturing maternity. The final step away from badgirlhood may be into motherhood rather than a nun's habit. Nevertheless, it is a strikingly asexual depiction of motherhood that leaves little room for eroticized marriage. Female sexuality is lodged entirely in the realm of bad girlhood, while adult womanhood (in the sense of a mature, maternal attitude) involves a turn to chastity. In this respect, *Girls Town* places morality in the role of motherhood that closes the film, but invests all the glamour of female sexuality in bad girlhood, just as it invests the sexiness of bad boy masculinity in characters such as Chip or Fred, rather than the domesticated male femininity of a Jimmy Parlow. The ideological force of the film belongs to the beginning and middle, with its exciting bad girl, rather than only to the uplifting end when, redeemed, she no longer has any fight.

The binary opposition also bears a racial component, as the name "Silver" itself implies. Though it designates her as white (like "Whitey," the Mickey Rooney character upon which she is based) and as precious in her substance, Silver begins the film not very white at all. Unlike the families of the boys, who have money, prestige, and a "name" to protect, Silver's behavior makes her an inappropriate love interest, someone so far down the social ladder that she lacks "breeding" altogether. Like Danny Fisher, Silver's sovereign personality, her self-interested toughness make her something of a "king creole," claiming independence by flamboyantly showing that she is not afraid to face down the niceties of an expected "whiteness." Her decision to forsake sexual rebelliousness near the film's end is thus the inversion of her return to the value of "Silver," a means of proving that she always was as white as she actually looks, the "real thing." Yet, as in *Rebel* or *Blackboard Jungle*, the appeal of the film does not concern the return to "goodness," but the badness that precedes it. Silver's appeal as a rebel, in short, concerns her *refusal* to be silver, by turning away from the whiteness of "good girl" femininity. Silver is a white girl who acts "black." As we shall see, under certain conditions the bad girl could also be a black girl who acts "white."

When an Imitation of an Imitation Is the Real Thing

Notwithstanding the minor fame achieved by Mamie Van Doren, the girls among Hollywood's "rebels" tended toward the periphery of the star system, just as they did in the emergent rock 'n' roll star system. Nevertheless, bad girls were not entirely denied mass cultural attention in the 1950s. To demonstrate this, I turn to a bad girl who inhabits a very different kind of film, an extravagant production that was celebrated both by reviewers in its day and subsequently by academic film critics. I am referring here to Douglas Sirk's *Imitation of Life*, which has received more scholarly attention than any other Hollywood film discussed in this book. This attention derives, however, not from any association with discourses of youth, but rather from the film's stature in the oeuvre of a renowned auteur, as well as its intriguing representation of motherhood. Reaching back to the German emigré Sirk's early work in Brechtian theater, film critics have viewed the director's weepy melodramas as brilliantly wrought works of irony whose uses of generic excess and cliché reveal a subtly achieved critical perspective on postwar America. Building upon this critical consensus, feminist critics in particular have lavished attention on *Imitation of Life*, Sirk's final feature film, as a sophisticated intervention into the "woman's film" in general, the maternal melodrama in particular. Like *Stella Dallas*, *Mildred Pierce*, and numerous other films, *Imitation of Life* features the story of a pained mother's desperate love for her daughter. *Imitation* in fact doubles the maternal narrative, yielding two pairs of mother and daughter, one white and one black, working out their respective mothering pains even while it adds race as an explicit complication to the tribulations of female subjectivity.

Sirk's *Imitation of Life* substantially revises earlier versions of the story,[4] reshaping the main character into the glamorous Lora Meredith, a blond beauty (played by Lana Turner) who must juggle her aspirations for a Broadway acting career with her domestic aspiration to find a husband and make a good mother. The film opens in 1947, one summer afternoon at

Coney Island, as Lora searches the crowd for her lost six-year-old daughter, Susie. During the search, Lora encounters three people who will become central to her future life. First, she meets Steve Archer, a handsome photographer with artistic aspirations, who will become her principal but troubled love interest for the remainder of the film. Second, she finds Susie in the company of an apparently white eight-year-old girl, Sarah Jane, who turns out to be the light-skinned daughter of her much darker, black mother, the good-hearted Annie Johnson. When she learns that they are homeless, Lora hesitantly offers Annie and Sarah Jane a bed for the night. Annie's help at home proves so indispensable to Lora, however, that it leads to a permanent arrangement.

In the scenes that follow, Steve the photographer actively pursues Lora's affections. A pattern quickly develops, however, in which Lora repeatedly sacrifices plans with Steve for the sake of theatrical opportunities. Annie, in pointed contrast to Steve, makes no demands, staying home to facilitate Lora's quest in every way possible. From the start, however, Annie's labors are burdened by her daughter, Sarah Jane, who wants to escape her mother as the burdensome sign of her own blackness. Sarah Jane refuses black dolls, calls herself white, and attempts to pass as white at school. The first half of *Imitation* reaches a climax when Steve abandons his artistic ambitions as a photographer to propose marriage to Lora, only to be rejected because she cannot bear to give up the theater for a married life. Infuriated, Steve walks out of Lora's life just as she is poised to succeed in her Broadway ambitions.

Sirk's *Imitation of Life* has been studied thoughtfully for its dynamics of race, gender, and even class.[5] Excepting the obvious oedipal dimension, however, little has been written about how age also structures the film in powerful ways. For instance, her status as mother notwithstanding, it is clear that, from the beginning, the aspiring quality of Lora Meredith's character gets associated with a girlish idealism over and against a womanly maturity that would be more appropriate to her age. As she herself notes (and as other characters such as the agent Loomis confirm), Lora is simply too old to pursue a career as a showgirl. Yet she insists that the delay she suffered when her former husband unexpectedly died has only intensified her youthful ambitions. To Steve, whose offer of marriage she refuses, Lora appears as a woman who cannot relinquish (as he has) an improbable adolescent dream for the sake of a more modest but certain happiness as wife and mother. "You're not a child anymore, and I might not be around this time to pick up the pieces."

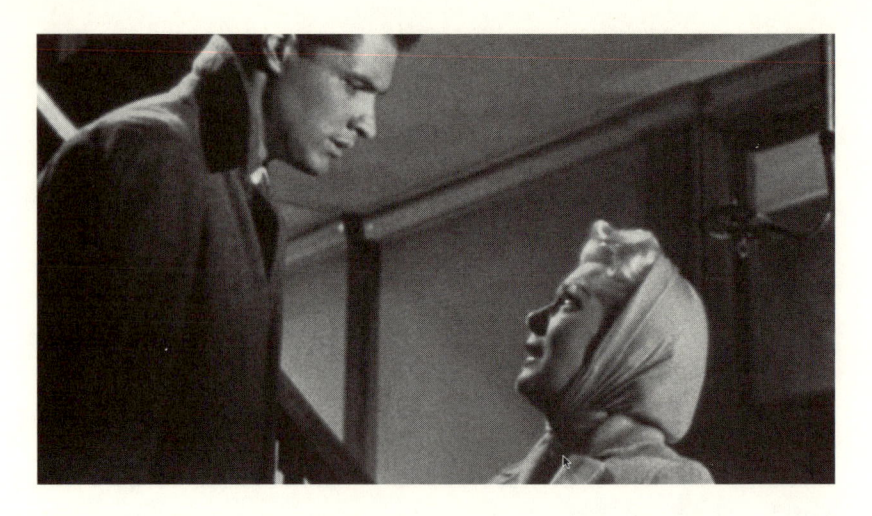

28. "Act your age," Steve demands of Lora in *Imitation of Life* (Universal, 1959).

The second half of the film begins with a success montage of Lora Meredith as she rockets to fame on Broadway between 1948 and 1958. This temporal ellipsis warrants several observations. First, the decade of this montage marks the transition from what was an uncertain postwar economic situation into full-blown Fordist affluence. Lora's success serves as a glamorized metonym for the expanding prosperity in these years of the American middle- and primary-sector working classes, a relation represented by Lora's move to a much fancier home. Like many Americans of those years, Lora suburbanizes her life, though on a far grander scale, relocating her family from its small New York apartment into a mansion located in the Connecticut suburbs. In addition to this nod to the suburbs, the second half of *Imitation* also registers the late fifties phenomenon of the mass-market youth culture. The two young girls of the first act, Susie and Sarah Jane, have become teenagers, implicit representatives of the emerging market's first generation of new consumers.

In place of the child actresses, two new performers appear in the adolescent roles: Sandra Dee as Susie and Susan Kohner as Sarah Jane. Each of these actresses, it should be noted, already had notable histories as participants in the developing genre of the teenpic. By the time she appeared in *Imitation*, Dee had already established herself as the single most famous teenpic actress of the 1950s, starring in such lucrative films as *The Reluctant Debutante* and *The Restless Years*. On the whole, Dee is remembered today as the paradigmatic good girl of the 1950s, a clean-cut, unambiguously heterofeminine girl on the threshold of romantic maturity. Yet, it is important to note that Dee's cultural signification in her films usually tended to involve a level of explicit resistance to adult expectations. She is always a *reluctant* debutante, she has entered the *restless* years, and, as we shall see later in this chapter, in *Gidget* her very willingness to behave like a girl becomes the central narrative issue. Susan Kohner was also considered an up-and-coming teen actress in the late fifties, and one with a far more overt flair than Dee for evoking badness in her characters. The intertext I would note here is her appearance in *Dino*, a juvenile delinquency film that starred Sal Mineo in a follow-up performance to his appearance in *Rebel without a Cause*. In that film, Kohner plays a young woman working at the orphan home for troubled boys, who falls in love with Dino. Although not a bad girl herself, she is set up as the kind of girl who empathizes with and romances bad boys. Kohner's acting persona, even before her appearance in *Imitation*, was thus already quite definitely associated with that of the teenpic problem girl.

Several critics of *Imitation* have rightly zeroed in on Sarah Jane, and her antagonistic attitude toward her mother's quiescence, as investing *Imitation of Life* with a powerful antisexist and antiracist subtext.[6] Yet, once again, without attending to age as a supplement to the standard analytic triad of race, class, and gender, the postwar conditions that enable a character such as Sarah Jane to create such meanings cannot be grasped. So, for example, when Marina Heung, in an otherwise brilliant essay on *Imitation*, suggests that the film depoliticizes racial and class conflict by familializing them, she misses the way in which the rebel youth narrative of the 1950s tended to *politicize* teenage-parent conflicts. As I have indicated in this book, the teenager's revolt was granted a social and not just a personal value, lodging its critique not only against the parental character in question but also against the parent culture at large. The force of Sarah Jane's ideological potency in *Imitation* derives from its *generic* redeployment of this narrative. The second half of the film functions, not merely as a maternal melodrama but also in accordance with the conventions of the teenpic, which grant Sarah Jane the status of a bad-girl protagonist. As we shall see, Sarah Jane draws upon the general authority of postwar teen revolt when she acts out her struggle against the class, race, and gender limitations embodied by her mother.

Though the family has relocated to Connecticut in the second half, a place with ample room and opportunity to allow the "togetherness" for which Lora increasingly longs, we quickly discover that the attention of both the teenage girls is focused elsewhere. Even the relatively dutiful Susie seems deeply engrossed in the romantic options posed by her new peer culture, asking herself, "[How can I] make a boy like me," and "Should I let him kiss me?" Sarah Jane, meanwhile, stops off at home only long enough to prepare for her excursions to the Village. Far from settling in Connecticut, Sarah Jane continues to find herself in New York, and more specifically in the bohemian New York of lower Manhattan. Even Lora, it turns out, is not quite ready for undiluted domesticity. Though thrilled when she reencounters Steve for the first time in ten years, Lora, only hours after promising everyone that she's not going to take on an acting role "for a long, long time," quickly succumbs to Italian director Enrico Felluci's offer of a starring role in his next feature film.

At this point, the plot of *Imitation of Life* bifurcates, alternately tracing the drama concerning each mother-daughter pair. Loosely, we may say that Lora and Susie's story pursues the tension between a bad mother and a more-or-less good daughter, while that of Annie and Sarah Jane observes the conflict between a good mother and a bad daughter. In both cases, however, the friction intensifies as the daughter exits the boundaries of the domestic relations in search of something else. Susie, already interested in boys, falls in love with Steve when he starts taking her out during Lora's film shoot. In keeping with Devlin's account of the postwar pyschoanalytic discourse on delinquent girls, Susie's romantic interest in her father figure is depicted as perfectly natural, a manifestation of her properly developing erotic interest in men. The problem emerges, not in Steve's properly paternal approach to Susie, but rather in the simple fact that Lora's lengthy delay in marrying Steve prevents him from seeming truly off limits to Susie. The blame, in other words, falls on Lora for not perceiving how badly she is needed at home, both as a mother who might counterbalance her daughter's teenage romanticism and as a wife whose timely union with Steve would have led Susie to sublimate her unrealizable crush. Although Annie attempts to offer Susie sound advice as to when she should or should not kiss the boys (when love is the motive, then kissing is like yeast to bread, Annie tells her), she does not listen. "Annie was always much more of a mother to me than you were," Susie sobs tearfully to Lora in their final confrontation, yet obviously she says this in order to move Lora back to the rightful place she must play as Susie's birth mother.

While Susie stays near to home in all respects, Sarah Jane emphatically steers away, passing on her own into a different world in Greenwich Village. Shortly after learning of Sarah Jane's excursions, the viewer hears more about the nature of this second life in a key scene. After feigning sickness to avoid a family outing, Sarah Jane sneaks back into the house only to be unexpectedly caught out by Susie. Quickly shushing her, Sarah Jane boldly confesses that she's just returned from a visit with her boyfriend in the Village, a fellow she's been seeing ever since he started whistling at her on visits to the jukebox at a Village ice cream parlor. Unlike Susie, who has barely begun thinking about boys, Sarah Jane relates that her boyfriend has even confessed wanting to "marry me someday." Taken by surprise, Susie asks her first and only question: "Is he colored?" Angered, Sarah Jane replies that the boy is white, and that if he ever finds out that she is trying to pass, she'll kill herself: "I'm white too. And if I have to be colored then I want to die. I want to have a chance in life. I don't want to come in through back doors or feel lower than other people or apologize for my mother's people. Don't say she can't help it. She can't, but I can. And I will." A rather transparent racial binary seems to undergird this comment. Whiteness, the color of her boyfriend and of their youth culture in the Village, connotes self-assertive freedom and confident possibility. Blackness, the color of her "mother's people," involves humiliating servility and a resignation to lack of possibility.

The meaning of race, however, is not actually so settled as Sarah Jane's words suggest. As this study has shown, the whiteness of fifties youth culture was no simple matter, for its character was repeatedly constituted over and against the whiteness associated with the domestic world of the suburbs. What in chapter 3 I called the suburban counterimaginary of rock 'n' roll is also operative in *Imitation of Life*. Sarah Jane literally flees from the false utopia of the new suburban home into the arms of a youthful bohemian world. Indeed, she replays precisely the romance celebrated in Chuck Berry's "School Days," seeking an emotively rich escape from a dreary teenage home life by visiting the local juke joint, where she has found someone who dances in step with her desire. And, who indeed does it turn out that Sarah Jane dances with, but Troy Donahue, the boy star of so many late fifties teenpics, appropriately dressed in the black-leather-and-jeans uniform of Marlon Brando's "wild one." While Sarah Jane tells Susie that the youthful scene to which she flees is a *white* world, it is not at all the same whiteness as that embodied by clean-cut Susie herself, nor even that of the glamorous Lora. Paradoxically, it resembles the whiteness borne by Norman Mailer's "white negro," a racialized hipster whose self-definition as a rebellious free spirit leans upon his uses of blackness for the purpose of countercultural self-fashioning. We can further see in her mirroring of

Chuck Berry's anthem that the blackness through which this white world constitutes itself differs strikingly from that which Sarah Jane disparages in her mother. Not the servility of the domestic servant but instead the assertive freedom of the jazz, blues, or rock musician becomes the racially coded basis of the white negritude secretly sought by Sarah Jane. In effect, Sarah Jane seeks to escape blackness in the very setting where it is emulated, but in so doing she establishes that setting (the beat or hipster world) as the guarantee of whiteness, understood as autonomy and freedom.

Sarah Jane's passing, therefore, is a far more complex operation than most critics have assumed, routed as it is through the racial transactions of fifties youth culture. Rather than crossing a boundary from a self-understood blackness to an equally coherent whiteness, we might say that Sarah Jane traffics between two sets of the black/white binary. In the first, she moves from her mother's servitude toward Lora's glamorous freedom; in the second she escapes suburban domesticated whiteness by traveling toward passionate urban blackness. Sarah Jane in effect traverses through the first of these racial boundaries, from black to white, so that she can position herself to cross back, at a different point in the racial divide, from white to black. Or, to put it another way, Sarah Jane must pass as white before she can fashion herself into a "white negro," a bad "white" girl with the spirit of social and sexual defiance against social limitations that has characterized her from the start of the film.

Earlier I noted how Sarah Jane emulates Lora by rejecting domesticity for the sake of youthful ambition. This relation gets reversed at least once, shedding light in the process on the political meaning of Sarah Jane's rebellion. In her final theatrical performance, Lora turns from her comedic mainstays to appear in *No Greater Glory*, a social drama about a social worker with "high dreams" that is apparently considered bold and controversial for its advocacy of black civil rights. In Lora's single greatest moment of theatrical triumph, the curtain call for this play, we see black faces in the theater for the first and only time, both on stage as principals in the cast, as well as in the audience that applauds them. Lora's ambitions are quite explicitly mapped in this scene onto black aspirations to transcend the social limits imposed by white supremacy. Ironically, of course, Lora achieves this symbolic triumph by exploiting Annie's willingness to labor under the limitations of her race, class, and gender, to seek "no greater glory" for herself than standing by Lora in *her* moment of triumph. Yet it is equally the case that Lora here parallels the spirit of Sarah Jane, echoing the latter's ambition to surpass the social liabilities imposed upon a black

29. Lora appears in a civil rights drama *No Greater Glory* in *Imitation of Life* (Universal, 1959).

person in America. Only Lora is allowed, in this narrative, to articulate a discourse of civil rights that demands something more, something better, for African Americans than that offered by white paternalism.

If we consider Lora and Sarah Jane as expressing similar ambitions of social transcendence, then it is striking that the similarities cease in their relation to marriage. Lora, as I noted, is associated early in the film with a youthfulness whose preservation requires her to reject marriage. Steve, like Lora, is young and artistically ambitious. But for him, falling in love signals the turn to maturity and thus to domestication. Marriage, for him, necessitates that they both "grow up" and move on to a more adult way of life. For Sarah Jane, however, a different kind of love seems possible, one that the actress Susan Kohner imports into the film from her previous history in the teenpic *Dino* and its beatnik follow-up in *The Gene Krupa Story*. The youth culture woven into the fabric of *Imitation of Life*'s second half includes the pattern of the bad-boy figure. Sarah Jane is of just the right age and growing up at precisely the right moment to fall in love with a passionate but delinquent young man. Unlike Lora, but like many female teenpic heroines (including, for instance, Judy in *Rebel without a Cause*) Sarah Jane need not refuse romance in order to avoid her own domestication because her beloved Frankie, played by the teenpic star Troy Donahue, himself embodies a male principle of antidomesticity. Frankie, a bad boy akin to the rebels whom Kohner had romanced in her previous films, is not the kind

30. "Are you black?" asks Frankie before beating Sarah Jane in *Imitation of Life* (Universal, 1959).

of man who (like Steve) craves domesticity, hence not the kind of man who would expect Sarah Jane to settle for a life resembling her mother's.

Brief but central to the teenpic thread in *Imitation of Life* is the scene in which Frankie's promise is first foregrounded, then voided. Donahue's single scene of the film occurs at night on the street of the Village, to the extradiagetic sound of cool jazz, which thematizes the urban bohemia where he and Sarah Jane have shared their romance. Attired in a standard rebel teen uniform, the handsome Donahue strides up to Sarah Jane, who emotionally proposes to Frankie that they run away together. Instead, it turns out that, through the innuendo of other kids, Frankie has discovered that Sarah Jane is black. As the jazz grows loud and discordant, Frankie, with increasing fury, slaps Sarah Jane down into the gutter. This scene, perhaps the most wrenching of the film, forces the viewer to witness a brutal act of punishment that is both explicitly racist and expressive of a frightening male rage toward women. Frankie's blows, however, seem most emotionally traumatizing in how they force Sarah Jane to confront the stinging knowledge that her mother's blackness will forever thwart her cherished hope of marrying into a bohemian life.

Critics have argued that Sarah Jane now descends into a grotesque parody of Lora's theatrical career. While pretending to her mother that she has taken a position at the New York Public Library, Sarah Jane actually becomes a performer at a nighclub. For Lauren Berlant, this signals Sarah

31. Sarah Jane as a "white negro" blues singer in *Imitation of Life* (Universal, 1959).

Jane's inability to match the success of Lora, the genuinely white showgirl of the film: Sarah Jane "is not good enough to achieve the self-iconicity of mass culture: she earns no success montage" (131). Yet in the scene of her performance at Harry's Club, it is hardly clear that we are witnessing failure. Sarah Jane's act, as Berlant observes, is a raunchy one in which she sings a seductive number about "her need to embody herself sexually, so that she might avoid the fate of passive, feminine women who have 'empty, empty arms'" (131). Her act, while admittedly raw, expresses an aggressive eroticism that meets the desire of the men in the audience with great success. Certainly, in comparison to Lora's clean and decent acts, Sarah Jane's world may appear sleazy. Yet, it is not difficult to discern a countercultural logic by which the raunch of Sarah Jane's bluesy come-ons seems more attractive and glamorous a style of femininity than the clean-cut white womanhood conveyed by Lana Turner in the flea powder advertisement. The compliments that she receives from the men ("I thought you were great tonight! Really great!") suggest that Sarah Jane might well have achieved her version of a success montage were *her* lucky break not derailed immediately thereafter when her mother arrives to bring her home. Sarah Jane forfeits her spot at the club the same way she loses Frankie, by being exposed as black through association with her all too visibly marked mother. Sarah Jane repeatedly creates for herself just the life she wants whenever she manages to pass as a "white negro" (here, a white woman who sings

[margin note: Idea of performative blackness]

the bawdy blues). She is thwarted whenever her blackness is unmasked as not merely performative but in her blood.

Rather than dismiss the final turns in Sarah Jane's life as parodic failure, it is worth seeing how she fashions herself as an alternative to her mother's docility as a black domestic. Simply put, Sarah Jane repeatedly opts to exert her will through a racially coded enactment of sexual freedom. She begins by finding a white boyfriend in the village. When that fails, she converts her heterosexuality-as-rebellion into an act at Harry's Club. As she puts it in her song to the audience:

> The loneliest word I've heard of is "empty"
> Anything empty is sad
> An empty purse can make a good girl bad
> You hear me, Dad?

Even as Sarah Jane explicitly names herself a bad girl in this song, she invests that badness with a specifically sexual content. Emptiness, of course, need not take on a sexual meaning. It can just as easily, for instance, express the feeling of one who has not been able to meet her "high ambitions," to paraphrase the title of Lora Meredith's final play, ambitions thwarted by the social barriers upheld against both blacks and women in postwar America. Like Martin Luther King in the title of his book *Why We Can't Wait*, Sarah Jane proclaims in her song that she "can't wait" any longer to bring her emptiness to an end. Yet, in her blues number, Sarah Jane converts her emptiness into sexual frustration, into the desperate need to refill her "empty empty arms" with the likes of the men in the audience. Frankie may be out of the picture, but Sarah Jane continues to assert her badness by reference to a postulated man who would want to be joined with a bad girl, a "white negress" blues singer. Even Sarah Jane's final incarnation—when she leaves for Los Angeles to become a chorus girl—positions her as an eroticized woman who plays to the gaze of an undomesticated playboy, a slightly older bad boy.

What explanation does *Imitation of Life* offer for the fact that, although the young Sarah Jane rebels against every possible manifestation of blackness and docile domesticity, by the time she becomes a teenage bad girl, her rebellion takes so specifically sexual a form in seeking romance with a bohemian or unconventional bad boy? One motivation may be discerned in the seemingly throwaway addressee of her raunchy song, "You hear me, Dad?" In its opening minutes, the film explains the peculiarity of a dark black woman like Annie giving birth to so light-skinned a daughter by way of an absent father. "Yes ma'am. It surprises most people. Sarah Jane favors her daddy. He was practically white. He left before she was born."

This explanation suggests a genealogy, not only for Sarah Jane's light skin color, but also for her rebellious character. Certainly much of *Imitation of Life*'s power lies in the painful fact that Sarah Jane is very much *not* Annie's daughter, departing from her mother not simply in her skin color but also in her ambitious and fiery disposition. All we know of her father is, first, that Sarah Jane "favors him," and second, that he left Annie. For all her touted "goodness," Annie fails as a mother in the film if one measures failure by her daughter's wish to abandon her. So too, years before we meet them, Annie had apparently failed in a similar measure of marriage. She could no more keep her husband than she can keep her daughter. This parallel, in which Sarah Jane follows her father in abandoning Annie, suggests a shared disposition. Though we have no information as to why Sarah Jane's father left Annie, by informing us that Sarah Jane favors him, *Imitation* projects a phantom father who, like Sarah Jane, apparently refused the social limitations placed on being black and who perhaps rejected the docility that would accompany a life of domestication by Annie. Cast in the form of an erotic freedom, this escape comes with the appropriation of whiteness, here understood as a personal liberation from the domestic servitude of blackness. Yet, as noted earlier, this is not a suburban whiteness but a bohemian one.

Imitation of Life has been widely understood as a maternal melodrama in the sense that it stresses the bittersweet love of mothers for their wayward daughters. Yet it is also possible to understand the film, from the perspective of the teenpic, as equally concerned with the love and desire of daughters for their fathers. Sarah Jane, in finding something in herself that resists identification with her mother, seeks a transcendence of blackness through an oedipal desire to become the kind of woman who could have successfully romanced her father. Relatedly, she seeks a man who, like her father, expresses a resistive relationship to the converging categories of blackness and domesticity. If the film offers us no black men passing as white, Sarah Jane at least finds a white boy who calls on the tropes of a rebellious black masculinity. And when even this romance fails, she continues seeking to fill her "empty arms" with a man very different from the kind who would stay with Annie, the kind who instead answers to the appeal "You hear me, Dad?"

If we consider the larger pattern of parentage and progeny in *Imitation of Life*, the question of maternity and paternity resolves curiously. The good girl, Susie, finds her proper parents, not in Lora (who is never around), nor in her blood father, who was a man of the theater and perhaps something of a bohemian, but in Annie, the good black woman who actually raises her, and in Steve, the good white man who was always more than willing to forfeit his artistic freedom, settle down and marry into the family. Susie's crush on Steve, obviously oedipal in that she desires her mother's love interest, also expresses a desire for a "good man," a proper husband and father who completes the domestic family space for which Susie has always longed. Sarah Jane, by contrast, finds her spiritual parentage in the absent father, the passing daddy for whom she continues to search as a bad girl, and in Lora, the woman who refuses domesticity, always seeking something more.

Imitation of Life resolves Sarah Jane's badness by symbolically incorporating her into a domesticated white family. When Annie dies at the end of the film, the fabric of the black social world of which she was apparently always a part appears for the first time on screen through the famous funeral performance of Mahalia Jackson and the hyperbolic funereal parade. Yet, when Sarah Jane arrives too late, grasping onto her mother's casket, she can no longer reclaim a connection to the body of her mother, so completely has she moved into the world of her father. Essentially successful as a "white negro" at the end of the film, Sarah Jane's grief for her lost black mother, at the end of the film, is what ironically allows her to be incorporated into the white family. In wanting to reclaim the domestic connection, the warmth of motherhood, Sarah Jane is prompted to leave her theatric world as a showgirl and enter the car that contains Lora, Susie, and Steve. Without Annie, no one in the family is visibly black. But with Lora finally reconciled to domesticity with Steve, no longer is anyone in the family undomesticated or bohemian. When Sarah Jane enters the vehicle, she thus joins a white, domesticated family and becomes, as she always wanted, white, but in her last-minute, penitent conversion, she is domesticated rather than bohemian in her whiteness: a good girl now, rather than a bad one.

In this respect, Sarah Jane is reconciled to domesticity much as Silver is in *Girls Town*. This narrative resolution makes these bad-girl texts neither more nor less ideologically conservative than most bad-boy narratives, which also offer closure to rebellion. Bad boys, after all, are usually reconciled with their families, brought back in as dutiful sons. Like their male counterparts, bad girls yield up their rebellion by the end of the story, but for a while at least, they enact revolts that express remarkably explicit criticisms of their social world and its expectations for them. What I do want to stress, however, is that in both examples, bad-girl revolt is grounded in a prior legitimacy of a bad-boy's rebellion. In *Girls Town*, Silver's badness rests on her sexual availability, her willingness to play with boys, which she justifies as the only way a girl can take care of herself in a world of bad boys out for kicks and adults who are unsympathetic at best, and actual class antagonists at worst. In *Imitation of Life*, Sarah Jane's badness emerges explicitly out of the "badness" of her absent father, the man whom her heart favors and for whom she seeks a substitute. If the bad boy cannot be coupled with a good girl lest he be domesticated, then one possible mate for him is a bad girl, whose rebellion is enacted through a sexualized femininity that bespeaks both desire for the bad boy and resistance to a domesticated future. Once the bad girl's rebellion is justified by its appeal to the bad boy, it can go on to express and bear a variety of socially and politically resistive meanings.

Tomboy: From Sexualized Femininity to Female Masculinity

The bad girl rebelled by enacting an alternative, antidomestic femininity that served as a romantic complement to the similarly antidomestic masculinity of the bad boy. Quite different is the way in which the tomboy girled the rebel narrative. In recent years, queer theorists have taken a deep interest in the tomboy as a prefigure for the butch dyke. Judith Halberstam in particular has observed a cycle of tomboy films from the late fifties through the late eighties that she deems as having "threatened an unresolved gender crisis and projected or predicted butch adulthoods" (193). For Halberstam, the tomboy represents the quintessential queer youth rebel whose early defiance of feminine expectations opens the possibility for queer adult female masculinities. Yet, despite this assertion of her importance to contemporary female queerness, the postwar tomboy figure's embeddedness in the general ideological matrix of rebel youth remains largely unexplored. So, for instance, Halberstam launches her discussion of tomboys by citing Jenni Olson's account of her own identification in childhood with Hollywood's tomboys (Tatum O'Neil, Jodi Foster, Kristy McNichol), an identification that she could not sustain into adulthood, once these tomboy actresses had themselves made a transition into "womanhood." Instead, Olson writes, "I turned to Marlon Brando and James Dean for my models of butchness" (175). For Halberstam, what is important here is simply that the Hollywood tomboy is sooner or late forced to "grow up" into femininity. Yet Olson's point also alludes to the history of a butchness that would trace lines of continuity between the tomboy and the star images of Dean or Brando. As we shall see, Olson's substitution remained within the same family of figures, for the first wave of postwar tomboy figures were themselves modeled quite directly on bad boys like Brando and Dean. It is not just any masculinity, therefore, that grounded tomboyhood, but the specifically rebel version that embodied the right to identity, with all the gender implications that it brought to bear upon that right. To put this even more strongly, the tomboy's aura as a gender outlaw, which is now of such interest to queer theorists, bears a close historical relationship to the bad boy's antagonism toward the gender norms of suburban domesticity.

It is important, for both historical and political reasons, not to privilege the tomboy over the bad girl, celebrating the former as the bold pioneer of female masculinity, while downplaying the latter as bearing a far less transgressive gender of "dangerous femininity." In point of fact, both the bad girl and the tomboy served as important alternative protagonists in a rebel youth narrative that usually featured bad boys. It is obviously true that the tomboy's transgenderedness allowed her defiance, unlike the bad girl's, to involve a *tout court* rejection of femininity as the obligatory gender for girls. It was usually the bad girl, however, who explicitly claimed a sexuality of her own when she rebelled. One might well argue, therefore, that she served as no less important a precursor for nonnormative female sexualities. Tomboy identity was primarily social rather than sexual in the primary narrative issues it raised, though this situation was in some respect a product of unspoken censorship. The tomboy offers a counterfactual to Paul Goodman's assertion that female delinquency always took a sexual form. Her delinquency instead concerned her direct, if precarious, participation in a homosocial community of rebel boys, precisely the one with which Goodman's book was so concerned. The tomboy's particular challenge to patriarchal gender relations concerned her assertion of female agency through capacities that (unlike the bad girl's) were not conditional upon a male gaze. Through such skills as fighting, racing, stealing, or surfing, boyish female masculinity signified the prospect of a nonsexual cultivation of autonomy for girls. Nevertheless, sexual risk remains a central narrative element in tomboy stories, as the following discussion of two exemplary texts will reveal.

Surfing with the Boys

It testifies to the figure's muted presence in postwar life that few people would remember *Gidget*, perhaps the single most popular teen girl text of the fifties, as a tomboy film. Released in 1959, the same year as *Imitation of Life*, it starred Sandra Dee in a role noteworthy both for its similarity to and its difference from Susie in the latter film. Slender, her medium-long blond hair often bunned or waved, with an inescapably clean-cut look, Dee might seem a quite conventionally feminine actress who was best suited to play good girls. Certainly, when compared to the rougher "wild one" styles of the fifties, or even to Mamie Van Doren, Dee comes off as a very good girl indeed.[7] In *Imitation of Life* this is how she appears when set in an obviously racialized comparison to Susan Kohner: where Sarah Jane is dark, reckless, and bad, Susie is fair, timid, and good. However, as I have already noted, Sandra Dee's characters almost always have a streak of rebelliousness to them, and Susie in *Imitation of Life* constitutes no exception. Although she never rejects her mother with the same absoluteness as did Sarah Jane, Susie does wage battle with Lora, in order to claim agency over her own sexuality, her right to erotic exploration with boys, and even makes a rivalrous play for her own mother's romantic partner. Where Sarah Jane's unnamed desire for someone like her absent father can only be approached indirectly through a kind of negative hermeneutics, Susie's finds expression right on the textual surface. In short, Susie might be viewed as herself a budding bad girl who only appears good because her rebelliousness is so decisively overshadowed by Sarah Jane's. In *Gidget*, as we shall see, Dee's body type signified quite differently. What seems important here is Dee's underdevelopment, the fact that her lack of a mature woman's curves gives her a presexual boyish character.

In *Gidget*, Dee plays Francie, a girl growing up in the suburbs of Los Angeles and who became famous as the icon of the girl surfer. What rarely gets remembered, however, is that Francie comes to surfing because she (still) lacks her girl friends' sexual interest in boys. The film begins on the fateful summer when Francie's girl friends, having all just crossed the line from children to sexualized young women, want to devote the summer to boys rather than to play. When the other girls drag the reluctant Francie with them to the beach, she shows none of their interest in the somewhat older gang of beach boys, at least not until the boys begin to surf. Only minutes into the film, Francie has abandoned her manhunting girl friends to devote her summer to joining the boys' surfing club.

Contra Paul Goodman, this desire to surf with the boys explicitly responds to a female version of "growing up absurd." Francie finds little meaning or interest in her friends' manhunt, which stands in as the exact equivalent of the rat race that Goodman decries. Why hunt for boys if it leads only to a staid and tedious life? Surfing is not exactly delinquency, but it approximates it insofar as it allows Francie to join a subcultural fellowship whose members all share values counter to those associated with a deadening maturity. The boys themselves are quintessential Goodmanian youths, presented with a dismal future as white-collar professional men and tract home husbands. In retreat from this "absurdity," the boys have found temporary refuge on the beaches of Malibu, which they use as a free zone of male cameraderie divorced from materialist and domestic "goals." Sharing what Barbara Ehrenreich calls the fifties male "flight from commitment," *Gidget*'s beach gang draws openly on beat generation discourse: a homosocial ethos of shared kicks that separate the youthful hipsters from the adult squares. Leading this teen- to college-aged gang is a somewhat older man, Kahuna, who promotes these beatnik surfer values, not merely as a transitory teen hesitation toward suburban manhood, but as a stable, alternative masculinity that enjoys genuine freedom.

Kahuna, having long ago discarded his original name, uses his surf moniker to mark out his new identity. If ordinary American names here connote a workaday American life, then "Kahuna," which signifies "honored chieftain" in native Hawaiian, plays with the long-standing colonial trope of the Pacific island as a tropical paradise where one might escape from the strictures of modernity. It also, like the name "King Creole," uses that racial hybridity to designate a sovereign self, someone who is the "chief" of his own destiny and the determiner of his own actions. Much like the city or the country in my discussion of rock 'n' roll, the beaches of the Pacific become yet another zone for the suburban counterimaginary, and one that also bears an affiliation to nonwhite peoples. A proudly self-proclaimed beach bum, Kahuna tells Francie that he dropped out of the workforce after the Korean War because jobs demanded "too many rules, hours" and ultimately chains on his daily life. To the boys in his gang, Kahuna represents a better kind of man than their organizational fathers, and their summertime emulation of him casts them as mild but definite bad-boy types. Following Kahuna, all the boys have adopted summertime nicknames. And at least one of them, Moondoggie (whose real name is Jeffrey), has already decided to embrace Kahuna's life in lieu of his father's. When the summer ends, Moondoggie plans to douse the expectations of his affluent father, quitting college to join Kahuna in a southward journey down to the Peruvian coast.

Like the boys, Francie's adoption of surfer masculinity challenges a developmental telos. The question arises, however, as to whether her challenge is any more or less serious than is theirs. Though the boys explicitly reject the manhood of their fathers by surfing, their rebellion from within masculinity can be taken as preparatory, an experiment in free living that serves as a valuable stage in their development into capable men. Francie's masculine urges place her outside any straightforward sequences of femininities that might lead her to someday resemble her mother. Nevertheless, the film *Gidget* periodically makes efforts to assimilate its protagonist's tomboyhood to a trajectory of housewifery. As the title song lets you know in the first few seconds, Gidget is

> a regular tomboy dressed for a prom,
> how cute can one girl be?
> Although she's not king-size, her finger is ring-size
> Gidget is the one for me.

This song ventriloquizes the voice of Moondoggie, the beach boy who will eventually be romantically united with Gidget. It also, overtly and ominously, presents our heroine's tomboyhood as a sexy prelude to her marriagability. Yet, at first, Gidget's urge to be one of the boys seems less cute than irritating to Moondoggie. "What are we running here, a baby farm?" he indignantly asks Kahuna. And in this, the other boys largely share Moondoggie's sentiment. "This beach is for surfers, not dames," says Stinkie, to which Francie replies "Oh, I'm no dame." When the boys coin her a surfing nickname, they come up with "Gidget," which they explain is short for "girl-midget," branding her as both different from and inferior to the rest. Nevertheless, by embracing her nickname, Gidget expresses both a power and pathos in her will to surf with which the film asks us to identify.

Gidget's affiliation with the gang climaxes in a scene in which the boys tell her that she must be initiated if she is to become one of them. They begin by taking her on a thrilling surfing ride. Then, far offshore, they circle around Gidget and take turns sadistically dunking her under the surface until at last, inhaling too much seawater, she passes out. Suddenly panicked, the boys bring Gidget ashore and lay her down in Kahuna's beach cabin. Despite this near death experience, when Gidget revives under the worried gaze of Moondoggie, she speaks as her first real thought, "I guess I'm a real member now." Sighing in apparent resignation, Moondoggie

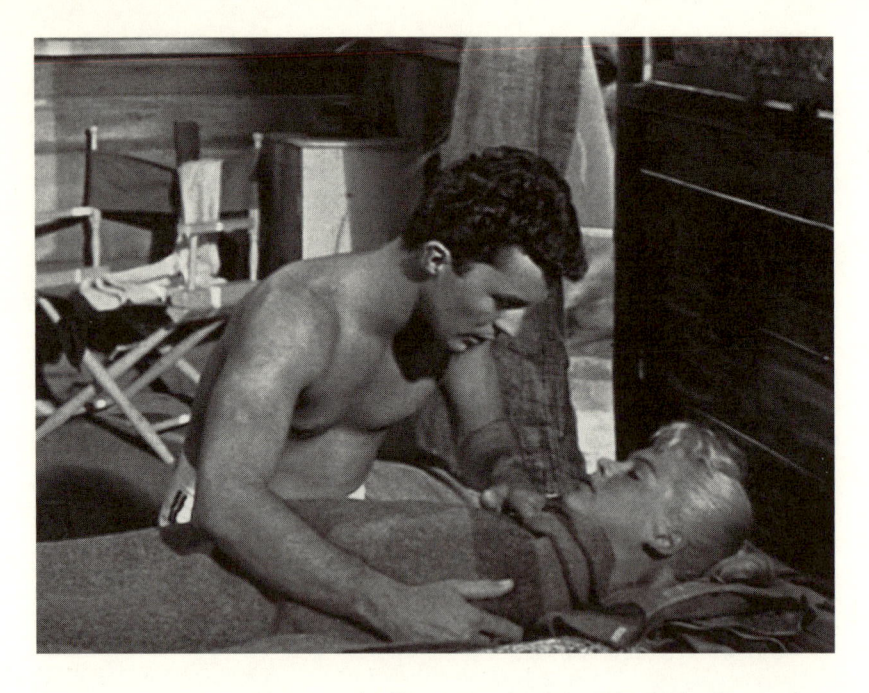

32. "I suppose you are, you crazy tomboy!" says Moondoggie in *Gidget* (Columbia, 1959).

responds, "I suppose you are, you crazy tomboy." This moment marks a crucial turning point in the plot of the film. Gidget has struggled, first against her girlfriends and parents, who expect her to behave like a girl, then against the boys, who resent that a young girl wants to join their surfing fellowship. Through tenacity and increasing skill as a surfer, Gidget has somehow succeeded; the "crazy tomboy" has doggedly made her way into the circle of boys.

Even as Moondoggie concedes her victory, however, he drops a record onto the phonograph, and as the familiar notes of the title song begin, he serenades her with the "Gidget" song. Suddenly, the cruel nickname that served to identify Francie as a junior member of the boy's club transforms itself as an object of Moondoggie's romantic admiration. This moment comes not only as a surreal and jarring break from the lowbrow but otherwise unbroken realist illusionism of the film. It also registers a serious break in the film's narrative direction. While Moondoggie playfully croons his attraction, Gidget finds herself unexpectedly overwhelmed with desire for Moondoggie. She asks him, when he finishes singing, to please take her home. But this request suddenly draws Moondoggie back into his own "reality." He suddenly remembers that he has a date with another girl and rushes off. Kahuna, who has sauntered in, asks Gidget how she is doing, and she replies that she has just been "hit by a sledgehammer," meaning of course that she has fallen in love. From here, the film shifts directions as Gidget stops working to become a fellow surfer and focuses instead on winning Moondoggie's affections by hook or by crook. In short, Gidget conducts the kind of scheming manhunt that she had once resisted.

In so doing, the film veers away from a very different conclusion in which Gidget might have become a girl surfer, an identity that could have steered her far and clear from suburban matronhood. To be sure, the film waves us off from this option as early as the title song, by presenting Gidget's tomboyhood as a kind of precocious presexual childhood. For her to remain a surfer would thus condemn her to a kind of eternal prepubescence, in the film's ideological terms as always too young for romance. However, the film also suggests a counterreading. Throughout *Gidget*, surfing itself is clearly presented as an erotic pursuit. Kahuna, for instance, questions the boys' commitment to surfing, saying, "For the others, it's a summer romance. For me it's a lifelong passion." In effect, Kahuna is permitted to romance surfing rather than a person as his long-term object choice, and while he too is condemned as immature, he is also granted opportunity to defend himself on both libidinal and philosophical terms. If Gidget verges on becoming the same kind of surfer fellow as Kahuna, then she also verges on cultivating a self-justifying bad-boyish identity that defends itself as living outside the limits and confines (both gendered and otherwise) of suburban living.

Despite the tendencies in the film to suggest that Gidget's sexualization will require her to give up tomboyhood and embrace femininity ("dressed for a prom"), at least two alternative sexual directions are also suggested in the film. The first of these is only hinted at, but it is present from the start. Of Francie's girlfriends whom we meet in the opening scene, one stands apart from all the others. Unlike Nan or Patti, this girl has short-cropped hair. In fact, she appears considerably more butch than Francie. Nor does she join the other girls on the beach to go manhunting. The actress, Sue George, had appeared just two years previously as a bad-girl outlaw in a western, *The Dalton Girls*. She had also appeared as a guest on a TV western, *The Californians*, in what appears to have been a tomboy episode titled "A Girl Named Sam." In *Gidget*, George's character goes by the initials "B.L.," and B.L. simply doesn't understand why the other girls would pressure Francie into a manhunt. "Oh, you're wearing Buck's fraternity pin, you've got social security," Nan retorts. Nan doesn't say that B.L. has a boyfriend,

33. Gidget rides the bed with B.L. in *Gidget* (Columbia, 1959).

only an alibi for one; perhaps it's her brother's fraternity pin, who knows? What we do know is that the only female friend Gidget retains through the summer is B.L., who appears in two later scenes with strong sexual undercurrents. In the first, Gidget practices surfing by having B.L. instruct her from a book while she rides a board on the bed, literalizing the eroticism of the sport to the point where Gidget ends with a big orgasmic crash on the mattress. In the next scene, B.L. keeps time for Gidget as she lifts freeweights in an absurd effort to grow her breasts. Both scenes have obvious comic intent, but the eroticized humor between the two tomboys also hints subtly at a lesboerotic solution to the question of how Gidget might cross the threshold into sexuality without disowning her tomboyhood.

The option taken up most explicitly in the film, however, concerns a romance with Kahuna himself. Unlike the boys, including Moondoggie, Kahuna never teases or dismisses Gidget. He remains her advocate in the surfing club, ostensibly because she is a "paying customer," but implicitly because she loves surfing, and that is all he thinks really matters. Gidget quizzes him repeatedly about his beatnik philosophy. Ironically, however, these exchanges lead not to Gidget's eventual bohemianization, but instead to Kahuna's domestication. Gidget's queries gradually bring Kahuna to confront the loneliness of his vagabond life and, by the film's conclusion, he has accepted a regular job as an airline pilot. "Okay, I can't kid anybody," he tells Francie. "You start a guy like me thinking, it's fatal." Transformed by Gidget from a bum into an aviator, Kahuna—now returned to his original name, Burt—even succumbs to the suburban gender philosophy espoused by Francie's mom. Echoing her earlier assertion to Gidget that "a real woman brings out the best in a man," Kahuna's last line of the film directs Jeffrey/Moondoggie to respect Gidget's feminine qualities: "Remember," he says, "she might be pint-sized, but she's quite a woman."

But Burt's story almost goes otherwise. In her effort to win Moondoggie's affection, Gidget employs jealousy, claiming that she's fallen in love with Kahuna. At first this assertion seems a mere scheme. But, late in the film, Gidget actually absconds with Kahuna from the end-of-season luau, joining him at a beach shack where she actively tries to seduce him. At this point, intentionality becomes quite blurry. Could Gidget be going this far just to make Moondoggie jealous? Or is she trying to lose her virginity, a goal she expresses in the second half of the film? Or is she genuinely infatuated with the chief surfer? Certainly, Kahuna makes his own feelings clear, pulling back at the last possible moment to say, "It's time to stop before I forget this is just a game." Kahuna's response suggests his desperate hope that Gidget could cure his loneliness as a wandering surf bum, with only a pet parrot for companionship on his trips. Moondoggie, with his reckless plans to join Kahuna after the summer, promises human company. The two men thus display a risky reciprocal homosocial desire, modeling a father-son relationship in which Kahuna would become Moondoggie's bohemian substitute daddy. Yet Kahuna distrusts Moondoggie's commitment to a shared life, repeatedly hinting at his expectation that Moondoggie is yet another "summer romantic" who will back out. Gidget and Kahuna, however, by virtue of the overt possibility of a sexual relationship, are another matter. In brushing so close to romance, Gidget and Kahuna anticipate a shared bohemian surfing life in which they might get it both ways. Gidget might find sex and romance without resigning herself to conventional femininity. Likewise, Kahuna might cure his loneliness without abandoning his life as a surfer.

In calling their near affair a "game," Kahuna implies that their age difference precludes any romantic possibility. Unlike Moondoggie, who is just a few years older than Gidget, Kahuna raises the specter of an eroticized daughterly-fatherly relationship. Despite their mutual sexual attraction, Kahuna ultimately distrusts the possibility that Gidget offers much as he does the promise of Moondoggie's companionship. Both Moondoggie and Gidget are too young, exploring surfing perhaps as a transitional moment in their lives rather than as a lifelong love affair in which they would stave off adulthood indefinitely to enjoy a youthful lifestyle.

The cross-generational relationship that Kahuna offers to both Gidget and Moondoggie plays explicitly off of each of the youth's oedipal relationships at home, expressing in the process the respective rebellious constitution of the tomboy and bad boy. Moondoggie's defiance of his father's tedious organizational manhood echoes not only Goodman's notion of "growing absurd," but also the standard father-son conflicts that we saw at work in *Rebel without a Cause* and *King Creole*. Gidget's dilemma at home encapsulates the tomboy's closely related struggle. At no point does Gidget enter into conflict with her mother, who instead continually offers solace and advice. At the same time, however, Mrs. Lawrence continually encourages the budding of Gidget's femininity. She accepts that her daughter might be entering a phase in which she takes an interest in surfing but does not yet take a sexual interest in boys. And later, when Gidget falls in love with Moondoggie, she advises Gidget not to feel herself a failure if her love is not immediately realized. Gidget's father, on the other hand, continuously intrudes into her personal affairs, expressing his suspicion that she might be consorting with the wrong sort of boys. Instead, Mr. Lawrence keeps proposing, to Gidget's endless irritation, that she date the son of his distinguished friend. In his desperate attempt to unite Gidget with a boy who resembles himself, Mr. Lawrence reveals a desire to control, perhaps even vicariously enjoy, the sexuality of his "little girl." The more involved Gidget becomes with the surfers, the more upset the blustering Mr. Lawrence grows, until the conflict climaxes on the evening of the gang's annual luau, when Gidget shamefully yet defiantly confesses that she has bought admission to the year-end surf party by promising to supply the boys with food. Mr. Lawrence is infuriated, but his bellows cause him to slip and fall onto the floor as Gidget walks off to her party in a huff. The rebellious Gidget thus finds her ire directed at her father, the parent who keeps insisting that Gidget behave like a "good girl": someone who will marry a domesticated man like himself.

Seen against these scenes of ruffled home life, the near romance with the adult Kahuna clarifies what sort of father Gidget implicitly wishes she could romance. Late on the night that Gidget leaves for the luau, Gidget's parents anxiously drive over to it, only to discover that Gidget has already left with Kahuna for a "private party." Terrified that their daughter is in

34. Facing off with Dad in *Gidget* (Columbia, 1959).

35. Gidget has a "private party" with Kahuna in *Gidget* (Columbia, 1959).

some sort of physical or sexual danger, they contact the police and track her down. Kahuna comes close to seducing Gidget in this climactic scene of their near relationship. But at the moment of truth, Kahuna turns out to have decided against the underaged Gidget. For all the hoopla with the police, nothing actually happens. Having now failed both as a tomboy and as a bad girl, not really a surfer yet still a virgin, Gidget departs with her parents, crushed by her rejection.

With summer nearly over, the defeated Gidget finally resigns herself to her father's dictate that she try a date with his friend's son, Jeffrey. And who should Jeffrey turn out to be but Moondoggie himself, a bad boy according to his summer nickname, but a good boy when under the academic-year sign of his real name. *Gidget* concludes with the proverbial happy ending, allowing its protagonist to retain the veneer of her tomboy desire but at no social cost. She ends up with a boy acceptable to her father, but who will call her Gidget, not Francie, and who understands her desire to surf. Nor need she pay the price of leaving her family for good to live as Kahuna's companion. As if to close off the option Kahuna represented for both Gidget and Moondoggie, it is at this very end of the film that they find him preparing to become an airline pilot, having himself relinquished bohemian surfdom as an immature and lonely way of life. *Gidget* shuts down its protagonist's option of female masculinity in fairly short order, allowing her to keep her nickname and the flavor of her beach passions but concluding her refusal of a conventional feminine life course. Nevertheless the film allows for the expression of female dissatisfaction with being paired off as a good girl with a good boy in order to produce a domesticated suburban family. And in so doing, it holds out the opportunity to imagine a female masculine alternative to womanhood for which the figure of youth, and more specifically of a tomboy, becomes a potent metaphor.

Toughing It Out as a Tomboy

Gidget's ideological recuperations in the second half of the narrative make a great deal of sense, given the generic constraints placed upon a mainstream Hollywood film. More daring in many ways was the pulp genre of crime fiction. In the late forties and fifties, a cycle of hard-boiled novels about juvenile delinquents was published, riding the coattails of the book industry's paperback revolution. One of the most popular novelists to write in this tradition, Hal Ellson, in 1950 published *Tomboy*, a novel so popu-

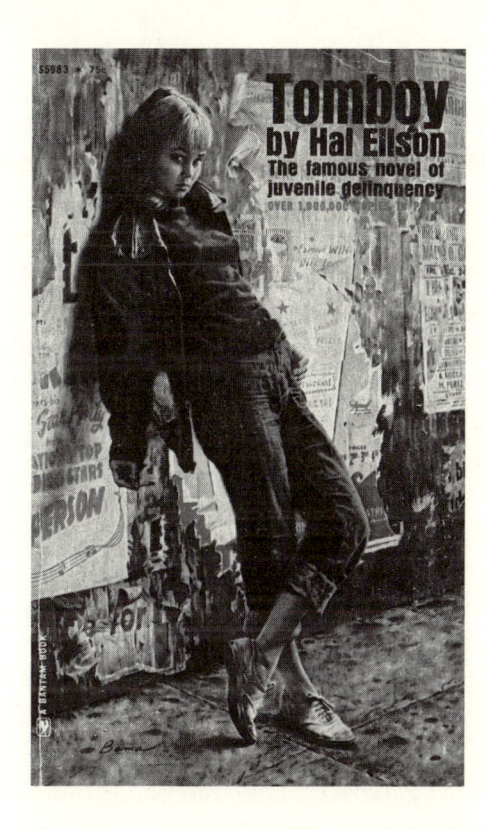

36. Cover design for a paperback edition of Hal Ellson's *Tomboy* (1950).

lar that by 1969, the year of its fifteenth edition, a million copies had been printed.

In stark contrast to the suburban backdrop to *Gidget*'s romantic comedy, the naturalistic street thrills of *Tomboy* are set in the tenements of upper Manhattan, where the Harps, a gang of local Irish boys, engage in petty theft while vying with nearby rivals. Contemptuous of adults in their impoverished neighborhood, who mouth a middle-class-derived work-and-marriage ethic even while they actually live out the humiliations of unemployment, alcoholism, and marital violence, the Harps constitute an alternative social network that guarantees its members income, family ties, and a sexual outlet. The gang is sharply divided along a sex-gender axis in which boys plan and carry out the capers and rumbles, while girls serve as loyal debs who provide the boys with company and sex. The girls are trafficked between the boys, who fight to possess them, staking their claim by scratching their initials onto their steady's arm.

Tomboy, the nickname of the novel's eponymous protagonist, occupies a unique position in the world of the Harps as the only girl who is not a deb but a gang member, indeed the one who plans the capers. Tomboy, as she confesses to her loyal friend Mick, "wishes she were a boy," which Mick understands because "it's kind of lousy to be a girl, I guess. A boy can do everything. Girls can hardly do anything" (24). Tomboy, of course, is the exception, the one girl who can "do anything like a boy" and be accepted as such. Pondering the other girls, who dream and talk only of boys, Tomboy (like Gidget) wonders, "Why am I different?" And as the narrator tells us, "in a way, she knew, knowing almost without thinking about it, that it was wrong to give herself as the other [girls] did, for that only meant to be talked about and to be passed on to another and another boy. This always happened, and she knew it could happen to her too, if she allowed it, if she gave in even once." (24).

Tomboy maintains her female masculinity, in short, because it provides her with agency and allows her to own herself and her self-respect. Yet this precarious path to bad-boy sovereignty is easily lost to the danger of feminization. The novel opens with Lucky, a strong and handsome boy whom Tomboy admires, goading her into a wrestling match during which he makes a grab at her breasts. Lucky, as it happens, is one of the least sexually abusive boys in the gang, the only one who objects in a later movie house scene to the way that the Alan Ladd character beats his women. Most of the other boys are considerably more aggressive with the girls. "They're too wise," Tomboy remarks in explaining why she doesn't like boys: "As soon as you get to be friends, they want to get too friendly" (25). Each pass that a boy makes at her places her masculinity at risk yet again. Tomboy defends herself by lathering on the boyish toughness, sternly threatening whoever comes on to her. Yet she must walk a tightrope with her response, for if she expresses too much hostility, Tomboy risks creating a permanent rift between herself and her fellow Harp. Moreover, as the novel soon reveals, Tomboy must keep at bay not only the desires of the other boys but her own. As the novel progresses, Tomboy gradually becomes aware of her attraction to Lucky, who is her closest buddy among the gang members. Yet giving in to these feelings, in Tomboy's estimation, would exact the same steep cost as responding to any of the other Harps' desire for her: the gang would surely strip her of her boy status, downgrading her to a deb.

Tomboy sidesteps the riskiness of sex for her tomboyhood by maintaining a Boston marriage with Mick, the one boy too weak and cowardly to threaten her sexually. Timid and ineffectual as a gang member, Mick is barely tolerated by the other Harps, who cannot fathom what Tomboy sees in him. At times Tomboy genuinely seems to care for Mick, defending him against his detractors and appreciating the reflective conversations she can hold only with him. Mick even has permission to call Tomboy by her proper name, Kerry, when they are alone. Yet, as Tomboy observes early on, "there was something girlish about him which was vaguely distasteful to her." As the novel indicates repeatedly, Tomboy despises girls for their submissive relation to the boys, a relation she associates with a lack of confidence and courage to cultivate their abilities. Mick's anxious ineffectuality thus strikes Tomboy as contemptuously effeminate. By contrast, Tomboy finds only pleasure in witnessing the comparatively taciturn Lucky's daring and self-reliance.

Ellson's novel is organized episodically around the gang's capers as well as its battles, whether internally between its members or with neighboring black and Puerto Rican gangs. Midway through the novel, Lucky inadvertently finds himself fighting another Harp who resents his own girlfriend Mary's infatuation with Lucky. When Lucky triumphs he also by default wins the right to her. Although Mary initiates Lucky into sexual activity, he quickly loses interest in her. Not realizing this, Tomboy grows jealous of their relationship. Her jealousy, however, hardly compares to that of Mary, who sees clearly that she cannot compete with Tomboy for Lucky's affections. Lucky and Tomboy are quite simply best friends, always together, whether carrying out capers or smoking cigarettes on the rooftop. They have an intimacy as boy friends that a mere girl like Mary simply cannot touch.

Late in the novel, Mick is run over in a freak auto accident. Her sexual cover blown, Tomboy finds the erotic tension with Lucky growing. Shortly thereafter, in the Harp clubhouse, Mary publicly accuses Tomboy of wanting her boyfriend. For the first time in the novel, Tomboy openly acknowledges her sexual interest with a terse "So what?" The girls fight and Tomboy quickly wins. In a fantastic mirror image of Lucky's earlier fight, Tomboy's victory wins her a lover. An anonymous voice calls out, "Hey, Lucky, it looks like you got a new chick on your hands now." This scene bears the clear weight of a fantasy structured from the psychic perspective of Tomboy, for at no point would the reader be led to believe that the world of this fiction would allow girls to fight over their claims on boys. The scene rather expresses a wish fulfillment in which Tomboy's skill at fighting could win her a boy lover just as the boys may win a girl.

Unlike *Gidget*, Ellson's novel never alludes to any lesboerotic interest. The other Harps clearly consider Tomboy queer; "She don't like to be manhandled.... You know what I mean," explains Happy to one of the girls, who replies by asking, "She doesn't like boys?" But the only interest Tomboy shows in other girls is sadistic and angry in nature, as seen in an earlier initiation scene far more brutal than *Gidget*'s where the Harps instruct Mary and one other prospective deb to strip off their clothes: "Everyone laughed but Tomboy, who stared at both girls with a sudden unreasoning hate in her eyes. She moved in, lifting her hand that held the belt and brought it down. The others followed her, and it was the girls who struck with greater force, but Tomboy struck savagely and was the last to stop and then only when Lucky grabbed her arm" (38). This scene, which comes well before Mary's involvement with Lucky, offers no explanation for Tomboy's brutality other than her basic contempt for feminine subjection and her notion of masculine pride. "Listen to them," says Tomboy, "momma's little babies," to which Mary responds by saying, "Yeah, I'd like to see you take it! ... You wouldn't laugh." Tomboy answers simply, "I don't have to take it.... I hand it out" (38). Beyond this pleasure in punishing femininity, Tomboy shows no interest in the other girls. Instead, as already noted, the novel indulges the romantic possibility of bringing Tomboy and Lucky together as a two-butch, heterosexual, but nonheteronormative couple. Together, as the narrator explains, the two establish "an implicit and stronger bond, and not only they but all the Harps recognized it. Tomboy was Lucky's steady now, yet not in the same sense that each of the other debs belonged to a boy. Acting with each other as they had before, Tomboy held him off with her manner, not letting him touch her, but this didn't seem to bother him" (133–134).

The relationship that Tomboy and Lucky forge differs noticeably from the one I discussed earlier between Moondoggie and Gidget, where the tomboy must girl herself in order to enter heterosexuality. In Ellson's novel, Tomboy never relinquishes her masculine status to become Kerry in the final pages. What happens instead has a twofold aspect. On the one hand, Tomboy and Lucky's bond takes the overt form of a boy-boy love affair: a tomboy and a bad boy. Tomboy's passion for Lucky eroticizes his masculine capability and physique, which she explicitly compares to her own (24). Lucky, meanwhile, finds Tomboy's more slender, effeminate build attractive, while also romancing her sharp wits, her all-around skills as a Harp boy, and most important perhaps, the intimate friendship they share only because she moves like him in masculine space. In the world of the Harps, Tomboy and Lucky become each other's erotic brother at arms. In this context, Tomboy's being a girl implies only one thing: their nominally heterosexual pairing spares them a homophobic reaction by the other Harps.

In positing this homoeroticism, however, it is important not to lose sight of the way in which Tomboy's femaleness determines the signification of their relationship. From the viewpoint of sexuality, the novel would surely challenge heteronormativity more explicitly were Tomboy really a boy and Ellson's novel addressing the challenge of a gay affair to the juvenile delinquent world of upper Manhattan. From the viewpoint of gender, however, Tomboy's *female* masculinity becomes the key difference. Tomboy and Lucky's mutually masculine romance takes a homosexual form precisely because of the rigidity and brutal inequality of the gender norms that dictate the shape of both heterosexuality and heterosociality among the Harps. Another necessary way to read Lucky and Tomboy's relationship, then, is as the emergence, in a manner that *Gidget* can only hint at, of a *sexual* Tomboy, the hollowing out of a new gendered space in which a girl can occupy a masculine rebel position without forgoing or deferring sexual agency.

As in *Gidget*, tomboyhood in Ellson's novel finds its narrative motivation through a conflictual relationship between daughter and father. Tomboy lives at home with her alcoholic father and his shrewish new lover, Molly, who makes a point of abusing him for drinking instead of finding a job. Like Jim Stark in *Rebel*, Tomboy responds to the scene of her father's humiliation by asking, "Why doesn't he smack her around a bit? Why doesn't he kick her out of the house?" It is Tomboy's anger at this scenario that drives her away from conventional heterosexuality. When she turns away from this sight, spotting a crayoned heart on the wall with the words "RAYMOND LOVES JANICE," Tomboy proceeds to erase the conjoining word. But it then occurs to her that this is not enough, since "with the two names together the meaning was still clear. For it meant love wherever a girl's name was joined with a boy's, in all the dark hallways of the city, in all the littered streets and on the high shadowed walls. For a moment she hesitated, then slowly, methodically, she moved the pencil back and forth till she blocked out the names completely and they were no more" (31).

Later, after another painful scene between her father and Molly, she tells Mick, "They were fighting in my house as usual. I wonder why people get married? I'll never get married." When Mick replies, "Everybody gets married," Tomboy emphatically responds, "Maybe every one does, but I won't, and I mean it" (53). Tomboy's union with Lucky offers the principal alternative to conventional marriage, a form she rejects because, in matching together a masculine and feminine partner, it results either in shameful abuse of the feminine partner (like the debs) or in the equally humiliating henpecking of the masculine partner (like Tomboy's father). Against such an outcome, Tomboy and Lucky's masculine cameraderie seems utopian as a relationship among sovereigns who each maintain her or his identity.

It is worth noting that Ellson's novel explicitly rejects bad girlhood as another option (alternative to tomboyhood) in the search for female autonomy. The novel establishes this through one of the debs, Lizzie, who represents the sexual precocity of the bad girl in *Tomboy*. Like Tomboy, Lizzie thinks that the boys are "all alike," but, in a conversation with Mary, Lizzie reveals that, rather than evading sex by boying herself (as Tomboy does), she deals with boys by playing the girl to the hilt: "Anyway it's fun.... I like doing it and I'm not afraid of saying so. I like doing it with lots of boys.... They're no better than we are. We can have our fun too" (123). Lizzie's response, however, comes at a moment when its efficacy seems highly questionable; only a short time earlier, at a party thrown by a rival gang to which all the debs had been sent to gather information, Lizzie's excessive flirtatiousness had encouraged four boys to gang-rape her. As we learned in the case of Silver's sister in *Girls Town*, the more sexual a girl makes herself, the greater her risk. Bad girlhood is even further stigmatized toward the end of the novel when Tomboy learns, in a stinging confrontation with her father's girlfriend, Molly, that her mother is not, as she thought, long dead. Instead, it turns out that her mother is a prostitute who, in leaving her father years ago, drove him to the bottle. Sexualized femininity is here strongly linked to everything that Tomboy fears and despises; it is blamed not only for breaking up her family but also for her father's emasculated dissipation. Tomboy's resistance to sex with boys and her hatred for sexual girls, which through the body of the novel has seemed inexplicable, at last receives a final justification in the traumatic history of her family.

Tomboy responds to this discovery in a complex manner. First, she runs away from home, but then, encountering Lucky, she joins him to hang out in their usual haunt on the roof of the club house. Tomboy at last succumbs to Lucky's advances, allowing him to make love to her. Yet, even now, she is described as only "half-willing, wanting to fight him and wanting to give in. And even when she gave in it was like that, for part of herself protested, telling her that she was doing wrong" (143).

It is wrong, not because of a blanket condemnation of premarital sex but rather because maintaining her autonomy requires Tomboy to avoid being girled by any man, which she cannot do without withholding sex. This half-willingness expresses a kind of compromise between Tomboy's desire to be paired intimately and erotically with Lucky, but also her resistance to becoming his deb, and thereby losing precisely what she values in her relationship to him. It is Tomboy's horror at the failure of her parents' marriage that spurs her decision to run away, and the escape she imagines expresses, in the only such moment in the book, an escape from the bleak despair of the city itself toward a pastoral suburban vision: "You know, I'd like to live in the country, Lucky, in a little house only one story high with not even a doorstep to climb" (142).

The city that Tomboy wishes to escape, throughout the novel, takes a strongly racial cast. The gangs that the Harps fight are black and Puerto Rican, and Harps are repeatedly described as under siege even in the squalor and misery of their tenement neighborhood, which "in spite of its desolation, knew the threatening pressure and growing pains of another on its border where a darker people lived and brawled yearning to break down the walls of its ghetto" (71).

Tomboy's yearning to escape thus recapitulates, in imaginative form, an impetus behind the postwar white flight from the cities into suburbs. Yet Tomboy and Lucky hardly strike one as a budding domestic couple who are hungry to settle down into the social and gender norms of the suburban ideal. Instead, one might well think of them at one and the same time as representing those white people who hope to save themselves from the rising tide of color in the city streets but also as a youthful couple who embody what in an earlier chapter I called the suburban counterimaginary.[8] Like Danny Fisher in *King Creole*, should they ever make their way into suburbia, they will bring with them a toughness of character and a commitment to their own autonomy and resourcefulness that suburban America deeply needs. In the closing scenes of the novel, Tomboy gathers money for their escape by planning a final heist in which she and the boys will steal a stash of money from Lizzie's aunt while Lizzie is babysitting for her. This theft, strikingly at the expense of the promiscuous bad girl who resembles Tomboy's mother, succeeds, but the police, in hot pursuit, nearly catch up with them. The novel closes with Lucky and Tomboy hopping a train together, escaping the city at last, but to a destination unknown.

Tomboy, like *Gidget*, demonstrates the narrative complications associated with a girl character who occupies the rebel masculinity of fifties youth narratives. Most obviously, both protagonists struggle for entrance as boys into the homosocial male community of a bad boy gang. Gidget barely receives admission to the rank of boy at all. Tomboy mostly succeeds. Yet both face a second round of trouble concerning their impossible place in the sexual order of their gangs. Getting involved with a boy jeopardizes their masculine status. Getting involved with a girl seems ruled out, primarily because femininity functions in both texts as that which is undesirable (although *Gidget* at least hints at the possibility of a lesboerotic bond).

Nevertheless, both *Gidget*'s unrealized narrative possibilities (with B.L. or Kahuna) and *Tomboy*'s actual conclusion indicate powerful utopian longings for compatibility between sexual passion and rebellious tomboy masculinity. While postwar youth rebellions expressed a general protopolitical longing for alternative futures to suburban maturity, the tomboy figure layered on a further longing for specific transformations of its attendant female gender and sexual norms. In addition to imagining space for girls as the heralds of masculine rebellion, tomboy narratives also instilled utopian fantasies about egalitarian heterosociality, deeper bonds between girls and boys that allowed for friendships of the sort usually reserved for homosocial intimacy. Moreover, they also hinted at lesboerotic and homoerotic sexualities as options that could begin to break down the gender norms that thwarted girls from finding agential positions as youth rebels.

These utopian longings also extracted serious ideological costs from the emancipatory possibilities of the rebel narrative. In large measure, they worked by elevating the "different" desires of the masculine girl and deriding feminine girls by contrast as conventional, masochistic, or complicit. The masculinity these narratives offered girls, in short, relied upon the all-too-ubiquitous misogyny of the generic fifties rebel narrative. Finally, in very different ways, both texts also mobilize racial desires that complicate the gender and sexual valence of the narrative. *Gidget* clearly envisions an escape from whiteness that draws upon a colonial myth of Hawaii as tropical paradise, and hence an outside to the world of work, marriage, and responsibility. *Tomboy*, in its portrayal of the conflicts between upper Manhattan's various gangs, expresses the degradation of the neighborhood through the lens of a beleaguered white working class hemmed in by black and brown people. The tomboy, then, like the bad boy, plays out her alternative status vis-à-vis suburban gender norms by drawing upon qualities of masculinity that are ideologically associated with a nonwhite urban world even when, as in *Tomboy*, people of color are presented as threats to the white heroine rather than as outlaw heroes in their own right.

Coupling Up

At first glance, the rebellious girls who appear in these various texts would not seem to have much in common. Silver is a poor girl who uses her sex to defy class injustice; Sarah Jane is a black girl who passes in order to obtain the sexual and social privileges of bohemian white femininity. Gidget is a white suburban girl who becomes a surfer in order to free her from romantic female adolescence. And, finally, Tomboy acts as a juvenile delinquent in order to avoid both the despair of her neighborhood's poverty and the sexual servitude of the other girls in her gang. Some of these girls are middle-class, others are not; most are white, but at least one is not; some of them embrace sexual femininity as their means of defiance, while others flee sexual femininity in favor of female masculinity. Finally, the two bad girls (Silver and Sarah Jane) express their rebelliousness in relation to mother figures, while the tomboys are motivated by their difficulties with their fathers. However, for all these striking differences, one thing holds all of these girls together: their rebellious acts find narrative expression in relationship to those of boys. Silver acts as a bad girl by playing sexually with untrustworthy bad boys such as Chip and Fred, eventually joining forces with a former bad boy, Jimmy Farlow. Sarah Jane seeks a companionate rebellion with a rebel boy, like Frankie, who at least implicitly resembles her lost father. Gidget turns away from her father by seeking to share in the life pursued by surfer boys such as Moondoggie and rebellious young men such as Kahuna. Finally, Tomboy responds to her father's inadequacy by becoming a Harp boy herself, and eventually partnering herself with Lucky, the bravest bad boy of the book. In short, bad girl or tomboy, poor or middle-class, white or black, the rebellious girl of these fifties texts must stake out her adversarial relation to her parent culture by affiliating it with a preexisting adversarial relation already held by one or more boys.

In this broad sense, it may be said that postwar girlhood obtained rebelliousness by establishing a romantic bond with the bad boy as companionate opponents of suburban domesticity. All of the girl characters under discussion here, in one way or another, become linked to a suburban counterimaginary through their romantic relations with a boy whose masculinity exceeds and challenges domesticated manhood. Silver acts out her hostility toward domestic sentimentality by flaunting her sex to attract bad boys for thoroughly unsentimental, fun encounters. Sarah Jane, more romantically, seeks a bohemian boy companion with whom she can escape the domestic thralldom of both suburban women and black servants. Gidget flees both her suburban family life and her heteronormative friends to share the comradery of the surf world. And Tomboy, finally, rejects the failure of her family's domestic life by turning to the delinquent gang life of the Harps. In each case, a bad boy of some sort becomes the rebellious girl's consort. In the case of Silver and Gidget, it is through her connection to the boy (Jimmy and Moondoggie) that the girl is domesticated in time for a happy ending. In *Tomboy*, the couple actually maintains their bond as delinquent partners right through the end of the narrative. Finally, in the tragic story of Sarah Jane, the right boy never turns up. Frankie's rejection leaves Sarah Jane empty and lonely in her rebelliousness, without the romantic companionship she craves to replace the maternal bond she deliberately rejects. In some of these narratives, then, the rebellious girl is won back to domesticity. In the more open, ideologically risky narratives, such reintegration may seem shaky, or even fail altogether. What draws these narratives together, however, is the shared implication that girls need to pass through a wild moment, a phase of intelligible and justifiable rebelliousness, before they can be expected to embrace, in their own way, the domestic values associated with suburban womanhood. During that phase, the bad girl may become a bad boy's glamorously erotic lover, or she may become his equally masculine comrade, but in either case she demonstrates her fundamental difference from the bad boy's mother, the one who presumably domesticated the bad boy's literal or figurative father. In this way, we can interpret both the bad girl and the tomboy as a possible Bonnie to the bad boy's Clyde. Partnered with him, both rebel girl types played to the idealized vision of a rebellious generation whose desire was to live differently from their parents.

The Vicissitudes of Girl Power

This overarching narrative of girls in revolt possessed both limitations and strengths. To be sure, it established female youth rebellion as a supplement to male rebellion rather than as a metanarrative in its own right. To that extent, most of the rebellious girls of the fifties were not definitively feminist figures, queer or otherwise. Yet they could rightly be called protofeminist characters who openly expressed female resistance to suburban gender norms, sexual hypocrisy, white supremacy, or class injustice. A path can thus be clearly traced from the fifties girl rebel to the radical politics of the lesbian and women's liberation movement.

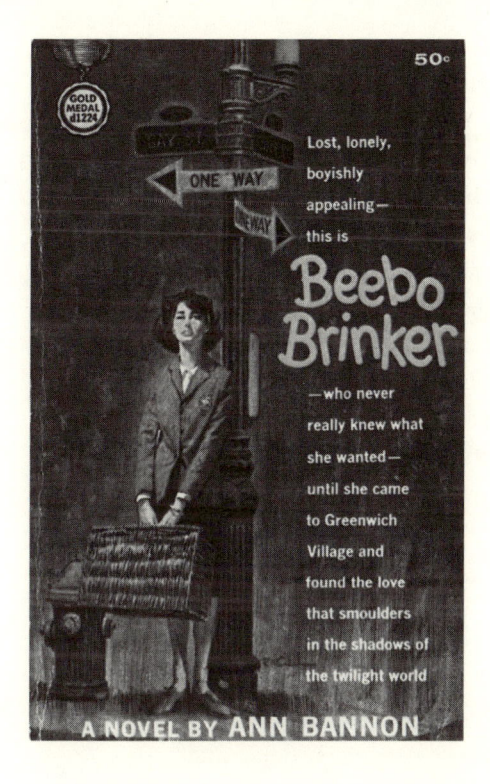

37. Original cover design for Ann Bannon's *Beebo Brinker* (1962).

In searching for the earliest postwar fictions of lesbian identity, queer literary historians have often attended to the work of Ann Bannon, author of pulp paperback novels in the late 1950s and 1960s that bespoke the trials and struggles of young women coming out as lesbians. Read in the context of this book, Bannon's novels exhibit a very familiar plot: the young rebel realizes that to assert a sovereign sense of herself she must refuse to "conform" to a sexually standardized world. Bannon clearly drew on the rebel figure's authority in a fashion very much akin to the literature of the beats. Her lesbian outlaws, moreover, drew upon both of the rebel girl types we have been discussing. Beebo Brinker, her most famous character, is a tough, heavy-drinking butch very much in the bad-boy mold, someone who (as we learn in the eponymous novel of 1961) lived her adolescence as a rebellious tomboy.

Bannon's first novel, *Odd Girl Out* of 1959, meanwhile, tells the story of two college girls, Beth and Laura, the former a glamorous rebellious type, and the latter a more introverted, seemingly conformist girl. As Beth falls in love with Laura, she takes increasing social risks, discovering in the process her lesbian identity. By the end of that novel, Laura has come to recognize that it is *she* (not the ultimately heterosexual Beth) who is fated always to be an "odd girl," a (homo)sexualized bad girl who bucks the norms of heteronormative domesticity. As in so many oedipalized rebel narratives of the era, we also learn that it is Laura's father, with his dictatorial demands on her academic and romantic life, who has driven her into a sexual revolt. Bannon's work establishes a genealogical link between the bad girls and tomboys of early postwar culture and the radicalization of gender and sexual identity propounded by the women's liberation movement. It is not for nothing that feminist historian Alice Echols chooses to title her study of the early women's movement *Daring to Be Bad*. But here we have left the "fifties" behind, and begun to describe the rise of identity discourse as a precondition for the radical politics of liberation in the sixties.

CONCLUSION

THE RISE AND FALL OF IDENTITY

I thought you were the most serious little thing I had ever seen—you said: (He imitates her [Beneatha]) "Mr. Asagai—I want very much to talk with you. About Africa. You see, Mr. Asagai, I am looking for my *identity*!"
—Lorraine Hansberry, *A Raisin in the Sun*

In a society degenerating into a form of totalitarianism . . . our concern for black power addresses . . . the necessity to reclaim our history and our identity from the cultural terrorism and depradation of self-justifying white guilt. To do this we shall have to struggle for the right to create our own terms through which to define ourselves and our relationship to the society, and to have these terms recognized. This is the first necessity of a free people.
—Stokely Carmichael, "Toward Black Liberation"

The yellow power movement has been motivated largely by the problem of *self-identity* in Asian Americans. The psychological focus of this movement is vital, for Asian Americans suffer the critical mental crises of having "integrated" into American society. . . . Now they are beginning to realize that this nation is a "White democracy" and that yellow people have a *mistaken identity*.
—Amy Uyematsu, "The Emergence of Yellow Power"

Pluralism is *radical* only to the extent that each term of this plurality of identities finds within itself the principle of its own validity, without this having to be sought in a transcendent or underlying positive ground for the hierarchy of meaning of them all and the source and guarantee

of their legitimacy. And this radical pluralism is democratic to the extent that the autoconstitutivity of each one of its terms is the result of displacements of the egalitarian imaginary.
—Ernesto Laclau and Chantal Mouffe, *Hegemony and Socialist Strategy*

Perhaps [gender] trouble need not carry such a negative valence. To make trouble was, within the reigning discourse of my childhood, something one should never do precisely because that would get one in trouble. The rebellion and its reprimand seemed caught up in the same terms. . . . Hence, I concluded that trouble is inevitable and the task, how best to make it, what best way to be in it.
—Judith Butler, *Gender Trouble*

In these five passages, one can chart the rise and fall of identity politics in the United States. Lorraine Hansberry's 1959 play marks a transition from the identity concept of the fifties toward the terrain of identity politics as we have come to know it. By the late sixties, in this pair of black and Asian American movement manifestos, identity has already become the occasion for full-blown radicalisms. Over the next ten years, the liberationist agendas of these radicalisms would moderate considerably, yet they would preserve their underlying metanarrative of identity as a struggle for psychopolitical emergence. What did change in this narrative during late seventies and eighties, however, was the *singularity* of its protagonist, who became pluralized as identity discourse increasingly staged a coalitional drama of "multiculturalism."

This multicultural turn in identity discourse must be understood in the determining context of Fordism's crisis in the seventies, for it was Fordism that had rendered intelligible the logic of the unitary rebel pitted against a mass society. As openly pluralist strategies of post-Fordist accumulation began to segment the cultural landscape, conformity's binary opponent—the rebel—gave way to Laclau and Mouffe's "radical plurality" of identities (1985), each mutually articulated with the others by a democratic vision that asserted a continuing radical project vis-à-vis the American social order. Despite Fordism's collapse, the continuation of the Cold War preserved democratic peoplehood as a viable first world political imaginary that identity struggles might still figure and deploy.

As the Cold War ended in the early nineties, however, the very basis of identity politics began to erode. Texts such as Judith Butler's *Gender Trouble* (1990) began to express a theoretical desire that is still with us: to abandon identity altogether as a ground for the politics of gender, race, and sexuality. Yet this desire to move past the politics of identity has remained predominantly theoretical and deeply ambivalent, often tacitly reinscribing identity even as it appears to repudiate it. This ambivalence, I submit, stems from the failure to establish a clear successor to identity with which to ground the post–Cold War politics of race, gender, and sexuality. Feminist, antiracist, and queer thinker-activists have therefore found it risky and difficult to forego identity politics even while sensing that the new global conditions require it. Let us trace the history that ends in this predicament more slowly.

In 1959, Lorraine Hansberry's play *A Raisin in the Sun* was performed for the first time at the Ethel Barrymore Theatre in New York City. Perhaps more than any other text of the fifties, *Raisin* captures the political direction in which the discourse of identity would move in the following decade. On the one hand, Hansberry's play is well remembered as the story of a black family, the Youngers, seeking to leave their cramped, worn-out apartment on the South Side of Chicago for an affordable home in a white "suburban" neighborhood, even as the local homeowners' association aims to prevent them. Hansberry's play was widely celebrated for dramatizing the new racism of postwar Fordist geography, and specifically for demanding that the suburbs be "integrated" so as to make room for a long history of black aspirations (the "dream deferred" of the play's title).

Yet *Raisin*'s apparent call for the integration of blacks into the promise of the suburbs in no way constituted a call for cultural "assimilation." On the contrary, the play is avowedly antiassimilationist in its rhetoric, making it clear by the final act that the Youngers embody a courageous challenge to the ideological racism of the white suburban imaginary, that their move augurs something akin to the impact of rock 'n' roll: the interjection of an oppositional "dream" or imagination into Fordist culture. It is not the Youngers who should change by moving to the suburbs; rather, the suburbs will need to change in order to accommodate their hopes. This point is brought home most strongly in Walter Younger's heroic transformation from a black man willing to bow and scrape for white approval, a figure of resentful racial obedience, into a paragon of black pride who defies the white homeowners association.

Black pride enters the play, however, not with the closing look toward the suburbs, but much earlier, in another glance that Walter's sister Beneatha trains upon African decolonization as figured by the Nigerian college student, Joseph Asagai. Throughout the play Asagai conveys an unwavering

THE RISE AND FALL OF IDENTITY 319

spirit of hope for the building of a prosperous and independent Nigerian homeland, reflecting thereby the Younger family's own dream of self-sufficiency that they must assert anew with each bout of disillusionment and despair. At the most general of levels, Asagai inspires the Youngers to believe in what black people might achieve by resisting white acts of racial oppression, whether in the form of red-lining in Chicago or colonialism in Africa.

Yet Asagai's ability to inspire derives not from some essentially black spirit that he shares with the Youngers but instead from a principle of youthful idealism that establishes the young Nigeria's affinity with what Asagai repeatedly calls the "New World" of Beneatha's America (116). Late in the play, for instance, when a large fraction of the Younger family's nest egg has been stolen, Asagai listens as Beneatha bitterly repudiates her naive childhood passion to become a doctor so she could cure the world. "Children see things very well sometimes—and idealists even better," Asagai responds (113). "You are still where I left off," responds Beneatha with irritation. "You with the dreams of the future will patch up all Africa—you are going to cure the Great Sore of colonialism with Independence" (113).

Asagai's presence in the play is itself dreamlike in that he never appears at a moment of dramatic action, but only in transitional scenes, as though he were an imaginary figure whose visitations nonetheless rejuvenate the Younger family, restore its youthful ability to "eye the prize" of self-sufficiency and defy those who would keep them in a state of subjection. Asagai acts not only as avatar of third world independence but, like Holden Caulfield or Elvis, as a charismatic figure for the identity concept itself, an image of the sovereign personality rightfully claimed by youth, whether as young individuals like Beneatha or new nations like Nigeria. "I am searching for my identity," Beneatha had told Asagai upon their first meeting. Though an American black, Beneatha looks to Asagai and to Africa for her identity because it is the "African" part of her African Americanness that keeps her "younger," allowing her to cling to her idealism and to resist capitulation to the suburban regime of American whiteness.

Raisin brings together many of the themes explored in this book: identity as a normative psychopolitical principle, as an idealization of youth rebellion, and most importantly as a grounding conflict between the "America" respectively associated with the "age of three worlds" and Fordist suburbia. Yet *Raisin* also looks forward to the identity politics of the sixties: in it identity has already been wedded to a narrative of *emergence* into black pride. Though Lorraine Hansberry died in 1965, she lived long enough to author a photo album of the Student Non-Violent Coordinating Committee's political activism. The following year, SNCC leader Stokely Carmichael would publish "Toward Black Liberation," one of the earliest of the liberationist manifestos, in which he posited identity as black power's most basic demand: the right to "define ourselves and our relationship to society and to have these terms recognized" as the "first necessity of a free people."

The psychopolitical sovereignty that had been figured by the young rebel was thus the first item on the agenda of the new liberation movements that emerged in the late 1960s, and these movements indeed articulated themselves precisely as young rebels pitted against the quasi-totalitarian state of "Amerika." Youthfulness remained central to this imagination, and it continued to come in manifestly white versions, embodied by the likes of SDS (Students for a Democratic Society) leaders, the yippies, or the new rock stars. But increasingly, the young rebel came to figure the challenge of people of color to the psychopolitics of white race privilege.

On the terrain of social theory, Irving Goffman's 1963 *Stigma: Notes on the Management of Spoiled Identity* represents an important transitional text. Although Goffman, working out of a Weberian framework, begins by loosely equating stigmatized "social identity" with stigmatized "social status," he cites the Eriksonian notion of self-identity as he begins to address the self's psychopolitical relationship to its own stigmatization. For Goffman, the stigmatized self can only consolidate his/her identity by negotiating a complex relationship with both "in-group" (the individual's aggregate "fellow sufferers" [112]) and "out-group" (the wider order that enforces the stigma and defines the "normal" [114]). In Goffman's view, stigma thus leads to an inevitable "politics of identity" with special application to race, disability, and sexual difference.

Goffman's analysis led smoothly into the logic of many early identity movement statements. Consider, for instance, Amy Uyematsu's 1969 manifesto on "yellow power," whose vital "psychological focus," she explains, stems from the movement's critical struggle to consolidate a self-identity that might replace the "mistaken identity" imposed by white America. Through their integration into a social order premised on white normality, Asian Americans had been pushed into "mental crises" that now required the politicization of "yellow" identity. As a counter to internalized stigma, argued Uyematsu, Asian Americans needed to become "proud of their physical and cultural heritages. Yellow power advocates self-acceptance as the first step toward strengthening personalities of Asian Americans" (191).

Often enough in the late sixties, it was still a proud bad boy who figured the new politics of racial identity: among politicos Stokely Carmichael himself or Eldridge Cleaver, in the domain of literature Amiri Baraka, Frank Chin, or Oscar Zeta Acosta, and Muhammed Ali or James Brown in pop culture. Likewise, political organizations such as the Black Panthers and the Young Lords typically articulated their collective identity project through the form of fraternity. The masculinist strain in sixties radicalism operated in a direct line of descent from the bad boy's oppositional relation to the "organization man," or the boy gang's struggle against an American "Moloch."

Yet the bad boy's monopoly on the discourse of identity was neither absolute nor unbreakable, as already demonstrated by Hansberry's Beneatha and the other girl rebels of the fifties, nor was it difficult to queer a bad boy who already embodied a homosocial and antidomestic male eroticism. By the late sixties, women, gays, and lesbians would also begin to figure new politics of identity in the form of the young rebel, often enough as a female or gay breakaway from a New Left organization that would itself come to stand in for the totalitarian conformity of Fordist America. "Goodbye, goodbye forever, counterfeit Left, counterleft, male-dominated cracked-glass-mirror reflection of the Amerikan Nightmare," wrote Robin Morgan in her famous manifesto "Goodbye to All That." If the bad boy's girlfriend was, as I have argued, an early female figure for identity, then Morgan's lines may be read as the last act in that figure's drama, wherein she finally "breaks up" with the bad boy, unmasked as a hypocritical reflection of the father that had prompted rebellion in the first place. Morgan's piece in fact ends with a litany of girlfriends (exploited partners to various new left boys) and a final refrain, "FREE OUR SISTERS! FREE OURSELVES!" (503). At times, the new feminist identity politics even oedipalized the "badness" of its rebel explicitly; Valerie Solanis's revolutionary society of bad girls (SCUM), whom she describes exactly as though it were a gang of female "king creoles," "dominant, secure, self-confident, nasty, violent, selfish, independent, proud, thrill-seeking, free-wheeling arrogant females, who consider themselves fit to rule the universe," contrast their defiance of the patriarch with their insipid good-girl counterparts, the "nice, passive, accepting, 'cultivated,' polite, dignified, subdued, dependent, scared, mindless, insecure, approval-seeking Daddy's Girls" (516).

As in the fifties, rebel identity in the sixties and seventies offered an American reflection of the young third-world nations struggling to liberate themselves. This was not only true of the black movement, finding inspiration in Kwame Nkrumah and sometimes casting itself as a "fifth column" of global third world revolution, but even of the gay liberation movement, which proclaimed that "the struggles of the peoples of the world are our fight as well" and demanded simultaneously the "right of self-determination for all Third World and gay people," so that together they might take up the psychopolitical task of exploring "how we view ourselves, and analyze the assumptions behind our self-identity" (601–602). As the imaginative locus of identity-in-struggle, the third world thus became the explicit model *within* the first world for liberation movements aiming to emancipate themselves from the repressive and subjectifying grip of a white, patriarchal, or heteronormative American mass mentality.

Sixties movements, then, did not merely borrow, appropriate, or restyle the Cold War concept of identity. We can trace the continuities in identity discourse far more deeply, from Erikson's "young Alyoshas" who see industrial America as a "hypnotized consumership," to Hansberry's "Asagai," helping the Youngers to defy the whiteness of suburbia, and finally to the social movements of the sixties, liberating their identities from postwar "Amerika" as if they were third world peoples. Born out of the Cold War/Fordist conjuncture, early identity discourse generated a mode of political thought and action that proved tremendously potent to all political agents who could be understood and imagined as *representing* (both depicting and speaking for) a collective self emerging into sovereignty. At this figurative level, James Dean, Holden Caulfield, or the beats were not very different from the political activists of the late sixties and early seventies, excepting for the vital fact that the latter's "emergent selves" deployed the politicized value of "identity" on behalf of social constituencies whose interests were strongly served for several decades by the force of its claims.

Sometime in the late seventies, the word "liberation" disappeared from the names of the various identity movements, to be gradually supplanted by a new narrative project associated with such terms as "multiculturalism," "coalition politics," "plurality," and "diversity." This shift may be understood in several ways. On the one hand, they might be read as a strategic retreat from the "revolutionary" expectations of identity politics in the late sixties, and as a strategic response to the right-wing political backlash that began gathering force in the mid-seventies. Certainly, the political independence of a "people" ceased to provide a simple model for the claims of identity. Rather, identity increasingly became a matter of *minoritarian* recognition, one whose aims always referred to the ultimate horizon of the

American polity. But this is not all. During the 1970s, identity was *diversified* on two distinct but related levels. First, identity was *divided* along the constitutive axes of race, gender, and sexuality, so as to pluralize its psychopolitics. Feminism was critical here as a site in which women of color critiqued the unity of "Woman" as an identity and a political agent, while also indicting the masculinist bad-boy figure that had been so widely deployed by black and brown power movements. "Woman," "black," or "Chicano" no longer appeared as a singular protagonist, struggling to consolidate a unique identity, but rather as compound identities—black woman or Chicana lesbian—challenging the fictitious unity of a movement that needed to recognize the *plurality* of identities actually making up its political subject. The narrative of identity thus became a linked series of subnarratives or subplots, nesting particular acts of identitarian recognition *within* more generalized others.

Even as the narration of identity was being thus divided—its plot fragmented and serialized, its protagonist hyphenated and compounded—it was also being *multiplied*. From a unitary narrative of liberation, identity was recast as a gathering of parallel struggles, uniting in a common struggle for greater inclusion or representation. Categories such as "people of color," for instance, presumed something very much like what Ernesto Laclau and Chantal Mouffe would shortly be calling the "articulation" of equivalence, expressing the comparability of identity projects in terms of mutual struggles for inclusion in the domain of political and cultural recognition. When fully generalized, this multiplication of identity even gained a name of its own. "Multiculturalism" may be understood as a reordering of identity politics in the late seventies and early eighties, now narrated as the coming together of various emergent identities into a unified struggle being waged for full inclusion by—but also a transformative democratization of—the American polity.

These diversifications of identity and its politics have been variously evaluated. While in the seventies some accused what I call the "division" of identity of splintering the shared (nationalist or radical feminist) cause, today it is usually lauded for having challenged the internal racism, sexism, or homophobia of the early identity movements, as well as for initiating an invaluable antiessentialist turn that would stress the constitutive role of difference in processes of identity formation. By contrast, the value of multiplying identity into the politics of "multiculturalism" remains contested. To borrow Avery Gordon and Christopher Newfield's incisive weighing of the debate, multiculturalism has been alternately viewed as offering a road to the "cultural autonomy" and "grassroots alliances" of identities, or else as threatening a return to "common culture" that primarily serves the interests of corporate "diversity management" (4–5).

Rather than judge these political changes on their own terms, I want instead to focus on their determination by a new social condition: the crisis of Fordism. It is well known that, in mutually reinforcing ways, the postwar systems of Taylorized mass production and suburban mass consumption went into a spiraling descent during the seventies.[1] As overall productivity in the United States declined relative to that of Japan, Europe, and even the early industrial economy of the "NICS" ("newly industrialized countries," such as South Korea or Taiwan), and as profits were squeezed, American capital began relocating its production processes abroad in an effort to recapture its competitive advantage. From both a regulatory and an ideological perspective, the national-industrial paradigm for economic growth began giving way to a transnational model that would eventually come to be known as "globalization." As U.S. industry shrank, American-based production became increasingly concentrated in three primary areas: "knowledge work" that required a highly skilled professional class, corporate and finance management (which remained stationed in the United States), and the sector of unskilled, nonunionized labor providing on-site service support for the new professional-managerial class.

The fallout from these developments cannot be adequately treated here, but a few observations are necessary. To begin with, the contraction of the "primary sector" industrial American workforce severely eroded the purchasing power of labor that had propped up Fordist consumption. American cities, which had already begun to suffer economically during the Fordist era due to the suburban exodus of the "white" working and middle class, now underwent an even more severe crisis as primary-sector industrial employment dried up for minority workers. But in the working-class suburbs too, mass consumption faltered as the unionized workforce shrank, and therefore so too did the underpinnings of a suburban imaginary predicated on the financial security of the domestic space. Meanwhile, a new international immigrant labor force also began to grow rapidly in the United States, due in part to new immigration laws and growing economic pressures in Latin America.[2]

As the Fordist mass market broke up into an increasingly uneven terrain of consumption, it became more important for capital to identify and to target particularized markets across sharpened lines of class, nationality, and ethnicity. It is this context that gave rise to "flexible specialization" as a post-Fordist accumulation strategy, one that delivered limited quantities of targeted goods to a multiple array of consumer groups ("niche markets") using newly developed "just-in-time" batch-production techniques.[3]

The pluralization of identity politics in the seventies bore a close relation to this rise of post-Fordist niche markets. This is not to suggest that the project of multiculturalism should be dismissed as the post-Fordist commercialization and thus the deradicalization of identity discourse. As this book has argued, identity discourse had been tied to a commodified youth culture from its earliest moments. The mere fact of identity's embeddedness in relations of consumption has thus never in itself ruled out its capacity to radicalize the politics of race, gender, or sexuality.

Indeed, the "break" between Fordist and post-Fordist consumption is far less sharp than many have argued, for the latter's "specialization" strategies were apparently developed out of the cultural history explored in this book. The consumption system of Fordism did not strictly apply a logic of mass standardization, for even in its postwar golden age it had bifurcated the marketplace into a so-called suburban mass market and what effectively became the first niche market—teen culture—itself already organized around the exchange value of identity. The commodification of difference under post-Fordism thus merely extended and pluralized Fordism's strategy of commodifying the "difference" of youth identity.

The politics of post-Fordist multiculturalism must therefore be specified by something other than a simple appeal to the status of identity as commodity. A more effective starting point might be to consider the increasingly cosmopolitan consumption patterns of the post-Fordist professional-managerial class. Compared to the standardized consumer goods produced under a Fordist national economy, the transnational processes of flexible production allowed for the cultivation of a previously unimaginable cultural diversity in this class's taste. And yet, this diversity was refunctioned (or to use my own term, transcommodified) for the new post-Fordist middle classes as a means to what might be called cross-cultural capital. What Martyn Lee calls the techniques of "blasphemous disruption" or "scandalous utilization" in postmodern cultural consumption, with their underlying testimony to the consumer's playful cosmopolitanism, constituted in Lee's view a "new mode of consumption [that] has the desired effect of being able to subjugate all other taste formations as its cultural inferiors" (172–173). This new mode of cross-cultural capital thus provided the professional-managerial class with its distinctions from the racialized service sector.[4]

The radical valence of multicultural identity politics in the post-Fordist moment might be measured against this context, for multiculturalism made the identitarian demand for "recognition" and psychopolitical sovereignty directly relevant to the new multicultural character of post-Fordist consumption. Where in the Fordist moment a simpler narrative of rebellion against conformity sufficed as an expression of sovereign personality, post-Fordism necessitated a pluralized narrative of multiple identities coming together in a democratic opposition to the hierarchical articulation of multiple cultures under post-Fordism. This is just the sort of project that Laclau and Mouffe expressed in their theory of the articulation of identities along chains of democratizing "equivalence." The aim of their politics remains one of democratic sovereignty, as can be seen in their assent to each identity's "internal principle of validity" or "autoconstitutivity," so long as it does not reinstate a hierarchy of value among the radical plurality.

The continued access to "democracy" as an overarching political imaginary in this multicultural moment is revealing of an important continuity with the earlier moment in identity politics. For while Fordism had entered into crisis by the 1970s, the Cold War and its "age of three worlds" were still going strong, despite the period of détente following the debacle of the Vietnam War that softened its geopolitical tensions for a brief time before the Reagan years. As in the preceding decades then, through the seventies and eighties American democratic freedom continued to demand definition against the "state slavery" of Soviet communism, while appealing to the desire for "freedom" in the third world. In reference to these imperatives, identity would continue to bear a deeply politicized meaning, not as a singular rebel or a boy gang, but instead as an alliance of rebels in a "rainbow coalition." Like its youth rebel predecessor, the new multicultural counterimaginary offered a "new image" of America, on the one hand meant to reflect the claims to leadership of the "free world," yet on the other demanding a radical acknowledgment of America's minority elements.

It is no coincidence that the culture wars over the proper image of America slowed just as the world established by the Cold War itself began to implode in 1989. For a brief moment, the political discourse of identity reached its apotheosis. The new regimes of Eastern Europe and South Africa were welcomed as the final triumph of youthful dissent, the coming to power of identities in struggle (exemplified in such figures as Vaclav Havel or Nelson Mandela; the media made numerous references to a "spiritual relationship" between these events and the American Revolution. Yet this climax quickly dimmed as the long Cold War drama of insurrectional citizenship reached its conclusion. With it the strategic force of identity claims has also faded. New narratives of political action have come to seem necessary, not because identity fails us as a coherent ontological category but rather because, one by one, we have left behind the historical contingencies that led it to be honored in the first place as the answer to the ideological impasse of its age.

Nevertheless, it seems difficult to give up on "identity" altogether, precisely because it is not clear where else to find the impetus to political action that it offers. Consider, for instance, the opening to Judith Butler's *Gender Trouble*, a text widely acclaimed for its challenge to the positing of gender identity as the ground for feminist politics.[5] In offering "gender trouble" in lieu of "gender identity" as the better road for feminism, Butler notes that, within the "reigning discourse" of her childhood, trouble was both the name for her rebellion and for the reprimand that she received when she was "bad." Already in her youth she had concluded that, since trouble was "inevitable," the task became "how best to make it, what best way to be in it" (vii). It should be obvious by now that what makes Butler's very notion of "trouble" appealing is precisely its saturation in the classical drama of identity. "Trouble," the rebellious acts of her youth expressively challenges the codes, laws, and standards to which a "good girl" is expected to conform. Evacuating from the word "identity" its notion of making trouble, Butler shifts it instead to the side of conformity, where it now names the very law against which she imagines the gender outlaw to rebel. But this is precisely a reinscription of identity discourse, a reinvigoration of the psychopolitical rebel who confronts the mass standard as a totalitarian iteration of the same. In the very same gesture with which Butler would displace identity from our feminist politics, she reinvokes it as motivation for making "gender trouble." And yet, so long as feminism is understood as a psychopolitical project, how could it be otherwise?

The genealogy of this book may be read by some as one more reason to reject identity as always already representing a failed or ideologically compromised politic. Yet identity cannot be reduced to a ruse of power or a counterfeit resistance simply because its meanings were embedded in the field of Cold War political discourse. Our understanding needs a greater analytic sophistication than that. Power generates its own resistance, Foucault teaches us, and "identity" represents a particularly potent recent example. Identity was the positive form of Cold War power, the site where we can see that it was not simply repressive, destructive (for example) of the Old Left but also politically productive. Within the historic conditions of its existence, identity offered a strategically effective discourse for the waging of radical politics. At a time when class radicalisms had been foreclosed by Cold War power, identity helped bring into existence new social movements whose invaluable effects on the conduct of contemporary political life we disregard whenever we proffer a transhistorical indictment.

Yet this genealogy is also no reason to wax nostalgic for the grandeur of the liberationist moment of the sixties and seventies. The end of the Cold War has also spelled the decline of identity as a potent banner for radical politicking. Yet race, gender, and sexuality present no less urgent political issues today than they did then, and we are confronted by the daunting task of determining how they might be articulated to the threats and promises of economic globalization and to the neoimperial "war on terror," the two tendencies that have supplanted for now the national-Fordist paradigm of world affairs that reigned in the Cold War era. This will likely require new, nonidentitarian strategies through which we pursue issues of social justice in some language other than that of sovereignty and recognition. The politics of class have always operated in a nonidentitarian mode, as a program of socioeconomic interests tied to a division of labor rather than a primary matter of psychopolitical self-determination. So too have the politics of ecology, which stress the embeddedness of social processes in fragile environmental systems. It is thus not surprising to see both revitalized today. But for the politics of race, gender, and sexuality, the road is far less clear. I offer this account of the origins of the age of identity in the modest hope that it will help all of us to better understand where we find ourselves in its political aftermath.

NOTES

1. Identitarian Thought and the Cold War World

1 Often these criticisms are taken as point of departure for reconstructing the politics of identity in a more sophisticated, anti- or postessentialist form. Paula Moya has proposed yet another theory of identity, now founded on a realist but still-antiessentialist ontology, that means to "rescue identity from the disrepute into which it has fallen" as a "theoretically incoherent and politically pernicious" category (1). Other critics, such as Cornel West, have attempted to reclaim identity simply by pluralizing it. Identity politics gives way to the identities politics of radical multiculturalism in what he calls a "postmodern politics of difference." All of these approaches, however, continue to take identity for granted as a universal norm.

2 Paul Gilroy's *Against Race*, for instance, asks us to discard raciological thinking altogether, while certain queer theorists, including Michael Warner and David Halperin, sometimes endorse the sexual politics of antinormalization over those that defend counternorms associated with gay and lesbian identity. See the introduction to Warner's *The Trouble with Normal* and Halperin's endorsement of "queer" as an "identity without an essence" or a "positivity" of its own in *Saint Foucault* (62).

3 Walter Benn Michaels proposes in *Our America* that the identity concept finds its origins in nativist modernism of the 1920s, but, notably, none of the literary texts that he cites ever use the word. I would argue that what Michaels actually demonstrates is that American nationality became racialized after World War I, but not that it became "identitarianized." To assert, as he does, that the formulation "blood is blood" in Faulkner "expresses the priority of identity over any other category of assessment" is to mistakenly equate the prioritization of race, a fixed category of descent, with the prioritization of racial identity, which I will

show to be a quite specific psychopolitical category (6). Ironically, Michaels, who loves nothing more than to taunt the presuppositions of identity politics, shares their axiomatic ontology. He does not dispute the existential ubiquity of identity, but only the account given by its partisans, which in his view "makes no sense" (142). A handful of critical works that actually map the lexical history of identity have provided me with crucial resources and insights for the writing of this book. Grant Farred has described what he calls the "New Left roots of identity politics" in the 1960s. In pushing this history back to the 1950s, I will be arguing conversely that the New Left finds its roots in a discourse of identity that predates it. To that end, Philip Gleason has written a brief but penetrating account of identity as a postwar concept in the social sciences, which includes an invaluable discussion of its invention by Erik Erikson. Extremely useful and inspiring has been Jonathan Arac's essay on a hidden or forgotten intellectual genealogy of "identity" that he traces through Kenneth Burke and Erik Erikson to Ralph Ellison, and to which, as he argues, contemporary celebrations of *Invisible Man* are tacitly indebted. In drawing our attention to Burke, Arac points to extremely early (and rare) usages of "identity" in the 1930s, ones that I would view as anticipating but not yet realizing contemporary meanings of the concept (*Toward* 201–203). My reading of identity discourse locates its origins in relation to a quite specific network of Cold War ideological grid.

4 Philip Gleason has observed that, as far back as the sixteenth century, "identity" could, according to the *Oxford English Dictionary*, refer in philosophical discourse to the "sameness of a person or thing at all times or in all circumstances; the condition or fact that a person or thing is itself and not something else" (911). This definition suggests an important source for what I will call the "psychopolitical" sense of identity. Nevertheless, for Locke, Hume, and other philosophers, "identity" was a property that applied to both objects and subjects. It did not depend on, nor in any way entail, a state of self-awareness. A comb possessed identity in this sense no less than a person. In the German idealist tradition too, the question of identity arises in determining the subject/object relation. Schelling called his philosophical system *Identitätsphilosophie* for the reason that he posited the identity or exact correspondence of the subject and object in order to derive from it a differentiated world. The "identity" of subject and object would persist as an issue in the Hegelian and Marxist tradition. This usage too differs substantially from the contemporary sense of identity, which is understood as describing the subject alone rather than a relation between subject and object.

5 See, for example, Linda Alcoff's "Cultural Feminism versus Post-Structuralism: The Identity Crisis in Feminist Theory," where she asserts erroneously that "identity politics" is a "concept that developed from the Combahee River Collective's "A Black Feminist Statement," a text that dates from 1977, at least ten years too late (431).

6 These passages greatly complicate Wendy Brown's Nietzschean critique of the "wounded attachments" of identity politics and their alleged affective invest-

ment in a relationship of ressentiment toward the dominant Other that has excluded or marginalized them (159–161). Ressentiment has certainly served as a genuine risk for politics of identity, but these early examples of identitarian politicking strike a very different tone of pride and empowerment, hardly the voice of Nietzsche's "slave morality." Brown is one of the very few theorists to attempt a genuinely historicized analysis of identitarian claims, but her reading deals so generically with the broad sweep of modernity and capitalism that it bypasses the actual historical archive of identity discourse. In light of the reading offered by this book, the psychology of ressentiment that Brown so effectively criticizes might be posited perhaps as a distressing of identity politics that has recurred when its political aims are thwarted or its assertions of power and pride are hollowed out by an unrelieved state of disenfranchisement. The rightward course of the 1980s and 1990s was surely fertile ground for the breeding of "wounded attachments" within identitarian movements, and no doubt this tendency signals a strategic weakness of its politics in trying times. On the other hand, nearly *all* political rhetorics flail in difficult historical situations. Was the Old Left tendency to fall back on the consolation of a deterministic eschatology of capitalism's future demise any better?

7   *Childhood and Society* figured prominently in the postwar popularization of ego psychology as America's distinct brand of psychoanalysis. Its importance, however, was far greater than this. As Gleason shows, Erikson's concept of identity took all of the social sciences by storm (912–915). Erikson biographer Lawrence Friedman observes that by 1955 Margaret Mead would announce "a new concept clamoring for acceptance—the concept of identity" and predict that Erikson would soon become a "central public figure" (Friedman, 303–304). Erikson was offered a professorship at Harvard University on the strength of the book's importance.

8   Arac, as noted earlier, discusses a considerably earlier psychopolitical usage of the term identity, in a section of Kenneth Burke's 1937 study *Attitudes toward History* entitled "Dictionary of Pivotal Terms" (*Toward*, 203). Burke's discussion, while also drawing loosely on psychoanalytic models, treats identity quite differently from the usage to which we are accustomed. For Burke, "identity" delineates the individual's "incorporation," his taking on of managerial, bureaucratic, or national autocratic interests through a process of symbolic exchange with the collectivity in question. Identity, in short, is used by Burke not to name a norm of subjectivity but to critique its political relation to the object world. As we shall see, the concept of identity as popularized by Erikson suggests almost the opposite: the idealized capacity of the self to resist and to challenge autocratic incorporation. I would see Burke's concept of identity as representing something of a path not taken, an intriguing tangent in the genealogy of identity. A clearer line of descent can be found in the anticipatory use of the word "identity" in *Escape from Freedom*, Eric Fromm's 1941 critique of the fascist personality. Fromm uses the word several times to describe the autonomous aspect of the normative self that is dissolved in the fascist mass.

This usage evidently influenced Erikson's elaboration of identity as the site of psychopolitical *challenge* to mass conformity (Friedman, 161–162). Fromm, however, never elevated "identity" to the status of a central concept, leaving Erikson to become its popularizer and advocate.

9 The classic statement is found in the opening sentence of Immanuel Kant's "What Is Enlightenment?": "Enlightenment is man's emergence from his own self-imposed nonage" (384).

10 A recent example of this may be found in Nancy Fraser's equation of identity politics with the "politics of recognition," which she distinguishes in her book *Justice Interruptus* from the socialist "politics of redistribution." Fraser herself borrows the language of "recognition" from Charles Taylor's *Multiculturalism and the "Politics of Recognition."*

11 Stephen Krasner distinguishes these two senses as "Westphalian sovereignty" and "international legal sovereignty" respectively, but in practice they are closely linked (9–25). A state's domestic autonomy is to be guaranteed by international recognition of its legitimacy (and thus its entitlement to Westphalian sovereignty).

12 For discussions of the "domestic analogy, see Michael Walzer's *Just and Unjust Wars* (58–63) and Martti Koskenniemi's *From Apology to Utopia* (68–73). In his classic *The Law of Nations*, J. L. Brierly finds the origins of the domestic analogy in the work of Emerich de Vattel, whose *Le Droit des gens* (1758) contended that "nations being composed of men naturally free and independent, and who before the establishment of civil societies lived together in a state of nature; nations or sovereign states must be regarded as so many free persons living together in the state of nature; and since men are naturally equal, so are states" (37).

13 In putting my point in such language, I have deliberately violated Michel Foucault's own distinction between sovereignty and governmentality. Foucault primarily addresses sovereignty as a juridical model of power that he considers a distraction from the rise of alternative operations of power: in disciplinary institutions and the capillary operations of biopolitics. Foucault's attack on the sovereignty model is most carefully developed in the second lecture of *Society Must Be Defended* (23–42). Governmentality, by contrast, represents a strategy of self-regulation closely connected to these alternative operations, most especially because it has no necessary relation to the sovereign state (see Foucault's essay on "Governmentality"). Because "identity" discourse detaches the principle of sovereignty from the state, it has tended to blur the sovereignty/governmentality distinction. This book, instead of dismissing sovereignty as an erroneous theory of power, as Foucault himself tended to do, treats it instead in accordance with Foucault's discourse analytics: as a politically productive discourse of personhood that authorizes a wide range of different struggles, including all those we consider identitarian. The political event that called itself "black power," to offer just one example, would not have been possible had it

not asserted "power" as the juridical right of sovereign (i.e., identity-bearing) peoplehood.

14 In significant ways, this national section of Erikson's study was actively commissioned by the U.S. national security state. The Germany chapter, for instance, which dealt with the psychological nature of Hitler's appeal to the German people, reworks two wartime essays Erikson had published as a resource for the Office of Strategic Services. Erikson only began working on the Russian chapter in 1948, at the dawn of the Cold War, at the behest of Margaret Mead and her Research in Contemporary Culture Program at Columbia, a project heavily funded by the Rand Corporation, a prominent Cold War think tank funded by the state.

15 In Erikson's model of the individual life cycle, adolescence and its ideal of identity begins immediately following a childhood stage concerned with the successful use of tools, the stage he associates with the ideal of "industry" (260). An unspoken analogy thus holds between individuals and nations so that a people's acquisition and implementation of industrial means of production corresponds to its national passage into adolescence.

16 Other theorists, notably Theodor Adorno and his coauthors of *The Authoritarian Personality*, made precisely the opposite charge: Nazism was the regime of excessive obedience. This latter view became the dominant one in postwar America, but the basic principle remained the same: sovereign political personality required a balance between the excesses of obedience and rebelliousness.

17 Much of this section is condensed from my "Cold War American Culture as the Age of Three Worlds."

18 See Carl Pletsch for his invaluable study of the origins of the "three worlds concept" in postwar social science. As Pletsch shows, a 1952 essay by French demographer Alfred Sauvy, "Three Worlds, One Planet," was seminal in defining the new spatial logic of the globe. Sauvy's essay explicitly calls the third world the "raison d'être" of the Cold War, the regions that the first and second world aim to win, leaving third world nations compelled to make a fateful choice between the first and second world approach to development (566–570).

19 One must not forget that this metanarrative of development, so reliant on age as its master metaphor, actively obscured the rich techniques of neocolonial domination simultaneously employed and disavowed by the United States, as we know from the invaluable tradition of U.S. imperial historiography as developed in such classic works as William Appleman Williams's *Empire as a Way of Life*, and Walter LeFeber's *The American Age* and *The New American Empire*.

20 The principal regulation school figures are Michel Aglietta, Alain Lipietz, and Robert Boyer. What follows here is a highly condensed summary of their position on the history of Fordism as lucidly analyzed by Martyn J. Lee in his excellent synthetic study, *Consumer Culture Reborn*. See particularly 59–85. Their work is echoed by another group of American economists, including Samuel Bowles and Herbert Gintis, sometimes known as the "social structure of accu-

mulation school," whose studies offer a very similar socioeconomic framework for postwar consumerism. Though the regulation school places less stress than the social structure of accumulation school on the role of class conflict and negotiations, for both schools, culture and social institutions are not superstructural effects or ideological supports of capitalism's economic base, but constitutive elements in any successful regime of capital accumulation. See David M. Kotz's "Comparative Analysis" for a detailed comparison of the two schools.

21 For an excellent analysis of the underlying problem with the cultural studies approach, see Janice Peck's "Itinerary of a Thought: Stuart Hall, Cultural Studies, and the Unresolved Problem of the Relation of Culture to 'Not Culture.'" Peck argues that, in positing the autonomy of culture, Hall and his disciples must also presume the autonomy of "not culture," which then "by default, becomes the 'base' or 'economy'" (207). Ironically then, Halls's version of cultural studies ends up reinstating economism (in the sense of a self-determining economy) in order to avoid any economic determination of culture. Peck recommends that in lieu of maintaining "the analytic separation of culture and 'not culture' and their autonomy," we should embark instead on a "long overdue investigation of the notion of the 'base'" (207). I am here using the regulation school for just such a purpose, as their approach allows for the integration (yet not the subordination) of cultural analysis with that of political economy.

22 The regulation school begins with the premise that neoliberal theories of capitalism's "equilibrium" are mistaken, and that capitalism's contradictions (such as short-term profit vs. long-term sustainability, or the need to lower wages vs. the need to sell commodities to workers) render strategies for accumulation fundamentally unstable and prone to crises. Precisely because it is not self-sustaining, capital accumulation therefore requires modes of regulation that can manage (or at least defer) these instabilities. Capital is therefore dependent on processes that are not themselves about accumulation but that establish a relatively stable social context within which predictable capital accumulation can occur. Capitalism, in this reading, does not possess a monologic. Not only are many accumulation strategies possible (production may be artisanal, assembly line, slave-based, flexibly specialized), and thus yield many variants of capitalisms, but so too are the many different cultural and political formations that may be mustered to sustain them. Economic analysis of capitalism therefore cannot be intelligibly separated from a historical study of its developments.

23 In contrast to an "extensive regime" (like that of nineteenth-century capitalism) in which business increases productivity by adding work hours or hiring additional workers, an "intensive regime" increases output by making more out of existing hour of labor through the broad application of Taylorist efficiency programs and the continuous development of labor-saving devices (Lee, 71).

24 Likewise on the international front, Fordism was regulated through an ensemble of Cold War programs and institutions, beginning with the Marshall

Plan's state-led rebuilding of Western European economies, but primarily built upon the institutional framework of the Bretton Woods agreement. Enrolling, as it largely did, only the industrial capitalist nation-states, this agreement fixed the borders of what would become known as the first world. These economic alliances found their political analog, of course, in such military organizations as NATO and SEATO.

25 The classic study of this development from the period itself is C. Wright Mills's 1951 *White Collar: The American Middle Classes*. In his chapter on white-collar unionism, Mills explicitly argued that, although white-collar workers were becoming proletarianized, a residual sense of status anxiety kept them from unionizing. For an historical overview, see *Fear of Falling*, Barbara Ehrenreich's excellent popular study of this class's self-image as it evolved from the 1940s to the 1980s. A brilliant re-examination of these questions is forthcoming in Andrew Hoberek's *The Twilight of the Middle Class*, a text I cite in the next chapter thanks to the author's generosity.

26 See George Lipsitz's essay "Against the Wind," in *Time Passages* (99–132), which touches thoughtfully on this history.

27 See Shelly Nickles's essay "More Is Better" for a rich elaboration of these dynamics of gender and class ideology in postwar consumption.

28 The scholarship on McCarthyism is immense, but Victor Navasky's *Naming Names*, Larry Ceplair and Steven Englund's *The Inquisition in Hollywood*, and Ellen Schrecker's *No Ivory Tower* are excellent points of entry. Matthew Ruben's "Suburbanization and Urban Poverty Under Neoliberalism" is an incisive critique of the suburb as ideological apparatus.

29 It was May who coined the concept of "domestic containment," a term meant to emphasize the fact that postwar women's consignment to family life was ideologically associated with safety from communism in the suburbs. John D'Emilio and Robert Corber have both explored the conflation of homosexuality and communism as alien threats to national security that required containment strategies. Gerald Horne has shown in *Black & Red* that the same was true of antiracist causes. Although Thomas Schaub's incisive book, *American Fiction in the Cold War*, never names the term "containment" directly, his analysis of the "new liberalism," a critical posture adopted by Cold War liberal intellectuals to repudiate their own prewar leftist commitments, thoughtfully demonstrates the intellectual containment of thirties progressivism. Andrew Ross, in a similar vein, argues that Cold War liberal intellectuals "contained culture" by attacking popular entertainment of the 1950s as a creeping Stalinization of American life. The study of Cold War culture as a strategy of "containment at home" reaches its apotheosis in Alan Nadel's book *Containment Culture*, the title of which he uses in broad reference to atomic age cultural production. Although containment undoubtedly represents a central political logic of Cold War culture, I believe that the three worlds imaginary generated a rival logic of emancipation whose consideration offers a more dialectically complex understanding of the era. For a more explicit version of this critique, which is here

embedded in my larger argument, see my essay "Cold War Culture in the Age of Three Worlds."

30 See, for instance, Robert Corber's *Homosexuality in Cold War America* and Steven Cohan's *Masked Men*, two excellent gay cultural studies of postwar masculinity as read through cinematic (and for Corber also literary) images. Both of these highly nuanced studies nonetheless tend to treat these male figures as representative of a hegemonic postwar ideal of manhood against which gay or queer masculinities increasingly needed to assert themselves. The positive reception of film noir and gay fiction cited by Corber, and the sexual/textual ambiguities of the "Organization Man" films that Cohan brilliantly explores, are in my view actually symptomatic of the profound ideological ambivalences that were condensed into these figures of Fordist manhood.

31 Though they did not function as norms, they nevertheless performed important ideological work in so far as they displaced depression and wartime images of working-class manhood. The new Fordist discourses of masculinity, sweeping aside prior debates over the autonomy of working men "on the line," declared that most men had now become suburban, "middle-class," and employees of the "organization." In the process, they displaced prior debates over the latter's autonomy on the job. Concerns over the fate of the working man in the age of mass industry would henceforth be played out on the ideologically safer terrains of professional and family life in an age of mass consumption.

32 For a classic example of the antisuburban critique, see Daniel Seligman's famous essay, "The New Masses." Whyte's *Organization Man* concludes with a lengthy section on his subject's new suburban homespace, about whose standardized quality even its residents crack "wry" or "sharp" jokes: " 'sorority house with kids,' a projection of dormitory life into adulthood, or, slightly better, a lay version of Army post life" (310).

33 Ever committed to a liberal ideal of neutral research, Riesman backpedals periodically in *The Lonely Crowd* so as to soften the reader's likely conclusion that the loss of "inner" directedness constituted a grave deterioration in America's political personality. In the 1960 preface to the book, Riesman complains that "the negative aspects of these [other-directed] qualities had been overemphasized by many readers . . . and the positive aspects underemphasized" (xx). Nevertheless, it is hard to mistake the tone of urgent concern expressed by *The Lonely Crowd* at the alleged reshaping of American character.

34 It is undoubtedly for this reason that Riesman was greatly drawn to Erikson's thinking. Riesman became Erikson's most important intellectual advocate in the 1950s, orchestrating a high-profile position for him in his own department at Harvard.

35 I owe this source to Thomas Doherty, whose extremely helpful *Teenagers and Teenpics* references Manchester's research in a footnote (67). Doherty's book brilliantly historicizes the teenager in relation to the new entertainment markets of the postwar years. Thomas Hine's *The Rise and Fall of the American Teenager* also provides a rich framework for understanding the political, cultural,

and economic vicissitudes of youth in general (i.e., understood as an intermediary category between childhood and adulthood, but is actually less specifically concerned with the postwar teenager than the title asserts.

36 "Adolescence" emerged as a normative form of youth subjectivity, measured and constructed in terms of everyday life for middle-class, usually native-born, youth. Where, for example, the "gang instincts" of middle-class boys were considered socially valuable since they could be routed through such organizations as the Boy Scouts, the same "instincts" among immigrant and lower-class boys who formed unsupervised gangs, became the alleged sources of juvenile delinquency. During the nineteenth century, the term "juvenile delinquent" came to designate the non-middle-class victim of a "wild" adolescence, a youth whose lack of adult guidance had derailed maturation and brought him or her into a state of lawless degeneracy. It is worth noting, as a preface to the "bad girl" figure of chapter 7, that the content of delinquency broke down across gender lines: for lower-class boys, delinquency signified gang violence and/or vandalism, while for girls it connoted promiscuity or prostitution.

37 The conservative reading of the teenager would reach its apotheosis in Grace and Fred M. Hechinger's book, *Teen-age Tyranny*, a polemic against the alleged abdication of adult responsibility and authority over youth.

38 The feared risk of delinquency explains the reassuring tone in the caption to Doyle's article on the rights of teenagers, which tells parents that they "must have the faith and courage" to overcome their understandable fears, but that all will turn out well with their teenagers if they allow them to "pursue happiness in their way, with a minimum of questioning and objection" (Doyle, 20).

39 See Landon Jones's book on the baby boom, *Great Expectations*, which begins with these statistics, arguing that the phenomenon was not, as some assume, "a short rise in the birthrate caused by returning GIs making up for lost time. It began that way in 1946, but instead of stopping in the 1950s (as in Europe), the tidal wave of births continued, affecting all races and classes with astonishing uniformity. . . . At least 4 million babies were born in each of the bumper-crop years from 1954 through 1964, the last real year of the baby binge. All totaled, 76,441,000 babies—one-third of our present population—arrived in the nineteen years from 1946 through 1964" (2).

40 Of course, this representation of the teenager as mere consumer was no less ideological than it was for adults. As James Gilbert points out, the employment of people in their teens, which had been dropping for the previous forty years, actually grew from 1940 to 1960 as more and more teenagers took part-time jobs (19–20). One could actually argue that teenagers became one of the most grossly exploited members of the American workforce (worst pay, lowest benefits, most easily laid off), who did not need to be fairly compensated because—as teenagers—their needs as workers were (and still are) not taken seriously.

41 Kenneth Davis's *Two-Bit Culture* offers the best survey of the postwar history of the book. See also Thomas L. Bonn's *Heavy Traffice & High Culture*.

42 Thomas Doherty documents this rise of the teen marketplace in Hollywood,

then goes on to sort the teenpic into these three general subgenres, to which he also adds the rock 'n' roll movie. See chapter 4 for a lengthier discussion of this history.

43 An upstanding, normatively bourgeois man, in the view of these novels, could easily have grown up in his youth as a ragged, horseplaying "bad boy." Mailloux points out that these "bad boy" novels broke with an earlier Christian discourse of morality, while anticipating the evolutionary model of adolescence that would be popularized by psychologist G. Stanley Hall in the following decade (110–113). It was useless, from this new perspective, to condemn the "savageness" of youth, which—like the working classes or the darker races—was in fact a natural sign of their early stage of development, but also therefore of their remarkable plasticity, their ability to grow and evolve as they received guidance from their more mature elders. The nineteenth-century bad boy was thus fundamentally compatible with the projects of bourgeois social reform and imperialism.

44 See Leslie Fiedler's "The Eye of Innocence," collected in *No! in Thunder: Essays on Myth and Literature* (251–91). This 1957 essay would later be incorporated into the text of *Love and Death in the American Novel*.

45 Obviously, I am not implying a one-to-one relation between Nietzsche and Fiedler's moral system. Nietzsche's genealogy merely helps us to unpack the distinction between the rival moralities of agency and altruism through which Fiedler formulates the good bad boy.

46 See Rogin's essay "Kiss Me Deadly" for a thoughtful discussion of these topics.

47 See Fiedler's "Come Back to the Raft Ag'n, Huck Honey," collected in *An End to Innocence*.

48 See Morris Dickstein's "On and Off the Road" for a similarly dialectical account of fifties culture, and which also seizes upon the motif of the young outsider.

49 Ironically, this account of the "other fifties" positions its agents in much the same terms as the containment logic of the Cold War: as subversives who threatened the given "consensus." Despite the fact that "consensus" and "subversion" are transvalued, the familiar plot line remains intact, offering a view of the Cold War order whose exercise of power, to paraphrase Foucault, was only ever repressive and normalizing. A particularly clear illustration of how reading the "other fifties" can mirror the logic of containment may be found in Milton Viorst's *Fire in the Streets: America in the 1960s*, where the beat writers are described as follows: "Most Americans behaved according to the strictures of Eisenhower's morality and McCarthy's politics, challenging little, daring less. They lived beneath a blanket of conformity, scarcely aware that it was suffocating. Only a few brave spirits were gasping for air, and they seemed like anomalies, perhaps even lunatics, agitators who scarcely threatened the society's placid temperament. It is only in retrospect that these few have been granted credit for tugging at the edges of the blanket, to admit a breeze that would ultimately permit Americans to breathe more freely" (55).

2. Cold War Literature and the National Allegory

1. Although the editorial statement does not specify its authorship, William Phillips, Philip Rahv, William Barrett, and Delmore Schwartz served as the *Partisan Review* editors in 1952, and the advisory board included James Burnham, Sidney Hook, James Sweeney, and Lionel Trilling. The editorial statement thus represented a quite broad cross-section of liberal opinion.
2. Only a small handful of respondents—Norman Mailer and C. Wright Mills among them—rejected absolutely the celebratory premise of the statement. Most aimed instead to finesse some of the more detailed claims.
3. Fredric Jameson once claimed national allegory to be the ubiquitous mode of third world literature, to considerable controversy ("Third World Literature," 1986). As I will show, it is less that Jameson was mistaken so much as that allegory took on a central importance in literary projects associated with all three worlds of the era. I will return to this point at the end of this chapter, when it can be better substantiated.
4. As Joel Fineman notes, allegory has been understood since at least the Renaissance as the "temporal extension of trope" (30).
5. In addition to Pease's "*Moby-Dick* and the Cold War," see also Geraldine Murphy's "Ahab as Capitalist, Ahab as Communist: Revising *Moby-Dick* for the Cold War" and William V. Spanos's *The Errant Art of Moby-Dick*. Pease's book *Visionary Compacts* traces the appropriation of the entire American Renaissance by a literary agenda. See especially his opening chapter "Visionary Compacts and the Cold War Consensus" (3–48).
6. This reading, moreover, flew in the face of how nineteenth-century publics actually understood *Huck Finn*. See Steven Mailloux's *Rhetorical Power*, which places its reception amidst the "bad-boy boom" of the late nineteenth century (100–129) and Arac's "Nationalism, Hypercanonization, and *Huckleberry Finn*," which stresses its reception as "local humor."
7. See Gayatri Spivak's "Can the Subaltern Speak?" (275–279). In "Analogies of the Aesthetic," David Lloyd terms this sense of "darstellen" the aesthetic "analogy" for politics (vertreten). For Lloyd, the former functions to forstall or defer politics (119–121). I would qualify this point by suggesting that, because each sense of representation functions as a supplement to the operations of the other, "darstellen" can also provide the precondition for the emergence of new political practices. In the context of criticism, for instance, the study of America's "democratic aesthetics" often served as a compensatory substitute for the political practice of democracy. And yet, to anticipate the argument that follows, the *figuring* of identity in criticism (by what I will call the "rebel allegory") also prepared the way for the rise of identity politics.
8. My argument is indebted to Donald Pease's brilliant reading of the political fantasy out of which Leslie Fiedler built his American canon. Pease takes a negative view of the national fantasy of democratic freedom that Fiedler asserted in

his canon, noting that, although Fiedler's metanarrative "call[s] for a political alternative to the Cold War mentality," it functions as "psychological compensation for the state coercion and social disrelations constructed out of the "Cold War mentality," thereby ultimately providing "ideological justification for that mentality" (158). More concretely, Fiedler managed to preserve liberal freedom on the level of literary fantasy even while lauding the state when it withheld those very freedoms from the Rosenbergs, Hiss, and other victims of the red scare. Yet the contradiction that Pease discloses between liberal anticommunism and the celebration of figures for social justice can be analyzed, not only as a process of compensatory justification but also as potentially authorizing social activism. Pease himself suggests as much when he reads the movements of the sixties as "literalization" or a "realization" of the principles embodied in Fiedler's archetypes. These archetypes served as a symbolic resource out of which such activism became possible, and in this respect we can see that Fiedler's fantasy had a radical as well as a conservative dimension. I choose to stress the former because the genealogy of New Left and identity politics that if offers has been so deeply disavowed.

9 Murphy takes her reading of the romance/novel binary further than I would. She too casts Chase's romance as an American self-characterization, but she also takes its opposite, the novel, to stand in for the second world. Chase's romance, she writes, "promoted freedom, just as American democracy did. . . . While the novel was not quite totalitarian, it was coercive insofar as it insisted on verisimilitude, narrative closure, and the reconciliation of the protagonist with society" (745). I detect more ambivalence toward the novel than Murphy suggests, which I believe stems from the slippage surrounding the "old world," as a site for both a tradition of monarchic tyranny that got attached to the second world, but also a legacy of Western Civilization and liberal values, which the United States now claimed to lead.

10 While the Invisible Man's political work with the Brotherhood turns out to be only a false rebellion, replacing one set of authority figures with another and one "false" identity with another, it establishes ever more clearly the struggle that one must wage to possess identity for oneself in a world of authoritative institutions.

11 See Hoberek's "Race Man, Organizational Man, *Invisible Man*," especially 101–104.

12 In Ellison's novel, as elsewhere, youth bears a special symbolic importance as the signifier for this promise of personal sovereignty. The novel embodies this promise most explicitly in Tod Clifton, the charismatic hipster leader of the Brotherhood's youth group, and more generally in the zoot suit subculture from which he springs. Clifton serves as a kind of double for the Invisible Man in the second half of the novel. It is precisely when Clifton shamefully acts out his own status as a puppet in the hands of the Brotherhood, selling Sambo dolls on the street, that the Invisible Man begins his final turn away from the Brotherhood.

13 See Pamela Hunt Steinle's *In Cold Fear* for an excellent review of the criticism's development over time. Steinle tends to uncritically embrace rather than to historicize the Adamic "national identity" reading of *Catcher*, but she does an excellent job reviewing both the celebratory approaches, as well as the conservative censorship campaigns against the novel. See especially 44–67.

14 See George Steiner's "The Salinger Industry" and Harvey Swados's "Must Writers Be Characters?" Both writers felt directly threatened by the critical obsession with *Catcher*. In the mid-1970s, a much more thoughtful critique of the Salinger craze was offered by Carol and Richard Ohmann, who contended that *Catcher*'s critics, under the baleful influence of postwar affluence, had taken such great interest in the novel because they could interpret it as a timeless psychological study of the pitfalls of growing up. In the process, critics depoliticized what was actually an insightful tale of class inequality in America. The Ohmanns, interpreting "phoniness" to name the cruelty of social status judgments, thus rebuked a generation of complacent postwar intellectuals for psychologizing Holden's social alienation, while ignoring the hierarchical relations that actually provoke his dismay. While it astutely aimed to historicize the unspoken determinants of Salinger criticism, this analysis missed the Cold War's decisive role in the psychologistic reading of *Catcher*. My own concern is less with the political failings of Salinger criticism, than with its political achievements, as it were. When read alongside the rise of the first world national allegory, Salinger criticism would seem not to have depoliticized *Catcher* at all, but rather to have supersaturated the novel with political meanings.

15 According to Hassan, Salinger's work reworks "the old story of the self against the world in outlines blurred by a mass society" (151).

16 Seng's developmental reading is quite straightforward and musters considerable supporting textual evidence. Built around the aphorism that Mr. Antolini offers to Holden, "The mark of the immature man is that he wants to die nobly for a cause, while the mark of the mature man is that he wants to live humbly for one" (Salinger, 188), Seng argues that Salinger provides critical distance from Holden's search for "simple truth," which is "doomed from the start: there are no simple truths. In a complex modern society truth too is complex, and a certain amount of social compromise is necessary" (77). Salinger's perceptive novel shares this Trillingesque vision of complexity, argues Seng. The fault lies with romanticizing critics who parade Holden "as the ideal youth, as a Galahad who carries his pure white banner undefiled through a world of sordid adults" (75).

17 In a similar vein, Edgar Branch wrote that "because Holden's [critical] vision is lit by the sick lamps of civilization, *The Catcher in the Rye* is as appropriate to our age as *Huckleberry Finn* is to an earlier America" (239).

18 As I noted in chapter 1, different sectors of the culture industry adopted the Fordist model in quite different ways and at different rates. Both the film and music industries, for example, had already taken a Fordist turn by the 1930s, well in advance of heavy industry. These differences in productive and con-

sumptive organization greatly affected how the various media actually incorporated early identity discourse and marketed its representative young rebel figures, as the next two chapters show in relation to the music and film industries respectively.

19 See James Gilbert's *A Cycle of Outrage* for how this belief operated in discussions of juvenile delinquency.

20 Steiner was not alone in this view. Harvey Swados and Mary McCarthy concurred that serious authors like themselves were being drowned out by the commercial success of mass market opportunists like Salinger.

21 Aijiz Ahmad in particular objected to the "rhetoric of otherness" with which Jameson cast Europe's former colonies as a culturally monolithic "third world," everywhere distinct from the industrialized first world. In Ahmad's view, the first/third world distinction, whether in literature or elsewhere, possesses "no theoretical status whatsoever" (4), for we all inhabit a single capitalist world-system whose internal differences represent, not a "binary opposition [between first and third world]," but a "contradictory unity, with differences, yes, but also with profound overlaps" (9). Only by acknowledging this unity might one think intelligibly about nonallegorical writing in the third world or about the "countless allegories" one also finds in first world black and feminist writing. However, one can relinquish the empirical validity of the spatial doctrine of the three worlds even while acknowledging that this doctrine generated all sorts of cultural and literary projects during the era of its imaginative appeal. The "real" of the third world concerned not a place but a project: the territorial setting was itself the effect of a narrative of national liberation that in turn underwrote a wide range of postwar anticolonial struggles.

22 The respective drives to allegorize the literature of both first world and third world nations were hardly unrelated to one another. In the era of global Fordism, national sovereignty was everywhere the form through which freedom—political, economic, or cultural—was imagined, even in the "people's democratic republics" of the second world.

3. Transcommodification

1 Many rock 'n' roll critics have questioned this origin story. Reebee Garofalo, for instance, calling this the "algebraic formula" of "r&b + c&w = r&r," grants it an element of truth, yet argues that it obscures rock's multiple sources of inspiration (94–95). Charles Gillett offers the alternative formula of five major sources for rock 'n' roll: northern band, New Orleans dance blues, Memphis country, Chicago R & B, and vocal group sounds (23–35). The combining of rural and urban, however, seems central to most narratives of rock 'n' roll's origins.

2 See Robert Fishman's *Bourgeois Utopias* for a brief but thorough review of the history of suburbia as a cultural ideal.

3 Roger Silverstone, for instance, who argues that "the suburb was an attempt, by and for the middle classes, to get the best of both worlds: the country and the

city," offers as evidence such early advocates as "Evenezer Howard, the founder of the Garden Cities Association [who] wrote in 1898, in what became a seminal treatise, that 'Town and country must be married and out of this joyous union will spring a new hope, a new life, a new civilization'" (58).

4. In *The Culture of Cities*, Lewis Mumford succinctly characterizes suburbia as "a collective effort to live a private life." This comment captures both suburbia's vision of privacy, as well as its implicit need to keep the "public" at a distance.

5. As Fishman puts it, "Suburbia can thus be defined first by what it includes—middle-class residences—and second (perhaps more importantly) by what it excludes: all industry, most commerce except for enterprises that specifically serve a residential area, and all lower-class residents (except for servants)" (6).

6. This conception, of course, obscured the suburban home as a site for domestic *labor* or housework. The suburban vision thus presumed a binary of labor and leisure modeled on patriarchal structures of experience that tended to render the lives of housewives as coterminous with leisure time. Consequences of this for the sexual politics of youth will be taken up in detail in the next two chapters.

7. These events in media transformation in fact reached their turning points in the same year. According to Lynn Spigel, 1955 was the year when enough televisions had been sold for the new medium to become a "viable reality" in Amerian life (32). Coincidentally, this is the same year conventionally offered by rock historians as the debut of rock 'n' roll as a mass media phenomenon, kicked off (as the next chapter explains) by the release of *Blackboard Jungle*.

8. J. Ronald Oakley even notes that early skeptics believed these sorts of problems with TV—its demands on space, including a "semi-darkened room," and on viewers, requiring their "continuous attention"—would restrict its appeal vis-à-vis radio (95).

9. As early as 1948 for instance, Levittown, the very first of the many postwar tract home developments, allowed buyers to have TV sets installed in the walls of their new living room, and to finance them with their mortgages (Spigel, 1).

10. For a brilliant discussion of the shows that were phased out by this transition, see George Lipsitz's essay "The Meaning of Memory" in *Time Passages*.

11. Garofalo claims that records had become the music industry's dominant product as early as 1952, even on radio where they came to replace live performances as the standard form of programming (84).

12. A scene in the early teenpic *Rock, Rock, Rock!* openly expresses (from a youth perspective, of course), this tension between the rock 'n' roll TV show and the family home. In the scene, a growing conflict between a teenage girl (Dori) and her father plays out over Alan Freed's "Rock 'n' Roll Dance Party." As Dori and her friend begin watching the show in the living room, father tries to read a magazine and smoke a pipe, using body language to express his exasperation with the girls. Soon enough, however, Dad himself becomes captivated by the music (including numbers by key black performers: the Flamingos, the Moonglows, Chuck Berry), and he is soon swaying and snapping his fingers

alongside his daughter. Each time a number ends, however, he returns to his feigned adult distaste for Freed's show. The scene, of course, means to comically express the hypocrisy of adult hostility toward the TV programming of rock 'n' roll (and it implicitly lauds the movies for offering the music a far more sympathetic screen to perform for).

13 See Glenn Altschuler's useful summary of *American Bandstand*'s disciplinary policies (82–87).

14 Related histories might easily be developed for the movement of other styles—western swing and black choral group sounds for instance—into the rock 'n' roll era, which would doubtlessly have somewhat different trajectories from R & B and country's contributions to the creation of rock 'n' roll.

15 See Ennis's detailed account of the converging streams, which he argues began with pop and R & B, followed shortly thereafter by country (161–228).

16 Domino in fact allegedly told a journalist in the late fifties, "What they call 'rock 'n' roll' now is rhythm & blues and I've been playing it for 15 years in New Orleans" ("Offbeat").

17 Like Domino, Haley was no icon of youth by the time this breakthrough happened, but a balding thirty-year old. That his sound might prove particularly so attractive to teenagers was far from obvious to him or his contemporaries. As Altschuler notes, Haley billed himself in the forties as the "Ramblin' Yodeler," and, wearing cowboy hats and boots, fronted a band that as late as the early fifties still went by the name of The Saddlemen (31).

18 Unlike Domino, whose style remained constant from the forties through the fifties, Haley achieved his success in part by modifying his earlier sound, principally by adding a bigger R & B beat to make his songs more danceable.

19 In point of fact, country and R & B had been sharing sounds from the start, so much so that it is sometimes difficult to distinguish between R & B, honky-tonk, roadhouse blues, rockabilly, and so forth. My point, however, is that rock 'n' roll actively tapped these blendings and confusions as means out of which it could condense a multilayered, and multilocational promise of "countering" suburbia.

20 Lewis only plugged in the high school reference because it had been commissioned as the title song to the teenpic *High School Confidential*, where in the opening shot Jerry Lee Lewis performs atop a flatbed truck as it drives by.

21 See Charles White's more thorough discussion of the Richard/Boone play around "Tutti Frutti" in *The Life and Times of Little Richard* (60).

22 I call these "landscapes" to call attention to the fact that they are imaginative settings. The R & B or country singer need not actually live (or have lived) in the sorts of material conditions s/he describes, nor need his/her music be meant primarily for audiences living in them. For all the reasons I am describing here, pre-Fordist social relations became imaginatively valuable in a music suited to the conditions of suburban teenagers in a Fordist world. It is the imaginative value of these pre-Fordist micronarratives for fifties suburbia that I am exploring here, not the pre-Fordist worlds from which they first sprang.

23 Each of these, it should be noted, corresponds to one of the three *Billboard* charts from the forties and fifties. From the industry's point of view, then, the advent of rock 'n' roll was initially marked by the repeated crossover of hits from the "specialty" R & B and country charts onto the mainstream pop chart or (to put this another way) the listing of hits on two (or even all three) charts at once.

24 Examples of such songs would include Pat Boone's "April Love" ("April love is for the very young"), Tab Hunter's "Young Love," and a plethora of Ricky Nelson's hits ("Be-Bop Baby," "A Teenager's Romance," and "Young Emotions," for instance).

25 For a detailed discussion of Berry's early life in suburban St. Louis, and its influence on his later music, see Howard DeWitt's *Chuck Berry* (1–17).

26 In "Johnny B. Goode," Berry did adapt a country music persona, singing about the guitar heroism of a poor country boy who goes neither to school nor to work, but just plays his magnificent sound by the railroad tracks. Here Berry approaches becoming a mirror image of Elvis Presley (a black man with a white sound vs. a white man with a black sound). Beyond this less acknowledged side of rock 'n' roll's racial inversions (i.e., blacks playing white music), Berry's innovations on behalf of fifties rock 'n' roll would be difficult to overestimate. Charles Gillett claims that, of all the early rockers, Berry had the greatest impact on his audience and on subsequent artists. Unlike most other early rock 'n' roll artists, Berry was his own songwriter, setting a precedent as a pop poet for later artists such as Bob Dylan and the Beatles. Berry is also credited for making the electric guitar into rock's chief instrument.

27 These substitutions are extended even further in the next verse, with a school-bell replacing the work whistle to signal a lunch break too short even to finish one's meal, and conducted in a room that's short of seats.

28 Derrida's critique of Ricoeur's model finds its primary statement in "White Mythologies." For Derrida, the literal is derivative of the figurative, not the other way round. Ricoeur's objections to Derrida's argument are responded to in a later essay, "The Retrait of Metaphor."

29 Yet, to return again to the Derridean observation, it is vital to recognize that these "literal" meanings of R & B and country were no less free of metaphoricity and displacement than, let us say, heavy metal music that today might appear to "literally" signify a suburban context. Just as rock 'n' roll and its descendants can be shown to have constituted themselves by transfiguring other sounds, so R & B and country are themselves the results of earlier transfigurations (involving rural blues, various folk musics, and Tin Pan Alley, extending along an endless chain of transcodal processes. R & B was itself composed through the transfiguration (into an urban, industrial context) of the rural connotations of the Delta blues. To the extent that literality is aligned with authenticity and metaphoricity with appropriation, it is crucial to recognize all musical sounds as either more or less obviously appropriative, but never self-identical with their social or cultural context.

30 Of course, many teenagers did in fact work jobs, and therefore had leisure time in the narrow sense. My point, however, is that, through rock 'n' roll, to imagine oneself as a teenager (working or not) meant to understand oneself as living a life that resembled (here is the metaphorical operation) one divided between labor and leisure.

4. Identity Hits the Screen

1 Teenpics sometimes also came in a "clean" flavor, as Doherty notes, depicting teenage romance rather than the explicit rebellion of the "juvenile delinquent" films. Yet even the "cleanies" ultimately centered on the ideal of teen sovereignty, much along the lines of "pop" rock 'n' roll as I outlined in the previous chapter. Indeed, many of the cleanies actually starred major pop rock 'n' roll performers like Pat Boone. The cleanies, furthermore, only began to appear in the late fifties, on the coattails of the rock 'n' roll and juvenile delinquency movies that had, by then, already drawn a sharp line between adult and youth pleasure.
2 These teenage responses to *Blackboard Jungle*, and the controversies over the film's meaning to which they gave rise, have continued in public debates over films like *Colors* and *Menace 2 Society*. In this respect, *Blackboard* is the progenitor of a significant post–rock 'n' roll film cycle playing off of adults' class- and race-based fears of urban youth gang violence.
3 James Gilbert's *A Cycle of Outrage* is the best study to date of adult anxiety in the fifties that mass media were encouraging juvenile delinquency. See especially 162–195 for a discussion of the debates over whether to censor Hollywood teenpics.
4 In effect, "Encoding/Decoding" aims to politicize Umberto Eco's notion of the "aberrant decoding," a situation that results when addresser and addressee of a message do not share the same codes. Hall uses Eco's concept to explain the dynamics that underlie what mass media studies have traditionally called communication "misunderstandings" or "failures." The discipline, Hall insists, must accept the fact that the interpretive (decoding) moment is not simply individual and idiosyncratic but, on the contrary, just as social as the production (encoding) moment. When different social identities in mass-mediated societies share a popular culture but apply different codes to it, this means that they are in a state of ideological contradiction that *potentially* may lead to overt social conflict.
5 Hall's theory of reading is deeply indebted to Gramsci's modification, through his theory of hegemony, of the Marxist theory of the state as instrument of the ruling class. Indeed, Hall's model of the popular text can best be understood as a semiotic hegemony (again as opposed to ideological instrument of the ruling class). For Gramsci, political hegemony involves manufacturing general consent to state power by way of its incorporation of the interests of classes and class fractions other than those of the "ruling" class (the coalition forming what

he calls a "historical bloc"). Similarly, Hall's popular text produces widespread semiotic consent to its preferred meanings by allowing most viewers to negotiate their own relationship to them.

6 See, for example, John Fiske's considerably later cultural studies classic *Television Culture*, in which Hall's theory of reading becomes the point of departure, allowing Fiske to argue that the political valence of popular culture inheres not in the ideological codes of the text but rather in the negotiation between these codes and their socially positioned viewers (64). Like Hall, Fiske contends that popular texts lack any intrinsic ideological closure. Closure instead becomes an effect intermittently imposed by dominant ideologies, which by leading subjects to prefer certain semiotic processes over others, will tend to limit the play of meaning in their readings of popular text. Indeed, a dominant reading can be defined as an instance where that tendency has won out: the reader has successfully decoded the text in an ideologically coherent manner and repressed any textual contradictions of that coherence.

7 Sidney Poitier would literally take on Glenn Ford's role later in his career, playing the part of the teacher in *To Sir with Love*.

8 Peter Biskind interprets Artie's reading in very similar generational terms, describing it as a threat to Dadier, who "can't allow the kids to heroize him [Jack] in these terms, to make him over into a juvenile Dillinger" (213). Artie's delinquent reading also bears a *racial* significance, just as Dadier's response (apparently a lesson on racism) includes a *generational* dimension. Racial and generational antagonism in this scene are thus always being articulated together, as indeed they are throughout the film.

9 Both James Baldwin and Lorraine Hansberry compellingly criticized Norman Mailer's romanticization of what is in effect the very segregationist's stereotype of the black man that he had presumably set out to demolish. They do so in rather different ways. Baldwin objects to the sexualization of that romance, to yet another use of black men as "walking phallic symbols" by someone who should have known better (172). Hansberry protests more generally to the wholesale association of African Americans with the marginal life of the street hustler. At bottom, Baldwin's and Hansberry's critiques of "The White Negro" share a dismay at the potential costs for black people of Mailer's obsessive masculinization of crossracial rebellion.

10 Another such oppositional scene takes place when the students, led by Artie (but conveniently missing Gregory), entice Dadier's fellow teacher Joshua Edwards into playing his jazz records for them. Disliking the Bix Beiderbecke record as wimpy, Artie puts on a fast-paced tune and then proceeds to break the entire collection while the other boys dance with one another in the classroom. The music is bop rather than rock 'n' roll, but once again the boys' wild dance is linked with their rebellious delinquency. As one might expect, their energy in this scene contrasts with Edwards's impotence.

11 Once again the film cautiously mediates its more dangerous racial meanings, using white characters (Jack in the cartoon, Bill Haley and the Comets for rock

'n' roll, the rapist in this scene), to signify a racial threat. This allows the film to engage white fears of integration, while maintaining a liberal position that avoids overt racial demonization in the reactionary tradition of *Birth of a Nation*.

12 McRobbie's critique is leveled at the canonical cultural studies texts on youth subcultures: Paul Willis's *Learning to Labour*, Dick Hebdige's *Subculture*, and the *Resistance through Ritual* anthology edited by Tony Jefferson and Stuart Hall.

13 I have written explicitly on rock 'n' roll's staging of masculinist rebellion in "Mapping the Rebel Image."

14 See Sara Evans's *Personal Politics* for a detailed history of how the women's movement emerged from the limitations of the New Left. See Dennis Altman's *Homosexual* for a meditation on the relationship of gay political consciousness to the counterculture and New Left. Particularly useful are chapters 5 and 6, where Altman elaborates his own metaphor of the "faggot as nigger" (152–226).

5. Oedipus in Suburbia

1 The two other threats noted by Erikson were the "machine," a symbol of the assembly-line mass stamping of Fordist culture, and the "boss," who represents the risk of a return to despotism via corporate hierarchy. In this chapter, I consider why "Mom" might represent the third emblem of Fordism's risks to the next generation of America's "freeborn sons."

2 Because they dramatize conflicts between sons and fathers, bad-boy identity dramas like *Rebel without a Cause* and *King Creole* beg to be read through a psychoanalytic lens. And yet it is crucial that this be done in a way that engages the historicity of psychoanalysis, particularly in an era such as the fifties, when it had come to dominate much of American social science. As Rob Corber has thoughtfully argued, film theorists have engaged in circular argumentation when they use films that consciously deploy Freudian themes—those of Alfred Hitchcock for instance—in order to rediscover the truth-value of psychoanalytic approaches to the cinema. Instead, Corber suggests, we should consider the specific ideological work that a movie's psychoanalytic codes perform. In the case of Hitchcock's films, Corber argues, oedipal narratives of psychic maturation were adapted to homophobic Cold War discourses of national security. My interest in the oedipal dimensions of *Rebel* and *King Creole* is very much in Corber's spirit. The point is not to confirm again the oedipality of all narrative, nor even the oedipality of all bad-boy narratives. Rather, the psychoanalytic elements in these films are important because they register the era's ideological struggles over domesticity, illuminating the conditions that led identity— itself a concept born out of Erikson's psychoanalytic work—to be normalized as a specifically if complexly masculine ideal and achievement. The same concerns govern my periodic use of Laura Mulvey's classic essay "Visual Pleasure and Narrative Cinema," with its brilliant account of the visual encoding of classic Hollywood masculinity. At certain critical moments oedipal bad-boy films feature a Mulveyan "male gaze," but these do not make them instances of a

monolithically patriarchal classic Hollywood cinema. Neither do certain anti-Mulveyan moments show them to be clandestine examples of some hidden countercinema. Rather, these films alternately enunciate and transgress the codes of the male gaze in ways that rendered a boy's unwillingness to "become his father" into the generic drama of identity struggle.

3 See Jessica Weiss's insightful discussion of the "new fatherhood" of the fifties, which circumscribed the role of breadwinner in order to open space for male domesticity. This trend, Weiss points out, was the culmination of a half-century trend underwritten by the suburbs and the new stress on family life (86–113).

4 At least one scholar, John Kreidl, claims that Ray and Lindner briefly met to discuss the film project (88).

5 This sudden obsession with male homosexuality of course derives from the 1948 Kinsey Report, *Sexual Behavior in the Human Male*, which revealed to an unsuspecting public that one out of every three American men had at some point practiced homosexual relations.

6 See Charles Gillett's *Sounds of the City* (7–18) and Rebeel Garofalo's *Rockin' Out* (43–91) for the development of the three-chart system (pop, race, and hillbilly) and its postwar transformations. Both writers stress that the rise of rock 'n' roll involved the crossing over of country and blues hits onto the more prestigious pop chart that had previously been monopolized by the products of Tin Pan Alley.

7 Marsh claims that the army service was actually a conscious ploy by the draft board to "rob him of everything—not just fame but also his wealth and whatever new dignity he had acquired" (126). Certainly, the timing was such that Presley left the musical world at the same moment as many other early rock 'n' rollers, and for an astonishing range of different reasons. The symbolic meaning of putting Presley, of all people, in uniform was surely lost on nobody.

8 See James Robertson's *The Casablanca Man* for a useful review of Crutiz's career in Hollywood. Particularly useful is the discussion of his wartime politics in chapter 5 (74–91).

9 See Marsh (62) for a quick account of Colonel Parker's moves to gain control over Presley as a commodity.

6. Beat Fraternity and the Generation of Identity

1 In the King James version of the Bible, "generation" is the word that translates (reasonably well) the Hebrew "dor."

2 Recognizing this problem, Mannheim draws a further distinction between a "generation" (sharing a common social location) and a "generation unit" (sharing a common perspective on that social location), admitting the likely existence of multiple generation units within any particular generation. This, however, ultimately begs the question of how a "generation unit" gets formed, and what its members could possibly share that a generation does not. Something beyond social location is needed to explain the emergence of what Mann-

heim calls "concrete bonds," namely some sort of theory of mediation availed by concepts such as ideology, representation, or articulation (125).

3 The gap in question is the same as *The Catcher in the Rye*'s, which was first published in 1951 but did not become an object of critical acclaim until about 1957.

4 See the articles "Generation of Esthetes" and "Luckiest Generation" in *Life*, "Explosive Generation" in *Look*, "Silent Generation" in *Harper*, and Harrison Salisbury's "Shook-up Generation." Of these, the last two were the strongest of the pretenders. The "silent generation" represented the young as apparently acquiescent and yet disconcertingly evasive when asked to express its social opinions. The "shook-up generation" represented a crime-prone and shocking youth whose delinquency needed to be explained in terms of social neglect. In interesting ways, the beat generation condensed these two representations, making room, as John Clellon Holmes explicitly states in "Philosophy of the Beat Generation," for both the young Republican who cynically plays the game and the hipster who hides out in a subterranean bohemian world.

5 John Horne Burns's 1952 novel was perhaps the earliest attempt at beat mass-marketing. The cover of the paperback edition called it a "merciless novel of America's 'Beat Generation.'" After 1957, however, "beat generation" became idiomatic as a signifier for the youth market. See for example, novels such as Nolan Miller's *Why Am I So Beat*, sociological studies such as Lawrence Lipton's *The Holy Barbarians*, Hollywood's *This Beat Generation*, and, somewhat later of course, the Beatles in pop music.

6 Barbara Ehrenreich makes this problematic but common claim in her otherwise excellent chapter on the beats in *The Hearts of Men*.

7 Consider, for example, the titles of articles on the beat generation, such as Paul O'Neil's "The Only Rebellion Around" or "Squaresville, U.S.A. vs. Beatsville."

8 In fact, when *On the Road* at last popularized the term "beat generation," in 1957, Kerouac himself was already thirty-five years old. Allen Ginsberg and John Clellon Holmes were thirty-one, and William Burroughs was forty-seven. Only the lesser known poet Gregory Corso was still in his twenties (twenty-seven, to be exact). I point this out only to emphasize that we are dealing here with representations of subjects and not with empirical age groups. That the beats were in fact considerably older than the beat generation they came to represent was not *necessarily* a problem. It did on occasion, however, make them vulnerable to attacks on their legitimacy as popular generational spokesmen.

9 This argument is partially inspired by Jane Tompkins's notion of the "cultural work" of fiction, meaning its historically efficacious rhetorical designs on a readership. Whereas she deploys it in *Sensational Designs* as a recuperative concept that allows her to evoke, for example, the sophistication of *Uncle Tom's Cabin*'s abolitionist appeal to white Christian women, I am putting it more in the service of an ideology critique. The problem with the beats is not that, like the writers of domestic fiction, their literature is not taken seriously. The problem is rather that the "cultural work" of their fiction has been misunderstood. Beat fiction does not express a generational experience. Rather, that experience

is a rhetorical effect of the fiction. My metaphor of the roadmap is also influenced by Janice Radway's discussion of the value of middlebrow fiction to its readership, who appreciate the literature not on aesthetic grounds (highbrow formalism), nor for the pleasure it gives them (lowbrow vulgar sensuality), but as a moral compass to daily life. Beat literature serves this sort of purpose too, I argue, but in the process of mapping a moral condition it also works to produce the generation held to be subject to it.

10   This role is usually played, biographically speaking, by each text's Neal Cassady character. In "Howl," however, Carl Solomon plays that role. And in *Go*, the Kerouac and Ginsberg characters are nearly as important as the Cassady character in representing beatness.

11   Sedgwick's intent was to draw possible lines of connection between feminist and queer politics by demonstrating that homophobia against men, when at work historically, is always misogynistic in that it constitutes a patriarchal repugnance for femininity. Another implication of Sedgwick's argument is that because their sexuality is not considered to be a way for men to promote the interests of men, men who find themselves on the wrong side of the homosocial divide (i.e., gay) engage in male-male relations that could be (though certainly need not be) compatible with an antipatriarchal struggle.

12   Barbara Ehrenreich has discussed the beats as part of American men's much broader postwar "flight from commitment" to marriage and family life since the fifties. Insofar as all the beat texts valorize male adolescence over male maturity, Ehrenreich's analysis conveys one of the most important dimensions of the public meanings of beat homosociality. Of all the principal beat texts, *On the Road*'s explicit posing of a conflict between heterosexuality and homosociality most closely adheres to Ehrenreich's thesis. As we shall see, *Go* and "Howl" work somewhat differently.

13   Shortly after this scene, impotence will become literalized. Hobbes takes the young woman home, but in his sense of loss and sadness he cannot get an erection when they make love.

14   The "kids" sketched here, incidentally, are easily recognizable as those Holmes describes as natural bohemians in his nearly contemporaneous article, "This Is the Beat Generation." Indeed, in the introduction to section 2 of his essay collection, *Passionate Opinions*, Holmes explicitly acknowledges his description of the Go Hole in *Go* as his first attempt to formulate the beat generation (50).

15   The one exception is Stofsky. His unique status as a gay beat troubles the gang/marriage binary at a basic level, as I will show momentarily.

16   Though the pool of individuals upon whom section 1 is based is quite small, the sheer number of events and their constantly shifting locales (New York, Laredo, New Jersey, Kansas, Idaho, the West Coast, Oklahoma, Colorado, etc.) create the impression that these "best minds" of a generation are loose everywhere in America. See Barry Miles's biography of Ginsberg for a historical key to "Howl" detailing what actually happened to whom (188–191).

17   Another excellent example of this motif can be found in Gregory Corso's poem

"Variations on a Generation": "The Hipster dressed in ermine in the golden halls of the Beat Generation will be the slayer of society, as is told in his enthusiastic eye. He will sack society with this sword of old prunes, climb the fortress with armies of penguins and fly away with the daughter of society. He will wed the daughter of society, and throughout all the nights of their marriage, he will drive her mad with descriptions of her father" (93).

18 Among all of Sedgwick's narrative variants of homosocial desire, the one that best approximates the beat homosociality occurs in her final chapter, where she considers English appropriations of what she calls Walt Whitman's vision of "manly love in the service of new democratic ideals." Although Sedgwick's book actually shows the diversity of the homosocial, it also tries in problematic ways to resolve it into a universal feminist problematic. This contradiction stems from a self-acknowledged tension in her methodology between a structuralist (and universalizing) approach to homosociality, which she associates with the radical feminist exchange-of-women thesis, and a historical approach, attributed to Marxist feminists and concerned with shifting class relations and family structures. Ultimately, however, I would argue that Sedgwick balances these two in favor of structuralism, by taking the asymmetrical, erotic triangle as an ahistorical patriarchal foundation upon which historically variable gender, class, and race relations have been built. The erotic triangle is, as she puts it, "a sensitive register precisely for delineating relationships of power and meaning, and for making graphically intelligible the play of desire and identification by which individuals negotiate with their society for empowerment" (27). While this elegant formulation appears to ease the tension between structuralist and historical approaches to sex and gender, it can only work by treating the form of the erotic triangle itself as an always already available barometer for sexual history. Like patriarchy itself, one can never explain how it came into being historically, or what it would take for it to disappear. It is simply always there, a minimal cultural constant across time and place that can be used to reveal the local plays and contingencies of power. If one begins, as Sedgwick does, with such an abstract, structural model for patriarchy, algebraically expressible in the exchange-of-women thesis and geometrically mappable in the erotic triangle, it then becomes extremely difficult to acknowledge different kinds of homosocial narratives as possessing varying relations to patriarchy since they all recapitulate its basic structure. It becomes equally difficult, for that matter, to consider major historical changes in the relations of gender and power.

19 The one exception is Freud's recapitulation of the revolutionary narrative in *Totem and Taboo*, where the sexual contract regarding the brothers' access to the primal father's women is made explicit (149–150).

20 See in particular the introduction to Nelson's masterful critique of American fraternity (1–28).

21 See Lisa Maria Hogeland's *Feminism and Its Fictions* for a historically grounded discussion of consciousness-raising as a tactic of early feminist literary politics, especially 23–53.

22 Unlike accounts of the beat fraternities, *Burning Questions* sexualizes its sisterhood. When Zane begins a relationship with Faith, another member of her "girl gang," she explains their heightened passion for each other as a function of their sisterly equality. However, Zane also names a homosocial passion that haunts the novel from beginning to end. She first sees Morgan Moore on the day that she steps off the bus that has taken her from Indiana to Greenwich Village, her first journey toward liberation. At the time, Morgan seems like just one more character in a larger tableau of beatnik freedom, but in fact Moore is "probably the number one exception in the Village." Morgan, it turns out, is a dyke, columnist, and master chess player who shadows Zane throughout the novel as a sort of romantic counterfigure, someone whose strong sense of individual autonomy Zane aspires to share. When years later (and at the close of the novel) the two women at last meet up and speak with mutual admiration as sister feminists, the passion that drives the entire novel is still there, and still unsexualized: who would think that "after half a lifetime of false starts I was now sitting equal and opposite Morgan Moore in an absolutely unprecedented New Space?" (354).

7. Where the Girls Were

1 This would include the conventional Sally Hayes in *Catcher*, Nelly in *King Creole*, as well as the wives and girlfriend of the beats in Kerouac and Holmes's novels. I have developed this argument about the gendering of rebellion elsewhere in "Mapping the Rebel Image."

2 *Girls Town* directly reworks the juvenile delinquent crime narrative of *Boys Town*. In the latter film of 1938, Mickey Rooney plays a cigar-puffing adolescent tough who is gradually reformed by Catholic schoolmaster Father Flanagan (Spencer Tracy). *Boys Town* spoke specifically to depression-era concerns about underclass street boys who, having been separated from their parents under economic pressures, seemed destined for a life of crime. Reflecting these fears, Rooney's character, Whitey, is the already angry and callous younger brother of a convicted felon whom Flanagan rescues from a repetition of his older sibling's fate. Whitey may be seen as the cinematic prototype of the romanticized lower-class urban delinquent so central to the rock 'n' roll rebellion featured in *Blackboard Jungle*. However, released as it was before the development of an age-segmented consumer culture, and thus before the advent of the teenpic, *Boys Town* lacks the teen-centered identification structures of *Blackboard Jungle* and most postwar teenpics, including *Girls Town*. *Boys Town* and *Girls Town* differ most obviously in that the latter immerses the viewer from its opening scene onward in a self-contained teen world, complete with its own lingo, its own forms of leisured freedom (rock 'n' roll, beach parties, drag racing), and a general sense of distantiation from adult life. By contrast, *Boys Town* begins by introducing the viewer to half an hour's worth of Father Flanagan's altruistic exploits before presenting the bad boy whom he will convert to goodness.

Boys Town marks itself as a pre–Cold War, pre-Fordist film precisely through its lack of any effort to bring its audience to identify with Whitey's side in the generational conflict with Flanagan.

3 Such sisterhood makes an interesting point of contrast with the fraternity of the beats, who (as we saw) also kept the sexual at bay in forming a brotherly generational cadre. Yet there are crucial differences as well. While the beats desexualized the bonds between brothers in order to form a generational unit, they celebrated sexual relations with women and sometimes men outside the social unit as a sign of their virility. For this sisterhood, sexuality simply has no place at all. Indeed, the sexual license of the individual bad girl must give way precisely to chastity if sisterhood is to emerge.

4 Fannie Hurst's original novel is much more faithfully translated in a 1930s film version directed by Robert Stahl.

5 See, in particular, the excellent essays by Sandy Flitterman-Lewis ("Imitation(s) of Life"), Lauren Berlant ("National Brands/National Body"), and Marina Heung ("What's the Matter with Sarah Jane?").

6 Flitterman-Lewis, for instance, perceives Sarah Jane as a transgressive mulatta whose challenge to prescribed categories of race and sex threatens "culturally determined racial and feminine boundaries" (327). Deploying a Lacanian model through which Sarah Jane can be seen to signify feminist resistance to the symbolic order of patriarchy, Flitterman-Lewis underscores the sexual substance of Sarah Jane's resistance, specifically her use of sex in the second half of the film to enact her refusal of Annie's servile position. Flitterman-Lewis concludes that, in terms of the narrative, her revolt must be a doomed one, yet it nevertheless manages to articulate an otherwise suppressed feminine voice objecting to the psychosocial terms of female and black subordination. In a considerably less optimistic reading, Marina Heung presents *Imitation* as a principally conservative text on the grounds that it first reduces class inequality to a matter of racial difference, then depoliticizes racism by displacing it from the social to the familial register through the "built-in theme of mother-daughter conflict" (312–313). She also proposes, however, that Sarah Jane's rebelliousness may be read subversively for its ability to activate otherwise disallowed meanings, specifically the legitimacy of a woman's resistance to female "confinement in the home" as well as to the "limitations placed on her by class and race structures" (314).

7 The Sandra Dee number in *Grease*, the fifties nostalgia musical of the mid-seventies, neatly encapsulates this memory of the actress. Rizzo, the bad-girl figure of that film, mocks her good-girl rival by associating her with Dee's preposterous protection of her virtue. I see this as a misleading postsixties reevaluation of Dee as a goody-two-shoes, when in fact Dee's characters almost never aim to protect their virginity but are usually bent on figuring out how to lose it.

8 This metaphor of a rising black tide that threatens the white self gets deployed with great explicitness in a key passage in which Tomboy, wandering through

the streets, sees "a vision of the city rise again, and this time all the faces were turned completely upward; black and turbulent water swirled through every street, rising higher and higher, and now she knew why the faces were turned that way, for these were the corpses of the drowned and among them she saw a small white hand rise above the water" (135).

Conclusion: The Rise and Fall of Identity

1. The pithiest description of Fordism's crisis within the United States, and of the transition into "flexible accumulation," remains David Harvey's *The Condition of Postmodernity* (140–192). I have here condensed the account of this crisis down to a bare minimum. Alain Lipietz's *Mirages and Miracles* takes a more global approach, showing how the crisis of Fordism in the "core" industrial economies actually gave rise to the success of a "peripheral Fordism" elsewhere, as industrial production relocated to what would become the NICS (newly industrializing countries).
2. See Roger Rouse's "Thinking through Transnationalism" for an excellent analysis of the reconfiguration of class relations in the United States that accompanied the post-Fordist transnationalization of production.
3. As Ash Amin points out, "flexible specialization" is an account of post-Fordist accumulation that has been elaborated, less by the regulation school writers themselves than by other theorists such as Piore and Sable in *The Second Industrial Divide*, who tend to make rather absolute—and often utopian claims—about a transition in twentieth-century capitalism from rigid mass-production systems to specialized, and potentially less hierarchical ones (6). See their well-known study *The Second Industrial Divide*.
4. See Rouse's insightful reading of "corporate-liberal multiculturalism" in relation to the post-Fordist class system (380–386).
5. Another quick example would be the critical legal theory collection boldly entitled *After Identity*, but which instantly reverses course when its editors (Dan Danielsen and Karen Engle) acknowledge as its goal the waging of "identity politics after identity" (xiii). Legal theories of identity appear inadequate, yet the editors still feel compelled to assert on principle the "vital importance of identity in people's lived experience" (xviii). "After identity" thus expresses a wish more than it does an existing politicotheoretical strategy.

WORKS CITED

Adorno, Theodor, Else Frenkel-Brunswik, Daniel J. Levinson, and R. Nevitt Sanford. *The Authoritarian Personality*. New York: Norton, 1950.

Ahmad, Aijaz. "Jameson's Rhetoric of Otherness and the 'National Allegory.'" *Social Text* 17 (fall 1987): 3–25.

Alcoff, Linda. "Cultural Feminism versus Post-Structuralism: The Identity Crisis in Feminist Theory. *Signs* 13, no. 3 (spring 1988): 405–436.

Aldridge, John W. *In Search of Heresy: American Literature in an Age of Conformity*. New York: McGraw-Hill, 1956.

Altman, Dennis. *Homosexual: Oppression and Liberation*. New York: Avon, 1973.

Altschuler, Glenn C. *All Shook Up: How Rock 'n' Roll Changed America*. Oxford: Oxford University Press, 2003.

Amin, Ash. "Post-Fordism: Models, Fantasies, and Phantoms of Transition." In *The Post-Fordism Reader*, edited by Ash Amin, 1–40. Oxford: Blackwell, 1994.

Anderson, Benedict. *Imagined Communities: Reflections on the Origin and Spread of Nationalism*. New York: Verso, 1983.

Andrews, Geoff. *The Films of Nicholas Ray*. London: Charles Letts, 1991.

Angels with Dirty Faces. Directed by Michael Curtiz. Warner Studio, 1938.

Aquila, Richard. *That Old Time Rock & Roll: A Chronicle of an Era, 1954–1963*. New York: Schirmer Books, 1989.

Arac, Jonathan, "Nationalism, Hypercanonization, and *Huckleberry Finn*." In *National Identities and Post-Americanist Narratives*, edited by Donald E. Pease, 14–33. Durham, N.C.: Duke University Press, 1994.

———. "Toward a Critical Genealogy of the U.S. Discourse of Identity: Invisible Man after Fifty Years." *boundary 2: An International Journal of Literature and Culture* 30, no. 2 (summer 2003): 195–216.

Arlow, Joanna E. "Not Just 'Chicks' and 'Boy Gangs': Gender, Sex, Writing, and the Beats in Postwar America, 1945–1965." Master's thesis, University of Oregon, 1998.

Auerbach, Erich. "'Figura.'" In *Scenes from the Drama of European Literature*, 11–76. Gloucester, Mass.: Peter Smith, 1973.

Baldwin, James. "The Black Boy Looks at the White Boy." In *Nobody Knows My Name: More Notes of a Native Son*, 161–190. New York: Laurel, 1961.

Balio, Tino, ed. *Hollywood in the Age of Television*. New York: Unwin Hyman, 1990.

Bannon, Ann. *Beebo Brinker*. San Francisco: Cleis, 1962.

———. *Odd Girl Out*. San Francisco: Cleis, 1957.

Baruch, Dorothy W. *How to Live with Your Teenager*. New York: McGraw-Hill, 1953.

———. *You, Your Children, and War*. New York: D. Appleton-Century, 1942.

Baudrillard, Jean. *For a Critique of the Political Economy of the Sign*. Translated by Charles Levin. New York: Tebs Press, 1981.

Beebe, Roger, Denise Fullbrook, and Ben Saunders, eds. Introduction to *Rock over the Edge: Transformations in Popular Music Culture*, 1–24. Durham, N.C.: Duke University Press, 2002.

Bellow, Saul. *The Adventures of Augie March*. Greenwich, Conn.: Crest Books, 1949.

Belton, John. *American Cinema/American Culture*. New York: McGraw Hill, 1994.

Benton, Nick. "Don't Call Me a Brother." In *The Gay Liberation Book*, edited by Len Richmond and Gary Noguera, 181–183. San Francisco: Ramparts Press, 1973.

Berlant, Lauren. "National Brands/National Body: Imitation of Life." In *Comparative American Identities: Race, Sex, and Nationality in the Modern Text*, edited by Hortense J. Spillers, 110–140. New York: Routledge, 1991.

Bettleheim, Bruno. "Fathers Shouldn't Try to Be Mothers." *Parents*, October 1954.

Biskind, Peter. *Seeing Is Believing: How Hollywood Taught Us to Stop Worrying and Love the Fifties*. New York: Pantheon, 1983.

Blackboard Jungle. Directed by Richard Brooks. Metro-Goldwyn-Meyer Pictures, 1955.

Bonn, Thomas L. *Heavy Traffic and High Culture: New American Library as Literary Gatekeeper in the Paperback Revolution*. New York: Meridian, 1990.

Bowles, Samuel, and Herbert Gintis. *Capitalism and Democracy: Property, Community, and the Contradictions of Modern Social Thought*. New York: Basic Books, 1987.

Boyer, Paul. *By the Bomb's Early Light: American Thought and Culture at the Dawn of the Atomic Age*. New York: Pantheon Books, 1985.

Branch, Edgar. "Mark Twain and J. D. Salinger: A Study in Literary Conti-

nuity." In *Salinger: A Critical and Personal Portrait,* edited by Henry Aratole Gronwald, 226–240. New York: Pocket Books, 1962.
Breines, Winifred. *Young, White, and Miserable: Growing Up Female in the 1950s.* Boston: Beacon Press, 1994.
Brierly, J. L. *The Law of Nations: An Introduction to the International Law of Peace.* New York: Oxford University Press, 1963.
Brown, Wendy. "Injury, Identity, Politics." In *Mapping Multiculturalism,* edited by Avery Gordon and Christopher Newfield, 149–166. Minneapolis: University of Minnesota Press, 1996.
Burke, Kenneth. *Attitudes toward History.* Los Altos: Hermes Publications, 1959.
Burns, John Horne. *A Cry of Children.* New York: Bantam, 1952.
Butler, Judith. *Gender Trouble: Feminism and the Subversion of Identity.* New York: Routledge, 1990.
Byars, Jackie. *All That Hollywood Allows: Re-Reading Gender in 1950s Melodrama.* Chapel Hill: University of North Carolina Press, 1991.
Camus, Albert. *The Rebel: An Essay on Man in Revolt.* New York: Vintage, 1957.
Carmichael, Stokely. "Toward Black Liberation." In *Black Fire: An Anthology of Afro-American Writing,* edited by Leroi Jones and Larry Neal, 119–132. New York: William Morrow, 1968.
Casablanca. Directed by Michael Curtiz. Warner Brothers Studios, 1942.
Castiglia, Christopher. "Rebel without a Closet." In *Engendering Men: The Question of Male Feminist Criticism,* edited by Joseph Boone and Michael Cadden, 207–221. New York: Routledge, 1990.
Ceplair, Larry, and Steven Englund. *The Inquisition in Hollywood: Politics in the Film Community, 1930–1960.* New York: Anchor Press. 1980.
Charters, Ann, ed. *The Portable Beat Reader.* New York: Viking. 1992.
Chase, Richard. *The American Novel and Its Tradition.* New York: Doubleday Anchor, 1957.
———. "One's Self I Sing." In *Interpretations of American Literature,* edited by Charles Feidelson Jr. and Paul Brodtkorb Jr., 176–185. New York: Oxford University Press, 1959.
Clark, Eric O. *Virtuous Vice: Homoeroticism and the Public Sphere.* Durham: Duke University Press, 2000.
Cleaver, Eldridge. *Soul on Ice.* New York: Ramparts, 1972.
Cohan, Steven. *Masked Men: Masculinity and the Movies in the Fifties.* Bloomington: Indiana University Press, 1997.
Cohen, Elliot E. "A 'Teen-Age Bill of Rights.'" *New York Times Magazine.* January 7, 1945: 16–18.
Cook, Bruce. *The Beat Generation.* New York: Charles Scribner's Sons, 1971.
Corber, Robert. *In the Name of National Security: Hitchcock, Homophobia, and the Political Construction of Gender in Postwar America.* Durham, N.C.: Duke University Press, 1993.

———. *Homosexuality in Cold War America: Resistance and the Crisis of Masculinity.* Durham, N.C.: Duke University Press, 1997.

Corso, Gregory. "Variations on a Generation." In *A Casebook on the Beat*, edited by Thomas Parkinson, 88–97. New York: Thomas Y. Crowell, 1961.

Danielsen, Dan, and Karen Engle, eds. *After Identity: A Reader in Law and Culture.* New York: Routledge, 1995.

Davis, Harriet. "How *Not* to Raise Our Children." *Parents* (October 1945): 17, 123–124.

Davis, Kenneth C. *Two-Bit Culture: The Paperbacking of America.* Boston: Houghton Mifflin, 1984.

D'Emilio, John. "The Homosexual Menace: The Politics of Sexuality in Cold War America." In *Passion and Power: Sexuality in History*, edited by Kathy Peiss and Christina Simmons, 226–240. Philadelphia: Temple University Press, 1989.

D'Emillio, John, and Estelle Freedman. *Intimate Matters: A History of Sexuality in America.* New York: Harper, 1988.

Derrida, Jacques. "The Retrait of Metaphor." *Enclitic* 2 (1978): 6–33.

———. "White Mythologies." In *Margins of Philosophy*, 207–272. Chicago: University of Chicago Press, 1984.

Devlin, Rachel. "Female Juvenile Delinquency and the Problem of Sexual Authority in America, 1945–1965." In *Delinquents and Debutantes: Twentieth-Century American Girls' Cultures*, edited by Sherrie Inness, 83–106. New York: New York University Press, 1998.

DeWitt, Howard. *Chuck Berry: Rock 'n' Roll Music.* Ann Arbor, Mich.: Pierian Press, 1985.

Dickstein, Morris. "On and Off the Road: The Outsider as Young Rebel." In *Beat Culture: The 1950s and Beyond*, 31–48. Amsterdam: VU University Press, 1999.

Doherty, Thomas. *Teenagers and Teenpics: The Juvenilization of American Movies in the 1950s.* New York: Unwin Hyman, 1988.

Doyle, Kathleen. "A Bill of Rights for Teen-agers." *Parents*, April 1948, pp. 20, 82–86.

Dyer, Richard. *Heavenly Bodies.* London: Macmillan, 1986.

Echols, Alice. *Daring to Be Bad: Radical Feminism in America, 1967–1975.* Minneapolis: University of Minnesota Press, 1989.

———. "We Gotta Get out of This Place: Notes toward a Remapping of the Sixties." *Socialist Review* 22, no. 2 (April–June 1992): 9–33.

Ehrenreich, Barbara. *Fear of Falling: The Inner Life of the Middle Class.* New York: Perennial, 1990.

———. *The Hearts of Men: American Dreams and the Flight from Commitment.* New York: Anchor, 1983.

Eisenschitz, Bernard. *Nicholas Ray: American Journey.* Translated by Tom Milne. London: Faber and Faber, 1993.

Ellison, Ralph. *Invisible Man.* New York: Random House, 1952.

Ennis, Philip H. *The Seventh Stream: The Emergence of Rock 'n' Roll in American Popular Music*. Hanover, N.H.: Wesleyan University Press, 1992.

Erikson, Erik H. *Childhood and Society*. New York: W. W. Norton & Company, 1950.

Esman, Aaron H. *Adolescence and Culture*. New York: Columbia University Press, 1990.

Evans, Sara. *Personal Politics: The Roots of Women's Liberation in the Civil Rights Movement and the New Left*. New York: Vintage, 1980.

Farber, Jerry. *The Student as Nigger*. New York: Pocket Books, 1972.

Farred, Grant. "Endgame Identity? Mapping the New Left Roots of Identity Politics." *New Literary History* 31, no. 4 (fall 2000): 627–648.

Fiedler, Leslie. *An End to Innocence*. New York: Stein and Day, 1971.

———. *No! In Thunder: Essays on Myth and Literature*. Boston: Beacon Press, 1960.

———. *Love and Death in the American Novel*. New York: Stein and Day, 1966.

———. *The Return of the Vanishing American*. New York: Stein and Day, 1969.

———. "Up from Adolescence." In *Salinger: A Critical and Personal Portrait*, edited by Henry Grunwald, 62–68. New York: Pocket Books, 1963.

Fineman, Joel. "The Structure of Allegorical Desire." In *Allegory and Representation*, edited by Stephen J. Greenblatt, 26–60. Baltimore: Johns Hopkins University Press, 1981.

Fishman, Robert. *Bourgeois Utopias: The Rise and Fall of Suburbia*. New York: Basic Books, 1989.

Fiske, John. *Television Culture*. New York: Methuen, 1987.

Fliegelman, Jay. *Prodigals and Pilgrims: The American Revolution against Patriarchal Authority, 1750–1800*. Cambridge: Cambridge University Press, 1982.

Flitterman-Lewis, Sandy. "Imitation(s) of Life: The Black Woman's Double Determination as Troubling 'Other.'" In *Imitation of Life: Douglas Sirk, Director*, edited by Lucy Fischer, 325–335. New Brunswick: Rutgers University Press, 1991.

Foreman, Joel. "Introduction." In *The Other Fifties: Interrogating Midcentury American Icons*, 1–23. Urbana: University of Illinois Press, 1997.

Foucault, Michel. "Governmentality." In *The Foucault Effect: Studies in Governmentality*, edited by Graham Burchell, Colin Gordon, and Peter Millers, 87–104. Chicago: University of Chicago Press, 1991.

———. *"Society Must Be Defended."* New York: Picador, 2003.

Frank, Thomas. *The Conquest of Cool: Business Culture, Counterculture, and the Rise of Hip Consumerism*. Chicago: University of Chicago Press, 1997.

Fraser, Nancy. *Justice Interruptus: Critical Reflections on the "Postsocialist" Condition*. New York: Routledge, 1997.

French, Warren G., ed. *The Fifties: Fiction, Poetry, Drama*. Deland, Flor.: Everett Edwards, 1970.

Freud, Sigmund. *Totem and Taboo*. New York: Norton, 1950.

Friedan, Betty. *The Feminine Mystique.* New York: Norton, 1963.

Friedman, Lawrence. *Identity's Architect: A Biography of Erik H. Erikson.* New York: Scribner's, 1999.

Frith, Simon. *Sound Effects: Youth, Leisure, and the Politics of Rock 'n' Roll.* New York: Pantheon, 1981.

Fromm, Eric. *Escape from Freedom.* New York: Farrar and Rinehart, 1941.

Garofalo, Reebee. *Rockin' Out: Popular Music in the USA.* Boston: Allyn and Bacon, 1997.

Gay Liberation Front Women. "Lesbians and the Ultimate Liberation of Women" (1970). Reprinted in *Takin' It to the Streets: A Sixties Reader*, edited by Alexander Bloom and Wini Breines, 605–606. New York: Oxford University Press, 1995.

Geismar, Maxwell. *American Moderns, From Rebellion to Conformity.* New York: Hill and Wang, 1958.

———. "J. D. Salinger: The Wise Child and the New Yorker School of Fiction." In *Salinger: A Critical and Personal Portrait*, edited by Henry Anatole Grunwald, 95–111. New York: Pocket Books, 1963.

George, Nelson. *The Death of Rhythm and Blues.* Boston: Plume, 1989.

Gilbert, James. *A Cycle of Outrage: America's Reaction to the Juvenile Delinquent in the 1950s.* New York: Oxford University Press, 1986.

Gillett, Charles. *The Sound of the City: The Rise of Rock and Roll.* New York: Outerbridge and Diensfrey, 1970.

Gillis, John R. *Youth and History: Tradition and Change in European Age Relations 1770–Present.* New York: Academic Press, 1974.

Gilroy, Paul. *Against Race: Imagining Political Culture beyond the Color Line.* New York: Belknap Press, 1991.

Ginsberg, Allen. "At the Conspiracy Trial." In *The Gay Liberation Book*, edited by Len Richmond and Gary Noguera, 200–202. San Francisco: Ramparts Press, 1973.

———. "Death to Van Gogh's Ear." In *The Beats*, edited by Seymour Krim, 149–153. Greenwich, Conn.: Fawcett, 1960.

———. *Gay Sunshine Interview: with Allen Young.* Bolinas, Calif.: Grey Fox Press, 1974.

———. *"Howl" and Other Poems.* San Francisco: City Lights, 1955.

———. "Poetry, Violence, and the Trembling Lambs." In *A Casebook on the Beat*, edited by Thomas Parkinson, 24–26. New York: Thomas Crowell, 1961.

Girls Town. Directed by Charles F. Haas. MGM, 1959.

Gitlin, Todd. *The Sixties: Years of Hope, Days of Rage.* New York: Bantam Books, 1987.

Gleason, Philip. "Identifying Identity: A Semantic History." *Journal of American History* 69, no. 4 (March 1983): 910–933.

Goffman, Irving. *Stigma: Notes on the Management of Spoiled Identity.* Englewood-Cliffs, N.J.: Prentice-Hall, 1963.

Goodman, Paul. *Growing Up Absurd: Problems of Youth in the Organized Society.* New York: Vintage, 1960.

Gordon, Avery, and Christopher Newfield. Introduction to *Mapping Multiculturalism*, 1–16. Minneapolis: University of Minnesota Press, 1996.

Gordon, Dorothy. "Youth's Right to Knowledge and Free Speech: The Challenge of Youth Forum Discussions." Speech delivered October 16, 1959. In *Vital Speeches of the Day*, volume 6, January 1, 1960, pp. 173–175. New York: City News Publishing Company, 1961.

Green, Martin. *The Great American Adventure.* Boston: Beacon Press, 1984.

Griswold, Jerry. *Audacious Kids: Coming of Age in America's Classic Children's Books.* New York: Oxford University Press, 1992.

Grossberg, Lawrence. *We Gotta Get Out of This Place: Popular Conservatism and Postmodern Culture.* New York: Routledge, 1992.

Grovogui, Siba N'Zatioula. *Sovereigns, Quasi Sovereigns, and Africans: Race and Self-Determination in International Law.* Minneapolis: University of Minnesota Press, 1996.

Grunwald, Henry Anatole. Introduction to *Salinger: A Critical and Personal Portrait*, ix–xxxiv. New York: Giant Cardinal, 1963.

———. "The Invisible Man: A Biographical Collage." In *Salinger: A Critical and Personal Portrait*, 1–23. New York: Giant Cardinal, 1963.

Guillory, John. *Cultural Capital: The Problem of Literary Canon Formation.* Chicago: University of Chicago Press, 1993.

Guttwillig, Robert. "Everybody's Caught The Catcher in the Rye." In *Studies in J. D. Salinger: Reviews, Essays, and Critiques of* The Catcher in the Rye *and Other Fictions*, edited by Robert Guttwillig, 1–6. New York: Odyssey Press, 1963.

Halberstam, Judith. *Female Masculinity.* Durham, N.C.: Duke University Press, 1998.

Hall, G. Stanley. *Adolescence: Its Psychology and Its Relations to Physiology, Anthropology, Sociology, Sex, Crime, and Religion.* New York: D. Appleton, 1904.

Hall, Stuart. "Encoding/Decoding." In *Culture, Media, Language*, edited by S. Hall, D. Hobson, A. Lowe, and P. Willis, 128–138. London: Methuen, 1982.

Hall, Stuart, and Tony Jefferson, eds. *Resistance through Rituals.* London: Hutchinson, 1976.

Halperin, David. *Saint Foucault: Towards a Gay Hagiography.* New York: Oxford University Press, 1996.

Hansberry, Lorraine. *A Raisin in the Sun.* New York: Vintage, 1994.

———. *To Be Young, Gifted, and Black.* New York: Vintage, 1996.

Harpers. "Silent Generation," *Harpers*, April 1953, pp. 34–36.

Harris, Oliver. "Queer Shoulders, Queer Wheel: Homosexuality and Beat Textual Politics." In *Beat Culture: The 1950s and Beyond*, edited by Cornelis

A. van Minnen, Jaap van der Bent, and Mel van Elteren. Amsterdam: VU University Press, 1999.

Harvey, David. *The Condition of Postmodernity*. Oxford: Blackwell, 1990.

Hassan, Ihab. *Radical Innocence: The Contemporary American Novel*. Princeton: Princeton University Press, 1961.

Hayek, F. A. *The Road to Serfdom*. Chicago: University of Chicago Press, 1994.

Hayden, Tom. "The Trial." In *Takin' It to the Streets: A Sixties Reader*, edited by Alexander Bloom and Wini Breines, 440–444. New York: Oxford University Press, 1995.

Hebdige, Dick. *Subculture: The Meaning of Style*. London: Methuen, 1979.

Hechinger, Grace, and Fred M. Hechinger. *Teen-Age Tyranny*. New York: Crest Books, 1963.

Heiserman, Arthur, and James Miller. "J. D. Salinger: Some Crazy Cliff." In *Salinger: A Critical and Personal Portrait*, edited by Henry Anatole Grunwald, 216–225. New York: Pocket Books, 1963.

Heung, Marina. "What's the Matter with Sarah Jane? Daughters and Mothers in Douglas Sirk's "Imitation of Life." In *Imitation of Life: Douglas Sirk, Director*, edited by Lucy Fischer, 302–324. New Brunswick: Rutgers University Press, 1991.

Hicks, Granville. "J. D. Salinger: Search for Wisdom." In *Salinger's* Catcher in the Rye: *Clamor vs. Criticism*, edited by Harold P. Simonson and Philip E. Hager, 88–91. Boston: D. C. Heath, 1963.

Higham, John. "The Cult of the American Consensus: Homogenizing Our History." *Commentary* 27 (1959): 93–100.

Hill, Trent. "The Enemy Within: Censorship in Rock Music in the 1950s." In *Present Tense: Rock & Roll and Culture*, edited by Anthony De Curtis, 39–72. Durham, N.C.: Duke University Press, 1992.

Hine, Thomas. *The Rise and Fall of the American Teenager*. New York: HarperCollins, 1999.

Hoberek, Andrew. "Race Man, Organizational Man, *Invisible Man*." *Modern Language Quarterly* 59, no. 1 (March 1998): 99–119.

———. *Twilight of the Middle Class: Post–World War II American Fiction and White-Collar Work*. Princeton: Princeton University Press, 2005.

Hobsbawm, Eric. *The Age of Extremes: A History of the World, 1914–1991*. New York: Vintage, 1994.

Hogeland, Lisa Maria. *Feminism and Its Fictions: The Consciousness-Raising Novel and the Women's Liberation Movement*. Philadelphia: University of Pennsylvania Press, 1998.

Holmes, John Clellon. *Go*. New York: New American Library, 1980.

———. "The Sexual Gentleman's Agreement." In *Passionate Opinions: The Cultural Essays*, 101–109. Fayetteville: University of Arkansas Press, 1988.

———. "Philosophy of the Beat Generation." In *Passionate Opinions: The Cultural Essays*, 65–77. Fayetteville: University of Arkansas Press, 1988.

———. "This Is the Beat Generation." In *Passionate Opinions: The Cultural Essays*, 57–64. Fayetteville: University of Arkansas Press, 1988.
Hoover, J. Edgar. "The Twin Enemies of Freedom: Crime and Communism." In *Vital Speeches of the Day*, volume 4 (December 1, 1956): 104–107.
Horne, Gerald. *Black and Red: W. E. B. Du Bois and the Afro-American Response to the Cold War, 1944–1963*. Albany: State University of New York Press, 1986.
Hunter, Evan. *The Blackboard Jungle*. New York: Arbor House, 1984.
Imitation of Life. Directed by Douglas Sirk. Universal Pictures, 1959.
Jackson, Kenneth T. *Crabgrass Frontier: The Suburbanization of the United States*. New York: Oxford University Press, 1985.
Jailhouse Rock. Directed by Richard Thorpe. Warner Studios, 1957.
James, David E. *Allegories of Cinema: American Film in the Sixties*. Princeton: Princeton University Press, 1989.
Jameson, Fredric. "Third World Literature in the Era of Multinational Capitalism." *Social Text*, no. 15 (fall 1986): 65–88.
Jezer, Marty. *The Dark Ages: Life in the United States, 1945–1960*. Boston: South End Press, 1982.
Johnson, Joyce. *Minor Characters*. Boston: Houghton Mifflin, 1982.
Johnson, Ronna C., and Nancy M. Grace. *girls who wore black: Women Writing the Beat Generation*. New Brunswick: Rutgers University Press, 2002.
Jones, Landon Y. *Great Expectations: America and the Baby Boom Generation*. New York: Coward, McCann and Geoghegan, 1980.
Jones, Ernest. "A Case History of Us All." In *If You Really Want to Know: A Catcher Casebook*, edited by Malcolm M. Marsden, 8–9. Chicago: Scott, Foresman, and Company, 1963.
Jones, Mark M. "The Position of Public School Education in 1958: The Number One Problem Is Parents." *Vital Speeches of the Day*, volume 21, (August 15, 1958): 661–665.
Kammen, Michael. *A Season of Youth: The American Revolution and the Historical Imagination*. New York: Knopf, 1978.
Kant, Immanuel. "What Is Enlightenment?" In *The Enlightenment: A Comprehensive Anthology*, edited by Peter Gay, 383–389. New York: Simon and Schuster, 1972.
Kaplan, Amy. "'Left Alone with America': The Absence of Empire in the Study of American Culture." In *Cultures of United States Imperialism*, edited by Amy Kaplan and Donald E. Pease, 3–21. Durham, N.C.: Duke University Press, 1993.
Kaplan, Charles. "Holden and Huck: The Odysseys of Youth." *College English* 18 (November 1956): 76–80.
Kazin, Alfred. "Everybody's Favorite." *Salinger: A Critical and Personal Portrait*, edited by Henry Anatole Grunwald, 47–57. New York: Pocket Books, 1963.
Kerouac, Jack. *On the Road*. New York: Penguin, 1976.
———. "The Origins of the Beat Generation." In *A Casebook on the Beat*,

edited by Thomas Parkinson, 68–76. New York: Thomas Y. Crowell Company, 1961.

Kett, Joseph F. *Rites of Passage: Adolescence in America, 1790 to the Present*. New York: Basic Books, 1977.

King Creole. Directed by Michael Curtiz. Paramount Pictures, 1958.

Kinsey, Alfred C., Wardell B. Pomeroy, Clyde E. Martin, and Paul H. Gebhard. *Sexual Behavior in the Human Male*. Philadelphia: W. B. Saunders, 1948.

Knight, Arthur, and Kit Knight, eds. *Kerouac and the Beats: A Primary Sourcebook*. New York: Paragon, 1980.

Knight, Brenda, ed. *Women of the Beat Generation: The Writers, Artists and Muses at the Heart of a Revolution*. Berkeley: Conari Press, 1996.

Koskenniemi, Martti. *From Apology to Utopia: The Structure of International Legal Argument*. Helsinki: Finnish Lawyers' Publishing Company, 1989.

Kotz, David M. "A Comparative Analysis of the Theory of Regulation and the Social Structure of Accumulation Theory." *Science and Society* 54, no. 1 (spring 1990): 5–28.

Krasner, Stephen D. *Sovereignty: Organized Hypocrisy*. Princeton, N.J.: Princeton University Press, 1999.

Kreidl, John Francis. *Nicholas Ray*. Boston: Twayne, 1977.

Laclau, Ernesto, and Chantal Mouffe. *Hegemony and Socialist Strategy: Towards a Radical Democratic Politics*. New York: Verso Press, 1989.

LeFeber, Walter. *The American Age: United States Foreign Policy at Home and Abroad, 1750 to the Present*. New York: Norton, 1994.

———. *The New American Empire: An Interpretation of American Expansion, 1860–1898*. New York: Comstock, 1998.

Lears, Jackson. "A Matter of Taste: Corporate Cultural Hegemony in a Mass-Consumption Society." In *Recasting America: Culture and Politics in the Age of Cold War*, edited by Lary May, 38–57. Chicago: University of Chicago Press, 1989.

Lee, Martyn J. *Consumer Culture Reborn: The Cultural Politics of Consumption*. New York: Routledge, 1993.

Leitch, David. "The Salinger Myth." In *Salinger: A Critical and Personal Portrait*, edited by Henry Anatole Grunwald. New York: Pocket Books, 1962.

Lewis, Jon. *The Road to Romance and Ruin: Teen Films and Youth Culture*. New York: Routledge, 1992.

Lewis, R. W. B. *The American Adam: Innocence, Tragedy, and Tradition in the Nineteenth Century*. Chicago: University of Chicago Press, 1955.

Life. "A Boon to the Household and a Boom to Industry: The New American Domesticated Male." *Life*, January 4, 1954, pp. 42–43.

———. "Generation of Esthetes." *Life*, November 26, 1951, p. 96.

———. "Luckiest Generation." *Life*, January 4, 1954, pp. 27–29.

———. "Squaresville, U.S.A. vs. Beatsville." *Life*, September 21, 1959, p. 7.

Lindner, Robert. "Homosexuality and the Contemporary Scene." In *Must You Conform?* New York: Grove Press, 1961.

———. *Prescription for Rebellion*. New York: Rinehart, 1952.
———. "Raise Your Child to Be a Rebel." *McCall's*, February 1956, pp. 31, 100–104.
———. *Rebel Without a Cause: The Hypnoanalysis of a Criminal Psychopath*. New York: Grune and Stratton, 1944.
Lipietz, Alain. *Mirages and Miracles: The Crises of Global Fordism*. London: Verso Press, 1987.
Lipsitz, George. *Class and Culture in Cold War America: "A Rainbow at Midnight."* New York: Praeger Press, 1981.
———. *Time Passages: Collective Memory and American Popular Culture*. Minneapolis: University of Minnesota Press, 2001.
Lipton, Lawrence. *The Holy Barbarians*. New York: Julian Messner, 1959.
Lloyd, David. "Analogies of the Aesthetic: The Politics of Culture and the Limits of Materialist Aesthetics." *New Formations* 10 (spring 1990): 109–126.
Look. "Explosive Generation." *Look*, January 3, 1961, pp. 16–25.
Love Me Tender. Directed by Robert Webb. Twentieth-Century Fox, 1956.
Loving You. Directed by Hal Kanter. Vidmark/Trimark Pictures, 1957.
MacDonald, Dwight. "A Theory of Mass Culture." In *Mass Culture: The Popular Arts in America*, edited by Bernard Rosenberg and David Manning White, 59–73. New York: Free Press, 1957.
Mackenzie, Catherine. "Recreation for Teen Ages." *New York Times Magazine*, June 6, 1943, p. 27.
Mailer, Norman. "The White Negro." In *Advertisements for Myself*, 298–322. New York: Signet, 1960.
Mailloux, Steven. *Rhetorical Power*. Ithaca: Cornell University Press, 1989.
Mannheim, Karl. *Essays on the Sociology of Knowledge*. London: Routledge, 1952.
Marcuse, Herbert. *One-Dimensional Man: Studies in the Ideology of Advanced Industrial Society*. Boston: Beacon Press, 1964.
Marsh, David. *Elvis*. New York: Thunder's Mouth Press, 1992.
Marx, Karl. "The Eighteenth Brumaire of Louis Bonaparte." In *The Marx-Engels Reader*, edited by Robert C. Tucker, 594–617. New York: Norton, 1978.
May, Elaine Tyler. *Homeward Bound: American Families in the Cold War Era*. New York: Basic Books, 1988.
May, Lary. Introduction to *Recasting America: Culture and Politics in the Age of Cold War*, 1–13. Chicago: University of Chicago Press, 1989.
McCann, Graham. *Rebel Males: Clift, Brando, and Dean*. New Brunswick: Rutgers University Press, 1993.
McGee, Mark, and R. J. Robertson. *The J.D. Films: Juvenile Delinquency in the Movies*. Jefferson, N.C.: McFarland, 1982.
McReynolds, David. "Hipsters Unleashed." In *The Beats*, edited by Seymour Krim, 202–210. Greenwich, Conn.: Fawcett Publications, 1960.

McRobbie, Angela. "Settling Accounts with Subcultures: A Feminist Critique." In *On Record: Rock, Pop, and the Written Word*, edited by Simon Frith and Andrew Goodwin, 66–80. New York: Pantheon, 1990.

Medovoi, Leerom. "Cold War American Culture as the Age of Three Worlds." Special Issue on 50s Culture, *Minnesota Review* 55–57 (2002): 167–186.

———. "Democracy, Capitalism, and American Literature: The Cold War construction of J. D. Salinger's Paperback Hero." In *The Other Fifties: Midcentury American Icons*, edited by Joel Foreman, 225–287. Urbana, Il.: University of Illinois Pres, 1997.

———. "Reading the Blackboard: Masculinity and the Racial Cross-Identification of White Youth." In *Race and the Subject of Masculinities*, edited by Harry Stecopoulos and Michael Uebel, 138–169. Durham, N.C.: Duke University Press, 1997.

———. "Mapping the Rebel Image: Postmodernism and the Masculinist Politics of Rock in the U.S.A." *Cultural Critique* 20 (winter 1991–92): 153–188.

Mellen, Joan. *Big Bad Wolves: Masculinity in the American Film*. New York: Pantheon, 1977.

Melley, Timothy. *Empire of Conspiracy: The Culture of Paranoia in Postwar America*. Ithaca: Cornell University Press, 1999.

Michaels, Walter Benn. *Our America: Nativism, Modernism, and Pluralism*. Durham, N.C.: Duke University Press, 1995.

Miles, Barry. *Ginsberg: A Biography*. New York: Simon and Schuster, 1989.

Miller, James. *"Democracy Is in the Streets": From Port Huron to the Siege of Chicago*. New York: Simon and Schuster, 1987.

Miller, Nolan. *Why Am I So Beat*. New York: Ace Books, 1954.

Mills, C. Wright. *White Collar: The American Middle Classes*. New York: Oxford University Press, 1951.

Mission to Moscow. Directed by Michael Curtiz. Warner Brothers, 1943.

Morgan, Robin. "Goodbye to All That." In *Takin' it to the Streets: A Sixties Reader*, edited by Alexander Bloom and Wini Breines, 499–583. New York: Oxford University Press, 1995.

Motion Picture Daily. "Girls Burn Barn In Memphis; Blame 'Blackboard Jungle,'" *Motion Picture Daily*, May 17, 1955, p. 2.

Moya, Paula M. L. "Introduction: Reclaiming Identity." *Cultural Logic* 3, no. 2 (spring 2000): 1–10.

Mulvey, Laura. "Visual Pleasure and Narrative Cinema." In *Movies and Methods*, vol. 2, edited by Bill Nichols, 2: 303–314. Berkeley: University of California Press, 1985.

Murphy, Alexander B. "The Sovereign State System as Political-Territorial Ideal: Historical and Contemporary Considerations." In *State Sovereignty as Social Construct*, edited by Thomas J. Biersteker and Cynthia Weber, 81–120. New York: Cambridge University Press, 1996.

Murphy, Geraldine. "Ahab as Capitalist, Ahab as Communist: Revising *Moby-Dick* for the Cold War." *Surfaces* 4, no. 201 (1994): 1–21.

———. "Romancing the Center: Cold War Politics and American Literature." *Poetics Today* 9, no. 4 (1988): 737–748.

Nadel, Alan. *Containment Culture: American Narratives, Post-modernism, and the Atomic Age*. Durham, N.C.: Duke University Press, 1995.

Navasky, Victor. *Naming Names*. New York: Viking Press, 1980.

Nelson, Dana. *National Manhood: Capitalist Citizenship and the Imagined Fraternity of White Men*. Durham, N.C.: Duke University Press, 1998.

Nickles, Shelley. "More Is Better: Consumption, Gender, and Class Identity in Postwar America." *American Quarterly* 54, no. 4 (2002): 581–622.

Noble, David. *Forces of Production: A Social History of Industrial Automation*. New York: Oxford University Press, 1986.

Oakley, Ronald J. *God's Country: America in the Fifties*. New York: Dembner Books, 1990.

"Offbeat Editorial: Fats Domino Status: RO." http://www.neosoft.com/~offbeat/text/fatsat70.html.

Ohmann, Carol, and Richard Ohmann. "Reviewers, Critics, and *The Catcher in the Rye*." *Critical Inquiry* 3, no. 1 (fall 1976): 15–38.

O'Neil, Paul. "The Only Rebellion Around." *Life*, November 30, 1959, p. 114.

Parents. "Help Make Democracy Live." *Parents*, January 1953, p. 10.

———. "One Way to Succeed as a Family." *Parents*, August 1948, pp. 27, 74–75.

———. "We're Tired of Juvenile Delinquency." *Parents*, August 1944, pp. 31, 130.

Parker, Christopher. "Why the Hell Not Smash All the Windows?" In *Salinger: A Critical and Personal Portrait*, edited by Henry Anatole Grunwald, 254–258. London: Peter Owen, 1964.

Partisan Review. "Our Country and Our Culture: A Symposium." *Partisan Review* 19, no. 3 (May–June 1952): 282–326.

Pateman, Carole. *The Sexual Contract*. Stanford: Stanford University Press, 1988.

Paterson, Thomas G., J. Garry Clifford, and Kenneth J. Hagan. *American Foreign Policy: A History since 1900*. Lexington, Mass.: D. C. Heath, 1983.

Pease, Donald. "Leslie Fiedler, the Rosenberg Trial, and the Formulation of an American Canon." *boundary 2* 17, no. 2 (1990): 155–198.

———. "*Moby-Dick* and the Cold War." In *The American Renaissance Reconsidered*, edited by Walter Benn Michaels and Donald Pease, 113–155. Baltimore: Johns Hopkins University Press, 1985.

———. *Visionary Compacts: American Renaissance Writings in Cultural Context*. Madison: University of Wisconsin Press, 1987.

Pease, Donald, and Amy Kaplan, eds. *Cultures of United States Imperialism*. Durham, N.C.: Duke University Press, 1993.

Peabody, Richard, ed. *A Different Beat: Writings by Women of the Beat Generation*. London: High Risk Books, 1997.

Peck, Janice. "Itinerary of a Thought: Stuart Hall, Cultural Studies, and the

Unresolved Problem of the Relation of Culture to 'Not Culture.'" *Cultural Critique* 48, no. 1 (2001): 200–249.

Pells, Richard H. *The Liberal Mind in a Conservative Age: American Intellectuals in the 1940s and 1950s*. New York: Harper and Row, 1985.

Peterson, Richard A. *Creating Country Music: Fabricating Authenticity*. Chicago: University of Chicago Press, 1999.

Piercey, Marge. "The Grand Coolie Damn." In *Sisterhood Is Powerful*, edited by Robin Morgan, 421–437. New York: Vintage, 1970.

Piore, M. J., and C. F. Sabel. *The Second Industrial Divide: Possibilities for Prosperity*. New York: Basic Books, 1984.

Pletsch, Carl. "The Three Worlds, or the Division of Social Scientific Labor, circa 1950–1975." *Comparative Studies in Society and History* 23, no. 4 (October 1981): 565–590.

Puffer, J. Adams. *The Boy and His Gang*. Boston: Houghton Mifflin, 1912.

Puner, Helen. "Is It True What They Say about the Suburbs?" *Parents*, July 1958, pp. 42–43, 96–97.

Radway, Janice. "Mail-Order Culture and Its Critics: The Book-of-the-Month Club, Commodification and Consumption, and the Problem of Cultural Authority." In *Cultural Studies*, edited by Lawrence Grossberg, Cary Nelson, and Paul Treichler, 512–530. New York: Routledge, 1992.

Rebel without a Cause. Directed by Nicholas Ray. Warner Brothers, 1955.

Reich, Wilhelm. *The Mass Psychology of Fascism*. New York: Orgone Institute Press, 1946.

Reising, Russell. *The Unusable Past: Theory and the Study of American Literature*. New York: Methuen, 1986.

Richards, Jeffrey, ed. *Imperialism and Juvenile Literature*. Manchester, England: Manchester University Press, 1989.

Ricoeur, Paul. *Hermeneutics and the Human Sciences: Essays on Language, Action, and Interpretation*. New York: Cambridge University Press, 1981.

Riesman, David, Nathan Glazer, and Revel Denney. *The Lonely Crowd: A Case Study of the Changing American Character*. New Haven: Yale University Press, 1971.

Robertson, James C. *The Casablanca Man: The Cinema of Michael Curtiz*. New York: Routledge, 1993.

Rock around the Clock. Directed by Fred Sears. Columbia Pictures, 1956.

Rock, Rock, Rock! Directed by Will Price. 1956.

Rogin, Michael. "Kiss Me Deadly: Communism, Motherhood, and Cold War Movies." In *Ronald Reagan, the Movie, and Other Episodes in Political Demonology*, 236–271. Berkeley: University of California Press, 1987.

Ross, Andrew. "Containing Culture in the Cold War." In *No Respect: Intellectuals and Popular Culture*, 42–64. New York: Routledge, 1989.

Rouse, Roger. "Thinking through Transnationalism: Notes on the Cultural Politics of Class Relations in the Contemporary United States." *Public

Culture: Society for Transnational Cultural Studies 7, no. 2 (winter 1995): 353–402.

Rowe, Joyce. "Holden Caulfield and American Protest." In *New Essays on* The Catcher in the Rye, edited by Jack Saltzman, 77–96. New York: Cambridge University Press, 1991.

Ruben, Matthew. "Suburbanization of Urban Poverty under Neoliberalism." In *New Poverty Studies: The Ethnography of Politics, Policy, and Impoverished People in the U.S.*, edited by Judith Goode and Jeffrey Maskovsky, 435–461. New York: New York University Press, 2001.

Rubin, Jerry. *Do It! Scenarios of the Revolution*. New York: Simon and Schuster, 1970.

Ruitenbeek, Henrik. *The Problem of Homosexuality in Modern Society*. New York: Dutton, 1963.

Salinger, J. D. *The Catcher in the Rye*. New York: Bantam Books, 1964.

Salisbury, Harrison E. *The Shook-up Generation*. New York: Crest Books, 1959.

Schatz, Thomas. *Boom and Bust: American Cinema in the 1940s*. Berkeley: University of California Press, 1997.

Schaub, Thomas Hill. *American Fiction in the Cold War*. Madison: University of Wisconsin Press, 1991.

Schlesinger, Arthur, Jr. *The Vital Center*. London: Andre Deutsch, 1970.

Schrecker, Ellen. *No Ivory Tower: McCarthyism and the Universities*. New York: Oxford University Press, 1986.

Scorpio Rising. Kenneth Anger. 1962.

Sedgwick, Eve Kosofsky. *Between Men: English Literature and Male Homosocial Desire*. New York: Columbia University Press, 1985.

Seligman, Daniel. "The New Masses." *Fortune*, May 1959, p. 108.

Seng, Peter. "The Fallen Idol: The Immature World of Holden Caulfield." In *If You Really Want to Know: A* Catcher *Casebook*, edited by Malcolm S. Marsden, 73–81. Chicago: Scott, Foresman, 1963.

Shulman, Alix Kates. *Burning Questions: A Novel*. New York: Thunder's Mouth Press, 1990.

Shumway, David. "Rock & Roll as a Cultural Practice." In *Present Tense: Rock & Roll and Culture*, edited by Anthony De Curtis, 117–134. Durham, N.C.: Duke University Press, 1992.

Silverstone, Roger. *Visions of Suburbia*. New York: Routledge, 1997.

SNCC (Student Non-Violent Coordinating Committee). "The Basis of Black Power." In *Takin' It to the Streets: A Sixties Reader*, edited by Alexander Bloom and Wini Breines, 152–158. New York: Oxford University Press, 1995.

Solanis, Valerie. "Excerpts from the SCUM (Society for Cutting Up Men) Manifesto." In *Sisterhood Is Powerful*, edited by Robin Morgan, 514–519. New York: Vintage, 1970.

Spanos, William V. *The Errant Art of* Moby-Dick. Durham, N.C.: Duke University Press, 1995.

Sperry, R. Letter to the editor. *Life*, January 11, 1954, p. 11.

Spigel, Lynn. *Make Room for TV: Television and the Family Ideal in Postwar America*. Chicago: University of Chicago Press, 1992.

Spivak, Gayatri. "Can the Subaltern Speak?" In *Marxism and the Interpretation of Culture*, edited by Cary Nelson and Lawrence Grossberg, 271–313. Urbana: University of Illinois Press, 1988.

Steiner, George. "The Salinger Industry." In *Studies in J. D. Salinger: Reviews, Essays, and Critiques of* The Catcher in the Rye, edited by Marvin Laser and Norman Fruman, 113–118. New York: Odyssey Press, 1963.

Steinle, Pamela Hunt. *In Cold Fear*: The Catcher in the Rye, *Censorship Controversies and Postwar American Character*. Columbus: Ohio State University Press, 2000.

Stevenson, David L. "The Mirror of Crisis." In *Salinger: A Critical and Personal Portrait*, edited by Henry Anatole Grunwald, 39–45. New York: Giant Cardinal, 1963.

Stimpson, Catherine. "The Beat Generation and the Trials of Homosexual Liberation." *Salmagundi*, nos. 58–59 (fall 1982–winter 1983): 373–392.

Swados, Harvey. "Must Writers Be Characters?" In *Studies in J. D. Salinger: Reviews, Essays, and Critiques of* The Catcher in the Rye, edited by Marvin Laser and Norman Fruman, 119–122. New York: Odyssey Press, 1963.

Take a Giant Step. Directed by Philip Leacock. United Artists, 1959.

Taylor, Charles. *Multiculturalism and "The Politics of Recognition": An Essay*. Princeton: Princeton University Press, 1992.

Theado, Matt. *The Beats: A Literary Reference*. New York: Carroll and Graff, 2001.

Third World Gay Liberation. "What We Want, What We Believe" (1971). In *Takin' It to the Streets: A Sixties Reader*, edited by Alexander Bloom and Wini Breines, 600–604. New York: Oxford University Press, 1995.

Thompson, Clara. "Changing Concepts of Homosexuality in Psychoanalysis." In *The Problem of Homosexuality in Modern Society*, 40–51. New York: Dutton, 1963.

Time. "Rebels or Psychopaths?" December 6, 1954, p. 64.

Tompkins, Jane. *Sensational Designs: The Cultural Work of American Fiction, 1790–1860*. New York: Oxford University Press, 1985.

Trilling, Lionel. *The Liberal Imagination: Essays on Literature and Society*. Garden City, N.Y.: Doubleday Anchor, 1953.

Truman, Harry S. "The Point IV Program." In *An American Primer*, edited by Daniel J. Boorstin, 916–922. Chicago: University of Chicago Press, 1968.

United States Congress. *Motion Pictures and Juvenile Delinquency: Report of the Committee on the Judiciary*. Washington: United States Government Printing Office, 1956.

Uyametsu, Amy. "The Emergence of Yellow Power." In *Takin' It to the Streets: A Sixties Reader*, edited by Alexander Bloom and Wini Breines, 190–192. New York: Oxford University Press, 1995.

Variety Weekly. "'Blackboard Jungle' Shapes as Top Metro Release in Some Time." *Variety*, May 18, 1955, p. 5.

———. "Police Seek to Finger 'Blackboard Jungle' As Root of Hooliganism." *Variety Weekly*, May 18, 1955, p. 5.

———. "Toronto Hubbub over 'Blackboard.'" *Variety Weekly*, May 25, 1955, p. 25.

Viorst, Milton. *Fire in the Streets: America in the 1960s*. New York: Simon and Schuster, 1979.

Von Eschen, Penny M. *Race against Empire: Black Americans and Anticolonialism, 1937–1957*. Ithaca: Cornell University Press, 1997.

Wakefield, Dan. "Salinger and the Search for Love." In *Salinger: A Critical and Personal Portrait*, edited by Henry Grunwald, 193–210. New York: Pocket Books, 1963.

Walzer, Michael. *Just and Unjust Wars: A Moral Argument with Historical Illustrations*. New York: Basic Books, 2000.

Warner, Michael. *The Trouble with Normal: Sex, Politics, and the Ethics of Queer Life*. Boston: Harvard University Press, 2000.

Weiss, Jessica. *To Have and to Hold: Marriage, the Baby Boom, and Social Change*. Chicago: University of Chicago Press, 2000.

West, Cornel. "The New Cultural Politics of Difference." *October* 53 (summer 1990): 93–109.

Wexman, Virginia Wright. *Creating the Couple: Love, Marriage, and Hollywood Performance*. Princeton: Princeton University Press, 1993.

White, Charles. *The Life and Times of Little Richard: The Quasar of Rock*. New York: Harmony Books, 1984.

White, David Manning. "Mass Culture in America: Another Point of View." In *Mass Culture: The Popular Arts in America*, edited by Bernard Rosenberg and David Manning White, 13–26. New York: Free Press, 1957.

Whyte, William H., Jr. *The Organization Man*. New York: Anchor Books, 1957.

The Wild One. Directed by Laslo Benedek. Columbia Pictures. 1954.

Willkie, Wendell L. "One World." In *An American Primer*, edited by Daniel J. Boorstin, 888–907. Chicago: University of Chicago Press, 1968.

Williams, William Appleman. *Empire as a Way of Life: An Essay on the Causes and Character of America's Present Predicament*. New York: Oxford University Press, 1980.

Williams, Raymond. *Keywords: A Vocabulary of Culture and Society*. New York: Oxford University Press, 1985.

Willis, Paul. *Learning to Labour*. London: Saxon House, 1977.

Wilson, Sloan. *The Man in the Gray Flannel Suit*. New York: Pocket Books, 1955.

Wise, Sue. "Sexing Elvis." In *On Record: Rock, Pop, and The Written Word*, edited by Simon Frith and Andrew Goodwin, 390–398. New York: Pantheon Books, 1990.

Wylie, Philip. *Generation of Vipers*. New York: Rinehart, 1942.

INDEX

Page numbers in italics refer to figures.

Adolescence, 6, 25, 134, 170, 339 n.36; and colonial nonage, 9–11; in contrast to teenager, 26–27; as dependence, 25; literature, role in, 70–71, 85; wartime crisis of, 26. *See also* Teenagers

Adorno, Theodor, 335 n.16

Adventures of Augie March, 65, 67–68, 74

Adventures of Huckleberry Finn, 39, 59, 74–75, 77

African Americans, 4, 5, 18; civil rights movement, 50, 286–87, 322–23; identity of, 49, 212, 214, 318–21 (*see also* Blackness); identity of, literary, 66–69, 85, 88; musical cultures of, 105–7, 110, 116, 152, 192–93; sensuality of, 150, 279–80, 286, 289–91; white identification with, 154–56, 164, 197–99, 202, 211

Ahmad, Aijaz, 85, 344 n.21

Alcoff, Linda, 332 n.5

Aldrich, Thomas, 39

Allegory: liberal (development) narrative, 60–61, 78, 79, 87, 335 n.19; nationalistic, 56–57, 59, 67, 71–72, 76, 78–79, 87–89, 257, 341 n.2; of rebellion, 61–64, 71, 74, 86, 87

Altman, Dennis, 350 n.14

American Adam, 62–66, 71, 75, 77, 84

American Bandstand, 103–4

American literature: canon of, 56–60, 66, 68, 85, 86–88, 341–42 n.8; commercialization of, 83–84, 217; democratization of, 79; generation, naming of, 216–19; multiculturalism of, 86–89; national allegorization of, 54–60, 61, 66, 86; nonconformity in, 59, 61, 63, 65, 75, 86; politicization of, 59–61, 79, 86–87; queer, 68–69, 261; realism, 58, 62; romance, 62–63; and third world, 87–88

American Renaissance, 61, 64

Amin, Ash, 357 n.3

Anka, Paul, 269, 271, 274–75

Anticommunism, 3, 13–14, 16, 28, 53–54, 58, 63, 176; in *Catcher* criticism, 73–74; as containment culture, 20; and Fordism, 19, 21; as liberal liter-

Anticommunism (*continued*)
ary criticism, 58–60, 65–66, 76–77, 174–75; and mass consumption, 172; momism, 44
Arac, Jonathan, 6, 56, 67, 332 n.3, 333 n.8, 341 n.6
Asian Americans, 317, 321–22
Auerbach, Erich, 56

Bad Boy, 40, 41
Bad boys, 24, 170, 274, 278, 287, 340 n.43, 350–51 n.2; defined, 39–40; "disidentification" of, 168–69, 180; fraternity between, 225, 264; masculinity of, 43, 156, 176–77, 182, 208–9, 324; marketing of, 217; as national character, 42–43, 71, 191; and race, 45, 322; erotic sexuality of, 45–47, 191, 194, 209, 212, 214, 251, 322; and women, 43, 49, 177. *See also* Juvenile delinquents; Rebels
Bad girls, 48–49, 210, 267; in film, 269, 280 (see also *Gidget*; *Girls Town*; *Imitation of Life*); and race, 268, 280–81, 283, 285–87, 289–92; sexual rebellion by, 187–88, 267–71, 294–95; transgender of, 294, 296–97, 299, 304, 306. See also *Tomboy*; Tomboys
Baldwin, James, 349 n.9
Bandung Conference, 13
Bannon, Ann, 49, 315–16
Bantam, 37, 80
Baruch, Dorothy, 27–28
Baudrillard, Jean, 128–29
Beats, 1, 39, 42, 46, 49, 323, 352 nn.8, 9; desexualization of, 225–26, 234; fraternity of, 225–26, 232–34, 236, 246, 254–58, 260, 262–63; homosexuality of, 225–28, 235, 242–49, 253, 260–63; and homosociality, 225–28, 235, 236, 238, 241–44, 247,
250, 252–53, 255, 264; and media, 220–21, 261–62; narrative of, 224–25; origins of, 215, 217–22; sexual lure of, 248–53; women and, 46, 230, 236, 241–46, 258–59, 263–64, 353 n.12. *See also* Burroughs, William; Ginsburg, Allen; Holmes, John; Kerouac, Jack
Beebo Brinker, 315
Bellow, Saul, 65, 67
Berlant, Lauren, 289
Berry, Chuck, 1, 47, 111, 121, 122–24, 126, 127, 286, 347 n.26
Bettleheim, Bruno, 175
Billboard, 105–6, 347 n.23
"Bill of Rights for Teenagers, A," 43
Blackboard Jungle, 38, 42, 110, 111, 135, 144, 145, 148, 151, 158, 160, 349 n.10; developmental narrative of, 141–42; homoeroticism in, 157–59, 161–62, 164; juvenile delinquency in, 137–43, 145–46, 149–53, 159, 164; patriotism in, 142, 145–46; political response to, 138–39, 143–44, 149–50; race in, 141, 144–56, 158, 164, 349 n.8, 349–50 n.11
Blackness, 47, 50, 107, 286; domestication of, 214; and servile/liberated binary, 285–86
"Blueberry Hill," 109
"Blue Monday," 108–9, 110
Book industry, 39; paperbacks, 37, 79–85, 217
Boone, Pat, 113–14
Boys Town, 269, 355–56 n.2
Brando, Marlon, 40, 169, 170
Breines, Wini, 265–66, 268
Brown, Wendy, 332 n.6
Brown v. Board of Education, 144
Burke, Kenneth, 333 n.8
Burning Questions: A Novel, 259, 355 n.22
Burroughs, Joan, 219

Burroughs, William, 219, 223
Butler, Judith, 2, 224, 318, 328

Carmichael, Stokely, 321–22
Carter, Angela, 273
Cash, Johnny, 111
Castiglia, Christopher, 186–89
Catcher in the Rye, The, 40, 65, 69–79, 81, 169, 170; canonization of, 37, 56–57, 88–89; marketing of, 79–85
Caulfield, Holden, 1, 39, 40, 69, 84, 169, 323, 343 nn.14, 16; as allegorical figure, 57, 71–76, 79, 87, 89; youth of, 77–79
"Charlie Brown," 116–17
Chase, Richard, 62
Childhood and Society, 5–6
Childrearing: and fascism, 173–75; in suburbs, 35
Civil rights. *See* Social movements
Clark, Dick, 104
Clark, Eric O., 261–62
Class, 105–6; in cultural studies, 163; and delinquency, 25, 29–30; as non-identitarian, 329; in R & B, 106; in rock 'n' roll culture, 94, 97, 110, 132–33, 192–97; suburban transformation of, 16–19, 95–96, 100; on TV, 99; uplift in, 141, 143; working, 17–18, 25, 29–30, 94, 97, 99–100, 110, 132–33, 177, 197, 211
Cleaver, Eldridge, 152–53
Coasters, the, 116–17, 121
Cochran, Eddie, 118–20, 121
Cohan, Steven, 338 n.30
Cohen, Elliot, 24
Cold War, 1, 8, 318, 328–29; as age of three worlds, 10–14; as containment culture, 19–20, 29; dialectics of, 24, 50–51; economics of, 16, 103; literarization of, 59; rebel culture of, 30–34; revolutionary motif of, 12–13, 256–57

Colonialism, 11–13, 14, 79
Containment, 19–20, 23, 29, 49, 50, 64, 211, 337 n.29, 340 n.49
Cook, Bruce, 218
Corber, Robert, 20, 50, 190, 337 n.29, 338 n.30, 350–51 n.2
Corso, Gregory, 219, 220, 352 n.8, 353–54 n.17
Country music, 38, 101, 105–6, 111–12, 114, 121, 126, 346 n.19
Cronin, James, 10
Cultural studies: and the rebel figure, 140, 162–64; vs. the Regulation School, 14–15, 336 n.21
Curtiz, Michael, 195

Dadism, 45. *See also* Fatherhood
Davis, Harriet, 173–74
Dean, James, 1, 34, 42, 169–71, 177–79, 191, 208, 220, 323
Dee, Sandra, 269, 282–83, 294, 356 n.7
D'Emilio, John, 20, 227, 337 n.29
Democracy, 65, 77; Cold War dialectics of, 59–60; cultural vs. political, 54–55; as family-type, 174–75; and masculinity, 45; post-Fordist multiculturalization of, 327; as principle of collective identity, 46
Derrida, Jacques, 130, 347 nn.28, 29
De Saussure, Ferdinand, 129
Devlin, Rachel, 266–67
Doherty, Thomas, 136, 338 n.35, 339–40 n.32, 348 n.1
Domino, Fats, 107, 108–10, 111, 114
Doo-wop, 111, 116
Dreiser, Theodore, 76–77
Dulles, John Foster, 12

Education, 25; desegregation of, 144–45, 151; teenage "slavery" in, 154–57. *See also Blackboard Jungle*

INDEX 379

Ehrenreich, Barbara, 21, 296, 337 n.25, 352 n.6, 353 n.12
Ellison, Ralph, 47, 65
Ellson, Hal, 304
Erikson, Erik, 1, 333 n.7, 335 nn.14, 15; identity concept by, 5–7, 8–10, 11, 13–14, 23, 27–28, 50, 169, 323, 350 n.1
Ethnicity, 4, 26, 68; and radio programming, 97; and rebel figures, 45, 47–48, 91; and suburbia, 18, 91, 95–97, 99–100. *See also* Race

Family: suburban nuclear, 18–20, 95, 103, 188–89; as cause of delinquency, 26, 167, 266–67; and Cold War, 44–45; and domestication of men, 171–76, 183, 195; and girl rebels, 266–67, 278–79, 292, 304, 310–11; and liberal anti-fascism, 173; and radio, 97; as site of rebel identity crisis, 177, 181–83, 189–90, 204, 208, 267; teenage consumer autonomy from, 35–36, 39, 102, 110, 136; and television, 39, 98–100, 104
Fanon, Frantz, 8
Farber, Jerry, 154–57, 164
Farred, Grant, 332 n.3
Fascism, 8–9, 28, 31, 333 n.8, 335 n.16; in parenting, 173, 179
Fatherhood, 44; disidentification with, 168–69, 171, 208, 211, 322; domesticated, 173–75, 182, 191, 208–10; inadequacy of, 45–46, 181, 195–96, 199, 201, 205, 208, 269, 309–10, 313
Feminism, 46–47, 51, 85, 254, 258–59, 264, 322, 324, 328
Fiedler, Leslie, 42–43, 47, 82
Film industry, 38, 135–36, 169, 177; anticommunism in, 178; exploitation genre in, 136; rock 'n' roll in, 136–37, 195. *See also* names of specific *films*; Teenpics
Fineman, Joel, 391 n.4

Fishman, Robert, 344 n.2, 345 n.5
Fiske, John, 349 n.6
Fliegelman, Jay, 256
Flitterman-Lewis, Sandy, 356 n.6
Ford, Henry, 15
Fordism, 51, 89, 322, 336–37 n.24; collapse of, 318, 325–26, 357 nn.1, 3; defined, 15–16; emasculating effects of, 172; resistance to, 21–22, 34, 48, 168; in suburbia, 17–19, 20, 21, 64, 96, 101–2, 119; and youth culture, 35, 36
Foreman, Joel, 50
Foucault, Michel, 2, 328, 334 n.13, 340 n.49
Fraser, Nancy, 334 n.10
Fraternity, 254–58; inequality of, 263–64; masculinized, 262–63
Freed, Alan, 103
Friedan, Betty, 268
Frith, Simon, 102
Fromm, Eric, 8, 333–34 n.8

Gangs, 45, 46, 163, 209, 296; desexualization of, 236, 241–44, 246, 254, 263; generational identity of, 238–39, 253, 256; girls in, 296–98, 305–12, 322
Garafalo, Reebee, 97, 99, 101, 121, 344 n.1, 345 n.11, 351 n.6
Gay Liberation Front Women, 5
Gender, 45; in nuclear family, 18, 20; politics of, 48–49, 51, 319, 329. *See also* Family; Feminism; Women
Gender Trouble, 2, 318, 328
Generational identity, 215–19, 223–24, 237, 239–41, 256, 351 n.2, 352 n.4; in "Howl," 247, 249, 251–53
George, Nelson, 106–7
George, Sue, 299
Gidget, 295–304
Gilbert, James, 26, 30, 137–38, 344 n.19, 348 n.3

380 INDEX

Gillett, Charles, 116, 351 n.6
Gilroy, Paul, 325 n.2
Ginsberg, Allen, 42, 219–20, 223, 227, 256–57, 352 n.8; homosexuality of, 226, 246, 260–63. *See also* "Howl"
Girls Town (film), 48, 270, 275, 277, 278, 355–56 n.2; race in, 279–80; rock 'n' roll in, 269, 271; sexuality in, 269–74, 276–79, 293, 313
"Girls Town" (song), 271
Gleason, Philip, 332 nn.3, 4, 333 n.7
Globalization, 3, 51, 325
Go, 219, 227, 236–37; homosociality in, 241–44; identity, generational, of, 238–41; women in, 241–45
Goffman, Irving, 321
Goodman, Paul, 34, 164, 168, 218, 267–68
Gordon, Avery, 324–25
Gordon, Dorothy, 28
"Great Balls of Fire," 112
Griswold, Jerry, 256–57
Grossberg, Lawrence, 92, 93–94, 127
Grovogui, Siba N'Zatioula, 11
Growing Up Absurd, 34, 164, 168, 267–68
Guillory, John, 85–86

Halberstam, Judith, 293–94
Haley, Bill, 110–11, 137, 151–52, 161, 346 nn.17, 18
Hall, Stuart, 139–40, 163, 348 nn.4–5
Halperin, David, 331 n.2
Hansberry, Lorraine, 49, 317–20, 349 n.9
Harris, Oliver, 249
Harvey, David, 357 n.1
Hassan, Ihab, 70–71, 78, 343 n.15
Hayden, Tom, 5
Hebdige, Dick, 162, 164
Heiserman, Arthur, 71–72, 75
Heterosexuality, 46, 49, 170, 204–5, 207; egalitarian, 185, 188, 203, 209; necessity of, 242–43; as phallic opposition, 158–59, 164, 186–87
Heung, Marina, 283, 356 n.6
Hill, Trent, 193–94
Hipsters, 150, 152, 164, 219, 354 n.17
Hoberek, Andrew, 67–68
Hobsbawm, Eric, 11
Hogeland, Lisa Maria, 354 n.21
Holmes, John Clellon, 46, 219–20, 223, 227, 236–37, 256. See also *Go*
Homosexuality, 20, 44–45, 84; and activism, 5, 46–47, 246, 254, 260–63, 264, 323; homophobia, 50, 226–27, 244–46, 252, 260–62, 353 n.11; lesbianism, 49, 293–94, 300–301, 315–16; politicization of, 190, 226, 319, 322, 331 n.2; and rebels, 47, 50, 158–59, 161–62, 164–65, 248–49, 253, 309, 322; as revolt against domestication, 188–91; in rock 'n' roll, 113
Homosociality, 46, 187; as articulated to fraternity, 254–55; as desire, 225–27, 228–30, 232–35, 250, 253, 262, 354 n.18; female, 258, 301; as rebellion, 236, 238, 241–44
Honky-tonk, 106, 112
Horne, Gerald, 20, 337 n.29
"Howl," 42, 46, 219, 227, 256; sexuality in, 247–53, 263
Huckleberry Finn, 74–75, 77
Hunter, Evan, 143

Identitarianism, 47, 55, 56, 87; decline of, 318–19
Identity: and authenticity, 93–94; defined, 3–8; as literary value, 53–57, 86; post-Fordist multiculturalization of, 318, 323–24, 327; as philosophical category, 332 n.4; as politics, 1–7, 23–24, 33–34, 51, 55–57, 66, 264, 321–29, 331 n.1, 332–33 nn.3, 4, 6, 341 n.7; psychopolitical paradigm of, 5–8, 89, 318, 320, 333 n.8

INDEX 381

Imitation of Life, 48, 280–81, 282, 287, 288, 289; class in, 283; motherhood in, 283–84, 291–92; race in, 283, 285–93, 295, 313, 356 n.6; sexuality in, 289–90, 293, 356 n.6
Industrialization, 8–9, 11, 13–14, 79
Intellectual: Cold War responsibilities of, 53–54, 58, 70
Invisible Man, 47, 65, 66–68, 74, 342 nn.10, 12

Jailhouse Rock, 194
Jameson, Fredric, 85, 87–89, 341 n.3
Jazz, 240
Jefferson, Tony, 163
Jews, 67–68, 88
Johnson, Joyce, 237
Jones, Ernest, 73
Jones, Mark, 176
Jordan, Louis, 107
Juvenile delinquency, 26, 30, 176, 339 nn.36, 38; and class, 29; emasculation, 182–83, 187; and ethnicity, 29; female, 266–67 (*see also* Bad girls); in film, 40, 137–43, 145–46, 149–53, 159, 164, 179, 180–81; in literature, 39–40, 304 (*see also* Beats; *Tomboy*); in music, 110, 116–17, 158; origins of, in family, 26, 167, 266–67; political purpose of, 32–33; and race, 150–56; redemption from, 39, 42; sexual deviance of, 187–91, 268–71, 309. *See also* Bad boys

Kant, Immanuel, 11, 261–62, 334 n.9
Kaplan, Amy, 12
Kaplan, Charles, 74–75
Kefauver, Estes, 149–50
Kennan, George, 19
Kerouac, Jack, 217–20, 223, 227, 256, 352 n.8
King, B.B., 107, 111
King Creole, 45, 171, 177, 197, 198, 200, 201, 203, 204, 207, 270; class in, 195, 196–97; emasculation in, 196–97, 201–2, 205–6, 210; fatherhood, failure of, 195–96, 199, 201–2, 205, 208–9; masculinity, sovereign, in, 195, 197, 201–2, 208–9; race in, 197–200, 202, 207; sexuality in, 191, 198–200, 202–7, 209–10
Knock on Any Door, 178
Kohner, Susan, 282–83
Krasner, Stephen, 334 n.11

Labor, 16, 25–26, 49, 325; in rock 'n' roll, 107, 111, 117, 123, 126, 128, 132–33; and suburbia, 17–19, 101; unions, 20; women, 172–73, 174, 345 n.6
Laclau, Ernesto, 317–18, 324
Lee, Martyn, 17, 326, 335 n.20
Leisure: and consumerism, 107, 132; and suburbia, 39, 105, 112–13; teenage, 35, 101–2, 114–15, 126, 133; undomesticated, 104, 107–8, 110, 114–15, 121
Levine, Evelyn, 217
Lewis, Jerry Lee, 111–12, 114
Lewis, R. W. B., 62–63, 64–65, 75
Liberalism, 53, 60–61, 63; identity's appeal to, 76–79; and nonconformity, 53–54, 56, 59–61, 68, 70, 79–80, 84, 86
Lindner, Robert, 31–34, 50, 179, 190
Lipietz, Alain, 335 n.20, 357 n.1
Lipsitz, George, 91, 92–94
Little Richard, 39, 47, 111, 113–14
Lloyd, David, 59, 341 n.7
"Lonely Boy," 275
Lonely Crowd, The, 21–22

MacDonald, Dwight, 82–83
Mailer, Norman, 34, 150, 152, 341 n.2, 349 n.9
Mailloux, Steven, 39–40, 340 n.43, 341 n.6

Mannheim, Karl, 215–16, 351–52 n.2
Marriage, 204, 231–33, 235, 353 n.12; and emasculation, 171–72, 196, 204, 230; exploitation of, 241–44, 246, 262; women, domestication of, 267–68, 287, 297, 299, 310
Marsh, David, 191–93, 351 nn.7, 9
Masculinity, 43, 260; adult, 142; defiant, 38; domesticated, 21, 22, 31–32, 46, 47, 48, 49, 168–69, 171–77, 180, 182–83, 189–91, 195–97, 201–2, 203–6, 208, 210, 230, 232, 235, 313, 338 n.31; eroticized, 193–94, 208; female, 48, 210, 267, 293–94, 297, 304, 306, 311–12; of public sphere, 262; of the rebel, 39, 43, 45–46, 48, 140, 157–59, 161–62, 164–65, 170–71, 211, 266; and violence, 208
Mass consumption, 14, 44, 95, 127, 172; domestic/youth binary of, 102–3; and Fordism, 15–19, 22, 36, 101, 325–26; as Fordist conformity, 20–22, 39, 91, 119, 122, 176; post-Fordist decline of, 325–26; and gender, 172; leisure, 107–8, 114; of literature, 80–81; semiotics of, 128–31; teenager as figure for, 30, 35–37, 43, 81–85, 114, 116, 136, 139, 217, 282; threat of, 21, 82–83, 88, 102
Mass media, 93, 97
May, Elaine Tyler, 18–19, 20, 337 n.29
McReynolds, David, 163
McRobbie, Angela, 162, 350 n.12
Mead, Margaret, 333 n.7
Melley, Timothy, 21
Metaphor, 130–33
Method acting, 169–70, 193
Michaels, Walter Benn, 331–32 n.3
Miller, James, 71–72, 75
Mills, C. Wright, 337 n.25, 341 n.2
Millstein, Gilbert, 218
Misogyny, 44, 161, 164, 288
Momism, 44, 169, 182–83, 189, 196

Morgan, Robin, 322
Mouffe, Chantal, 317–18, 324
Moya, Paula, 331 n.1
Multiculturalism, 86–89, 95–96, 318, 323–24, 327, 331 n.1; in radio, 97, 105–6; of rock 'n' roll, 92–94, 105, 110–12, 116, 127
Mulvey, Laura, 182–84, 210, 350–51 n.2
Murphy, Alexander, 7–8
Murphy, Audie, 40, 342 n.9
Murphy, Geraldine, 58, 342 n.9
Music: Afro-American, 91, 105–6; industry, 37–39; rural, 105; working-class, 91, 105–6, 110. *See also specific types of music*
Must You Conform?, 33, 179

Nadel, Alan, 20, 73–74, 266, 337 n.29
Nash, Johnny, 47, 212
Nationalism, 2, 331 n.3; as allegory, 78–79; literary production of, 54–60, 61–64, 67–68, 71–72, 74–75, 87–89, 256
Nelson, Dana, 256, 354 n.20
New American Library, 37, 80
Newfield, Christopher, 324–25
New Left, 3, 4, 210–11, 322
New World Writing, 84

Odd Girl Out, 49, 315–16
Ohmann, Carol, 343 n.14
Ohmann, Richard, 343 n.14
Olson, Jenni, 293–94
On the Road, 46, 217, 218, 220, 221, 227; homosocial desire in, 228–30, 233–35; women in, 48, 231–33
Organization Man, 20–21, 67, 168, 196, 322

Paramount Decision, 135–36
Parent Culture, 1, 3, 163
Parrington, Vernon, 76–77

Partisan Review, 53–54, 55, 58, 59, 65
Pateman, Carole, 254–56, 262, 263
Patriarchy, 209, 258; in family hierarchy, 173–75; fraternal, 254–56. *See also* Fatherhood
Pease, Donald E., 58–59, 341 n.5; and Cold War political fantasy, 341–42 n.8
Peck, Janice, 336 n.21
Perkins, Carl, 111
Pletsch, Carl, 335 n.18
Pocket Books, 37, 80
Poitier, Sydney, 47, 349 n.7
Postmodernism, 89
Presley, Elvis, 39, 47, 111, 114, 171, 210–11, 220; films by, 193–95 (see also *King Creole*); and race, 192–95; sexuality of, 191, 193–94, 198; as "teddy bear," 205
Psychology, 4; of rebellion, 31–33; of subjugation, 8. *See also* Erikson, Erik
Psychopolitics, 5, 67, 318, 332 n.4; in human development, 6–8; rebel allegory, 64; of sovereign rights, 24, 30

Race, 2, 47, 50, 51, 141, 159, 331–32 n.3; desegregation, 26, 144–45, 151, 156, 192; rebel, identity of, 153–56, 164, 211–12, 214, 268, 280–83, 285–93; and rock 'n' roll, 49, 93–94, 105–7, 110–12, 113–14, 116, 127, 192–93, 286; politics of, 214, 283, 318–19, 322, 324, 329; and sexuality, 279–80, 286, 289–91, 293; social regulation of, 20; and suburbia, 18, 91, 95–97, 99–100, 311. *See also* African Americans; Blackness
Radio, 37–38, 97–98, 103, 114–15, 131, 136; and record companies, 99–101
Radler, D. H., 28–29
A Raisin in the Sun, 49, 319–20
Ray, Nicholas, 178, 179

Reading strategies: dominant, 140–41; negotiated, 140; oppositional, 140, 146, 152, 154, 158, 161
Reagan, Ronald, 135, 139
Rebel, 1, 21, 34, 93; allegory of, 57, 61–64, 71, 86; decline of, 318; female, 265–67, 322 (*see also* Bad girls); in films, 38, 136–37, 140, 169–71, 177; masculinity of, 39, 43, 157–59, 161–62, 164–65, 169–71, 211; as metanarrative, 24, 30, 50; political purpose of, 3, 23–24, 30–34, 55, 179, 211, 283; racialization of, 150–56, 159, 165, 211–12, 214, 321. *See also* Bad boys; Beats; Caulfield, Holden; Dean, James; Juvenile delinquency; Presley, Elvis
Rebel without a Cause (book), 31, 35, 179
Rebel without a Cause (film), 34, 40, 45, 48, 177, 179, *180*, *183*, *184*, *185*; bad girl in, 188; delinquency in, 184–85, 187, 188, 190–91; emasculation in, 180, 182–83, 187, 189–90; fathers in, 180–81, 186, 208; homoeroticism of, 186–90; impact of, 170; masculinity, sovereign, in, 171, 177, 183–86, 191; sex in, 184–86, 188, 191
Record companies, 99–101
Regulation school, 14–15, 336 nn.20, 22
Reich, Wilhelm, 8
Reisman, David, 21–22, 338 n.34
Remmers, Herman, 28–29
Rhythm and blues, 38, 101, 105, 115, 127–28, 131–32, 346 nn.14, 19; and leisure, 107, 110–12, 114, 121, 123, 125–26; and race, 106–7, 110–11
Ricoeur, Paul, 92, 130, 131, 347 n.28
"Rip It Up," 113
Rockabilly, 111–12
"Rock around the Clock," 42, 110–11, 137, 139, 151–52

Rock 'n' roll, 37–38, 42, 49; and class, 97, 110, 132–33, 192–93; and delinquency, 116–18, 151, 158; in films, 136–37, 151, 161, 195, 200–202, 204–5, 269; labor in, 107, 111, 117, 123, 126, 128, 132–33; leisure in, 101, 104–5, 107–8, 110, 112–15, 120–21, 124–26, 132–33; marketing of, 92–94, 105, 114, 217; multiculturalism of, 92–94; politics of, 91; pop, 115–16, 121, 124, 131; and race, 49, 94–95, 105, 110–14, 116, 127, 151–52, 192–93, 286; in school, 122–23, 126; and sexuality, 113–14, 164, 271; sources of, 38, 108, 109, 344 n.1, 346 n.19; and suburbanization, 94, 97, 109–12, 114–28, 132–34; transcommodification of, 130–31, 133; on TV, 103–4

Rogin, Michael Paul, 340 n.46
Ross, Andrew, 20, 337 n.29
Rouse, Roger, 357 nn.2, 4
Rubin, Jerry, 210–11

Salinger, J. D., 37, 40, 56, 65, 69, 71–73, 76, 78, 84–85, 170, 343 n.14
Sands, Tommy, 115–16, 121, 124
Schaub, Thomas, 60, 66, 337 n.29
"School Days," 123–26, 131
Schulman, Irving, 179
Sedgwick, Eve, 186, 225–26, 228, 235, 251, 254–55, 353 n.11; stucturalist limits in, 354 n.18
Seng, Peter, 74
Sex and sexuality, 18, 43–44, 191; as anti-suburban, 45–46, 188–89, 209–11, 250–51, 268–69; female, 43–44, 184–88, 203–4, 209, 211, 268–74, 279–80, 286, 289–91; lure of, 250–53; in music, 112–14, 204, 207; norms of, 44; politics of, 51, 164, 208, 262, 268, 283, 319, 329; and race, 279–80, 286, 289–91. *See also* Heterosexuality; Homosexuality; Masculinity

Shulman, Alix Kates, 259
Shumway, David, 194
Silverstone, Roger, 96, 132, 344 n.3
Sirk, Douglas, 280–81
Social location, 215
Social movements, 86–87, 210; and identity politics, 2–5, 46–47, 50–51, 164–65, 258, 260, 314–16, 318–29
Solanis, Valerie, 322
Solomon, Carl, 247
Soul on Ice, 152
Sovereignty, 334 n.13; as basis for identity psychopolitics, 7–8; collective, 215; individual, 22–23, 55, 64, 72, 79, 92, 168, 204, 215, 269; of nation states, 23, 46, 79, 257; phallic male, 157, 174, 197, 201–2; politics of, 24, 174, 321
Soviet Union, 8–10, 13, 22, 28; Cold War with, 1, 10–14, 16, 20, 59; national identity of, 9–10, 32; and third world, 13
Spanos, William V., 341 n.5
Spigel, Lynn, 98, 345 nn.7, 8
Spivak, Gayatri, 59, 341 n.7
Steinle, Pamela, 333 n.13
Stevenson, David L., 69
Stigma, 321
"Student as Nigger, The," 154–57
Suburbia, 1, 35, 94–96, 172, 319, 345 nn.5, 6; and delinquency, 29; emasculation by, 45, 168–69, 171–77, 190–91, 208, 210; and Fordism, 17–19, 96, 101–2; mass media in, 97–101; resistance to, 21, 22, 39, 42, 47, 49, 92–95, 103–5, 109–11, 114–16, 119–21, 127, 131–33, 168, 260, 296; rise of, 17–18, 92; sexual deviance in, 189–91, 227; women in, 266
"Summertime Blues," 120

Take a Giant Step, 212, 213, 214
Taylor, Charles, 334 n.10
"Teen-Age Bill of Rights, A," 24, 26–27, 35
"Teenage Crush," 115, 124, 126
"Teenage Heaven," 118–19
Teenagers, 34, 43, 72; independence or autonomy of, 27–30, 79, 118, 134; and consumerism, 30, 35–37, 43, 81–82, 117–18, 136, 139, 339 n.40; identity crisis of, 169, 171; identity of, and rock 'n' roll, 92–93, 101, 109–10, 119–24, 126, 131–34; and race, 153–55; rights of, 24, 26–27, 35–36, 43, 74, 120, 161, 162, 339 n.38. *See also* Juvenile delinquents
Teenpic, 38, 136, 146, 170, 217, 283, 348 n.1; juvenile delinquent in, 136–37, 139, 269. *See also names of specific films*
Television, 37, 39, 91, 97, 98–99, 114, 136, 345 nn.7–9; music shows on, 103–4, 345–46 n.12
Third world, 1, 10, 257, 344 n.21; identity of, 11, 23–24, 32, 322–23; ideological competition for, 12–14; literary conception of, 63–64, 87–88
Tomboy (novel), 304–5, 314; fatherhood in, 309–10, 313; female masculinity in, 306, 311–12; homoeroticism in, 309; race in, 311–12, 356–57 n.8; sex in, 306, 310–11
Tomboys, 48, 210, 313; femininity of, 299–302, 304; and lesbianism, 293–94, 300; masculinity of, 267, 293–94, 297, 304. *See also Gidget; Tomboy*
"Too Much Monkey Business," 122–23, 126
Torme, Mel, 269
Transcommodification, 93–94, 127–31, 326; and structural analysis, 128–30

Trilling, Lionel, 75–77, 341 n.1
"Trouble," 167
Truman, Harry, 12
Tubbs, Ernest, 111
"Tutti-Frutti," 113
Twain, Mark, 39, 59, 75–77

United States of America: idealization of, 22, 75–77, 78; identity of, 13, 23, 32, 34–35, 42, 53, 77; industrialization of, 8–9; and Soviet Union, 1, 10, 12; and third world, 12–14
Urban culture, 38, 94–95; delinquency in, 26, 143; in music, 93, 100, 106–8, 110–11, 114–16, 124, 128; and race, 106–7, 110–11, 116, 311
Uyematsu, Amy, 317, 321

Van Doren, Mamie, 269, 280
Vattel, Emerich de, 334 n.12
Viking Press, 220
Von Eschen, Penny, 10

Wakefield, Dan, 84–85
Walzer, Michael, 334 n.12
Warner, Michael, 331 n.2
Waters, Muddy, 107, 111
Weiss, Jessica, 351 n.3
West, Cornel, 331 n.1
Wexman, Virginia, 169–70
White negro, 150–52, 285–86, 289–90, 292
"White Negro, The," 34, 47, 150, 152, 164
Whiteness: hybridity of bohemian whiteness, 192, 279, 285–86, 291; and identification, 150–51, 164; racialized rebellion against, 50–51, 197, 313, 319; as suburban norm, 47, 96
Whitman, Walt, 62, 261
"Whole Lotta Shakin' Goin' On," 112
Whyte, William, 20–21, 168, 338 n.32
Wilde, Marty, 42

Wild One, The, 40, 170
Wilkie, Wendel, 12
Williams, Hank, 106
Wilson, Sloan, 20–21
Wise, Sue, 205
Women, 49, 88; and bad boys, 43, 177, 265–67, 290, 293, 302, 304, 306, 308, 312, 313–14, 322; in beat novels, 236, 241–46, 259, 263; domestication of, 48, 51, 266–68, 277–79, 286–88, 291–92, 297, 299–300, 314, 345 n.6; equality of, 167, 254–55, 314, 316; in labor force, 26, 172–74; misogyny, 44, 161, 164; and momism, 44–45, 169, 182–83, 189, 196; sexuality of, 43–44, 184–88, 189, 194, 199, 203–4, 209, 211, 268–74, 279–80, 286, 289–91, 306, 308–16; sisterhood, 258–59; social regulation of, 20, 51. *See also* Bad girls; Feminism; Tomboys
Wood, Natalie, 181, 266, 269
Wylie, Philip, 169

"Yakkety Yak," 117–18, 126
Youth, as identity formation, 6–7; as third world metaphor, 64
Youth culture, 35; beat generation, 217, 220; consumption in, 93, 217, 282, 326; leisure politics of, 101–2, 114–15, 126, 133; in rock 'n' roll, 112, 115–16, 119–20, 125–27, 131; suburban, 94, 103, 105, 114–16, 126–27; unity in, 163–64

LEEROM MEDOVOI is an assistant professor of English at Portland State University and the director of the Portland Center for Cultural Studies.

Library of Congress Cataloging-in-Publication Data
Medovoi, Leerom
Rebels : youth and the Cold War origins of identity / Leerom Medovoi.
p. cm. — (New Americanists)
Includes bibliographical references and index.
ISBN 0-8223-3680-4 (cloth : alk. paper)
ISBN 0-8223-3692-8 (pbk. : alk. paper)
1. United States — Intellectual life — 20th century. 2. United States — Social conditions — 1945- 3. Group identity — United States — History — 20th century. 4. Cold War — Social aspects — United States. 5. Alienation (Social psychology) — United States — History — 20th century. 6. Alienation (Social psychology) in literature. 7. Alienation (Social psychology) in motion pictures. 8. Youth in literature. 9. Youth in motion pictures. 10. Popular culture — United States — History — 20th century.
I. Title. II. Series.
E169.12.M425 2005
302.5'4'0973 — dc22   2005012087